Selected Short Works
of Richard Wagner

Richard Wagner

Translated by William Ashton Ellis

DODO PRESS

CONTENTS

PASTICCIO

BY CANTO SPIANATO.

(1)

The old Italian mode of Song was based on so-called sostenuto singing, demanding a *formare, fermare* and *finire* of the vocal tone. It certainly allowed much elasticity, but every passage must conform to the character of the human voice itself. The modern method, on the contrary, only secondarily consists of melodious phrases, whose cut has been so uniformly made upon one last, that we recognise it instantly, for all its trimmings. This odious mania for copying the instruments shews a misunderstanding of both Song and human Voice. Erewhile men deemed the voice the noblest of all instruments and, rightly to enjoy its charm, accompanied it as discreetly as possible; now they bury it beneath a load of senseless instrumenting, and, without regard to the dramatic situation, they make it gurgle arabesques that tell us nothing. These gurglings, sure enough, are often mastered, but they rebel against the throat as obstinately as a hard nut against a worn-out tooth.

That the Singing-voice, like every other instrument, needs schooling, and indeed a very careful schooling, in which the *production* of the voice is dealt with quite apart from the *rendering* (taste and expression), no connoisseur will deny; but where, in all our German fatherland, are there training-schools for higher vocal culture?— True, we have Singakademieen, Gesangvereine, Seminaries, and may boldly assert that Chorus-singing in Germany and Switzerland has reached a technical perfection to be sought in vain in Italy itself, the land of song; but the higher vocal art, of solo-singing, is in manifest decline, and many a mile might we journey before we could assemble a couple of dozen good singers really worthy of the name, singers who should possess not only a *well-trained organ*, but also a *good delivery, correct declamation, pure enunciation, sympathetic expression and thorough knowledge of music*. Merely gauge the majority of our celebrated singers male and female by *this* standard!—Certain highly important endowments must be set to the credit of certain individuals, but nowadays we could but rarely and exceptionally convene a whole such as not only our fancy might dream of, and our higher aspirations wish for, but also is humanly realisable, and in former times has actually been realised. To-day one hardly ever hears a truly beautiful and finished *trillo*; very rarely a perfect *mordente*; very seldom a well-rounded *coloratura*, a genuine unaffected, soul-stirring *portamento*, a complete equalisation of the vocal register and perfect maintenance of intonation throughout the varying nuances of increase and diminution in the volume of sound. Most of our singers, so soon as they attempt the noble art of *portamento*, fall out of tune; and the public, accustomed to imperfect execution, overlooks the defects of the singer if he only is an able actor and versed in stage-routine.

> "The tricky roulade, be it neat or a smear,
> Will draw sure applause, as the onion the tear."
> C. M. VON WEBER. (2)

The German singer gladly sinks himself in the character he has to represent. That deserves all praise, but has its own grave dangers. If the singer lets himself be carried away by his rôle; if he does not stand absolute master *over* the whole of his portrayal: then all, as a rule, is lost. He forgets himself, he no longer sings, but screams and moans. Then Nature none too seldom fleeces Art, and the hearer has the unpleasant surprise of suddenly finding himself in the gutter. If in addition to this, each performer tries to set *his* part in the best and most striking light, without regard for his companions, it is all over with the harmony of play and song. Hence it comes, that our ordinary stage-performances in Germany pitch down from the height of rapt emotion to the depths of fussy dulness, and lack the outward stimulus of sustained artistic charm.

Many German singers regard it, in a certain sense, as a point of honour to be willing to sing *anything*, no matter if it suit their voice or not. The Italian does not hesitate to say right out that such and such a part he cannot sing, since it is ungrateful to his voice through height or depth, its trick of ornament, or other qualities. In this he often goes too far, and as good as demands that all his parts shall be written expressly for him: but the German, whether from free will or force of circumstances, too often and too readily accommodates himself to every rôle, thereby ruining both it and his voice as well. The singer should never attempt a part for which he is not qualified

a.   *physically*—in respect of vocal compass, timbre, and power of lung;

b.   *technically*—in respect of throat-dexterity; and

c.   *psychically*—in respect of expression.

German dramaturgists say: "The actor should accommodate himself to the rôle, not the rôle itself to the actor." The maxim—as it stands—may be true; but unreservedly applied to the stage-singer, it is downright false: for the human voice is no lifeless instrument, like the pianoforte, and our German vocal composers, alas! too often are very sorry lords of Song.—Every sterling Instrumental composer must have studied the character of the various instruments, before he can produce true instrumental effects. Let a composer write for any instrument in the orchestra a passage against its nature; let him assign it notes the player can but bring out badly, or which do not lie in its register—his condemnation is pronounced at once, and rightly. "The man," so the verdict goes, "is a musical bungler; he presumes to compose, and knows nothing of instrumentation! These are pianoforte, not clarinet passages; that cantilena is in the compass of the violin, but not of the violoncello." In short, let the composition breathe never so much life and spirit, it is thrown aside; for the man has not learnt his business—"He writes things that nobody could execute!" Hand on your heart, ye song-composers of our latter days, have ye zealously studied the peculiarities of the human voice? Know ye what it is, to write singably? I will answer:—Ye behold the mote that is in your brother's eye, but consider not the beam that is in your own eye; therefore shall ye be doubly judged.

3

Most truly does C. M. v. Weber say: The singer's individuality is the actual unconscious colorist of every rôle. The possessor of an agile and flexible throat, and he of a volume of tone, will render one and the same rôle quite differently. The first will be several degrees more animated than the second, and yet the composer may be satisfied with both, insofar as each according to his measure has rightly grasped and reproduced the gradations of passion prescribed.

It will always remain the hardest of tasks, so to combine the vocal and instrumental parts of a rhythmic composition that they shall melt into each other, and the last not only carry and relieve the first, but also help its utterance of passion; for Song and Instrument stand opposed. Breathtaking and articulation of the words enjoin on Song a certain undulation in the bar, not unlike the uniform swell of the waves. The Instrument, especially the stringed instrument, divides the time into sharp-cut sections, like the strokes of a pendulum. Truth of expression demands the blending of these opposite peculiarities. The beat, the Tempo, must never resemble a mill-clack in its tyrannical slowing or speeding, but to the piece of music it must be what the pulse-beat is to the life of man. Yet most of our modern vocal composers in Germany appear to regard the human voice as a mere portion of the instrumental mass, and misconceive the distinctive properties of Song. The instruments should form a guard of honour to the voice: with us they have become the singer's catch-polls, gagging him and casting him into chains at his first sign of free expression of feeling.

Mozart has irrefutably proved that, with the most complex, ingenious, and even massive orchestration, one still may leave the singer in full exercise of his rights; nowadays the human voice is degraded to an instrument. What has been gained?—Nothing!—The efforts of the human voice, even that of a Sontag, are outdone by instrumental virtuosi; a whole choir of bravura singers would never be able to bring out a thousandth of the tone-figures which have sprung up in our instrumental music since the time of *Bach*; and with this expansion of the art of instrumenting the inventiveness of our tone-artists has shot heaven-high above the bounds of Song.—The genuine art of Song depends on a Cantabile in keeping with the text and a Bravura in keeping with the voice. But since we fell into a depreciation of true Italian vocal beauty, we have departed more and more from the path which Mozart struck for the weal of our dramatic music. With the revival of the, in many respects, classical music of the period of Bach, much too little attention is paid to a really singable cantabile. All the masterworks of Sebastian Bach are as rich in invention as possible within the form of Fugue and Double Counterpoint in general. His inexhaustible creative-force ever drove him on to introduce into each of his products the highest and richest of specific tonal figures, forms, and combinations. But with this super-abundance of purely musical, or rather, instrumental contents, the word must needs be often thrust into its place beneath the note by force; the human voice, as a special organ of tone, was not at all considered by him; its peculiar office he never sufficiently appraised: and as a vocal composer of Cantabile he is nothing less than classical, however much the blind adorers of this master may cry out "Fie!"

Our worthy opera-composers must take a course of lessons in the good Italian cantabile style, guarding themselves against its modern outgrowths, and, with their superior artistic faculty, turn out good work in a style as good. Then will Vocal art bear fruit anew; then a man will some-day come, who in this good style shall re-establish on the stage the shattered unity of Poetry and Song.

Among us there is an archipatriarchal sect which refuses the name of beauty to any but quite simple singing, and utterly condemns all art of ornament. Let these judges turn back from their wretched one-sidedness, their taking of the choice of *means* as sole object for consideration, praise or blame, often blinding them to the *effect* itself! Art should be free. No school, no sect, must arrogate the title of the only bliss-purveyor. The simple, smooth and metric song has its great value—provided its setter is really a good vocal composer: only, it is not the sole true path of salvation, and the goal—the expression and communication of feeling—may be reached on other roads as well. The solo-singer ought to be an *artist* of song; as such, he may also give vent to his feelings in an enhanced and ornate art-form. Is that passion less true, forsooth, which takes the air with a volley of words, than that which breathes itself in few? Is not now this, now that, included in the individuality of this or that subject? Should not a speech in Parliament be different in form, to boot, from a sermon to a village parish? May not a sumptuous mould of periods, a flowery, decorative diction, a complex and ingenious scheme of verse, a rare but effective rhythm, be conditioned by aesthetic necessity?—We in nowise are opening the door to those meaningless flourishes by which unthinking singers too often, alas! betray their poverty of proper feeling, either to display their nimbleness of throat, or to mask their lack of portamento; but the nobler art of ornament has not yet reached with us its actual bloom; in our modern operatic singing we have merely the stereotyped *volutes of song*, which our singers and composers slavishly copy from the Italians, and wedge in everywhere without taste or psychological necessity.

The Public is at sea with Art, and the Artists have lost touch with the People. Why is it, that no German opera-composer has come to the front of late?—Because none has known how to gain the voice of the Folk,—in other words, *because none has seized true warm Life as it is.* The essence of dramatic art does not consist in the specific subject or point of view, but in this: that the inner kernel of all human life and action, the Idea, be grasped and brought to show. (3) By this standard alone should dramatic works be judged, their special points of view and subjects being simply regarded as special varieties of this Idea. Criticism makes a radically false demand on Art, when it requires the art of the Beautiful to do nothing else than idealise. For without all Ideality, so-called, Dramatico-musical art can take many a form. If the librettist has the true poetic spirit, in him there lies the universe of human moulds and forces, his figures have an organic core of life; let him unroll the heavenly, or the earthly chart of human characters, we shall always find them lifelike, even though we never may have met their like in actual life. But our modern Romantic manikins are nothing but lay-figures. Away with them all—give us *passion*! Only in what is human, does man feel interest; only the humanly-feelable, can the dramatic singer represent. You have been often enough told, but refuse to believe it, that *one* thing alone is needful for Opera—namely *Poesy*!—Words and tones are simply its expression. And yet the most of our operas are a mere string of musical numbers without all psychologic union, whilst our singers ye have degraded into musical-boxes set to a series of tunes, dragged on to the stage, and started by the wave of the conductor's baton. The public no longer believes the opera-singer, since it knows that he is only singing it a thing no heart of man can feel. Mark the age, ye composers, and diligently seek to cultivate new forms; for he will be master, who writes neither Italian nor French—nor even German. But would ye warm, and purify, and train yourselves by models; would ye make shapes instinct with musical life: then take the masterly declamation and dramatic power of *Gluck* and combine it with *Mozart's* contrasted melody, his art of orchestration and ensemble; and ye will produce dramatic works to satisfy the strictest criticism.

Notes

1

Pasticcio means a "pasty," an "olla podrida"; it is a term applied to a curious form of entertainment, somewhat common in earlier days, consisting of arias, duets etc., selected from different operas and served up almost at random.

Canto spianato, the pseudonym adopted by the author, is the Italian for "smooth singing."—Tr.

2

> "Auf die Roulade, gut oder übel,
> Folgt das Geklatsch wie die Thrän' auf die   Zwiebel."—

Wagner would appear to have quoted the couplet from memory, for he has substituted *"die Roulade"* for *"den Laufer"* (runs, or scales), and

"*Geklatsch*" for "*Gepatsch*" (clapping, or slapping)—unless the latter be a misprint in the *N.Z.f.M.*, repeated in the *Bayr. Bl.* of Nov. 1884. The original lines appeared in a half humorous, half serious sketch contained in certain fragmentary chapters of a "A Tone-artist's Life" posthumously published in Weber's *Hintergelassene Schriften* (Dresden 1828) and edited by C. G. T. Winkler, the "Councillor Winkler" referred to in Wagner's *Letters to Uhlig*. In the same collection of Weber's 'remains' occurs the following epigram upon "Bravura-singeress" Tembila: "Man muss es gesteh'n, dass ihr Trillern gelingt, Nur Schade, dass sie vor Singen nicht singt." —"One must freely admit that her trills are the thing; Yet with all her fine singing, 'tis sad she can't sing." —Tr.

3

It is somewhat remarkable to find the author thus early propounding the Platonic "Idea" as a basis of Æsthetics, and in fact of Life itself. As may be seen upon turning to Vol. VII. p. 134, the thought recurs to him in 1841, with special reference to Music. Therefore we are perfectly justified in chiming for Wagner an independent insight into one of Schopenhauer's main principles fully twenty years before he made acquaintance with that philosopher's system. —Tr.

Summary

Merits of old Italian mode of writing for the voice, and singing. In Germany good chorus-singing, but dearth of soloists with a well-trained organ, good delivery, correct declamation, pure enunciation, sympathetic expression, and thorough knowledge of music (60). Necessity of dramatic singer's exercising self-control; ensemble to be considered. Italians decline rôles unsuited to their voice etc.; Germans undertake anything, suitable or not. Human voice no lifeless instrument; must be studied by composers (62). Liberty accorded to singer; modifying tempo; the instruments should be a guard of honour to the voice, not its catch-polls. Mozart's orchestration: cantabile and bravura. Bach treats voice as an instrument. Take a lesson from the Italians, and then a man will some day come to re-establish the lost unity of Poetry and Song (64).

Pedantic onesidedness of the sect which abjures all ornament. A parliamentary speech should differ from a village sermon; a sumptuous mould etc. may be demanded by æsthetic necessity. Composers have lost touch with the people: essence of dramatic art the Idea behind all human actions; give us passion! One thing needful for Opera—*poesy*: words and tones are simply its expression. The future master (66).

ON GERMAN OPERA

When we talk of German Music, and especially when we listen to talk about it, the same confusion of ideas always appears to prevail as in the conception of freedom by those old-German black-frocked demagogues who curled their noses at the results of modern reforms abroad with just as much contempt as our Teutomaniac music-savants now shrug their shoulders. By all means, we have a field of music which belongs to us by right,—and that is Instrumental-music;—but a German Opera we have not, and for the selfsame reason that we own no national Drama. We are too intellectual and much too learned, to create warm human figures. Mozart could do it; but it was the beauty of Italian Song, that he breathed into his human beings. Since the time when we began to despise that beauty again, we have departed more and more from the path which Mozart struck for the weal of our dramatic music. Weber never understood the management of Song, and Spohr wellnigh as little. But Song, after all, is the organ whereby a man may musically express himself; and so long as it is not fully developed, he is wanting in true speech. In this respect the Italians have an immeasurable advantage over us; vocal beauty with them is a second nature, and their creations are just as sensuously warm as poor, for the rest, in individual import. Certainly, in the last decad or two the Italians have played as many pranks with this second nature-speech as the Germans with their learning,—and yet, I shall never forget the impression lately made on me by a Bellinian opera, after I had grown heartily sick of the eternally allegorising orchestral bustle, and at last a simple noble Song shewed forth again. (1)

French music acquired its tendency from Gluck, who, albeit a German, has had far less influence on ourselves than on the Frenchmen. He felt and saw what the Italians lacked, namely an individuality in their figures and characters, which they sacrificed to vocal beauty. He created Dramatic Music, and bequeathed it to the French as their possession. They have pursued its cultivation, and from Grétry to Auber dramatic truth has remained a first principle of the Frenchmen.

The talents of the good German opera-composers of modern times, of Weber and Spohr are unequal to the dramatic province. Weber's talent was purely lyrical, Spohr's elegiac; and where those bounds were overstepped, art and the expenditure of abnormal means had to supplement what their nature failed in. Thus Weber's best work is in any case his "Freischütz," since he here could move in his appointed sphere; the mystic weirdness of Romanticism, and that charm of the Folk-melody, belong peculiarly to the domain of Lyrics. But turn to his Euryanthe! What splitting of hairs in the declamation, what fussy use of this or that instrument to emphasise a single word! Instead of throwing off a whole emotion with one bold freehand stroke, he minces the impression into little details and detailed littlenesses. How hard it comes to him, to give life to his Ensembles; how he drags the second Finale! Here an instrument, there a voice, would fain say something downright clever, and none at last knows what it says. And since the audience is bound to admit in the end that it hasn't understood a note of it, people have to find their consolation in dubbing it astoundingly *learned*, and therefore paying it a great respect.—O this wretched erudition—the source of every German ill!

There was a time in Germany when folk knew Music from no other side than Erudition—it was the age of Sebastian Bach. But it then was the form wherein one looked at things in general, and in his deeply-pondered fugues Bach told a tale as vigorous as Beethoven now tells us in the freest symphony. The difference was this: those people knew no other forms, and the composers of that time were truly learned. To-day both sides have changed. The forms have become freer, kindlier, we have learnt to live,—and our composers no longer are learned: the ridiculous part of it, however, is that they want to pose as learned. In the genuine scholar one never marks his learning. Mozart, to whom the hardest feat in counterpoint had become a second nature, simply gained thereby his giant self-dependence;—who thinks of his learning, when listening to his Figaro? But the difference, as said, is this: Mozart *was* learned, whilst nowadays men want to *seem* so. There can be nothing wronger-headed than this craze. Every hearer enjoys a clear, melodious thought,—the more seizable the whole to him, the more will he be seized by it;—the composer knows this himself,—he sees by what he makes an effect, and what obtains applause;—in fact it comes much easier to him, for he has only to let himself go; but no! he is plagued by the German devil, and must shew the people his *learning* too! He hasn't learnt quite so much, however, as to bring anything really learned to light; so that nothing comes of it but turgid bombast. But if it is ridiculous of the composer to clothe himself in this nimbus of scholarship, it is equally absurd for the public to give itself the air of understanding and liking it; it ends in people being ashamed of their fondness for a merry French opera, and avowing with Germanomaniac embarrassment that it would be all the better for a little learning.

This is an evil which, however ingrained in the character of our nation, must needs be rooted out; in fact it will annul itself, as it is nothing but a self-deception. Not that I wish French or Italian music to oust our own;—that would be a fresh evil to be on our guard against—but we ought to recognise the *true* in both, and keep ourselves from all self-satisfied hypocrisy. We should clear ourselves a breathing-space in the rubble that threatens to choke us, rid our necks of a good load of affected counterpoint, hug no visions of forbidden fifths and superfluous ninths, and become men at last. Only by a lighter and freer touch can we hope to shake off an incubus that has held our music by the throat, and especially our operatic music, for many a year. For why has no German opera-composer come to the front since so long? Because none knew how to gain the voice of the people,—that is to say, because none has seized true warm Life as it is.

For is it not plainly to misconstrue the present age, to go on writing Oratorios when no one believes any longer in either their contents or their forms? Who believes in the mendacious stiffness of a Schneiderian fugue, and simply because it was composed *to-day* by Friedrich Schneider? What with Bach and Händel seems worshipful to us in virtue of its truth, necessarily must sound ridiculous with Fr. Schneider of our day; for, to repeat it, no one *believes* him, since it cannot be his own conviction. We must take the era by the ears, and honestly try to cultivate its modern forms; and he will be master, who neither writes Italian, nor French—nor even German.

Notes

1

In March 1834 the young man had heard Frau Schröder-Devrient as "Romeo" in Bellini's Montecchi e Capuleti at Leipzig. It should be remarked that the term "Song" (*Gesang*) is used by Richard Wagner throughout to signify the whole manner both of writing for, and of using the singing-voice.—Tr.

Summary

The Germans too learned to create warm human figures. Mozart *v.* Weber and Spohr. Bellini and Italian Song. Gluck's influence on the French; Grétry and Auber. Weber's *Freischütz* and his *Euryanthe*. Bach's vigour; Mozart's command of counterpoint. In the truly learned one never marks his learning. Modern pretence of erudition: none has seized warm life as it is. He will be master, who writes neither French, nor Italian, nor even German (58).

BELLINI († 1835)

A WORD IN SEASON

BELLINI'S music, i.e. Bellini's music for the voice, has latterly made such a stir and kindled such enthusiasm, even in highly-learned Germany, that the phenomenon itself perhaps is worth a closer scrutiny. That *Bellinian* Song enraptures Italy and France, is natural enough, for in Italy and France men hear with their ears,—whence our phrases such as "ear-tickling" (presumably in contrast to the "eye-ache" caused us by the reading of so many a score of our newer German operas);—but that even the German music-scholar should have taken the spectacles from his fagged-out eyes, and given himself for once to reckless delight in a lovely song, this opens us a deeper glimpse into the inner chamber of his heart,—and there we spy an ardent longing for a full and deep-drawn breath, to ease his being at one stroke, and throw off all the fumes of prejudice and pedantry which so long have forced him to be a German music-scholar; to become a Man instead at last, glad, free, and gifted with every glorious organ for perceiving beauty, no matter the form in which it shews itself.

How little we are really convinced by our pack of rules and prejudices! How often must it have happened that, after being transported by a French or Italian opera at the theatre, upon coming out we have scouted our emotion with a pitying jest, and, arrived safe home again, have read ourselves a lecture on the danger of giving way to transports. Let us drop for once the jest, let us spare ourselves for once the sermon, and ponder what it was that so enchanted us; we then shall find, especially with *Bellini*, that it was the limpid Melody, the simple, noble, beauteous Song. To confess this and believe in it, is surely not a sin; 'twere no sin, perchance, if before we fell asleep we breathed a prayer that Heaven would one day give German composers such melodies and such a mode of handling Song.

Song, Song, and a third time Song, ye Germans! For Song is once for all the speech wherein Man should musically express himself; and if this language is not made and kept as self-dependent as any other cultivated Speech, then nobody will understand you. The rest of the matter, what is bad in Bellini, any of your village schoolmasters could better; we admit it. To make merry over these defects, is quite beside the question: had Bellini taken lessons from a German village-schoolmaster, presumably he would have learnt to do better; but that he perhaps would have unlearnt his Song into the bargain, is certainly to be very much feared.

Let us therefore leave to this lucky Bellini the cut of his pieces, habitual with all the Italians, his crescendos, tutti and cadenzas that regularly succeed the theme, and all those other mannerisms which so disturb our spleen; they are the stable forms than which the Italians know no other, and by no means so dreadful in many respects. If we would only consider the boundless disorder, the jumble of forms, periods and modulations, of many a modern German opera-composer, distracting our enjoyment of the single beauties strewn between, we often might heartily wish this frayed-out tangle put in order by that stable Italian form. As a matter of fact the instantaneous apprehension of a whole dramatic passion is made far easier, when with all its allied feelings and emotions that passion is brought by one firm stroke into *one* clear and taking melody, than when it is patched with a hundred tiny commentaries, with this and that harmonic nuance, the interjection of first one instrument and then another, till at last it is doctored out of sight.

How much the Italians are helped by their form and manner, especially with certain operatic subjects,—whatever that form's onesidedness and tawdriness in degeneration,—of this Bellini affords a proof in his *Norma*, beyond dispute his most successful composition. Here, where the poem itself soars up to the tragic height of the ancient Greeks, this form, pronouncedly ennobled by Bellini, does but exalt the solemn, grandiose character of the whole; all the passions which his Song so notably transfigures, thereby obtain a majestic background, on which they hover not in vaguest outlines, but shape themselves to one vast and lucid picture, involuntarily recalling the creations of Gluck and Spontini.

Accepted with this free, untroubled self-abandonment, *Bellini's* operas have found applause in Italy, in France and Germany; why should they not find the like in Lithuania? (1)

O.

Notes

1

For his benefit at the Riga theatre (Dec. 1837) the author had chosen the production of *Norma*; the above article was intended as its avant-courière.—Tr.

Summary

"Ear-tickling" v. "eye-ache". Music-scholars should remove their spectacles, and listen for once; give up their sermonising and learn the lesson of a noble melody. Dramatic passion and its expression: *Norma* and Greek Tragedy (69).

ON GERMAN MUSIC

THANKS to the exertions of a number of distinguished artists, who seem to have combined expressly for this purpose,—thanks to them and their good services, the highest products of German Music are no longer unknown to the Parisian public; they have been set before it in the worthiest fashion, and received by it with the greatest enthusiasm. (1) People have begun to demolish the barriers which, destined perhaps to eternally sever the nations themselves, yet should never separate their arts; one may even say that through their ready acknowledgment of foreign productions the French have distinguished themselves more than the Germans, who are generally more prone to fall beneath a foreign influence than is good for the preservation of a certain self-dependence. The difference is this:—the German, not possessing the faculty of initiating a Mode, adopts it without hesitation when it comes to him from abroad; in this weakness he forgets himself, and blindly sacrifices his native judgment to the foreign gauge. But this chiefly refers to the mass of the German public; for on the other side we see the German musician by profession, perhaps from very revolt against this universal weakness of the mass, too sharply cutting off himself therefrom, and becoming one-sided in his falsely patriotic zeal and unjust in his verdict on extraterritorial wares.—It is just the reverse with the French: the mass of the French public is perfectly contented with its national products, and does not feel the least desire to extend its taste; but the higher class of music-lovers is all the broader-minded in its recognition of foreign merit; it loves to shew enthusiasm for whatever comes to it of beautiful and unknown from abroad. This is plainly proved by the reception so quickly accorded to German Instrumental-music. Whether the Frenchman *understands* German music for all that, is another question, and one whose answer must be doubtful. Of course it would be impossible to maintain that the enthusiasm called forth by the masterly execution of a Beethoven Symphony by the orchestra of the Conservatoire is an affected one; nevertheless it would suffice to learn the views, ideas and fancies roused in this or that enthusiast by the hearing of such a symphony, to perceive at once that the German genius has not as yet been thoroughly understood.—Let us therefore cast a more comprehensive glance upon Germany and the state of its music, to afford a clearer notion of how it should be taken.

Somebody once said: The Italian uses music for love, the Frenchman for society, but the German as science. Perhaps it would be better put: The Italian is a singer, the Frenchman a virtuoso, the German a—musician. The German has a right to be styled by the exclusive name "Musician," for of him one may say that he loves Music for herself,—not as a means of charming, of winning gold and admiration, but because he worships her as a divine and lovely art that, if he gives himself to her, becomes his one and all. The German is capable of writing music merely for himself and friend, uncaring if it will ever be executed for a public. The desire to shine by his creations but rarely seizes him, and he would be an exception if he even knew how to set about it? Before what public should he step?— His fatherland is cut up into a number of kingdoms, electoral principalities, duchies and free towns; he dwells, let us say, in a market-borough of some duchy; to shine in such a borough never occurs to him, for there isn't so much as a public there; if he is really ambitious, or compelled to support himself by his music,—he goes to the residential city of his duke; but in this little *Residenz* there are already many good musicians,—so it is terrible uphill work to get on; at last he makes his way; his music pleases; but in the next-door duchy not a soul has ever heard of him,—how, then, is he to begin to make a name in Germany? He tries, but grows old in the attempt, and dies; he is buried, and no one names him any more. This is pretty well the lot of hundreds; what wonder that thousands don't even bestir themselves to adopt the career of Musician? They rather choose a handicraft to earn their living, and give themselves with all the greater zest to music in their leisure hours; to refresh themselves, grow nobler by it, but not to shine. And do you suppose they make nothing but handicraft-music? No, no! Go and listen one winter-night in that little cabin: there sit a father and his three sons, at a small round table; two play the violin, a third the viola, the father the 'cello; what you hear so lovingly and deeply played, is a quartet composed by that little man who is beating time.—But he is the schoolmaster from the neighbouring hamlet, and the quartet he has composed is a lovely work of art and feeling. (2) —Again I say, go to that spot, and hear that author's music played, and you will be dissolved to tears; for it will search your heart, and you will know what German Music is, will feel what is the German spirit. (3) Here was no question of giving this or that virtuoso the opportunity of earning a storm of applause by this or that brilliant passage; everything is pure and innocent, but, for that very reason, noble and sublime.—But set these glorious musicians before a full-dress audience in a crowded salon,—they are no longer the same men; their shame-faced bashfulness will not allow them raise their eyes; they will grow timid, and fear their inability to satisfy you. So they inquire by what devices other people please you, and for sheer lack of self-confidence they'll abandon their nature in shame, to pick up arts they only know by hearsay. Now they will make their fingers ache in practising gymnastics for you; those voices, which sang the lovely German *Lied* so touchingly, will make all haste to learn Italian colorature. But these passages and colorature refuse to suit them; you have heard them performed much better, and are bored by the bunglers.—And yet these bunglers are the truest artists, and in their hearts there glows a finer warmth than ever has been shed on you by those who hitherto have charmed you in your gilded salons. What then has ruined them?—They were too modest, and ashamed of their own true nature. This is the mournful chapter in the history of German Music. (4)

Alike the nature and the constitution of his fatherland have set the German artist iron bounds. Nature has denied him that flexibility of one chief organ which we find in the throats of the happy Italians;—political barriers obstruct him from higher publicity. The opera-composer sees himself obliged to learn an advantageous treatment of Song from the Italians, yet to seek external stages for his works themselves, as he can find none in Germany on which to present himself before a nation. So far as concerns this hatter point, you may take it that the composer who has produced his works at Berlin, stays unknown at Vienna or Munich for that very reason; only from abroad, can he succeed in attracting the whole of Germany. Their works are therefore like nothing more than provincial products; and if a whole great fatherland is too small for an artist, how much smaller must one of its provinces be! The exceptional genius may soar above these limitations, but for the most part only through the sacrifice of a certain native self-dependence. So that the truly characteristic of the German always remains provincial, in a sense, just as we have Prussian, Swabian, Austrian folk-songs, but nowhere a German national anthem.—

This want of centralisation, albeit the reason why no great national work of music will ever come to light, is nevertheless the cause of Music's having preserved through out so intimate and true a character among the Germans. Just because there is no great Court, for instance, to gather all that Germany possesses in the way of artistic forces, and thrust it in one joint direction toward the highest-attain able goal,—just for this reason we find that every Province has its artists who independently exert their dear-loved art. The result is a general extension of music to the most unlikely neighbourhoods, down to the humblest cots. It is surprising and astonishing, what musical forces one often finds combined in the most insignificant towns of Germany; and though there is an occasional dearth of singers for the Opera, you everywhere will find an orchestra that as a rule can play Symphonies quite admirably. In towns of 20,000 to 30,000 inhabitants you may count on not *one*, but two to three well-organised bands, (5) not reckoning the countless amateurs who frequently are quite as good, if not still better-educated musicians, than the professionals. And you must know what one means by a German bandsman: it is rare indeed for the most ordinary member of an orchestra not to be able to play another instrument besides the one for which he is engaged; you may take it as a rule that each is equally expert on at least three different instruments. But what is more,—he is commonly a composer too, and no mere empiric, but thoroughly versed in all the lore of harmony and counterpoint. Most of the members of an orchestra that plays a Beethovenian Symphony know it by heart, and their very consciousness of this gives rise to a certain presumption that often turns out badly for the performance; for it will sometimes tempt each unit in the band to pay less heed to the ensemble, than to his individual conception.

We therefore may justly contend that Music in Germany has spread to the lowest and most unlikely social strata, nay, perhaps has here its root; for higher, showier society in Germany must in this respect be termed a mere expansion of those humbler, narrower spheres. Maybe in these quiet unassuming families German Music finds herself at home; and here in fact, where she is not regarded as a means of display, but as a solace to the soul, Music *is* at home. Among these simple homely hearts, without a thought of entertaining a huge mixed audience, the art quite naturally divests herself of each coquettish outward trapping, and appears in all her native charm of purity and truth. Here not the ear alone asks satisfaction, but the heart, the soul demands refreshment; the German not merely wants to feel his music, but also to think it. Thus vanishes the craze to please the mere sensorium, and the longing for mental food steps in. It not being enough for the German to seize his music by the senses, he makes himself familiar with its inner organism, he studies music; he learns the laws of counterpoint, to gain a clearer consciousness of what it is that drew him so resistlessly in master-works; he goes to the toot of the art, and becomes in time a tone-poet himself. This need descends from father to son, and its satisfaction thus becomes an essential part of bringing-up. All the difficulties on the scientific side of music the German learns as a child, parallel with his school-lessons, and as soon as he is at an age to think and feel for himself nothing is more natural than that he should include music in his thought and feeling, and, far from looking on its practice as an empty entertainment, religiously approach it as the holiest precinct in his life. He accordingly becomes a fanatic, and this devout and fervent *Schwärmerei*, with which he conceives and executes his music, is the chief characteristic of German Music.

Alike this bent and, perhaps, the lack of fine voices direct the German to instrumental music.—If we may take it as a general principle that every art has one particular genre that represents it at its purest and most independent, this certainly may be said to be the case with Music in its instrumental genre. In every other branch a second element combines that necessarily destroys the unity and self-dependence of the first, and yet, as we have experienced, can never raise itself to a level with it. Through what a mass of extras from the other arts must one not wade, in listening to an opera, to arrive at the real drift of the music itself! How the composer feels obliged to almost completely subordinate his art, here and there, and often to things beneath the dignity of any art. In those happy instances where the value of the services rendered by the auxiliary arts attains an equal height with the music itself, there arises indeed a quite new genre, whose classic rank and deep significance have been sufficiently acknowledged; but it must always stay inferior to the genre of higher instrumental music, as at least the independence of the art itself is sacrificed, whereas in instrumental music the latter gains its highest scope, its most complete development.—Here, in the realm of Instrumental music, the artist, free of every foreign and confining influence, is brought the most directly within reach of Art's ideal; here, where he has to employ the means the most peculiar to his art, he positively is bound to stay within its province.

What wonder if the earnest, deep and visionary German inclines to this particular genre of music more fondly than to any other? Here, where he can yield himself entirely to his dream-like fancies, where the individuality of a definite and bounded passion lays no chains on his imagination, where he can lose himself unhampered in the kingdom of the clouds,—here he feels free and in his native country. To realise the masterpieces of this genre of art it needs no glittering frame, no dear-paid foreign singers, no pomp of stage-accessories; a pianoforte, a violin, suffice to call awake the most enrapturing imaginations; everybody is master of one or other of these instruments, and in the smallest place there are enough to even form an orchestra capable of reproducing the mightiest and most titanic creations. And is it possible, with the most lavish aid of all the other arts, to erect a sublimer and more sumptuous building than a simple orchestra can rear from one of Beethoven's symphonies? Most surely not! The richest outward pomp can never realise what a performance of one of those master-works sets actually before us.

Instrumental music is consequently the exclusive property of the German,—it is his life, his own creation! And just that modest, bashful shyness, which constitutes a leading feature in the German character, may be a weighty reason for the thriving of this genre. It is this shamefacedness that prevents the German from parading his art, that inner halidom of his. With innate tact he feels that such a showing-off would be a desecration of his art, for it is so pure and heavenly of origin that it easily becomes defaced by worldly pomps. The German cannot impart his musical transports to the mass, but only to the most familiar circle of his friends. In that circle, however, he gives himself free rein. There he lets flow the tears of joy or grief unhindered, and therefore it is here that he becomes an artist in the fullest meaning of the word. If this circle is scant, it is a piano and a pair of stringed instruments that are played on;—one gives a sonata, a trio or a quartet, or sings the German four-part song. If this familiar circle widens, the number of instruments waxes too, and one undertakes a symphony.—This justifies us in assuming that Instrumental-music has issued from the heart of German family-life; that it is an art which can neither be understood nor estimated by the mass of a crowded audience, but solely by the home-like circle of the few. A pure and noble *Schwärmerei* is needed, to find in it that ecstasy it sheds on none but the initiate; and this can only be the true musician, not the mass of an entertainment-craving public of the salon. For everything the latter takes and greets as piquant, brilliant episodes, is therewith quite misunderstood, and what sprang from the inmost kernel of the noblest art is consequently classed with tricks of empty coquetry.

We will now attempt to shew how all of German music is founded on the selfsame basis.

The reason has already been given above, why the Vocal genre is far less native to the Germans than that of Instrumental music. It is not to be denied that Vocal music has also taken a quite special direction of its own, with the Germans, which likewise had its starting-point in the people's needs and nature. Yet the grandest and most important genre of vocal music, the Dramatic, has never attained a height and independent evolution on a par with that of Instrumental music. The glory of German vocal music appeared in the Church; the Opera was abandoned to the Italians. Even Catholic church-music is not at home in Germany, but exclusively Protestant. Again we find the reason in the simplicity of German habits, which were far less suited to the priestly splendour of Catholicism than to the unpretentious ritual of the Protestant cult. The pomp of Catholic Divine Service was borrowed by courts and princes from abroad, and all German Catholic church-composers have been imitators, more or less, of the Italians. In the older Protestant churches, however, in place of all parade there sufficed the simple Chorale, sung by the whole congregation and accompanied on the organ. This chant, whose noble dignity and unembellished purity can only have sprung from simple and sincerely pious hearts, should and must be regarded as an exclusively German possession. In truth its very structure bears the impress of all German art; in its short and popular melodies, many of which shew a striking likeness to other secular but always inoffensive folk-songs, one finds expressed the nation's liking for the *Lied*. The rich and forceful harmonies upon the other hand, to which the Germans set their choral melodies, evince the deep artistic feeling of the nation. Now this Chorale, in and for itself one of the worthiest events in the history of Art, must be viewed as the foundation of all Protestant church-music; on it the Artist built, and reared the most imposing fabrics. The first expansion of the Chorale we have to recognise in the *Motet*. These compositions had the same church-songs, as the Chorale, for their basis; they were rendered by voices alone, without accompaniment by the organ. The grandest compositions in this genre are those of *Sebastian Bach*, who must also be regarded as the greatest Protestant church-composer in general.

The Motets of this master, which filled a similar office in the ritual to that of the Chorale (saving that, in consequence of their great artistic difficulty, they were not delivered by the congregation, but by a special choir), are unquestionably the most perfect things we possess in independent vocal-music. Beside the richest application of a profoundly thoughtful art they shew a simple, forcible and often most poetic reading of the text in a truly Protestant sense. Moreover the perfection of their outward forms is so high and self-delimited, that nothing else in art excels it. But we find this genre still further magnified and widened in the great Passions and Oratorios. The Passion-music, almost exclusively the work of great Sebastian Bach, is founded on the Saviour's sufferings as told by the Evangelists; the text is set to music, word by word; but between the divisions of the tale are woven verses from the Church's hymns appropriate to the special subject, and at the most important passages the Chorale itself is sung by the whole assembled parish. Thus the performance of such a Passion-music became a great religious ceremony, in which artists and congregation bore an equal share. What wealth, what fulness of art, what power, radiance, and yet unostentatious purity, breathe from these unique master-works! In them is embodied the whole essence, whole spirit of the German nation; a claim the more justified, as I believe I have proved that these majestic art-creations, too, were products of the heart and habits of the German people.

Church-music therefore owed alike its origin and consummation to the people's need. A like need has never summoned up Dramatic music, with the Germans. Since its earliest rise in Italy the Opera had assumed so sensuous and ornate a character, that in this guise it could not possibly excite a need of its enjoyment in the earnest, steady-going German. Opera, with its pomps of spectacle and ballet, so very soon fell into the disrepute of a mere luxurious pastime for the Courts, that in former times, as a matter of fact, it was kept up and patronised by them alone. Naturally also, as these Courts, and especially the German ones, were so completely severed from the people, their pleasures could never become at like time those of the Folk. Hence in Germany we find the Opera practised as an altogether foreign art-genre down almost to the end of the past century. Every court had its Italian company, to sing the operas of Italian composers; for at that time no one dreamt of Opera being sung in any but the Italian language and by Italians. The German composer who aspired to write an opera, must learn the Italian tongue and mode of singing, and could hope to be applauded only when he had completely denationalised himself as artist. Nevertheless it was frequently *Germans*, who took first rank in this genre as well; for the universal tendency of which the German genius is capable made it easy to the German artist to naturalise himself on a foreign field. We see how quickly the Germans feel their way into whatever the national idiosyncrasy of their neighbours has brought to birth, and thereby win themselves a fresh firm stand-point whence to let their innate genius spread creative wings long leagues beyond the cramping bounds of Nationality. The German genius would almost seem predestined to seek out among its neighbours what is not native to its motherland, to lift this from its narrow confines, and thus make something Universal for the world. Naturally, however, this can only be achieved by him who is not satisfied to ape a foreign nationality, but keeps his German birthright pure and undefiled; and that birthright is Purity of feeling and Chasteness of invention. Where this dowry is retained, the German may do the grandest work in any tongue and every nation, beneath all quarters of the sky.

Thus we see a German raising the Italian school of Opera to the most complete ideal at last, and bringing it, thus widened and ennobled to universality, to his own countrymen. That German, that greatest and divinest genius, was *Mozart*. In the story of the breeding, education, and life of this unique German, one may read the history of all German Art, of every German artist. His father was a musician; so he too was brought up to music, apparently with the mere idea of turning him into an honest professional who could earn his bread by what he had learnt In tenderest childhood he was set to learn the very hardest scientific branches of his art; he naturally became their perfect master as soon as boy; a pliant, childlike mind and intensely delicate senses allowed him at like time to seize the inmost secrets of his art; but the most prodigious genius raised him high above all masters of all arts and every century. Poor all his life to the verge of penury, despising pomp and advantageous offers, even in these outward traits he bears the perfect likeness of his nation. Modest to shamefacedness, unselfish to the point of self-oblivion, he works the greatest miracles and leaves posterity the most unmeasured riches, without knowing that he did aught save yield to his creative impulse. A more affecting and inspiring figure no history of art has yet to shew.

Mozart fulfilled in its highest power all that I have said that the universality of the German genius is capable of. He made the foreign art his own, to raise it to a universal. His operas, too, were written in the Italian tongue, because it was then the only one admissible for song. But he snatched himself so entirely from all the foibles of the Italian manner, ennobled its good qualities to such a pitch, so intimately welded them with his inborn German thoroughness and strength, that at last he made a thing completely new and never pre-existing. This new creation was the fairest, most ideal flower of Dramatic music, and from that time one may date the naturalisation of Opera in Germany. Thenceforward national theatres were opened, and men wrote operas in the German tongue.

While this great epoch was in preparation, however, while Mozart and his forerunners were developing this novel genre from Italian music itself, from the other side there was evolving a popular Stage-music, through whose conjunction with the former at last arose true German Opera. This was the genre of German Singspiel, which, distant from the glare of Courts, sprang up in the people's midst and from its heart and customs. This German Singspiel, or Operetta, bears an unmistakable likeness to the older French *opéra comique*. The subjects for its texts were taken from the people's life, and mostly sketched the customs of the lower classes. They were generally of comic type, full of blunt and natural wit. The pre-eminent home of this genre was Vienna. In general it is in this Kaiser-city, that the greatest stamp of nationality has always been preserved; the gay and simple mind of its inhabitants has always been best pleased with what made straight for its mother-wit and buoyant fancy. In Vienna, where all the folk-plays had their origin, the popular Singspiel also thrived the best. The composer, indeed, would mostly restrict himself to Lieder and Ariettas; however, one met among them many a characteristic piece of music, for instance in the excellent "Dorfbarbier," that was quite capable, if expanded, of making the genre more important in time, had it not been doomed to die out through absorption into the grander class of opera. This notwithstanding, it had already reached a certain independent height; and one sees with astonishment that at the very time when Mozart's Italian operas were being translated into German, and set before the whole public of his fatherland immediately after their first appearance, that Operetta also took an ever ampler form, appealing to the liveliest fancy of the Germans by an adaptation of folk-sagas and fairy-tales.—Then came the most decisive stroke of all: Mozart himself took up this popular line of German Operetta, and on it based the first grand German opera: *die Zauberflöte*. The German can never sufficiently estimate the value of this work's appearance. Until then a German Opera had as good as not existed; with this work it was created. The compiler of the text-book, a speculating Viennese Director, meant to turn out nothing further than a right grand operetta. Thereby the work was guaranteed a most popular exterior; a fantastic fable was the groundwork, supernatural apparitions and a good dose of comic element were to serve as garnish. But what did Mozart build on this preposterous foundation? What godlike magic breathes throughout this work, from the most popular ballad to the sublimest hymn! What many-sidedness, what marvellous variety! The quintessence of every noblest bloom of art seems here to blend in one unequalled flower. What unforced, and withal what noble popularity in every melody, from the simplest to the most majestic!—In fact, here genius almost took too giant-like a stride, for at the same time as it founded German Opera it reared its highest masterpiece, impossible to be excelled, nay, whose very genre could not be carried farther. True, we now see German Opera come to life, but going backwards, or sicklying into mannerism, to the full as quickly as it raised itself to its most perfect height.— The directest imitators of Mozart, in this sense, were undoubtedly *Winter* and *Weigl*. Both joined the popular line of German Opera in the honestest fashion, and the latter in his "Schweizerfamilie," the former in his "unterbrochener Opferfest," proved how well the German opera-composer could gauge the measure of his task. Nevertheless the broader popular tendence of Mozart already loses itself in the petty, with these his copiers, and seems to say that German Opera was never to take a *national* range. The popular stamp of rhythms and melismi stiffens to a meaningless rote of borrowed flourishes and phrases, and above all, the indifferentism with which these composers approached their choice of subjects betrays how little they were fitted to give to German Opera a higher standing.

Yet we see the popular musical drama once more revive. At the time when Beethoven's all-puissant genius set open in his instrumental music the realm of daringest romance, a beam of light from out this magic sphere spread also over German Opera. It was *Weber* who breathed a fair warm life again into stage-music. In his most popular of works, the "Freischütz," he touched once more the people's heart. The German fairy-tale, the eerie saga, here brought the poet and composer into immediate touch with German folk-life; the soulful, simple German Lied was the foundation, so that the whole was like a long-drawn moving Ballad, attired in noblest dress of breeziest romanticism, and singing the German nation's fondest fantasies at their most characteristic. And indeed both Mozart's Magic Flute and Weber's Freischütz have proved with no uncertain voice that in this sphere German Musical Drama (*opéra*) is at home, but beyond it lie stern barriers. Even Weber had to learn this, when he tried to lift German Opera above those bounds; for all its beauty of details, his "Euryanthe" must be termed a failure. Here, where Weber meant to paint the strife of great and mighty passions in a higher sphere, his strength forsook him; his heart sank before the vastness of his task, he sought by toilsome painting-in of single features to make up for a whole that could only be drawn with bold and vigorous strokes; thus he lost his unconstraint and became ineffective. (6) 'Twas as if Weber knew that he here had sacrificed his own chaste nature; in his Oberon he returned with the sad sweet smile of death to the Muse of his former innocence.

Spohr also sought to make himself a master of the German stage, but never could arrive at Weber's popularity; his music lacked too much of that dramatic life which should radiate from the scene. To be sure, the products of this master must be called completely German, for they speak in deep and piercing accents to the inner heart. They entirely lack, however, that blithe and naïve element so characteristic of Weber, without which the colour of dramatic music grows too monotonous and loses all effect.

The last and most important follower of these two we recognise in *Marschner*; he touched the selfsame chords that Weber struck, and thereby swiftly gained a certain popularity. But with all his innate force, this composer was powerless to keep erect that German Opera so brilliantly revived by his predecessor, when the products of the newer French school began to make such strides in the enthusiastic welcome of the German nation. In effect, the newer French dramatic music dealt such a crushing blow at German popular Opera, that the latter may now be said to have wholly ceased to exist. Yet some further mention must be made of this last period, as it has exerted a most powerful influence on Germany, and it really seems as though the German after all would rise to be its master too. (7)

We can but date the commencement of this period from the advent of *Rossini*; for, with that brilliant audacity which alone could compass such a thing, he tore down all the remnants of the old Italian school, already withered to a meagre skeleton of empty forms. His lustful-jovial song went floating round the world, and its advantages—of freshness, ease and luxury of form—were given consistence by the French. Among them the Rossinian line gained character and a worthier look, through national stability; on their own feet, and sympathising with the nation, their masters now turned out the finest work that any folk's art-history can shew. Their works incorporated all the merits and character of their nation. The delicious chivalry of ancient France breathed out from *Boieldieu's* glorious *Jean de Paris*; the vivacity, the spirit, wit, the grace of the French re-blossomed in that genre exclusively their own, the *opéra comique*. But its highest point was reached by French dramatic music in *Auber's* unsurpassable "Muette de Portice" ,—a national-work such as no nation has more than one at most to boast of. That storm of energy, that sea of emotions and passions, painted in the most glowing tints, drenched with the most original melodies, compact of grace and vehemence, of charm and heroism,—is not all this the true embodiment of latter-day French history? Could this astounding art-work have been fashioned by another than a Frenchman? There is no other word for it,—with this work the modern French school had reached its apex, and with it the hegemony of the civilised world. (8)

Small wonder, if the impressionable and impartial German did not delay to recognise the excellence of these products of his neighbours with unassumed enthusiasm. For the German, in general, can be juster than many another nation. Moreover these foreign imports met a genuine need; for it is not to be denied that the grander genre of Dramatic music does not flourish in Germany of itself; and apparently for the same reason that the higher type of German, play has never reached   its fullest bloom. On the other hand it is more possible for the German, than for anyone else, on foreign soil to bring a national artistic epoch to its highest pitch and universal acceptation. (9)

As regards Dramatic music, then, we may take it that the Germans and the French at present have but one; though their works be first produced in *one* land, this is more a local than a vital difference. In any case the fact that these two nations now are stretching hands to one another, and lending forces each to each, is a preparation for one of the greatest artistic epochs. May this propitious union ne'er be loosed, for it is impossible to conceive two nations whose fraternity could bring forth grander and more fruitful results for Art, than the German and the French, since the genius of each of these two nations is fully competent to supply whatever may be lacking in the one or other.

Notes

1

Under the title of "De la Musique Allemande" this article originally appeared in the *Gazette Musicale* of July 12 and 26, 1840, forming Richard Wagner's earliest contribution to that journal.—Tr.

2

To many a foreigner the above little picture may appear exaggerated; it is therefore particularly apropos that we read in a sketch of August Manns (*Musical Times*, March 1898) the following:

"August Friedrich Manns was born at Stolzenburg, a village near Stettin, in North Germany, March 12, 1825. His father was a glass-blower, with a pound a week and ten children, of whom August was the fifth. When the father returned from his day's work he would take down his fiddle from the wall and make music to his children. . . . At the age of six August was sent to the village school, where the day's work always commenced with a hymn sung from a figure-notation upon the ancient 'movable doh' system. In course of time the father's fiddle was augmented by another, a violoncello, and a horn, played by August's elder brothers, and later on by an old F flute, played by the future conductor of the Crystal Palace orchestra. . . . At the age of ten, August temporarily took the place of one of his brothers at the factory. . . . At the age of twelve he was sent to a school, kept by his uncle, at Torgelow, a neighbouring village. Here he became a musical pupil of Herr Tramp, the village musician. Up to this time the boy had been self-taught, and Tramp soon put him into the pathway of acquiring the proper fingering of both the flute and clarinet; but his chief instrument was the violin. As he had no means of buying an instruction hook, he copied out the greater part of Rode, Kreutzer, and Baillot's book on the violin."

As this quotation deals with the very decad in which Wagner was writing, it is of peculiar interest in the present connection. A few lines farther in the *Musical Times* article, we read how at fifteen young Manns was apprenticed to Urban, the town-musician of Elbing, whose boys "were taught every instrument in the orchestra," and how "in his third year Manns played first violin in the string-band and first clarinet in the wind band of Urban's Town-band," which confirms a general statement of Wagner's a few pages ahead.—Tr.

3

"One sees that the author was young, and not yet acquainted with our elegant modern music-Germany.—The Editor" (i.e. R. Wagner in 1871).

4

"It would seem that in our days this grief and shame have been happily overcome.—Ed." (i.e. R. W. in 1871).

5

"This was the actual experience of our friend at *Wurzburg* in his time, where, besides a full orchestra at the theatre, the bands of a musical society and a seminary gave alternate performances.—Ed." (R. W. in '71).

6

"Methinks my friend would have learnt in time to express himself more guardedly on this point.—Ed." (i.e. R. Wagner).

7

Evidently referring to Meyerbeer; for the master does not appear to have realised at this epoch that the composer of the *Huguenots* was not a German, but a Jew.—Tr.

8

"Mephistopheles: 'You already speak quite like a Frenchman!'—Ed." (R. W.).

9

A longish passage appeared in the French, between this sentence and the succeeding paragraph, as follows: "Haendel et Gluck l'ont prouvé surabondamment, et de nos jours un autre Allemand, Meyerbeer, nous en offre un nouvel exemple.—Arrivé au point d'une perfection complète et absolue, le système français n'avait plus en effet d'autres progrès à espérer, que de se voir généralement adopté et de se perpétuer au même degré de splendeur; mais c'était aussi la tâche la plus difficile à accomplir. Or, pour qu'un allemand en sit tenté l'épreuve et obtenu la gloire, il fallait sans contredit qu'il fût doué de cette bonne foi désintéressée, qui prévaut tellement chez ses compatriotes, qu'ils n'ont pas hésité à sacrifier leur propre scène lyrique pour admettre et cultiver un genre étranger, plus riche d'avenir et qui s'adresse plus directement aux sympathies universelles. En serait-il autrement quand la raison aurait anéanti la barrière des préjugés qui séparent les différents peuples, et quand tous les habitants du globe seraient d'accord pour ne plus parler qu'une seule et même langue?"—Tr.

PERGOLESI'S "STABAT MATER"

(1)

THERE still are good musicians who find their keenest joy in searching the chefs-d'œuvre of ancient masters, to fill themselves with their incomparable beauties; and when one brings to such a study so much zeal and intelligence as the author of whom we are about to speak, the results deserve no less esteem and recognition than if they were original works. It would be a great mistake to ascribe to M. Lvoff the claim of having added to the perfection of the work of Pergolesi, for it is evident that his only aim has been to remind the modern school of a sublime exemplar, and to get it enrolled in the repertoire of contemporary performances. Under influence of this conviction, and in spite of all aesthetic scruples excited by this mode of secondary arrangement, it is impossible to deny the interest and importance of the publication now before us.

At an epoch like ours, when the different branches of the art of Music have taken such divergent lines, often to the point of a most abnormal transformation, it is an essential need and noble duty to ascend to primal sources for new elements of force and fecundity. But to usefully re-knit these ties of parentage with the great masters of the past, the practice of their compositions—adapted, if necessary, to the exigences of modern taste—will always be more efficacious than a pale and mediocre imitation of their wondrous style. In fact the last procedure offers all the danger of a retrogression, for such copiers are but too frequently inclined to reproduce in their concoctions those superannuated forms which purity of taste reproves.

The exclusive admirers of the ancient school have fallen into a vicious exaggeration, through attaching the same value to its imperfect canons as to the depth and thought revealed in its works.

Grand and noble as are those thoughts, the details of material execution shew inexperience and the gropings of a science in its infancy; and it is impossible to call in doubt the greater perfecting of form, if not in our day, at least during the intermediary period that succeeded to this golden age of musical art.

It was with Mozart, the chief of the Idealistic school, that religious music really touched its apogee in point of structure; and if I did not fear being misinterpreted, I should venture to express the wish that all the works of the preceding period had been transmitted to us clad in forms analogous, for the perfection of these latter would have been ample recompense for the pains of such a transformation; nor would the difficulty have been very great, since Mozart was not too distant from the primitive epoch, and his manner still preserved its sentiment and characteristic traits. On the contrary, he has brilliantly proved how much the older masterpieces could be enhanced by a vivacity and freshness of colour, without losing aught of their intrinsic merit, so to say, and notably by his arrangement of Haendel's oratorio *The Messiah*.

We are far from blaming those who would only have Haendel's oratorio performed in a cathedral with a chorus of from three to four hundred voices, supported by organs and a quartet of stringed instruments of proportionate number, to enjoy the whole splendour and primitive energy of the composition. For the individual anxious to appreciate the historic value of Haendel's music it would no doubt be preferable to hear it rendered by such potent means,—a thing almost impossible to realise to-day for reason of one notorious circumstance, namely that Haendel himself improvised the accompaniments on the organ for the first performances of the *Messiah*. Is it not permissible to assume that the composer, unacquainted with the more perfect modern use of the 'wind,' employed the organ to produce the same effects that Mozart entrusted later to the improved wind-instruments of his day?

In any case, Mozart's instrumentation has embellished the work of Haendel in the general interest of art. It needed, in truth, the genius of a Mozart, to accomplish such a task in so complete a measure. He who undertakes a similar work to-day, can therefore do no better than adopt that for his model, without seeking to complicate its simple and natural lines; for an application of the resources of modern orchestration would be the surest means of travestying the theme and character of ancient works.

And such has been the laudable desire of M. Lvoff. An examination of his score will demonstrate that he has taken his type from the discreet instrumentation of Mozart. Three trombones, two trumpets, the drums, two clarinets and two bassoons,—such are the elements added to the original orchestra. And most frequently it is only the clarinets and bassoons that take an active part in the accompaniment, following the precedent of the bassoons and basset-horns in Mozart's *Requiem*. The greatest difficulty must have resided in the general revision of the string-quartet, as Pergolesi had written it entirely in the naïve style of olden days, limiting himself for most of the time to three parts, and sometimes even to two. Very often the complementary harmonic part was a matter of course, and one finds it hard to explain why the composer omitted to write it, thereby producing very perceptible gaps. But in other places the filling-up presented serious difficulties, especially where the melody seems to admit of only three parts, or sometimes two, and where a supplementary voice might be considered superfluous, if not harmful. Nevertheless this great obstacle has always been happily surmounted by M. Lvoff, whose general discretion is beyond all praise. The wind-instruments which he introduces, far from ever smothering or altering the original theme, serve on the contrary to throw it into higher relief. They even have a certain independent character that contributes to the effect of the ensemble, entirely after the rules adopted by Mozart, and in this regard we may particularly instance the fourth strophe, *Quæ mœrebat*. Only occasionally, for example at the beginning of the first number, was it wrong, perhaps, to transfer the part of the violins to the bassoons and clarinets; not that the author has here misjudged the character of these latter instruments, but since the bass, retained for the lower strings, appears too full and too sonorous for its new superstructure.

It is astonishing, however, that the author of so conscientious a work should have let himself be once betrayed into altering the bass: namely at the commencement of the second strophe, where M. Lvoff has modified the entire phrase, greatly to the disadvantage of the original melody. No doubt he did it to avoid a passage of a certain crudity which Pergolesi had given to the part of the alto; but in our opinion there were other ways of remedying this harshness, without sacrificing the great composer's lovely bass. For the rest, it is the solitary instance, in all the work, of a change both useless and unfavourable. With scarcely another exception, we have witness of the most conscientious zeal and a highly delicate appreciation of the old chef-d'œuvre, down to tiny details of a character a trifle superannuated.

Beyond dispute the most audacious step in M. Lvoff's undertaking is the addition of choruses, since Pergolesi wrote his *Stabat* for but two voices, the one soprano and the other high contralto. Strictly speaking, it would have been better to respect the original intention of the master; but as this introduction of choruses has in no way spoilt the work, and as, moreover, the two original solo parts have been preserved in their integrity, it would be impossible to seriously blame the adaptor; in fact one must even acknowledge that he has added to the richness of the ensemble, for this adjunction has been effected with a rare address and a superior understanding of the text.

Thus in the first number the intermittent fusion of the choral with the solo voices reminds us happily of the manner in which the two choirs are treated in Palestrina's *Stabat*. However it is principally upon the choir, that weighs the difficulty of adding complementary parts in the places aforesaid where Pergolesi had designed his melody exclusively for two or three. Here the arranger is obliged to restrict the rôle of the chorus to three parts at most, not to absolutely mar the original harmony and disfigure its noble simplicity. This is especially perceptible in the fugal passages, such as the *Fac ut ardeat*. Further, the vocal theme is never in the tenor register, but devolves exclusively on either the soprano or alto, as in the original composition, or the bass which it was easy to extract from the primary accompaniment. Above all, the reviser must have been embarrassed by the *Amen*, expressly written by Pergolesi for two voices alone.

Apropos of No. 10, *Fac ut portem*, we must remark that it would have been better to omit the accompaniment by the choir, as also the concluding cadence, these two accessories reminding one too much of modern Opera, and ill according with the character of the sacred work.

But if we have felt it our duty to point out the reefs presented by so rare a task, we have also to frankly avow that the modern composer has given proof of great ability in doubling them. It would be impossible to praise too much the noble aim that has governed M. Lvoff's enterprise; for if an intelligent admiration and an ardent sympathy for so great a masterpiece alone were capable of prompting anyone to such a labour, there also is no doubt that M. Lvoff took the perfect measure of its difficulty and extent. It therefore is no more than just to recognise not merely the talent, but also the courage necessary to accomplish a labour where the artist has to make complete denial of, and constantly efface himself, to let the superior genius to whom he renders loving homage shine in all his glory.

R. WAGNER.

Notes

1

This "revue critique" of the "*Stabat Mater* de Pergolèse, arrangé pour grand orchestre avec chœurs par Alexis Lvoff, membre des Académies de Bologne et de Saint-Pétersbourg" appeared in the *Gazette Musicale* of Oct. 11, 1840. Although it is not included in the *Ges. Schr.*, having evidently been regarded by the author as simply a pot-boiler, I fancy that many of its sentences will justify my rescuing it from oblivion. Col. Alexis Lvoff, or Lwoff, was the composer of the Russian National Anthem.—Tr.

Summary

Importance of reviving old masterpieces for performance: limits to be observed by the adaptor; Mozart's revision of Handel's *Messiah* a model (104). Detailed criticism of M. Lvoff's adaptation; difficulties he has overcome (107).

ART AND CLIMATE

Translator's Note

In a letter to Uhlig, dated February 8th, *1850,* Wagner writes: "To the March number of the *Deutsche Monatsschrift* (Stuttgart) I have promised to contribute an article, 'Art and Climate.' The good friend in the *Allgemeine Zeitung* has determined me to expose the lazy, cowardly, preposterous objection of 'climate,' in all its emptiness." A nervous illness intervened between this letter and the following, undated but apparently written towards the end of the month, where he says: "Since yesterday I have been writing away at the article for the March number of the *Monatsschrift.*" In the succeeding letter (March 13th, *1850*), in which he also refers to "Wieland" as previously cited, Wagner says: "*Kunst und Klima* appears in the Stuttgart *Deutsche Monatsschrift*, in the March, or, at latest, in the April number. The article is important." — In the April number of that review (edited by Adolph Kolatschek) the article accordingly appeared. —

Upon referring to the *Deutsche Allgemeine Zeitung*, we find in the issue for Jan. *15, 1850* a criticism of *Art and Revolution* containing the remarks here referred to by our author. They run as follows: "Whence, beneath *our Northern skies*, shall we derive that rapt intoxication of the sense of beauty, which even upon the Ionic horizon did not loom so pure as we are wont to conceive when we sum up the æsthetic life of olden times in the principle of Hellenism?. . . These wailings are fantastic, unfruitful, and can be answered by no kind of Revolution, excepting by that of the whole *Earth-rind*, and a new cycle of the world." —

ART AND CLIMATE

THE author's publicly expressed views on the future of Art, in step with the advance of the human race to perfect Freedom, have been met with this objection, among others: that he has failed to take account of the *influence of Climate upon man's capacity for Art*, and has, for instance, presupposed of the modern Northern-European nations a future imaginative and constructive art-faculty to which the natural characteristics of their native skies are entirely opposed.

It may therefore be deemed of some importance to lay bare the lack of understanding which lies at the bottom of this objection, by a general survey of the actual relations between Art and Climate; leaving, for the present, the kindly reader to complete the individual details by their further consequences.

Just as we know that there are heavenly bodies which have not as yet, or never will have, attained the birth of those conditions fundamentally necessary to the existence of human beings: so do we know that at one time our own Earth, also, had not as yet evolved such attributes. The present physiognomy of our planet shows us that, even now, the life of Man is by no means permitted on every portion of its surface: where its climatic mood proclaims itself in unbroken exclusiveness, as on the fiery plains of the Sahara, or mid the Northern ice-steppes, there Man is an impossibility. Only where this 'Climate' resolves the fixed and all-dominating uniformity of its influence into a pliant chain of broken contrasts, do we see arise that infinitely manifold series of organic creations whose highest grade is conscience-gifted Man.

Yet where Climatic Nature draws Man beneath the all-sheltering influence of her rankest prodigality, and rocks him in her bosom as a mother rocks her child,—where we must therefore place the cradle of newborn mankind—there has Man remained a child forever—as in the Tropics,—with all an infant's good and evil qualities. First where she drew this all-conditioning, over-tender influence back, when she handed Man, like a prudent mother her adult son, to himself and his own free self-devisings,—where Man, then, mid the waning warmth of the directly fostering care of Climate, was forced to cater for himself,—do we see him ripening to the full unfoldment of his being. Only through the force of such a Need as surrounding Nature did not, like an over-careful mother, both listen for and still at once ere it had scarcely risen, but for whose appeasement he must himself provide, did he gain consciousness not only of that need but also of his *power*. This consciousness he reached through learning *the distinction between himself and Nature*; and thus it was that she, who no more *offered* him the stilling of his need, but from whom he now must *wrest* it, became the object of his observation, inquiry, and dominion.

The progress of the human race in the development of its innate capabilities of winning from Nature the contentment of those needs that waxed with its ever-waxing powers, is the *history of Culture*. In it Man evolves his own qualities in *counterpoise* to Nature, and thus acquires *independence* of her. Only man become independent of Nature by his personal energy, is the *historical* Man and only the historical Man has summoned *Art* to life, but not the primitive Man in Nature's leading-strings.

Art is the highest common life-expression of the man who, after self-fought-out contentment of his natural needs, displays himself to Nature in all the flush of triumph. His art-works as though fill up the gaps which she had left for Man's free personal activity; they form the closing harmony of her majestic whole, in which self-conscious, independent Man is thus included as her highest factor. Wherefore, where *Nature* in her overfill was All, we neither light upon free Man nor genuine *Art*; but where—as we have phrased it—she left those empty gaps, where she thus made room for the free self-evolution of Man and of his need-grown energy, was Art first born.

Granted, that Nature has also had her share in the birth of Art, just as the highest expression of the latter is the brilliant 'close,' the conscious reunion of Nature with Man, effected by his understanding of her. Her share, however, was this: that she abandoned Man, the creator of Art, to the conditions which must necessarily spur him on to self-gained consciousness,—inasmuch as she retreated before him and merely exerted a conditional influence over him, in place of holding him a prisoner in the bosom of her full and unconditional sway. From the over-tender mother, she became to him a bashful bride, whom he now must win by vigour and loveworthiness for his—endlessly enhanced—fruition; a bride who, vanquished thus by mind and valour, made offering of herself to Love's embraces. Not, therefore, in the teeming Tropics, not in the sensuous flower-land of India, was born *true Art*; but on the naked, sea-plashed rocks of Hellas, upon the stony soil and beneath the scanty shadows of the olive-trees of Attica, was set her cradle:—*for here, amid privations, strove Hercules and suffered*—here was the first *true Man* begotten.— —

When we survey the history of Hellenic culture, we are above all struck by *those* circumstances which favoured the development of Man to his highest energy, and thereby to independence of Nature and finally of those cramping human relationships which sprang directly from his natural surroundings. We certainly shall find these circumstances markedly involved in the characteristics of the 'scene of action' of Hellenic history; but the decisive feature of these characteristics lies herein, that Nature did not *pamper (v e r wöhnte)* the Hellenes by her influence, but *weaned (e n t wöhnte)* them from her care; that she *be-schooled (e r zog)*, and not *be-lapped (v e r zog)* them like the softer Asiatics. Every other determining factor in the Hellenic evolution may be referred to the individual manysidedness of the numerous racial stems which crowded close together in rich variety. The natural characteristics of their respective dwelling-places had, sure enough, an essential effect upon their individuality, and therefore upon that of the whole nation, but only in the sense of spurring them to free activity; so that the work of forming and developing these diverse individualities must be ascribed far more to History than to Nature.

The motive force of Hellenic history is thus the *vigorous (thätige) Man*; and its fairest fruit, the crown of Hellenic self-consciousness, is the *purely human Art*, i.e. that art which found its stuff and object in actual Man, man self-acknowledged as Nature's highest product. The later *Plastic art* was the luxury and superfluity of Hellenic Art: in it the flower of Greece shed down on its surroundings the overfill of its rich sap, secreted by the fibres of the humanistic art-work, and erstwhile kept close-locked within its maiden chalice: it is the squandered seed of bursting, over-ripe Hellenic Art. This seed glanced off from Man, fell back upon surrounding Nature, and on her soil twixt trees and bushes, from mountain, brook and meadow, brought forth those teeming pictures of man's art which signal for us, to this very day, the tidings of the overfill of human faculty.

In the plastic arts, Man undoubtedly brought himself once more into direct relationship with surrounding climatic Nature; but only herein, that he weighed his needs and forces against hers, and set his purely human will and pleasure in unison with the Necessity of her demeanour. *Only the free and full-fledged man*, however, such as he had evolved himself by combat with the parsimony of Nature, could throughly understand her, and wist at last to spend the overfill of his own being on that harmonic complement of Nature which should answer to his power of enjoyment. The creative faculty lay therefore ever grounded on Man's *independence of Nature*—yea, on the overfill of that quality—and not in any directly productive *operation of natural Climate*.

But the voiding of that overfill was also the death-knell of this art-creative man: the more he strewed his seed beyond the confines of his Hellenic motherland, the farther he shed this overfill toward Asia, and led back thence its lavish stream into the pragmatic-prosaic and grossly sensual world of Rome: so much the more visibly did his creative force die out; to make place, at his eventual death, for the worship of an *abstract* God who, in melancholy joy of immortality, wandered aimlessly between the splendid works of statuary and architecture which decked the burying-place of this departed Man. Thenceforth God *ruled* the world,—God, who had *made* all Nature for the glory of his name. From that time forward, man's affairs are governed by the '*incomprehensible will*' of God; no longer by the instinct and necessity of Nature,—and it is therefore a highly unchristian action, on the part of our modern Christian art-producers, to appeal to "Climate" and "Natural soil" as hindering or favouring conditions for the birth of Art.—Let us consider what has become of art-fit Man, under the dispensation of Jehova!

The first thing that strikes us, in glancing at the evolution of our modern nations, is this: that it has only most conditionally been governed by the influence of *Nature*, but quite unconditionally by the confounding and distorting operation of an alien Civilisation; that, as a matter of fact, our Culture and Civilisation have not sprung upwards from the nether soil of Nature, but have been poured down upon us from above, from the Heaven of the priests and the *Corpus Juris* of Justinian.

With its entrance upon history, the natural stock of each new European nation was grafted with a cutting from the tree of Roman-dom and Christendom, and the fruit of the thus-engendered artificial shoot, which bushed out on every hand in cripple-like monstrosity, we are now tasting in our barbaric civilisation. Hindered from the first in their self-unfolding, we can form no estimate of the shape which the original characteristics and climatic idiosyncrasies of those nations might perchance have evolved. Even though we should set down the degree of artistic culture, which they might be trusted to have attained on the path of self-unfolding, at ever so little (an assumption, however, which would be thoroughly onesided and unjust!), yet we have here no need to vex ourselves with that question; but simply to confess that such an undisturbed self-development has actually had no chance of taking place. Whosoever may choose to reply, that at all events our native idiosyncracy has had a well-marked influence on the shaping of imported elements of culture, is completely in the right when, for example, he asserts that the Christianity of Nicæa was a different matter from that of Berlin; but he would only make himself ridiculous, if he should attempt—as has already occurred to certain pious persons—to prove an innate predisposition of the Germanic races toward Christianity from the contents of the Eddas.

True, that into the evolutionary channel of the modern nations their 'climatic' origin poured its waters too, (1) and that from the perennial torrent of the Folk, with its own peculiar strain of poetry and intuition; only—it was but in an incomplete and spasmodic, a fragmentary and unsubstantial manner, that the true Folk-spirit could ever manifest itself, beneath the 'influences' that pressed upon it from outside and above. Our spiritual development has therefore been a mass of tangled contradictions: *not* the product of Nature and

Climate, nor of a cycle of culture that had shaped itself in strict conformity therewith; but the result of a violent counter-thrust against this Nature, of a wilful disregard of both Nature and Climate, of the frenzied strife twixt soul and body, "will" and "can." The desolate battlefield, across which this crazy fight swept howling, is the plain of the Middle Ages. Undecided, as of its very nature it could not but remain, the battle wavered to and fro; until the Turks came to our help, and hunted over to us, in the Occident, the last professors of Hellenic art.

Art's *renaissance*—mark well! not any *birth*—now set in with full force: the last remains of Greek art-beauty were *taught* to us. The tombstones from the burial-place of long-deceased Greek art, those weather-beaten forms of bronze and marble, denuded of their living garb of colour,—were unriddled for us by these learned men, so well as their own scant stock of understanding still permitted. And just as those monuments were, as we said, the merest gravestones of the once living Hellenic artist-man,—the last ghostlike, pallid death-abstraction from his onetime warmly-feeling, nobly-doing life,—so have we learnt from them to regard *Art* itself as an *abstract notion*, which we fancy we must pour down from above—as we had erstwhile done with the immaterial god of Heaven—into the mould of actual Life. From this abstract notion has our Modern Art been *constructed*: meaning thereby our *plastic* art, i.e. that art which, of our need of Luxury, we have *imitated* from the plastic art of Greece, itself the mere luxurious appanage of Grecian Art; and, in troth, have not imitated in the fulness wherewith it once took rise from Life and stood erect in living bloom,—but according to the sorrowful disfigurement in which alone it offered itself to us, beaten by the storms of time, torn from its natural bearings, and scattered in capricious fragments here a little and there a little. And thus we take these monuments—robbed of their warming and protecting deckery of tint— drag them naked and frostbitten through the Christian-German sand of "Mark" Brandenburg, set them up amidst the windy firs of "Sans-Souci," and chatter from between our teeth a learned sigh anent the *unfavourableness of our climate*. But that, midst this "unfavourableness," our Berlin art-pedants have not yet gone completely crazy, we ascribe with justice to the undeserved grace of God!

By all means these learned men are right, when, beholding the work of their own luxurious caprice, they find that in that work we are merely bunglers, prompted by neither necessity nor self-dependence; that in our "climate" the imitated plastic art of Greece can only be a hothouse growth, and not a natural plant This verdict, however, can but open the eyes of any man of common sense, to the fact that our whole art is good for nothing *because* it has had no origin in our actual being, nor in any harmonic supplementing of the "climatic" Nature which surrounds us. But this in nowise proves that, in our climate, an art could not unfold itself in answer to our veritable human needs; for we have never yet reached the point of developing our artistic powers, without let or hindrance, according to *our own* associate need.

A survey of our modern art thus teaches us that we absolutely do *not* stand under the influence of climatic *Nature*, but of a *History* at entire variance with that Nature. We must, therefore, first realise that our history of to-day is made by the selfsame *men* who once brought forth the Grecian art-work, and, that done, ask ourselves: *what* is it, that has changed these men so utterly, that Those created works of Art whilst We but turn-out costly wares of Industry? Then shall we also recognise that, as our essence is at bottom one and the same, so, however wide apart our starting-points, our termini must one day light upon each other, though approached on different paths. The Greek, proceeding from the bosom of Nature, attained to Art when he had made himself independent of the immediate influence of Nature: *we*, violently debarred from Nature, and proceeding from the drillground of a heaven-rid and juristic Civilisation, shall first reach Art when we completely turn our backs on such a civilisation and once more cast ourselves, with conscious bent, into the arms of Nature.

We have not, therefore, to turn to the consideration of Climatic Nature, but of *Man*, the only creator of Art, in order to discover what has made this modern European man art-impotent. Then shall we perceive with full distinctness, that this evil influence is none other than our present *Civilisation*, with its complete indifference to Climate. It is not our atmosphere, that has reduced the proud warriors of the North, who shattered once the Roman world, to servile, crass, weak-nerved, dim-eyed, deformed and slovenly cripples;—not it, that has turned the blithesome, action-lusting, dauntless sons of heroes, whom we cannot now conceive aright, into our hypochondriacal, cowardly and cringing citizens;—not it, that has brought forth from the hale and hearty Teutons our scrofulous linen-weavers, weaved themselves from skin and bones; from the Siegfried of olden days a "Gottlieb"; from spear-throwers our logic-choppers, our counsellors and sermon-spinners. No, the glory of this splendid work belongs to our clergy-ridden *Pandect-civilisation*, with all its fine results; among which, beside our Industry, our worthless, heart-and-soul-confounding *art* fills out its seat of honour. For the whole posse must be set down to this Civilisation, in its entire variance with our nature, and not to any Nature-born *necessity*.

Wherefore, not from that Civilisation, but from the future true and genuine *Culture, which shall bear a right relation to our climatic Nature,* will one day also bloom that Artwork which is now denied both breath and air to breathe in, and as to whose peculiar properties we shall never be able to form a notion until *we Men*, the creators of that artwork, can conceive ourselves as developed to a rational concord *with this Nature*.

From the kernel of our history therefore, have *we*, for now, to draw conclusions on our Future; from the character of Man, such as our history shows us working-out himself to free self-destination, under the merest conditional influence of Nature, have we to enquire how the free and veritable Men of the Future will take their stand twixt Art and Nature.

What then is the kernel of this history?

We shall surely not go far astray, if we describe it briefly thus:—

In Greekdom, we find Man evolving to full and conscious self-discrimination from Nature: the artistic monument in which this conscious man objectified himself, is the tintless marble statue,—the idea, expressed in stone, of the pure human form; which idea Philosophy, again, dissolved from out the stone and resolved into a pure 'abstraction' of the human essence. Into this solitary man, existing at last in naught but the idea,—this man in whom, amid the physical lack of all community of the species, the essence of the sheer personality was represented as the essence of the species,—the People's Christianity instilled the lifebreath of passionate heart's-desire. The error of the philosopher became the madness of the masses. This frenzy's scene of action is the Middle Ages: on it we see the Nature-sundered man—taking his personal, egoistic, and therefore impotent being for the essence of the human species—with greed and haste, by physical and moral mutilation, (2) hunt after his redemption into *God*; under whose image, by an instinctive error, he expressed the idea of the in truth con summate essence of the human race and Nature. (3)

As the only possible, true, therefore unconsciously and at last consciously striven-for, redemption from this state of misery, we then see loom before us the ascension of the *egoistic* essence of the individual into the *communistic* essence of the human race; the concretion of the abstract idea of Man into the actual, true and blissful common-being of *Mankind*. If, therefore the kernel of the world's history, from the Asiatic down to the close of the Grecian period, was the emanation of the *unit Man* from Nature: so is the kernel of the newer European history the resolution of this idea into the actuality of *Men*.

But to men who know themselves united in one all-capable species, the natural character of this or that particular Climate can no longer set up cramping bounds: to them, as a species at one with itself, the total like-united Nature of this Earth alone can form a confine. To this whole Earth-Nature, in measure as she is known to them in all her wide connexion with the World-All, will the Men and Brothers of the Future turn; yet no longer turn as to a barrier—such as the

Egoist deemed the circle of his natural surroundings—but as the prime condition of their existence, their life and handiwork.

In this vast and blest conjunction, shall we first attain the artist's true creative-force; when first *the Artists* are to hand, then will *Art* herself be present. But these Artists are *human beings*; not trees, nor waves, nor skies. This brotherhood of artist-men will mould its works of art in unison with, in complement and rounding-off of Mother Nature; accenting every quality and individual trait evoked by special need, in answer to the special call of Nature's individual features, but marching forward from the base of this particularity towards a common pact with common Nature—as toward the utmost fulness of man's being.

Before, however, men shall once more shape their artworks by their Need, and not as now by Luxury and Caprice, they will neither have the wit to bring their works to needful unison with Nature. But if they shape from Need—and the true need of Art can only be one felt in common—then no Climate upon earth, that allows at all of man's existence, can hinder them from Art-work; the rather will the niggardness of outward Nature but whet the more their purely human artist-zeal.

As for the objection that, even for the generation of the *art-need*, peculiar favouring conditions of Climate—such as Ionic skies—are indispensable: it is, in the sense in which it is nowadays brought forward, either bigoted or hypocritical, and in its very gist unmanly. Wherever Climate does not forbid men living *free* and *healthy* lives, neither will it hinder them from bodily beauty and the feeling of the need of art. Climate can only pronounce its fatal veto where, through the invincibility of its influence, it stays true Men from being bred, and merely lets the human *animal* vegetate. Yet even these men-beasts will one day vanish before the march of truer culture; just as so many of their like have already vanished, or through exchange of climate and intermingling of varieties, have thriven into normal men. But, as we have said above, where men attain to mastery of their dependence on climatic Nature, they will necessarily—in their ever broader *historical* contact with all those men who have reached like independence—stride onward also to the mastery of each dependence on those oppressive tenets which have clung to them as the result of erroneous conceptions harboured in the time of that war-of-emancipation with Nature, and have ruled both the religious and political conscience of mankind with equal cramping dictates of authority. The common creed of those Men of the Future must therefore necessarily take this form:—

There exists no higher *Power* than *Man's Community*; there is naught so *worthy Love* as the *Brotherhood of Man*.

But only through the *highest power of Love* can we attain to *perfect Freedom*; for there exists no genuine Freedom but that in which *each Man hath share*.

The mediator between Power and Freedom, the redeemer without whom Power remains but violence, and Freedom but caprice, is therefore—Love; yet not that revelation from above, imposed on us by precept and command,—and therefore never realised,—like the Christian's: but *that* Love which issues from the Power of true and undistorted human nature; which in its origin is nothing other than the liveliest utterance of this nature, that proclaims itself in pure delight at physical existence and, starting from marital love, strides forward through the love for children, friends and brothers, right on to *love for Universal Man.*

This Love is thus the wellspring of all true Art, for through it alone can the natural flower of *Beauty* bloom from Life. Yet Beauty, too, is now only one of our abstract notions, and verily no notion deduced from actual Life, but from the *lesson-ed* Grecian art. That which can only be perceived and felt in the full warm joy of all the senses, has become the object of æsthetic speculation; and, confronted with the axioms of the Metaphysician, our modern art- professor sighs again for Ionic skies, beneath which alone (in his opinion) can Beauty ever thrive. But here, again, he keeps his eyes involuntarily fixed on the only remaining, dull and faded link that connects the art of Greece with our own time, the *plastic* art and notably the natural Material from which it fashioned forms. He thus forgets entirely that the fashioner of those statues was first and foremost an artist Man, and that he only *copied* in those works the actual artwork he had *carried out* upon and with his own warm, living body. The Beauty to which the artist at last erected marble statues, he had *felt* before, and *tasted*, with the highest joy of sense; to him this tasting had been a true instinctive *need*, and this need was none other than—Love. How high this love-need could mount within the exclusive circle of the Grecian nation, we learn from the course of their historical evolution. Because it was no more than the need of a peculiar people, it remained hedged about with Egoism; and could therefore only squander, so to speak, its force on wantonness at last, and, after all this prodigality, die out in philosophical abstractions, renewed by not one spark of counter-love. If, on the other hand, we weigh the instinctive impulse of the men of present history,—if we recognise that they can only reach redemption by the realisation of God in the physical verity of the Human Race,—that their most burning need can only still itself in Universal Human Love, and that, by an infallible necessity, it must one day attain this stilling,—then we can but look with full assurance to a future element of life in which this Love, extending its own need into the widest circles of broad humanity, must needs give birth to works undreamt as yet; works which, moulded by unheard-of manysidedness of *felt and living* sense of Beauty, shall turn those mouldering remains of Grecian art to unregarded playthings for peevish children.

Let us therefore conclude thus:—

That which a man loves, that *deems* he beautiful; that which strong, free Men—who in community are all that of their essence they can be—that which *they* love in common, that *is* in very surety beautiful. No other natural standard exists for true, not inculcated, Beauty. In their joy at this beauty, will the Freemen of the Future fashion works of Art such as they needs *must* fashion to content their measurelessly heightened need. Everywhere, in every Climate, will these works be suchwise fashioned as to answer to the purely human need inspired by native skies: they will be beautiful alike and perfect, for reason that in them the highest need of Man is *satisfied*. But in the boundless intercourse of Future Men, the thousand individual qualities that shall have sprung from human Need, in answer to the divers idiosyncracies of Climate,—so *soon as ever they have raised themselves to the height of the universal Human, and therefore universally Intelligible,*—will mutually react on one   another in fertilising interchange, and blossom forth to joint 'all-human' artworks, of whose amplitude and splendour our art-sense of to-day, with its eternal clinging to the fetters of the old and dead, can conceive no jot or tittle.

To clear the ground for such a Work of the Future, must the Earth, then, take the human race once more into her womb, and bear herself and it anew?

In troth, she'd play us thus a sorry trick!—for then would Mother Earth destroy at one fell swoop all those conditions whose actual presence, just as they are, now shows us—rightly understood—the Necessity of such a framing of the human Future as we have here but barely hinted. For we can gain no hope, no courage, no confident assurance of the Future, till we convince ourselves that the fulfilment of our soul's best wish hangs not upon the old erroneous supposition that men must needs be what our wilful notions, abstracted from the Past, dictate that they *should* be; but on the certain knowledge, that they require alone to be what by their very nature they *can* be, and *therefore shall and will be*. Not *Angels*; but precisely *Men*!

The *Climate* about which alone we can talk, in any reasonable fashion, as fundamentally conditioning Art, is therefore:

The actual—and not the fancied—essence of the Human Race.

Notes

1

The original text runs: "Wohl ist im Entwickelungsgange der modernen Nationen ihre klimatische Originalität ebenfalls mit eingeflossen, und zwar aus dem unversiegbaren Strome des Volkes,..." The author has here indulged in a rhetorical play of words, quite impossible to reproduce in another tongue; taking the word "influence" from the mouths of his opponents, he has, in this sentence, restored it to its primitive meaning, viz., "to flow into" (cf. *influx*), a sense still preserved in the German verb "einfliessen." To complete his metaphor, he has further employed the "gang" of "Entwickelungsgang" (course of evolution) in its sense of "conduit," a meaning retained in the English "water-course." — TR.

2

Compare *Parsifal*, Act i. "an sich legt er die Frevelhand," where Gurnemanz refers to Klingsor's egoistic endeavours to force his way to the *Gral.* — TR.

3

"Unter welchem er das in Wahrheit vollkommene Wesen der menschlichen Gattung und der Natur nach unwillkurlichem Irrthume begriff." — The meaning of this passage, and of that which follows, will become clearer by reference to Ludwig Feuerbach's *Essence of Christianity* (for Wagner's partial thought-indebtedness whereto, see the Preface to the present volume and also p. 25), in the first chapter of which we find: "Religion is nothing else than the consciousness which man has of his own, not finite and limited, but infinite nature"; again: "The antithesis of divine and human is nothing else than the antithesis between human nature in general and the individual"; and later: "God is the concept of the species as an individual: the idea, or rather the essence of the species, that, while a universal being, the epitome of all perfections, of all attributes set free from the limits existing in the mind and feeling of the individual, is withal an individual *personal* being......Man supplies the absence of the idea of the species by the idea of God, — as of a Being who is free from the limits and wants which oppress the individual, and, in his judgment (since he identifies the species with the individual), the species itself." — TR.

A PILGRIMAGE TO BEETHOVEN

Prefatory Note

Shortly after the modest funeral of my friend R..., lately deceased in Paris, I had set to work and written the brief history of his sufferings in this glittering metropolis, in accordance with the dead man's wish, when among his papers—from which I propose to select a few complete articles in the sequel—there came into my hands the fond narration of his journey to Vienna and visit to Beethoven. There I found a wonderful agreement with what I already had jotted down. This decided me to print that fragment of his journal in front of my own account of his mournful end, since it deals with an earlier period of his life, and also is likely to wake a little prior interest in my departed friend.

A PILGRIMAGE TO BEETHOVEN

(01)

WANT-AND-CARE, thou patron-goddess of the German musician, unless he happens to be Kapellmeister to a Court-theatre or the like, (02) —Want-and-care, thine be the name first lauded even in this reminiscence from my life! Ay, let me sing of thee, thou staunch companion of my life-time! Faithful hast thou been to me, and never left me; the smiles of Inconstance thou hast ever warded off, and shielded me from Fortune's scorching rays! In deepest shadow hast thou ever cloaked from me the empty baubles of this earth: have thanks for thy unwearying attachment! Yet, might it so be, prithee some day seek another favourite; for, purely out of curiosity, I fain would learn for once how life might fare *without* thee. At least, I beg thee, plague especially our political dreamers, the madmen who are breathless to unite our Germany beneath *one* sceptre:—think on't, there then would be but one Court-theatre, one solitary Kapellmeister's post! What would become of my prospects, my only hopes; which, even as it is, but hover dim and shadowy before me— e'en now when German royal theatres exist in plenty? (03) But I perceive I am turning blasphemous. Forgive, my patron-goddess, the dastard wish just uttered! Thou know'st my heart, and how entirely I am thine, and shall remain thine, were there a thousand royal theatres in Germany. (04) Amen!

Without this daily prayer of mine I begin nothing, and therefore not the story of my pilgrimage to Beethoven!

In case this weighty document should get published after my death, however, I further deem needful to say who I am; without which information much therein might not be understood. Know then, world and testament-executor!

A middle-sized town of middle Germany is my birthplace. I'm not quite certain what I really was intended for; I only remember that one night I for the first time heard a symphony of Beethoven's performed, that it set me in a fever, I fell ill, and on my recovery had become a musician. This circumstance may haply account for the fact that, though in time I also made acquaintance with other beautiful music, I yet have loved, have honoured, worshipped Beethoven before all else. Henceforth I knew no other pleasure, than to plunge so deep into his genius that at last I fancied myself become a portion thereof; and as this tiniest portion, I began to respect myself, to come by higher thoughts and views — in brief, to develop into what sober people call an idiot. My madness, however, was of very good-humoured sort, and did no harm to any man; the bread I ate, in this condition, was very dry, and the liquid that I drank most watery; for lesson-giving yields but poor returns, with us, O honoured world and testament-executor! (05)

Thus I lived for some time in my garret, till it occurred to me one day that the man whose creations I reverenced above all else was still *alive*. It passed my understanding, how I had never thought of that before. It had never struck me that Beethoven could exist, could be eating bread and breathing air, like one of us; but this Beethoven was living in Vienna for all that, and he too was a poor German musician!

My peace of mind was gone. My every thought became one wish: *to see Beethoven*! No Mussulman more devoutly longed to journey to the grave of his Prophet, than I to the lodging where Beethoven dwelt.

But how to set about the execution of my project? To Vienna was a long, long journey, and needed money; whilst I, poor devil, scarce earned enough to stave off hunger! So I must think of some exceptional means of finding the needful travelling-money. A few pianoforte-sonatas, which I had composed on the master's model, I carried to the publisher; in a word or two the man made clear to me that I was a fool with my sonatas. He gave me the advice, however, that if I wanted to some day earn a dollar or so by my compositions, I should begin by making myself a little renommée by galops and pot-pourris.—I shuddered; but my yearning to see Beethoven gained the victory; I composed galops and pot-pourris, but for very shame I could never bring myself to cast one glance on Beethoven in all that time, for fear it should defile him.

To my misfortune, however, these earliest sacrifices of my innocence did not even bring me pay, for my publisher explained that I first must earn myself a little name. I shuddered again, and fell into despair. That despair brought forth some capital galops. I actually touched money for them, and at last believed I had amassed enough to be able to execute my plan. But two years had elapsed, and all the time I feared that Beethoven might die before I had made my name by galops and pot-pourris. Thank God! he had survived the glitter of my name!—Saint Beethoven, forgive me that renommée; 'twas earned that I might see thee!

Joy! my goal was in sight. Who happier than I? I might strap my bundle and set out for Beethoven at once. A holy awe possessed me when I passed outside the gate and turned my footsteps southwards. Gladly would I have taken a seat in the diligence, not because I feared footsoreness—(what hardships would I not have cheerfully endured for such a goal!)—but since I should thus have reached Beethoven sooner. I had done too little for my fame as galop-composer, however, to be able to pay carriage-fare. So I bore all toils, and thought myself lucky to have got so far that they could take me to my goal. O what I pictured, what I dreamed! No lover, after years of separation, could be more happy at returning to his youthful love.

And so I came to fair Bohemia, the land of harpists and wayside singers. In a little town I found a troop of strolling musicians; they formed a tiny orchestra, composed of a 'cello, two violins, two horns, a clarinet and a flute; moreover there was a woman who played the harp, and two with lovely voices. They played dances and sang songs; folk gave them money and they journeyed on. In a beautiful shady place beside the highway I found them again; they had camped on the grass, and were taking their meal. I introduced myself by saying that I too was a travelling musician, and we soon became friends. As they played dance-music, I bashfully asked if they knew my galops also? God bless them! they had never heard of my galops. O what good news for me!

I inquired whether they played any other music than dances.

"To be sure," they answered, "but only for ourselves; not for gentlefolk."

They unpacked their sheets, and I caught sight of the grand Septuor of Beethoven; astonished, I asked if they played that too?

"Why not?"—replied the eldest,—"Joseph has hurt his hand, and can't play the second violin to-day, or we'd be delighted to give it at once."

Beside myself, I snatched up Joseph's violin, promised to do my best to replace him, and we began the Septuor.

O rapture! Here on the slope of a Bohemian highway, in open air, Beethoven's Septuor played by dance-musicians with a purity, a precision, and a depth of feeling too seldom found among the highest virtuosi!—Great Beethoven, we brought thee a worthy offering.

We had just got to the Finale, when—the road bending up at this spot toward the hills—an elegant travelling-carriage drew slowly and noiselessly near, and stopped at last close by us. A marvellously tall and marvellously blond young man lay stretched full-length in the carriage; he listened to our music with tolerable attention, drew out a pocket-book, and made a few notes. Then he let drop a gold coin from the carriage, and drove away with a few words of English to his lackey; whence it dawned on me that he must be an Englishman.

This incident quite put us out; luckily we had finished our performance of the Septuor. I embraced my friends, and wanted to accompany them; but they told me they must leave the high road here and strike across the fields, to get home to their native village for a while. Had it not been Beethoven himself who was awaiting me, I certainly would have kept them company. As it was, we bade each other a tender good-bye, and parted. Later it occurred to me that no one had picked up the Englishman's coin.—

Upon entering the nearest inn, to fortify my body, I found the Englishman seated at an ample meal. He eyed me up and down, and at last addressed me in passable German.

"Where are your colleagues?" he asked.

"Gone home," I replied.

"Just take out your violin, and play me something more," he continued, "here's money."

That annoyed me; I told him I neither played for money, nor had I any violin, and briefly explained how I had fallen in with those musicians.

"They were good musicians," put in the Englishman, "and the Symphony of Beethoven was very good, too."

Struck by this remark, I asked him if he practised music?

"*Yes*," he answered, "twice a week I play the flute, on Thursdays the French horn, and of a Sunday I compose."

That was a good deal, enough to astound me. In all my life I had never heard tell of travelling English musicians; I concluded that they must do very well, if they could afford to make their tours in such splendid equipages. I asked if he was a musician by profession?

For long I got no answer; finally he drawled out, that he had plenty of money.

My mistake was obvious to me now, for my question had plainly offended him. At a loss what to say, I devoured my simple meal in silence.

After another long inspection of me, the Englishman commenced afresh.

"Do you know Beethoven?"

I replied that I had never yet been in Vienna, but was on my way there to fulfil my dearest wish, to see the worshipped master.

"Where do you come from?" he asked.

"From L...."

"That's not so far! I've come from England, and also with the intention of seeing Beethoven. We both will make his acquaintance; he's a very famous composer."

What a wonderful coincidence!—I thought to myself. Mighty master, what divers kinds thou drawest to thee! On foot and on wheels they make their journey.—My Englishman interested me; but I avow I little envied him his equipage. To me it seemed as though my weary pilgrimage afoot were holier and more devout, and that its goal must bless me more than this proud gentleman who drove there in full state.

Then the postilion blew his horn; the Englishman drove   off, shouting back to me that he would see Beethoven before I did.

I scarce had trudged a few miles in his wake, when unexpectedly I encountered him again. It was on the high road. A wheel of his carriage had broken down; but in majestic ease he sat inside, with his valet mounted up behind him, notwithstanding that the vehicle was all aslant. I learnt that they were waiting for the return of the postilion, who had run off to a somewhat distant village to fetch a blacksmith. As they had already been waiting a good long time, and as the valet spoke nothing but English, I decided to set off for the village myself, to hurry up smith and postilion. In fact I found the latter in a tavern, where spirits were relieving him of any particular care about the Englishman; however, I soon brought him back with the smith to the injured carriage. The damage was mended; the Englishman promised to announce me to Beethoven, and—drove away.

Judge my surprise, when I overtook him again on the high road next day! This time, however, no wheels were broken; drawn up in the middle of the road, he was tranquilly reading a book, and seemed quite pleased to see me coming.

"I've been waiting a good many hours for you," he said, "as it occurred to me on this very spot that I did wrong in not inviting you to drive with me to Beethoven. Riding is much better than walking. Come into the carriage."

I was astonished again. For a moment I really hesitated whether I ought not to accept his invitation; but I soon remembered the vow I had made the previous day when I saw the Englishman rolling off; I had sworn, in any circumstances to pursue my pilgrimage on foot. I told him this openly. It was now the Englishman's turn to be astonished; he could not comprehend me. He repeated his offer, saying that he had already waited many hours expressly for me, notwithstanding his having been very much delayed at his sleeping-quarters through the time consumed in thoroughly repairing the broken wheel. I remained firm, and he drove off, wondering.

Candidly, I had a secret dislike of him; for I was falling prey to a vague foreboding that this Englishman would cause me serious trouble. Moreover his reverence for Beethoven, and his proposal to make his acquaintance, to me seemed more the idle whim of a wealthy coxcomb than the deep inner need of an enthusiastic soul. Therefore I preferred to avoid him, lest his company might desecrate my pious wish.

But, as if my destiny meant to school me for the dangerous association with this gentleman into which I was yet to fall, I met him again on the evening of that same day, halting before an inn, and, as it seemed, still waiting for me. For he sat with his back to the horses, looking down the road by which I came.

"Sir," he began, "I again have waited very many hours for you. Will you drive with me to Beethoven?"

This time my astonishment was mingled with a secret terror. I could only explain this striking obstinacy in the attempt to serve me, on the supposition that the Englishman, having noticed my growing antipathy for him, was bent on thrusting himself upon me for my destruction. With undisguised annoyance, I once more declined his offer. Then he insolently cried:

"Goddam, you little value Beethoven. *I* shall soon see him." Post haste he flew away.—

And that was really the last time I was to meet this islander on my still lengthy road to Vienna. At last I trod Vienna's streets; the end of my pilgrimage was reached. With what feelings I entered this Mecca of my faith! All the toil and hardships of my weary journey were forgotten; I was at the goal, within the walls that circled Beethoven.

I was too deeply moved, to be able to think of carrying out my aim at once. True, the first thing I did was to inquire for Beethoven's dwelling, but merely in order to lodge myself close by. Almost opposite the house in which the master lived there happened to be a not too stylish hostelry; I engaged a little room on its fifth floor, and there began preparing myself for the greatest event of my life, a visit to Beethoven.

After having rested two days, fasting and praying, but never casting another look on the city, I plucked up heart to leave my inn and march straight across to the house of marvels. I was told Herr Beethoven was not at home. That suited me quite well; for it gave me time to collect myself afresh. But when four times more throughout the day the same reply was given me, and with a certain increasing emphasis, I held that day for an unlucky one, and abandoned my visit in gloom.

As I was strolling back to the inn, my Englishman waved his hand to me from a first-floor window, with a fair amount of affability.

"Have you seen Beethoven?" he shouted.

"Not yet; he wasn't in," I answered, wondering at our fresh encounter. The Englishman met me on the stairs, and with remarkable friendliness insisted upon my entering his apartment.

"*Mein Herr*," he said, "I have seen you go to Beethoven's house five times to-day. I have been here a good many days, and have taken up my quarters in this villainous hotel so as to be near Beethoven. Believe me, it is most difficult to get a word with him; the gentleman is full of crotchets. At first I went six times a-day to his house, and each time was turned away. Now I get up very early, and sit at my window till late in the evening, to see when Beethoven goes out. But the gentleman seems *never* to go out."

"So you think Beethoven was at home to-day, as well, and had me sent away?" I cried aghast.

"Exactly; you and I have each been dismissed. And to me it is very annoying, for I didn't come here to make Vienna's acquaintance, but Beethoven's."

That was very sad news for me. Nevertheless I tried my luck again on the following day; but once more in vain,—the gates of heaven were closed against me.

My Englishman, who kept constant watch on my fruitless attempts from his window, had now gained positive information that Beethoven's apartments did not face the street. He was very irritating, but unboundedly persevering. My patience, on the contrary, was wellnigh exhausted, for I had more reason than he; a week had gradually slipped by, without my reaching my goal, and the returns from my galops allowed a by no means lengthy stay in Vienna. Little by little I began to despair.

I poured my griefs into my landlord's ear. He smiled, and promised to tell me the cause of my bad fortune if I would undertake not to betray it to the Englishman. Suspecting my unlucky star, I took the stipulated vow.

"You see," said the worthy host, "quite a number of Englishmen come here, to lie in wait for Herr von Beethoven. This annoys Herr von Beethoven very much, and he is so enraged by the push of these gentry that he has made it clean impossible for any stranger to gain admittance to him. He's a singular gentleman, and one must forgive him. But it's very good business for my inn, which is generally packed with English, whom the difficulty of getting a word with Herr Beethoven compels to be my guests for longer than they otherwise would. However, as you promise not to scare away my customers, I hope to find a means of smuggling you to Herr Beethoven."

This was very edifying; I could not reach my goal because, poor devil, I was taken for an Englishman. So ho! my fears were verified; the Englishman was my perdition! At first I thought of quitting the inn, since it was certain that everyone who lodged there was considered an Englishman at Beethoven's house, and for that reason I also was under the ban. However, the landlord's promise, to find me an opportunity of seeing and speaking with Beethoven, held me back. Meanwhile the Englishman, whom I now detested from the bottom of my heart, had been practising all kinds of intrigues and bribery, yet all without result.

Thus several fruitless days slipped by again, while the revenue from my galops was visibly dwindling, when at last the landlord confided to me that I could not possibly miss Beethoven if I would go to a certain beer-garden, which the composer was in the habit of visiting almost every day at the same hour. At like time my mentor gave me such unmistakable directions as to the master's personal appearance, that I could not fail to recognise him. My spirits revived, and I resolved not to defer my fortune to the morrow. It was impossible for me to meet Beethoven on his going out, as he always left his house by a back-door; so there remained nothing but the beer-garden.

Alas! I sought the master there in vain on that and the two succeeding days. Finally, on the fourth, as I was turning my steps towards the fateful garden at the stated hour, to my despair I noticed that the Englishman was cautiously and carefully following me at a distance. The wretch, posted at his eternal window, had not let it escape him that I went out every day at a certain time in the same direction; struck by this, and guessing that I had found some means of tracking Beethoven, he had decided to reap his profit from my supposed discovery. He told me all this with the calmest impudence, declaring at the same time that he meant to follow wherever I went. In vain were all my efforts to deceive him and make him believe that I was only going to refresh myself in a common beer-garden, far too unfashionable to be frequented by gentlemen of his quality: he remained unshaken, and I could only curse my fate. At last I tried impoliteness, and sought to get rid of him by abuse; but, far from letting it provoke him, he contented himself with a placid smile. His fixed idea was to see Beethoven; nothing else troubled him.

And in truth I was this day, at last, to look on the face of great Beethoven for the first time. Nothing can depict my emotion, and my fury too, as, sitting by side of my gentleman, I saw a man approach whose looks and bearing completely answered the description my host had given me of the master's exterior. The long blue overcoat, the tumbled shock of grey hair; and then the features, the expression of the face,—exactly what a good portrait had long left hovering before my mental eye. There could be no mistake: at the first glance I had recognised him! With short, quick steps, he passed us; awe and veneration held me chained.

Not one of my movements was lost on the Englishman; with avid eyes he watched the newcomer, who withdrew into the farthest corner of the as yet deserted garden, gave his order for wine, and remained for a while in an attitude of meditation. My throbbing heart cried out: 'Tis he! For some moments I clean forgot my neighbour, and watched with eager eye and speechless transport the man whose genius was autocrat of all my thoughts and feelings since ever I had learnt to think and feel. Involuntarily I began muttering to myself, and fell into a sort of monologue, which closed with the but too meaning words:

"Beethoven, it is thou, then, whom I see?"

Nothing escaped my dreadful neighbour, who, leaning over to me, had listened with bated breath to my aside. From the depths of my ecstasy I was startled by the words:

"Yes! this gentleman is Beethoven. Come, let us present ourselves to him at once!"

In utter alarm and irritation, I held the cursed English man back by the elbow.

"What are you doing?" I cried, "Do you want to compromise us—in this place—so entirely without regard for manners?"

"Oh!" he answered, "it's a capital opportunity; we shall not easily find a better."

With that he drew a kind of notebook from his pocket, and tried to make direct for the man in the blue overcoat. Beside myself, I clutched the idiot's coat-tails, and thundered at him, "Are you possessed with a devil?"

This scene had attracted the stranger's attention. He appeared to have formed a painful guess that he was the subject of our agitation, and, hastily emptying his glass, he rose to go. No sooner had the Englishman remarked this, than he tore himself from my grasp with such violence that he left one of his coat-tails in my hand, and threw himself across Beethoven's path. The master sought to avoid him; but the good-for-nothing stepped in front, made a superfine bow in the latest English fashion, and addressed him as follows:

"I have the honour to present myself to the much renowned composer and very estimable gentleman, Herr Beethoven."

He had no need to add more, for at his very first words, Beethoven, after casting a glance at myself, had sprung on one side and vanished from the garden as quick as lightning. Nevertheless the irrepressible Briton was on the point of running after the fugitive, when I seized his remaining coat-tail in a storm of indignation. Somewhat surprised, he stopped, and bellowed at me:

"Goddam! this gentleman is worthy to be an Englishman! He's a great man, and no mistake, and I shall lose no time in making his acquaintance."

I was petrified; this ghastly adventure had crushed my last hope of seeing my heart's fondest wish e'er fulfilled.

It was manifest, in fact, that henceforth every attempt to approach Beethoven in an ordinary way had been made completely futile for me. In the utterly threadbare state of my finances I now had only to decide whether I should set out at once for home, with my labour lost, or take one final desperate step to reach my goal. The first alternative sent a shudder to the very bottom of my soul. Who, so near the doors of the highest shrine, could see them shut for ever without falling into annihilation?

Ere thus abandoning my soul's salvation, I still would venture on one forlorn hope. But *what* step, what road should I take? For long I could think of nothing coherent. Alas! my brain was paralysed; nothing presented itself to my overwrought imagination, save the memory of what I had to suffer when I held the coat-tail of that terrible Englishman in my hand. Beethoven's side-glance at my unhappy self, in this fearful catastrophe, had not escaped me; I felt what that glance had meant; he had taken me for an Englishman!

What was to be done, to lay the master's suspicion? Everything depended on letting him know that I was a simple German soul, brimful of earthly poverty but over-earthly enthusiasm.

So at last I decided to pour out my heart upon paper. And this I did. I wrote; briefly narrating the history of my life, how I had become a musician, how I worshipped him, how I once had come by the wish to know him in person, how I had spent two years in making a name as galop-composer, how I had begun and ended my pilgrimage, what sufferings the Englishman had brought upon me, and what a terrible plight my present was. As my heart grew sensibly lighter with this recital of my woes, the comfortable feeling led me to a certain tone of familiarity; I wove into my letter quite frank and fairly strong reproaches of the master's unjust treatment of my wretched self. Finally I closed the letter in genuine inspiration; sparks flew before my eyes when I wrote the address: "*An Herrn Ludwig van Beethoven.*" I only stayed to breathe a silent prayer, and delivered the letter with my own hand at Beethoven's house.

Returning to my hotel in the highest spirits—great heavens! what brought the dreaded Englishman again before my eyes? From his window he had spied my latest move, as well; in my face he had read the joy of hope, and that sufficed to place me in his power once more. In effect he stopped me on the steps with the question: "Good news? When do we see Beethoven?"

"Never, never"!—I cried in despair—"*You* will never see Beethoven again, in all your life. Leave me, wretch, we have nothing in common!"

"We have much in common," he coolly rejoined, "where is my coat-tail, sir? Who authorised you to forcibly deprive me of it? Don't you know that you are to blame for Beethoven's behaviour to me? How could he think it *convenable* to have anything to do with a gentleman wearing only one coat-tail?"

Furious at seeing the blame thrown back upon myself, I shouted: "Sir, your coat-tail shall be restored to you; may you keep it as a shameful memento of how you insulted the great Beethoven, and hurled a poor musician to his doom! Farewell; may we never meet again!"

He tried to detain and pacify me, assuring me that he had plenty more coats in the best condition; would I only tell him when Beethoven meant to receive us?—But I rushed upstairs to my fifth-floor attic; there I locked myself in, and waited for Beethoven's answer.

How can I ever describe what took place inside, *around* me, when the next hour actually brought me a scrap of music-paper, on which stood hurriedly written: "Excuse me, Herr R..., if I beg you not to call on me until tomorrow morning, as I am busy preparing a packet of music for the post to-day. To-morrow I shall expect you.—Beethoven."

My first action was to fall on my knees and thank Heaven for this exceptional mercy; my eyes grew dim with scalding tears. At last, however, my feelings found vent in the wildest joy; I sprang up, and round my tiny room I danced like a lunatic. I'm not quite sure what it was I danced; I only remember that to my utter shame I suddenly became aware that I was whistling one of my galops to it. (06) This mortifying discovery restored me to my senses. I left my garret, the inn, and, drunk with joy I rushed into the streets of Vienna.

My God, my woes had made me clean forget that I was in Vienna! How delighted I was with the merry ways of the dwellers in this empire-city. I was in a state of exaltation, and saw everything through coloured spectacles. The somewhat shallow sensuousness of the Viennese seemed the freshness of warm life to me; their volatile and none too discriminating love of pleasure I took for frank and natural sensibility to all things beautiful. I ran my eye down the five stage-posters for the day. Heavens! On one of them I saw: *Fidelio*, an opera by Beethoven.

To the theatre I must go, however shrunk the profits from my galops. As I entered the pit, the overture began. It was the revised edition of the opera, which, to the honour of the penetrating public of Vienna, had failed under its earlier title, *Leonora*. (07) I had never yet heard the opera in this its second form; judge, then, my delight at making here my first acquaintance with the glorious new! A very young maiden played the rôle of Leonora; but youthful as she was, this singer seemed already wedded to Beethoven's genius. With what a glow, what poetry, what depth of effect, did she portray this extraordinary woman! She was called *Wilhelmine Schröder*. (08) Hers is the high distinction of having set open this work of Beethoven to the German public; for that evening I saw the superficial Viennese themselves aroused to the strongest enthusiasm. For my own part, the heavens were opened to me; I was transported, and adored the genius who had led me—like Florestan—from night and fetters into light and freedom. (09)

I could not sleep that night. What I had just experienced, and what was in store for me next day, were too great and overpowering for me to calmly weave into a dream. I lay awake, building castles in the air and preparing myself for Beethoven's presence.—At last the new day dawned; impatiently I waited till the seemly hour for a morning visit;—it struck, and I set forth. The weightiest event of my life stood before me: I trembled at the thought.

However, I had yet one fearful trial to pass through.

Leaning against the wall of Beethoven's house, as cool as a cucumber, my evil spirit waited for me—the Englishman!—The monster, after suborning all the world, had ended by bribing our landlord; the latter had read the open note from Beethoven before myself, and betrayed its contents to the Briton.

A cold sweat came over me at the sight; all poesy, all heavenly exaltation vanished: once more I was in *his* power.

"Come," began the caitiff, "let us introduce ourselves to Beethoven."

At first I thought of helping myself with a lie, and pretending that I was not on the road to Beethoven at all. But he cut the ground from under my feet by telling me with the greatest candour how he had got to the back of my secret, and declaring that he had no intention of leaving me till we both returned from Beethoven. I tried soft words, to move him from his purpose—in vain! I flew into a rage—in vain! At last I hoped to outwit him by swiftness of foot; like an arrow I darted up the steps, and tore at the bell like a maniac. But ere the door was opened the gentleman was by my side, tugging at the tail of my coat and saying: "You can't escape me. I've a right to your coat-tail, and shall hold on to it till we are standing before Beethoven."

Infuriated, I turned about and tried to loose myself; ay, I felt tempted to defend myself against this insolent son of Britain by deeds of violence:—then the door was opened. The old serving-maid appeared, shewed a wry face at our queer position, and made to promptly shut the door again. In my agony I shouted out my name, and protested that I had been invited by Herr Beethoven himself.

The old lady was still hesitating, for the look of the Englishman seemed to fill her with a proper apprehension, when Beethoven himself, as luck would have it, appeared at the door of his study. Seizing the moment, I stepped quickly in, and moved towards the master to tender my apologies. At like time, however, I dragged the Englishman behind me, as he still was holding me tight. He carried out his threat, and never released me till we both were standing before Beethoven. I made my bow, and stammered out my name; although, of course, he did not hear it, the master seemed to guess that it was I who had written him. He bade me enter his room; without troubling himself at Beethoven's astonished glance, my companion slipped in after me.

Here was I—in the sanctuary; and yet the hideous perplexity into which the awful Briton had plunged me, robbed me of all that sense of well-being so requisite for due enjoyment of my fortune. Nor was Beethoven's outward appearance itself at all calculated to fill one with a sense of ease. He was clad in somewhat untidy house-clothes, with a red woollen scarf wrapped round his waist; long, bushy grey hair hung in disorder from his head, and his gloomy, forbidding expression by no means tended to reassure me. We took our seats at a table strewn with pens and paper.

An uncomfortable feeling held us tongue-tied. It was only too evident that Beethoven was displeased at receiving two instead of one.

At last he began, in grating tones: "You come from L...?" I was about to reply, when he stopped me; passing me a sheet of paper and a pencil, he added: "Please write; I cannot hear."

I knew of Beethoven's deafness, and had prepared myself for it. Nevertheless it was like a stab through my heart when I heard his hoarse and broken words, "I cannot hear." To stand joyless and poor in the world; to know no uplifting but in the might of Tone, and yet to be forced to say, "I cannot hear!" That moment gave me the key to Beethoven's exterior, the deep furrows on his cheeks, the sombre dejection of his look, the set defiance of his lips—*he heard not!*

Distraught, and scarcely knowing what, I wrote down an apology, with a brief account of the circumstances that had made me appear in the Englishman's company. Meanwhile the latter sat silently and calmly contemplating Beethoven, who, as soon as he had read my lines, turned rather sharply to him and asked what he might want.

"I have the honour —" commenced the Briton.

"I don't understand you!" cried Beethoven, hastily interrupting him; "I cannot hear, nor can I speak much. Please write down what you want of me."

The Englishman placidly reflected for a moment, then drew an elaborate music-case from his pocket, and said to me: "Very good. You write: 'I beg Herr Beethoven to look through my composition; if any passage does not please him, will he have the kindness to set a cross against it.'"

I wrote down his request, word for word, in the hope of getting rid of him at last. And so it happened. After Beethoven had read, he laid the Englishman's composition on the table with a peculiar smile, nodded his head, and said, "I will send it."

With this my gentleman was mighty pleased; he rose, made an extra-superfine bow, and took his leave. I drew a deep breath:—he was gone.

Now for the first time did I feel myself within the sanctuary. Even Beethoven's features visibly brightened; he looked at me quietly for an instant, then began:

"The Briton has caused you much annoyance? Take comfort from mine; these travelling Englishmen have plagued me wellnigh out of my life. To-day they come to stare at a poor musician, to-morrow at a rare wild beast. I am truly grieved at having confounded you with them.—You wrote me that you liked my compositions. I'm glad of that, for nowadays I count but little on folk being pleased with my things."

This confidential tone soon removed my last embarrassment; a thrill of joy ran through me at these simple words. I wrote that I certainly was not the only one imbued with such glowing enthusiasm for every creation of his; that I wished nothing more ardently than to be able to secure for my father-town, for instance, the happiness of seeing him. in its midst for once; that he then would convince himself what an effect his works produced on the entire public there.

"I can quite believe," answered Beethoven, "that my compositions find more favour in Northern Germany. The Viennese annoy me often; they hear too much bad stuff each day, ever to be disposed to take an earnest thing in earnest."

I ventured to dispute this, instancing the performance of "Fidelio" I had attended on the previous evening, which the Viennese public had greeted with the most demonstrative enthusiasm.

"H'm, h'm!" muttered the master. "Fidelio! But I know the little mites are clapping their hands to-day out of pure conceit, for they fancy that in revising this opera I merely followed their own advice. So they want to pay me for my trouble, and cry bravo! 'Tis a good-natured folk, and not too learned; I had rather be with them, than with sober people.—Do you like Fidelio now?"

I described the impression made on me by last night's performance, and remarked that the whole had splendidly gained by the added pieces.

"Irksome work!" rejoined Beethoven. "I am no opera-composer; at least, I know no theatre in the world for which I should care to write another opera! Were I to make an opera after my own heart, everyone would run away from it; for it would have none of your arias, duets, trios, and all the stuff they patch up operas with to-day; and what I should set in their place no singer would sing, and no audience listen to. They all know nothing but gaudy lies, glittering nonsense, and sugared tedium. Who ever wrote a true musical drama, would be taken for a fool; and so indeed he would be, if he didn't keep such a thing to himself, but wanted to set it before these people."

"And how must one go to work," I hotly urged, "to bring such a musical drama about?"

"As Shakespeare did, when he wrote his plays," was the almost passionate answer. Then he went on: "He who has to stitch all kinds of pretty things for ladies with passable voices to get *bravi* and hand-claps, had better become a Parisian lady's-tailor, not a dramatic composer.—For my part, I never was made for such fal-lals. Oh, I know quite well that the clever ones say I am good enough at instrumental music, but should never be at home in vocal. They are perfectly right, since vocal music for them means nothing but operatic music; and from being at home in that nonsense, preserve me heaven!"

I here ventured to ask whether he really believed that anyone, after hearing his "Adelaide," would dare to deny him the most brilliant calling as a vocal composer too?

"Eh!" he replied after a little pause,—"Adelaide and the like are but trifles after all, and come seasonably enough to professional virtuosi as a fresh opportunity for letting off their fireworks. But why should not vocal music, as much as instrumental, form a grand and serious genre, and its execution meet with as much respect from the feather-brained warblers as I demand from an orchestra for one of my symphonies? (10) The human voice is not to be gainsaid. Nay, it is a far more beautiful and nobler organ of tone, than any instrument in the orchestra. Could not one employ it with just the same freedom as these? What entirely new results one would gain from such a procedure! For the very character that naturally distinguishes the voice of man from the mechanical instrument would have to be given especial prominence, and that would lead to the most manifold combinations. The instruments represent the rudimentary organs of Creation and Nature; what they express can never be clearly defined or put into words, for they reproduce the primitive feelings themselves, those feelings which issued from the chaos of the first Creation, when maybe there was not as yet one human being to take them up into his heart. 'Tis quite otherwise with the genius of the human voice; that represents the heart of man and its sharp-cut individual emotion. Its character is consequently restricted, but definite and clear. Now, let us bring these two elements together, and unite them! Let us set the wild, unfettered elemental feelings, represented by the instruments, in contact with the clear and definite emotion of the human heart, as represented by the voice of man. The advent of this second element will calm and smooth the conflict of those primal feelings, will give their waves a definite, united course; whilst the human heart itself, taking up into it those primordial feelings, will be immeasurably reinforced and widened, equipped to feel with perfect clearness its earlier indefinite presage of the Highest, transformed thereby to godlike consciousness." (11)

Here Beethoven paused for a few moments; as if exhausted. Then he continued with a gentle sigh: "To be sure, in the attempt to solve this problem one lights on many an obstacle; to let men sing, one must give them words. Yet who could frame in words *that* poesy which needs must form the basis of such a union of all elements? The poem must necessarily limp behind, for words are organs all too weak for such a task.—You soon will make acquaintance with a new composition of mine, which will remind you of what I just have touched on. It is a symphony with choruses. I will ask you to observe how hard I found it, to get over the incompetence of Poetry to render thorough aid. At last I decided upon using our Schiller's beautiful hymn 'To Joy'; in any case it is a noble and inspiring poem, but far from speaking *that* which, certainly in this connection, no verses in the world could say."

To this day I scarce can grasp my happiness at thus being helped by Beethoven himself to a full understanding of his titanic Last Symphony, which then at most was finished, but known as yet to no man. I conveyed to him my fervent thanks for this rare condescension. At the same time I expressed the delightful surprise it had been to me, to hear that we might look forward to the appearance of a new great work of his composition. Tears had welled into my eyes,—I could have gone down on my knees to him.

Beethoven seemed to remark my agitation. Half mournfully, half roguishly, he looked into my face and said: "You might take my part, when my new work is discussed. Remember me: for the clever ones will think I am out of my senses; at least, that is what they will cry. But perhaps you see, Herr R., that I am not quite a madman yet, though unhappy enough to make one.—People want me to write according to *their* ideas of what is good and beautiful; they never reflect that I, a poor deaf man, must have my very own ideas,—that it would be impossible for me to write otherwise than I feel. And that I cannot think and feel their beautiful affairs," he added in irony, "is just what makes out my misfortune!"

With that he rose, and paced the room with short, quick steps. Stirred to my inmost heart as I was, I stood up too;—I could feel myself trembling. It would have been impossible for me to pursue the conversation either by pantomimic signs or writing. I was conscious also that the point had been reached when my visit might become a burden to the master. To *write* a farewell word of heartfelt thanks, seemed too matter-of-fact; so I contented myself with seizing my hat, approaching Beethoven, and letting him read in my eyes what was passing within me.

He seemed to understand. "You are going?" he asked. "Shall you remain in Vienna awhile?"

I wrote that my journey had no other object than to gain his personal acquaintance; since he had honoured me with so unusual a reception, I was overjoyed to view my goal as reached, and should start for home again next day.

Smiling, he replied: "You wrote me, in what manner you had procured the money for this journey.—You ought to stop in Vienna and write galops,—that sort of ware is much valued here."

I declared that I had done with all that, as I now knew nothing worth a similar sacrifice.

"Well, well," he said, "one never knows! Old fool that I am, I should have done better, myself, to write galops; the way I have gone, I shall always famish. A pleasant journey,"—he added—"think of me, and let that console you in all your troubles."

My eyes full of tears, I was about to withdraw, when he called to me: "Stay, we must polish off the musical Englishman! Let's see where to put the crosses!"

He snatched up the Briton's music-case, and smilingly skimmed its contents; then he carefully put it in order again, wrapped it in a sheet of paper, took a thick scoring-pen, and drew a huge cross from one end of the cover to the other. Whereupon he handed it to me with the words: "Kindly give the happy man his masterwork! He's an ass, and yet I envy him his long ears!—Farewell, dear friend, and hold me dear!"

And so he dismissed me. With staggering steps I left his chamber and the house.

At the hotel I found the Englishman's servant packing away his master's trunks in the travelling-carriage. So his goal, also, was reached; I could but admit that *he*, too, had proved his endurance. I ran up to my room, and likewise made ready to commence my homeward march on the morrow. A fit of laughter seized me when I looked at the cross on the cover of the Englishman's composition. That cross, however, was a souvenir of Beethoven, and I grudged it to the evil genius of my pilgrimage. My decision was quickly taken. I removed the cover, hunted out my galops, and clapped them in this damning shroud. To the Englishman I sent his composition wrapperless, accompanying it with a little note in which I told him that Beethoven envied him and had declared he didn't know where to set a cross.

As I was leaving the inn, I saw my wretched comrade mount into his carriage.

"Good-bye," he cried. "You have done me a great service. I am glad to have made Beethoven's acquaintance.—Will you come with me to Italy?"

"What would you there?"—I asked in reply.

"I wish to know Mr. Rossini, as he is a very famous composer."

"Good luck!"—called I: "I know Beethoven, and that's enough for my lifetime!"

We parted. I cast one longing glance at Beethoven's house, and turned to the north, uplifted in heart and ennobled.

Notes

01

This imaginary story originally appeared in the *Revue et Gazette Musicale de Paris* for Nov. 19, 22 and 29, and Dec. 3, 1840, with the title "Une visite à Beethoven: épisode de la vie d'un musicien allemand." Its German original, "Eine Pilgerfahrt zu Beethoven," first appeared in Nos. 181-86 of the Dresden *Abend-Zeitung*, July 30 to August 5, 1841, under the heading, "Zwei Epochen aus dem Leben eines deutschen Musikers" ("Two epochs from the life of a German musician," applying to the present article and its immediate successor) and with the additional sub-title "Aus den Papieren eines wirklich verstorbenen Musikers" ("From the papers of an actually deceased musician"). With that German version of 1841 the text in the *Gesammelte Schriften* agrees entirely, saving for two or three minute emendations of style and the omission of a tiny clause (p. 32 *inf.*) describing Beethoven as sitting "with his hands crossed over his stick" (*"die Hände über seinen Stock gelehnt"*). The prefatory note, on the opposite page, also appeared in the *Abend-Zeitung* (but not in the *Gazette*), with exception of the few words between the dashes.—Tr.

02

From "unless" to "like" does not appear in the French.—Tr.

03

These two sentences are absent from the French.—Tr.

04

"Were there a thousand royal theatres in Germany" is also absent from the French, and presumably was an addition made in 1841. On the other hand, instead of the two next short paragraphs there appeared, "L'adoption de cette prière quotidienne doit vous dire assez que je suis musicien et que L'Allemagne est ma patrie." — Tr.

05

From "O honoured" to "executor," of course, is also absent from the French. — Tr.

06

In the French the last part of this sentence ran: "Je m'interrompis subitement en entendant quelqu'un qui semblait m'accompagner en sifflant l'air d'un de mes galops." This reference to supernatural presences is significant, as Richard Wagner's favourite author, in early life, was the fantastic E. A. Hoffmann. The invisible whistler of 1840 is represented in 1841 by the *"around me"* of a previous sentence, which does not appear in the *Gazette*. — Tr.

07

Between this and the succeeding sentence there appeared in the French: "On ne peut nier, à la vérité, que l'ouvrage n'ait beaucoup gagné à son remaniement; mais cela vient surtout de ce que l'auteur du second libretto offrit au musicien plus d'occasions de développer son brillant génie; *Fidelio* possède d'ailleurs en propre ses admirables finales et plusieurs autres morceaux d'élite. Je ne connaissais du reste que l'opéra primitif." — Tr.

08

In the French this was followed by: "Qui ne connaît aujourd'hui la réputation européenne de la cantatrice qui porte maintenant le double nom de Schrœder-Devrient?" — In 1871 Frau Schröder-

Devrient had been dead eleven years; her praises are constantly sung in the master's prose-works, especially at the close of *Actors and Singers* (Vol. V.).—Tr.

09

This sentence is simply represented in the French by "Pour ma part, j'étais ravi au troisième ciel."—Tr.

10

From "and its execution," to the end of the sentence, did not appear in the French.—Tr.

11

In the French the last clause of this sentence presents a slight shade of difference, perhaps due to the translator, "Alors le cœur humain s'ouvrant à ces émotions complexes, agrandi et dilaté par ces pressentiments infinis et délicieux, accueillera avec ivresse, avec conviction, cette espèce de révélation intime d'un monde surnaturel."—Tr.

THE VIRTUOSO AND THE ARTIST

(1)

ACCORDING to an ancient legend there is somewhere an inestimable jewel whose shining light bestows forthwith, upon the favoured mortal whose glance rests on it, all gifts of mind and every joy of a contented spirit. But this treasure lies buried in unfathomed depths. The story goes, that eyes of happy mortals once were blest with superhuman power to pierce the ruins heaped above it like gateways, pillars, and misshapen fragments of a giant palace: through this chaos then there leapt to them the wondrous splendour of the magic jewel, and filled their hearts with bliss untold. Then yearning seized them to remove the pile of wreckage, to unveil to all the world the glory of the magic treasure at which the very sun would pale its fires when *its* glad rays should fill our heart with love divine, our mind with heavenly knowledge. But in vain their every effort: they could not move the inert mass that hid the wonder-stone.

Centuries passed by: the spirit of those rarest favoured ones still mirrored on the world the radiance of that starry light which once had shone upon them from the glinting jewel; but no one could draw near itself. Yet tidings of it still existed; there were traces, and men conceived the thought of burrowing for the wonder-stone with all the arts of mining. Shafts were sunk, levels and cross-cuts were driven into the bowels of the earth; the most ingenious of subterranean tactics were pursued, and one dug afresh, cut winzes and new galleries, until at last the labyrinth grew so confusing that all remembrance of the right direction was lost for good. And so the whole great maze, in whose behalf the jewel itself was finally forgotten, lay useless quite: men gave it up. Abandoned were adits, shafts and raises: already they were threatening to cave in, when—so they say—a poor miner from Salzburg came that way. He carefully surveyed the work of his forerunners: full of astonishment he paced the countless mazes, whose useless plan he half surmised. Of a sudden he feels his heart beat high for very rapture: through a chink the jewel flashes on him; with a glance he takes the measure of all the labyrinth: the longed-for pathway to the wonder-stone itself grows plain; led by its light he dives into the deepest cavern, to it, the heavenly talisman itself. A wondrous luminance then filled the world with fleeting glory, and every heart was thrilled by ecstasy untold: but the miner from Salzburg no man saw again.

Then came once more a miner, this time from Bonn in the Siebengebirge; he wished to search in the abandoned levels for the missing Salzburger: he lit full soon upon his track, and so suddenly the splendour of the wonder-jewel smote his eye, that it struck him blind. A foaming sea of light surged through his senses, he flung himself into the chasm, and down the timbers crashed upon him: a fearful din went up, as though a world had foundered. The miner from Bonn was never seen again.

And so, like every miner's-story, this ended—with a falling in. Fresh ruins overlay the old; yet to this day men shew the site of the ancient workings, and recently have even begun to dig for the two lost miners, as kind good people think they still might be alive. With breathless haste the pits are sunk afresh, and get much talked of; the curious come from far and near, to view the spot: fragments of schist are taken away as souvenirs, and paid a trifle for, for everyone would like to have contributed to such a pious work; moreover one buys the life-account of the two entombed, which a Bonn professor (2) has carefully drawn up, yet without being able to tell exactly how the accident occurred, which nobody knows but the Folk. And things have come to such a pass at last, that the real original legend is clean forgotten, whilst all kinds of minor modern fables take its place, *e.g.* that quite prolific veins of gold have been discovered in the diggings, and the solidest ducats struck therefrom. Indeed there seems some truth in this; for people think less and less about the wonder-stone and those two poor miners, although the whole exploit still bears the title of a rescue-party.—

Perhaps the whole legend, with its subsequent fable, is to be understood in an allegoric sense: on that hypothesis, its meaning would soon be apparent if we took the wonder-jewel to be the *genius of Music*; the two incarcerated miners would be no less easy to divine, and the debris that covers them would lie before our feet when we gird ourselves to pierce to those enshrined elect. In truth, on whom that wonder-stone has shone in fabled dreams o'night, whose soul has felt the fire of Music in the holy hours of ecstasy,— would he fain arrest that dream, that ecstasy, *i.e.* if he would seek the tools therefor, he first of all will stumble on that heap of ruins: there he has then to dig and delve; the place is filled with gold-diggers; they pile the debris ever denser, and, would you make for the forgotten shaft, they fling down slag and cat-gold in your way. The rubble waxes high and higher, the wall grows ever thicker: sweat pours in rivers from your brow. Poor fellows! And they laugh at you.

Yet the thing may have a serious side.—

What you have written down in notes, is now to sound aloud; you want to hear it, and let others hear it. Very good: the weightiest, nay, the ineluctable concern for you, is to get your tone-piece brought to hearing exactly as you felt it in you when you wrote it down: that is to say, the composer's intentions are to be conscientiously reproduced, so that the thoughts of his spirit may be transmitted unalloyed and undisfigured to the organs of perception. The highest merit of the executant artist, the Virtuoso, would accordingly consist in a pure and perfect reproduction of that thought of the composer's; a reproduction only to be ensured by genuine fathering of his intentions, and consequently by total abstinence from all inventions of one's own. It follows that a performance directed by the composer in person alone can give a full account of his intentions; nearest to him will come the man sufficiently endowed with creative power to gauge the value of observing another artist's intentions by that he sets upon his own, and it will be an advantage to him to have a certain loving pliability. After these most authorised would come such artists as make no claim to productivity, and belong to art, so to say, merely in virtue of their aptitude for making a stranger's artwork their intimate possession: these would have to be modest enough to so entirely sink their personal attributes, in whatever they may consist, that neither their defects nor their advantages should come to light in the performance; for it is the artwork in its purest reproduction, that should step before us, in nowise the distracting individuality of the performer.

Unfortunately however, this very reasonable demand runs counter to all the conditions under which artistic products win the favour of the public. This latter's first and keenest curiosity is addressed to art-dexterity; delight in that is the only road to notice of the work itself. Who can blame the public for it? Is it not the very tyrant whose vote we sue? Nor would things stand so bad with this failing, did it not end by corrupting the executant artist, and make him forget at last his own true mission. His position as vehicle of the artistic intention, nay, as virtual representative of the creative master, makes it quite peculiarly his duty to guard the earnestness and purity of Art in general: he is the intermediary of the artistic idea, which through him, in a sense, first attains to physical existence. The real dignity of the Virtuoso rests therefore solely on the dignity he is able to preserve for creative art: if he trifles and toys with this, he casts his own honour away. To be sure, 'tis small matter to him, should he not have grasped that dignity at all: though he be no artist, he yet has art-dexterities to hand: these he lets play; they do not warm, but glitter; and at night it all looks very nice.

There sits the virtuoso in the concert-hall, and entrances purely for himself: here runs, there jumps; he melts, he pines, he paws and glides, and the audience is fettered to his fingers. Go and watch the strange Sabath of such a soirée, and try to learn how you should make yourselves presentable for this assemblée; you will find that, of all that passes before your eyes and ears, you understand about as much as probably the Witches'-master there of what goes on within your soul when music wakes in you and drives you to produce. Heavens! You are to dress your music to suit this man? Impossible! At each attempt you would miserably fail. You can swing yourselves into the air, but cannot dance; a whirlwind lifts you to the clouds, but you can make no pirouette: what would you succeed in, if you took him for. model? A vulgar catherine-wheel, no more,—and everyone would laugh, even if you did not get hurled from the salon.

Plainly we have nothing to do with this virtuoso. But presumably you mistook your locality. For indeed there are other virtuosi, and among them true, great artists: they owe their reputation to their moving execution of the noblest tone-works of the greatest masters; where would the public's acquaintance with these latter be slumbering, had not those eminently pre-elect arisen from out the chaos of music-makery, to shew the world who These really were and what they did? There sticks the placard, inviting you to such a lordly feast: one name shines on you: *Beethoven!* Enough. Here is the concert-room. And positively, Beethoven appears to you; all round sit high-bred ladies, row after row of high-bred ladies, and in a wide half-moon behind them lively gentle men with lorgnettes in the eye. But Beethoven is there, midst all the perfumed agony of dream-rocked elegance: it really is Beethoven, sinewed and broad, in all his sad omnipotence. But, who comes there with him? Great God:— Guillaume Tell, Robert the Devil, and—who after these? *Weber*, the tender and true! Good! And then:—a "Galop." (3) O heavens! Who has once written galops himself, who has had his stir in Potpourris, knows what a want can drive us to it when it is a question of drawing near to Beethoven at all costs. I took the measure of the awful need that could drive another man to-day to Potpourris and Galops, to gain the chance of preaching Beethoven; and though I must admire the virtuoso in this instance, I cursed all virtuosity.—So falter not, true disciples of Art, upon the path of virtue: if a magic power drew you to dig for the silted shaft, be not misguided by those veins of gold; but deeper, ever deeper delve towards the wonder-stone. My heart tells me, those buried miners are living yet: if not, why! still believe it! What harms you the belief?

But come, is it all mere foppery? You need the Virtuoso, and, if he's the right sort, he needs you too. So, at least, it must once have been. For something happened, to cause a division between the Virtuoso and the Artist. In former times it certainly was easier to be one's own virtuoso; but you waxed overweening, and made things so hard for yourselves that you were obliged to turn their execution over to a man who has quite enough to do, his whole life long, to bear the other half of your labour. Indeed you should be thankful to him. He is the first to face the tyrant: if he doesn't do his business well, nobody asks about your composition, but *he* is hissed off the boards; can you be cross with him then, if, when applauded, he takes that also to himself, and does not specially return his thanks in name of the composer? Nor would that be quite what you want: you want your piece performed precisely as you thought it; the virtuoso is to add nothing to it, leave nothing from it; he is to be *your second self* But often that is very hard: let one of you just try, for once, to sink himself so entirely in another! —

Lo there the man who certainly thinks least about himself, and to whom the personal act of pleasing has surely nothing special to bring in, the man beating time for an orchestra. He surely fancies he has bored to the very inside of the composer, ay, has drawn him on like a second skin? You won't tell me that *he* is plagued with the Upstart-devil, when he takes your tempo wrong, misunderstands your expression-marks, and drives you to desperation at listening to your own tone-piece. Yet *he* can be a virtuoso too, and tempt the public by all kinds of spicy nuances into thinking that it after all is *he* who makes the whole thing sound so nice he finds it neat to let a loud passage be played quite soft, for a change, a fast one a wee bit slower; he will add you, here and there, a trombone-effect, or a dash of the cymbals and triangle; but his chief resource is a drastic cut, if he otherwise is not quite sure of his success. Him we must call a virtuoso of the Baton; and I fancy he's none too rare, especially in opera-houses. So we shall have to arm ourselves against him; and the best way will probably be to make sure of the real original, not second-hand virtuoso, to wit the *singer*.

Now the composer so thoroughly impregnates the Singer, that he streams from his throat as living tone. Here, one would think, no misunderstanding is possible: the Virtuoso has to pick here and there, all round him; he may pick the wrong thing: but there, in the Singer, we sit with our melody itself. It will be a bad job, by all means, if we are not sitting in the right spot of him; he, too, has picked us up from outside: have we got down as far as his heart, or simply stuck in his throat? We were digging, for the jewel in the depths: are we caught in the toils of the gold-veins?

The human voice, as well, is an instrument; it is rare, and paid for dearly. How it is shaped, is the first care of the inquisitive public, and its next *how* it is played with: *what* it plays, is immaterial to the generality. The Singer knows better: for what he sings must be so formed, as to make it easy for him to play on his voice to great credit. How small, in comparison, is the heed the Virtuoso has to pay to *his* instrument: it stands ready-made; if it suffers harm, he gets it repaired. But this priceless, wondrously capricious instrument of the Voice? No man has quite found out its build. Write how you will, ye composers, but mind it is something the singer sings gladly! How are you to set about it? Why, go to concerts, or better still, to salons!—We don't want to write for these, but for the theatre, the Opera,—dramatic music.—Good! Then go to the Opera, and discover that you still are merely in the salon, the concert-room. Here, too, it is the Virtuoso with whom you must first come to terms. And this virtuoso, believe me, is more perilous than all the rest; for wherever you encounter him, he'll slip between your fingers.

Look at those most celebrated singers in the world: from whom would you learn, if not from the artists of our great Italian Opera, who are worshipped as positively superhuman beings, not only by Paris, but by every capital in the world? Here learn what really is the *art* of Song; from them the famous singers of the French Grand Opéra first learnt what singing means, and that it's no joke, as the good German scrape-throats (*Gaumen-Schreihälse*) dream when they think the thing done if their heart is in the right place, namely seated tight upon their stomach. There you also will meet the composers who understood how to write for real singers: they knew that through these alone could they arrive at recognition, eh! existence; and as you see, they are there, doing well, nay, honoured and glorified. But you don't want to compose like these; your works shall be respected; it is from them you require an impression, not from the success of the throat-feats of the singers to whom those others owe their fortune?—Look a little closer: have these people no passion? Do they not tremble and heave, as well as lisp and gurgle? When they sing *"Ah! Tremate!"* it sounds a little different from your "Zittre, feiger Bösewicht!" Have you forgotten that *"Maledetta!"* at which the best-bred audience turned into a Methodist-meeting of niggers?—

But to you it doesn't seem the genuine thing? You think it a pack of Effects, at which all reasonable men should laugh?

However, this also is art, and one these celebrated singers have carried very far. With the singing-voice. too, one may toy and juggle as one pleases; but the game must lastly be related to some passion, for one does not pass so altogether needlessly from rational talk to the decidedly much louder noise of singing. Ah! now you have it: the public wants an emotion it cannot get at home, like whist or dominoes. This, also, may have been quite otherwise at one time: great masters found great pupils among their singers; the tradition still lives of the wonderful things they brought to light together, and often is renewed by fresh experience. Most certainly one knows and wills that Song should also work dramatically, and our singers therefore learn so thorough a command of Passion that it looks as if they never left it. And its use is quite reduced to rule: after cooing and chirping, an explosion makes a quite unparalleled effect; its not being an actual matter of fact, why! that is just what makes it art.

You still have a scruple, founded principally on your contempt for the sickly stuff those singers sing. Whence springs it? Precisely from the will of those singers, on whose behalf it is cobbled up. What in the world can a true musician wish to have in common with this handiwork? But how would it stand if these fêted demigods of the Italian Opera were to undertake a veritable art-work? Can they truly catch fire? Can they bear the magic lightnings of that wonder-jewel's flash?

See: "Don Giovanni"! And really by Mozart! So reads the poster for to-day. Let us go to hear and see.

And strange things happened to me, when I actually heard "Don Juan" lately with the great Italians: it was a chaos of every sensation in which I was trundled to and fro; for I really found the perfect artist, but close beside him the absurdest virtuoso, who sent him to the wall. Glorious was *Grisi* as "Donna Anna" unsurpassable *Lablache* as "Leporello." The grandest, richest-gifted woman, inspired with but one thought: to be Mozart's own "Donna Anna": there all was warmth and tenderness, fire, passion, grief and woe. Oh! *she* knew that the buried miner still is living, and blessedly she fortified my own belief. But the silly soul consumed herself for Signor *Tamburini*, the world-most-famous barytone who sang and played "Don Juan": the whole evening through, the man could not rid himself of the log of wood that was tied to his legs with this fatal rôle. I had previously once heard him in an opera of Bellini's: there we had *"Tremate!" "Maledetta,"* and all the Passion of Italy rolled into one. Nothing of the sort to-day: the brief swift pieces whizzed past him like fugitive shadows; much airy Recitative all stiff and flat; a fish on the sands. But it seemed that the whole audience was stranded too: it remained so decorous that no one could trace a sign of its usual frenzy. Perhaps a worthy mark of homage to the true genius who swayed his wings to-night throughout the hall? We shall see. In any case the divine *Grisi* herself did not peculiarly entrance: nobody could quite appreciate her secret passion for this tiresome "Don Juan." —But there was *Lablache*, a colossus, and yet to-night a "Leporello" every inch. How did he manage it? The enormous bass-voice sang throughout in the clearest, most superb of tones, and yet it was more like a chattering, babbling, saucy laughing, hare-footed scampering; once he absolutely piped with his voice, and yet it always sounded full, like distant church-bells. He neither stood nor walked, nor did he dance; but he was always in motion; one saw him here, there, everywhere, and yet he never fidgeted; always on the spot, before you knew it, wherever a fine sense of humour could scent out fun or frolic in the situation. *Lablache* was not applauded once in all this evening: that might be reasonable, a token of dramatic *goût* in the audience. But the latter seemed really annoyed that its authorised favourite, Madame *Persiani* (one's heart convulses at mere mention of that name !), was ill at ease in the music for "Zerlina." I perceived that one had quite prepared oneself to be charmed beyond all bounds with her, and whoever had heard her a short while before in the *"Elisire d'amore"* could not be gainsaid such a verification. But *Mozart* was decidedly to blame, that the charm refused to work to-night: more sand, for such a lively fish! Ah! what would not audience and Persiani have given to-day, had it been held decent to infuse a drop from that Elixir of Love! In effect, I gradually remarked that both sides were bent on an excess of decency: there reigned a unanimity which I was long in accounting for. Why, since to all appearance one was "classically" minded, did the magnificent and perfect execution of that glorious "Donna Anna" not carry everyone into that sterling ecstasy which seemed to be the only thing proposed to-day? Why, as in the strictest of senses one was ashamed of being carried away, had one come to a performance of "Don Juan" at all? Verily the whole evening seemed a voluntary act of penance, imposed on oneself for some unknown reason: but to what end? Something must really be gained by it; for such a Paris audience will spend much, 'tis true, but always expects a return for its money, be it only a worthless one.

This riddle also solved itself: *Rubini fired off this night his famous trill from A to B!* The whole thing flashed on me. How could I have expected much from poor "Don Ottavio," the so often mocked-at tenor-stopgap of Don Juan? Indeed I long felt truly sorry for the so unrivalledly adored *Rubini*, the wonder of all tenors, who on his side went quite crossly to his Mozart-sum. There he came, the sober, solid man, passionately dragged on by the arm by the divine "Donna Anna," and stood with ruffled peace of mind beside the corpse of his expected father-in-law, who now no more could breathe his blessing on a happy marriage. Some say that Rubini was once a tailor, and looks just like one; I should have credited him with more agility in that case: where he stood he stayed, and moved no further; for he could sing, too, without stirring a muscle; even his hand he brought but seldom to the region of his heart. This time his singing never touched him at all; he might fitly save his fairly aged voice for something better than to cry out words of comfort, already heard a thousand times, to his beloved. That I understood, thought the man sensible, and, as he took the same course throughout the opera whenever "Don Ottavio" was at hand, I fancied at last it was over, and still more anxiously inquired the meaning, the purpose of this extraordinary night of abstinence. Then slowly came a stir: unrest, sitting-up, shrewd glances, fan-play, all the symptoms of a sudden straining of attention in a cultured audience. "Ottavio" was left alone on the stage; I believed he was about to make an announcement, for he came right up to the prompter's box: but there he stayed, and listened without moving a feature to the orchestral prelude to his *B flat* aria. This ritornel seemed to last longer than usual; but that was a simple illusion: the singer was merely lisping out the first ten bars of his song so utterly inaudibly that, on my discovery that he really was giving himself the look of singing, I thought the genial man was playing a joke. Yet the audience kept a serious face; it knew what was coming; for at the eleventh bar Rubini let his F swell out with such sudden vehemence that the little reconducting passage fell plump upon us like a thunderbolt, and died away again into a murmur with the twelfth. I could have laughed aloud, but the whole house was still as death: a muted orchestra, an inaudible tenor; the sweat stood on my brow. Something monstrous seemed in preparation: and truly the unhearable was now to be eclipsed by the unheard-of. The seventeenth bar arrived: here the singer has to hold an F for three bars long. What can one do with a simple F? Rubini only becomes divine on the high B flat: *there* must he get, if a night at the Italian Opera is to have any sense. And just as the trapezist swings his bout preliminary, so "Don Ottavio" mounts his three-barred F, two bars of which he gives in careful but pronounced crescendo, till at the third he snatches from the violins their trill on A, shakes it himself with waxing vehemence, and at the fourth bar sits in triumph on the high B flat, as if it were nothing; then with a brilliant roulade he plunges down again, before all eyes, into the noiseless. The end had come: anything that liked might happen now. Every demon was unchained, and not on the stage, as at close of the opera, but in the audience. The riddle was solved: this was the trick for which one had assembled, had borne two hours of total abstinence from every wonted operatic dainty, had pardoned Grisi and Lablache for taking such music in earnest, and felt richly rewarded by the coming-off of this one wondrous moment when Rubini leapt to B flat!

A German poet once assured me that, in spite of all, the French were the true "Greeks" of our era, and the Parisians in particular had something Athenian about them; for really it was they who had the keenest sense of "Form." This came back to me that evening: as a fact, this uncommonly elegant audience shewed not a spark of interest in the stuff of our "Don Juan"; to them it was plainly a mere lay-figure on which the drapery of unmixed Virtuosity had first to be hung, to give the music-work its formal right to existence. But *Rubini* alone could do this properly, and so it was easy to guess why just this cold and venerable being had become the darling of the Parisians, the chartered "idol" of all cultivated friends of Song. In their predilection for this virtuosic side of things they go so far as to give it their whole æsthetic interest, while their feeling for noble warmth, nay even for manifest beauty, is more and more amazingly cooling down. Without one genuine throb they saw and heard that noble *Grisi*, the splendid woman with the soulful voice: perhaps they fancy it too realistic. But *Rubini*, the broad-built Philistine with bushy whiskers; old, with a voice grown greasy, and afraid of over-taxing it: if *he* is ranked above all others, the charm can't reside in his substance, but purely in a spiritual Form. And this form is forced upon every singer in Paris: they all sing *à la* Rubini. The rule is: be inaudible for awhile, then suddenly alarm the audience by a husbanded explosion, and immediately afterwards relapse into an effect of the ventriloquist. Mons. *Duprez* already quite obeys it: often have I hunted for the substitute, hidden somewhere beneath the podium like the mother's voice trumpet in "Robert the Devil," that seemed to take the part of the ostensible singer at the prompter's box, who now wasn't making a sign. But that is "art." What do we block-heads know about it?—Taken all in all, that Italian performance of "Don Giovanni" has helped me to great consolation. There really are great artists among the virtuosi, or, to put it another way: even the virtuoso can be a great artist. Unfortunately they are so entangled with each other, that it is a sorrowful task to sift them out. That evening *Lablache* and the *Grisi* distressed me, while *Rubini* diverted me hugely. Is there something corruptive, then, in setting these great differences side by side? The human heart is so evil, and hebetude so very sweet! Take care how you play with the Devil! He'll come at last when you least expect him. That's what happened to Sig. Tamburini that evening, where he surely would never have dreamt it. Rubini had happily swung himself up to his high B flat: he looked simpering down, and quite amiably upon the Devil. I thought to myself: God, if he'd only take that one!—

Presumptuous thought! The whole audience would have plunged to Hell after him.—

(To be continued in the next world!)

Notes

1

Under the title of "Du métier de Virtuose et de l'indépendance des Compositeurs: Fantaisie esthétique d'un musicien," this article appeared in the *Gazette Musicale* of Oct. 18, 1840; its French form, however, differs so greatly from the German of the *Ges. Schr.*, after the first page or two, that I reproduce it in its entirety *et seq.* — Tr.

2

Otto Jahn, whose Life of Mozart appeared in 1856-59, with a second edition in 1867; he also wrote for the *Grenzboten* an exhaustive review of the Complete Edition of Beethoven's works, with biographical information, re-published in his Collected Essays on Music in 1868, and was collecting materials for a minute biography of Beethoven at the time of his death in 1869. So that this clause at anyrate is an interpolation of 1870-71, having probably been represented in the original German manuscript by a reference to Schindler's biography of Beethoven, which made its first appearance in 1840; one of Wagner's Letters from Paris of 1841 (to appear in Vol. VIII.) alludes at greater length to Schindler. — Tr.

3

On April 20, 1840, Liszt had given a concert in the Salle Erard, playing Beethoven's Pastoral Symphony (for two hands), a fantasia on airs from *Lucia*, Schubert's *Serenade* and *Ave Maria*, and winding up with a *Galop Chromatique*. His *Robert le diable* fantasia would pretty certainly have figured also, if only as encore. — Tr.

Summary

Fable of the magic jewel and the two poor miners — Mozart and Beethoven — succeeded by the gold-diggers (110). The composer's intention and its interpreters; after *himself* would come an executant endowed with some creative power and much affection; then the man who, no producer, will sink himself in the performance. But the public wants trick; Thalberg contrasted with Liszt, though even Liszt makes concessions (113). Conductor as virtuoso, with false tempi, added instruments, and cuts (114). Singers: surely here are the true artists, for the composer's music comes from *inside* them; but the human voice is an expensive instrument, and needs humouring; you'll have to write to please them. The Italians, see how they're glorified! Can they really catch fire at the wonder-stone? (117). "Don Giovanni" at the *Italiens*: Grisi and Lablache, true artists, make no effect; the whole audience strangely impassive; why this abstinence? Don Ottavio (Rubini) duller than ever; till at last the fans begin to stir, the audience wakes up, for—Rubini is about to do his trick: an inaudible tenor suddenly explodes, and lands on his high B flat. Take care how you play with the Devil (122).

ON THE OVERTURE

Translator's Note

The following article originally appeared in the *Gazette Musicale* of January 10, 14 and 17, 1841 under the title "De L'Ouverture." The few variants between the French and German forms I have noted *in loco*.

On the Overture

IN earlier days a prologue preceded the play: it would appear that one had not the hardihood to snatch the spectator from his daily life and set him at one blow in presence of an ideal world; it seemed more prudent to pave the way by an introduction whose character already belonged to the sphere of art he was to enter. This Prologue addressed itself to the spectator's imagination, invoked its aid in compassing the proposed illusion, and supplied a brief account of events supposed to have taken place before, with a summary of the action about to be represented. When the whole play was set to music, as happened in Opera, it would have been more consistent to get this prologue sung as well; instead thereof one opened the performance with a mere orchestral prelude, which in those days could not fully answer the original purpose of the prologue, since purely instrumental music was not sufficiently matured as yet to give due character to such a task. These pieces of music appear to have had no other object than to tell the audience that singing was the order of the day. Were the weakness of the instrumental music of that epoch not in itself abundant explanation of the nature of these early overtures, one perhaps might suppose a deliberate objection to imitate the older prologue, as its sobering and undramatic tendence had been recognised; whichever way, one thing is certain—the Overture was employed as a mere conventional bridge, not viewed as a really characteristic prelude to the drama.

A step in advance was taken when the general character of the piece itself, whether sad or merry, was hinted in its overture. (01) But how little these musical introductions could be regarded as real preparers of the needful frame of mind, we may see by Händel's overture to his *Messiah*, whose author we should have to consider most incompetent, had we to assume that he actually meant this tone-piece as an Introduction in the newer sense. In fact, the free development of the Overture, as a specifically characteristic piece of music, was still gainsaid to those composers whose means of lengthening a purely instrumental movement were confined to the resources of the art of counterpoint; the complex system of the "Fugue"—the only one at command for the purpose—had to help them out with their prologues to an oratorio or opera, and the hearer was left to decipher the fitting mood from "dux" and "comes," augmentation and diminution, inversion and stretto.

The great inelasticity of this form appears to have suggested the need of employing and developing the so-called "symphony," a conglomerate of diverse types. Here two sections in quicker time were severed by another of slower motion and soft expression, whereby the main opposing characters of the drama might at least be broadly indicated. It only needed the genius of a. Mozart, to create at once a master-model in this form, such as we possess in his symphony to the "Seraglio"; it is impossible to hear this piece performed with spirit in the theatre, without obtaining a very definite notion of the character of the drama which it introduces. However, there was still a certain helplessness in this division into three sections, with a separate tempo and character for each; and the question arose, how to weld the isolated fractions to a single undivided whole, whose movement should be sustained by just the contrast of those differing characteristic motives.

The creators of this perfect form of overture were Gluck and Mozart.

Even Gluck still contented himself at times with the mere introductory piece of older form, simply conducting to the first scene of the opera—as in *Iphigenia in Tauris*—with which this musical prelude at anyrate stood mostly in a very apt relation. Though even in his best of overtures the master retained this character of an introduction to the first scene, and therefore gave no independent close, he succeeded at last in stamping on this instrumental number itself the character of the whole succeeding drama. Gluck's most perfect masterpiece of this description is the overture to *Iphigenia in Aulis*. Here the master draws the main ideas of the drama in powerful outline, and with an almost visual distinctness. We shall return to this glorious work, by it to demonstrate that form of overture which should rank as the most excellent.

After Gluck, it was Mozart that gave the Overture its true significance. Without toiling to express what music neither can nor should express, the details and entanglements of the plot itself—which the earlier Prologue had endeavoured to set forth—with the eye of a veritable poet he grasped the drama's leading thought, stripped it of all material episodes and accidentiæ, and reproduced it in the transfiguring light of music as a passion personified in tones, a counterpart both warranting that thought itself and explaining the whole dramatic action to the hearer's feeling. On the other hand, there thus arose an entirely independent tone-piece, no matter whether its outward structure was attached to the first scene of the opera or not. To most of his overtures, however, Mozart also gave the perfect musical close, for instance, those to the *Magic Flute*, to *Figaro* and *Tito*; so that it might surprise us to find him denying it to the most important of them all, the overture to *Don Giovanni* were we not obliged to recognise in the marvellously thrilling passage of the last bars of this overture into the first scene a peculiarly pregnant termination to the introductory tone-piece of a *Don Giovanni*.

The Overture thus shaped by Gluck and Mozart became the property of Cherubini and Beethoven. Whilst Cherubini (02) on the whole remained faithful to the inherited type, Beethoven ended by departing from it in the very boldest manner. The former's overtures are poetical sketches of the drama's main idea, seized in its broadest features and musically reproduced in unity, concision and distinctness; this notwithstanding, we see by his overture to the *Water-Carrier (Deux Journées)* how even the dénouement of a stirring plot could be expressed in that form without damage to the unity of the artistic setting. Beethoven's overture to *Fidelio* (in E major) is unmistakably related to that of the *Water-Carrier*, just as the two masters approach the nearest to each other in these operas themselves. That Beethoven's impetuous genius in truth felt cramped by the limits thus drawn around it, however, we plainly perceive in several of his other overtures, above all in that to *Leonora*. Beethoven, never having obtained a fit occasion for the unfolding of his stupendous dramatic instinct, here seems to compensate himself by throwing the whole weight of his genius upon this field left open to his fancy, from pure tone-images to shape according to his inmost will the drama that he craved for; that drama which, freed from all the petty make-weights of the timid playwright, in this overture he let spring anew from a kernel magnified to giant size. One can assign no other origin to this wondrous overture to *Leonora*: far from giving us a mere musical introduction to the drama, it sets that drama more complete and movingly before us than ever happens in the broken action which ensues. This work is no longer an overture, but the mightiest of dramas in itself.

Weber cast his overtures in Beethoven's and Cherubini's mould, and though he never dared the giddy height attained by Beethoven with his *Leonora*-overture, he happily pursued the dramatic path without wandering to a toilsome painting-in of minor details in the plot. Even where his fancy bade him embrace more subsidiary motives in. his musical picture than were quite consistent with the form of overture expressly chosen, he at least knew always to preserve the dramatic unity of his conception; so that we may credit him with the invention of a new class, that of the "dramatic fantasia," whereof the overture to *Oberon* is one of the finest examples. This piece has had great influence upon the tendency of more recent composers; in it Weber took a step that, with the truly poetic swing of his musical inventiveness, as we have seen, could but attain a brilliant success. Nevertheless it is not to be denied that the independence of purely-musical production must suffer by subordination to a dramatic thought, if that thought is not grasped in one broad trait congenial to the spirit of Music, and that the composer who would fain depict the details of an action cannot carry out his dramatic theme without breaking his musical work to atoms. As I propose to return to this point, for the moment I will content myself with the remark that the manner last described led necessarily downwards, inclining more and more towards the class of pieces branded with the name of "potpourri."

In a certain sense the history of this Potpourri begins with Spontini's overture to the *Vestale*: whatever fine and dazzling qualities one must grant this interesting tone-piece, it already shews traces of that loose and shallow mode of working-out which has become so prevalent in the operatic overtures of most composers of our age. To forecast an opera's dramatic course, it was no longer a question of forming a new artistic concept of the whole, its complement and counterpart in music; no, one culled from here and there the most effective passages, less for their importance than their showiness, and strung them bit by bit together in a banal sequence. This was an arrangement often even still more tellingly effected by potpourri-concoctors working on the same material later. (03) Highly admired are the overture to *GuillaumeTell* by Rossini and even that to *Zampa* by Herold, plainly because the public here is much amused, and also, perhaps, because original invention is undeniably displayed, especially in the former: but a truly artistic ideal is no longer aimed at in such works, and they belong, not to the history of Art, but to that of theatrical entertainment. —

Having briefly reviewed the development of the Overture, and cited the most brilliant products of that class of music, the question remains: To what mode of conception and working-out shall we give the palm of fitness, and consequently of correctness? If we wish to avoid the appearance of exclusiveness, an entirely definite answer is no easy matter. Two unexampled masterpieces lie before us, to which we must accord a like sublimity both of intention and elaboration, yet whose actual treatment and conception are totally distinct. I mean the overtures to *Don Giovanni* and *Leonora*. In the first the drama's leading thought is given in two main features; their invention, as their motion, belongs quite unmistakably to nothing but the realm of Music. A passionate burst of arrogance stands in conflict with the threatenings of an implacable over-power, to which that Arrogance seems destined to submit: had Mozart but added the fearful termination of the story, the tone-work would have lacked nothing to be regarded as a finished whole, a drama in itself; but the master lets us merely guess the combat's outcome: in that wonderful transition to the first scene he makes both hostile elements bow beneath a higher will, and nothing but a wailing sigh breathes o'er the place of battle. Clearly and plainly as is the opera's tragic principle depicted in this overture, you shall not find in all the musical tissue one single spot that could in any way be brought into direct relation with the action's course; unless it were its introduction, borrowed from the ghost-scene—though in that case we should have expected to meet the allusion at the piece's end, and not at its beginning. (04) No: the main body of the overture is free from any reminiscence of the opera, and whilst the hearer is fascinated by the purely-musical development of the themes, his mind is given to the changing fortunes of a deadly duel, albeit he never expects to see it set before him in dramatic guise.

Now, that is just the radical distinction of this overture from that to *Leonora*; while listening to the latter, we can never ward off that feeling of breathless apprehension with which we watch the progress of a moving action taking place before our eyes. In this mighty tone-piecer as said before, Beethoven has given us a musical drama, a drama founded on a playwright's piece, and not the mere sketch of one of its main ideas, or even a purely preparatory introduction to the acted play: but a drama, be it said, in the most ideal meaning of the term. (05) The master's method, so far as we here can follow it, lets us divine the depth of that inner need which must have ruled him in conceiving this titanic overture: his object was to condense to its noblest unity the *one* sublime action which the dramatist had weakened. and delayed by paltry details in order to spin out his tale; to give it a new, an ideal motion, fed solely by its inmost springs. This action is the deed of a staunch and loving heart, fired by the one sublime desire to descend as angel of salvation into the very pit of death. One sole idea pervades the work: the freedom brought by a jubilant angel of light to suffering manhood. We are plunged into a gloomy dungeon; no beam of day strikes through to us; night's awful silence breaks only to the moans, the sighs, of a soul that longs from its deepest depths for freedom, freedom. As through a cranny letting in the sun's last ray, a yearning glance peers down: 'tis the glance of the angel that feels the pure air of heavenly freedom a crushing load the while its breath cannot be shared by you, close-pent within the prison's walls. Then a swift resolve inspires it, to tear down all the barriers hedging you from heaven's light: higher, higher and ever fuller swells the soul, its might redoubled by the blest resolve; 'tis the evangel of redemption to the world. (06) Yet this angel is but a loving woman, its strength the puny strength of suffering humanity itself: it battles alike with hostile hindrances and its own weakness, and threatens to succumb. But the suprahuman Idea, which ever lights its soul anew, lends finally the superhuman force: one last, one utmost strain of every fibre, and the last bolt falls, the latest stone is heaved away. In floods the sunlight streams into the dungeon: "Freedom! Freedom!" shouts the redemptrix; "Freedom! Godlike freedom!" the redeemed.

This is the Leonora-overture, *Beethoven's* poem. Here all is alive with unceasing dramatic progress, from the first yearning thought to the execution of a vast resolve.

But this work is unique of its kind, and no longer can be called an Overture, if we mean by that term a tone-piece destined for performance before the opening of a drama, merely to prepare the mind for the action's character. On the other hand, as we now are dealing, not with the musical artwork in general, but with the true vocation of the Overture in particular, this overture to *Leonora* cannot be accepted as a model, for it offers us in all-too-warm anticipation the whole completed drama in itself; consequently it either is un-understood or misconstrued by the hearer not already well-acquainted with the story, or, if thoroughly understood, it undoubtedly weakens the enjoyment of the explicit dramatic artwork it precedes.

Let us therefore leave this prodigious tone-work on one side, and return to the overture to *Don Giovanni*. Here we found the drama's leading thought delineated in a purely musical, but not in a dramatic shape. We unhesitatingly declare this mode of conception and treatment to be the fittest for such pieces, above all because the musician here withdraws himself from all temptation to outstep the bounds of his specific art, i.e., to sacrifice his freedom. Moreover, the musician thus most surely attains the Overture's artistic end, to act as nothing but an ideal prologue, translating us to that higher sphere in which to prepare our minds for Drama. Yet this in nowise prevents the musical conception of the drama's main idea being given most distinct expression, and brought to a definite close; on the contrary, the overture should form a musical artwork entire in itself.

In this sense we can point to no clearer and finer model for the Overture than that to Gluck's *Iphigenia in Aulis*, and will therefore endeavour to illustrate by this particular work our general conclusions as to the best method of conceiving an overture. (07)

Here again, as in the overture to *Don Giovanni*, it is a contest, or at least an opposition of two hostile elements, that gives the piece its movement. The plot of *Iphigenia* itself includes this pair of elements. The army of Greek heroes is assembled for a great emprise in common: under the inspiring thought of its execution, each separate human interest pales before this one great interest of the gathered mass. Now this is confronted with the special interest of preserving a human life, the rescue of a tender maiden. With what truth and distinctness of characterisation has Gluck as though personified these opposites in music! In what sublime proportion has he measured out the two, and set them face to face in such a mode as of itself to give the conflict, and accordingly the motion! In the ponderous unison of the iron principal motive we recognise at once the mass united by a single interest; whilst in the subsequent theme that other interest, that interest of the tender suffering individual, forthwith arrests our sympathy. This solitary contrast is pursued throughout the piece, and gives into our hands the broad idea of old Greek Tragedy, for it fills us with terror and pity in turn. Thus we attain that lofty state of excitation which prepares us for a drama whose highest meaning is revealed to us already, and thus are we led to understand the ensuing action in this meaning.

May this glorious example serve as rule in future for the framing of all overtures, and demonstrate withal how much a grand simplicity in the choice of musical motives enables the musician to evoke the swiftest and the plainest understanding of his never so unwonted aims. How hard, nay, how impossible would a like success have been to Gluck himself, had he sorted out all kinds of minor motives to signal this or that occurrence of the drama's, and worked them in between these eloquent chief-motives of his overture; they here would either have been swallowed up, or have distracted and misled the attention of the musical hearer. Yet, despite this simplicity in the means employed, to sustain a longer movement it is permissible to give wider play to the drama's influence over the development of the main musical thought in its overture. Not that one should admit a motion such as dramatic action alone can supply, but merely such as lies within the nature of instrumental music. The motion of two musical themes assembled in one piece will always evince a certain leaning, a struggle toward a culmination; then a sure conclusion seems indispensable for our appeasement, as our feeling longs to cast its final vote on one or other side. As a similar combat of principles first lends to a drama its higher life, it is thus by no means contrary to the purity of music's means of effect to give its contest of tone-motives a termination in keeping with the drama's tendence. Cherubini, Beethoven, and Weber, were led by such a feeling in the conception of most of their overtures; in that to the *Water-Carrier* this crisis is painted with the greatest definition; the overtures to *Fidelio, Egmont, Coriolanus,* with that to the *Freischütz,* quite clearly express the issue of a strenuous fight. The point of contact with the dramatic story would accordingly reside in the character of the two main themes, as also in the motion given to them by their musical working-out. This working-out, on the other hand, would always have to spring from the purely musical import of those themes; never should it take account of the sequence of events in the drama itself, since such a course would at once destroy the sole effectual character of a work of Tone.

In this conception of the Overture, then, the highest task would be to reproduce the characteristic idea of the drama by the intrinsic means of independent music, and to bring it to a conclusion in anticipatory agreement with the solution of the problem in the scenic play. For this purpose the composer will do well to weave into the characteristic motives of his overture certain melismic or rhythmic features which acquire importance in the dramatic action itself: not features strewn by accident amid the action, but such as intervene therein with determinant weight, and thus can lend the very overture an individual stamp—demarcations, as it were, of the special domain on which a human action runs its course. Obviously these features must be in themselves of purely musical nature, therefore such as bring the influence of the sound-world to bear upon our human life; whereof I may cite as excellent instances the trombones of the Priests in the *Magic Flute*, the trumpet-signal in *Leonora*, and the call of the magic horn in *Oberon*. (08) These musical motives from the opera, employed at a decisive moment in its overture, here serve as actual points of contact of the dramatic with the musical motion, and thus effect a happy individualisation of the tone-piece, which in any case is meant as a suggestive introduction to one particular dramatic story.

Now if we allow that the working-out of purely musical elements in the overture should in so far accord with the dramatic idea that even its issue should harmonise with the dénouement of the scenic action, the question arises whether the actual development of the drama or the changes in the fortunes of its principal personages should exert an immediate influence on the conception of the overture, and above all on the characteristics of its close. Certainly we could only adjudge that influence a most conditional exercise; for we have found that a purely musical conception may well embrace the drama's leading thoughts, but not the individual fate of single persons. In a very weighty sense the composer plays the part of a philosopher, who seizes nothing but the *idea* in all phenomena; his business, as that of the great poet, lies solely with the victory of an Idea; the tragic downfall of the hero, taken personally, does not affect him. (09) From this point of view, he holds aloof from the entanglements of individual destinies and their attendant haps: he triumphs, though the hero goes under. Nowhere is this sublimest conception more finely expressed than in the overture to *Egmont*, whose closing section raises the tragic idea of the drama to its highest dignity, and at like time gives us a perfect piece of music of enthralling power. (10) On the other hand I know but one exception, of the first rank, which seems to flatly contradict the axiom just laid down: the overture to *Coriolanus*. If we view this mighty tragic artwork closer, however, the different conception of the subject is explained by the tragic idea here lying solely in the hero's personal fate. An inconciliable pride, an overbearing, overpowering, and overweening nature can only rouse our sympathy through its collapse: to make us forebode this, horror-struck see it arrive, was the master's incommensurable work. (11) But with this overture, as with that to *Leonora*, Beethoven stands alone and past all imitation: the lessons to be drawn from creations of such high originality can only be of fruit for us when we combine them with the legacies of other masters. In the triad, *Gluck, Mozart*, and *Beethoven* we have the lodestar whose pure light will always lead us rightly even on the most bewildering paths of art; but who should single *one* of them for his exclusive star, of a surety would fall into the maze from which but one has ever issued victor, that one Inimitable.

Notes

01

From here to the end of this paragraph the French differs a little: "Ces ouvertures étaient courtes, consistaient souvent en un seul mouve ment lent, et l'on pent retrouver les exemples les plus frappants de ce mode de construction, quoique étendu considérablement, dans les oratorios de Haendel. Le libre développement de l'ouverture fut paralysé par cette fâcheuse circonstance qui arrêtait les compositeurs dans les premières périodes de la musique, savoir l'ignorance où us étaient des procédés sûrs par lesquels on peut, l'aide des hardiesses légères et des successions de fraîches nuances, étendre un morceau de musique de longue haleine. Cela ne leur était guère possible qu'au moyen des finesses du contre-point, la seule invention de ces temps qui permit un compositeur de dévider un thème unique en un morceau de quelque durée. On écrivait des fugues instrumentales; on se perdait dans les détours de ces curieuses monstruosités de la spéculation artistique. La monotonie et l'uniformité furent les produits nets de cette direction. Ces sortes de compositions étaient surtout impuissantes exprimer un caractère déterminé et individuel.

Haendel lui-même ne parait pas s'être aucunement soucié que l'ouverture s'accordât exactement avec la pièce ou l'oratorio. Il est par exemple impossible de pressentir par l'ouverture du *Messie* qu'elle doit servir d'introduction une création aussi fortement caractérisée, aussi sublime que l'est ce célèbre oratorio." — Tr.

02

The French had: "Il faut seulement remarquer que dans la manière de voir de ces deux grands compositeurs, qui ont du reste de nombreux points d'affinité, Cherubini" etc. — Tr.

03

This sentence was represented in the French by: "Pour un public auquel on demandait ainsi moins de réflexion profonde, la séduction de cette manière de procéder consistait tout la fois dans un choix habile des motifs les plus brillants et dans le mouvement agréable, dans le papillotage varié qui résultait de leur arrangement. C'est ainsi que naquirent l'ouverture si admirée de *Guillaume Tell*" etc. — Tr.

04

From "unless" to the end of the sentence, did not appear in the French. — Tr.

05

This last clause was absent from the French. — Tr.

06

From "higher" to the end of the sentence was represented in the French by: "Semblable à un second messie, il veut accomplir l'oeuvre de rédemption." — Tr.

07

See also the special article upon this work in Vol. III.—Tr.

08

In the French this sentence took the following form: "Mais on ne doit jamais perdre de vue qu'ils doivent être de source entièrement musicale et non emprunter leur signification aux paroles qui les accompagnent dans l'opéra. Le compositeur commetrait alors la faute de se sacrifier lui et l'indépendance de son art devant l'intervention d'un art étranger. Il faut, dis-je, que ces éléments soient de nature purement musicale, et je citerai comme exemples" etc. —Tr.

09

In the French this sentence ran: "Le compositeur ne doit résoudre que la question supérieure et philosophique de l'ouvrage, et exprimer immédiatement le sentiment qui s'y répand et le parcourt dans toute son étendue comme uin fil conducteur. Ce sentiment arrive-t-il dans le drame à un dénouement victorieux, le compositeur n'a guère à s'occuper que de savoir si le héros de la pièce remporte cette victoire, ou s'il éprouve une fin tragique." —Tr.

10

The French contained the following additional passage: "Le destin élève [?-enlève] ici par un coup décisif le héros au triomphe. Les derniers accents de l'ouverture qui se montent à la sublimité de l'apothéose, rendent parfaitement l'idée dramatique, tout en formant l'œuvre la plus musicale. Le combat des deux éléments nous entraîne ici impérieusement, même dans la musique, à un dénouement nécessaire, et il est surtout de l'essence de la musique de faire apparaître cette conclusion comme un fait consolateur." —Tr.

11

The second half of this sentence is not represented in the French.—Tr.

AN END IN PARIS

(1)

WE have just laid him in the earth. It was cold and dreary weather, and few there were of us. The Englishman, too, was there: he wants to erect a memorial to him; 'twere better he paid our friend's debts.

It was a mournful ceremony. The first keen wind of winter cut the breath; no one could speak, and the funeral oration was omitted. Nevertheless I would have you to know that he whom we buried was a good man and a brave German musician. He had a tender heart, and wept whenever men hurt the poor horses in the streets of Paris. He was mild of temper, and never put out when the street-urchins jostled him off the narrow pavement. Unfortunately he had a sensitive artistic conscience, was ambitious, with no talent for intrigue, and once in his youth had seen Beethoven, which so turned his head that he could never set it straight in Paris.

It is more than a year since I one day saw a magnificent Newfoundland dog taking a bath in the fountain of the Palais Royal. Lover of dogs that I am, I watched the splendid animal; it left the basin at last, and answered the call of a man who at first attracted my attention merely as the owner of this dog. The man was by no means so fair to look on, as his dog; he was clean, but dressed in God knows what provincial fashion. Yet his features arrested me; soon I distinctly remembered having seen them before; my interest in the dog relaxed; I fell into the arms of my old friend R . . . .

We were delighted at meeting again; he was quite overcome with emotion. I took him to the *Café de la Rotonde*; I drank tea with rum, — he, coffee with tears.

"But what on earth," I began at last, "can have brought you to Paris—you, the musical hermit of the fifth floor of a provincial back-street?"

"My friend," he replied, "call it the over-earthly passion for experiencing what life is like on a Parisian sixth, or the worldly longing to see if I might not be able in time to descend to the second, or even the first,—I myself am not quite certain which. At anyrate I couldn't resist the temptation of tearing myself from the squalor of the German provinces, and, without tasting the far sublimer pinches of a German capital, throwing myself straight upon the centre of the world, where the arts of every nation stream together to one focus; where the artists of each race find recognition; and where I hope for satisfaction of the tiny morsel of ambition that Heaven—apparently in inadvertence—has set in my own breast."

"A very natural desire," I interposed; "I forgive it you, though in yourself it astonishes me. But first let us see what means you have of pursuing your ambitious purpose. How much money a-year can you draw?—Oh, don't be alarmed! I know that you were a poor devil, and it is self-evident that there can be no question of a settled income. Yet I am bound to suppose either that you have won money in a lottery, or enjoy the protection of some rich patron or relative to such a degree that you are provided for ten years, at least, with a passable allowance."

"That is how you foolish people look at things!" replied my friend, with a good-humoured smile, after recovering from his first alarm. "Such are the prosaic details that rise at once before your eyes as chief concern. Nothing of the kind, my dear friend! I am poor; in a few weeks, in fact, without a sou. But what of that? I have been told that I have talent;—was I to choose *Tunis* as the place for pushing it? No; I have come to *Paris*! Here I shall soon find out if folk deceived me when they credited me with talent, or if I really own any. In the first case I shall be quickly disenchanted, and, clear about myself, shall journey back contented to my garret-home; in the second case I shall get my talent more speedily and better paid in Paris, than anywhere else in the world.—Nay, don't smile, but try to raise some serious objection!"

"Best of friends," I resumed, "I smile no longer; for I now am possessed by a mournful compassion for yourself and your splendid dog. I know that, however frugal yourself, your magnificent beast will eat a good deal. You intend to feed both him and yourself by your talent? That's grand; for self-preservation is the first duty, and human feeling for the beasts a second and the noblest. But tell me: how are you going to bring your talent to market? What plans have you made? Let me hear them."

"It is well that you ask for my plans," was the answer. "You shall have a long list of them; for, look you, I am rich in plans. In the first place, I think of an opera: I am provided with finished works, with half-finished, and with any number of sketches for all kinds—both grand and comic opera.—Don't interrupt!—I'm well aware that these are things that will not march too quickly, and merely consider them as the basis of my efforts. Though I dare not hope to see one of my operas produced at once, at least I may be permitted to assume that I shall soon be satisfied as to whether the Directors will accept my compositions or not—For shame, friend—you're smiling again! Don't speak! I know what you were going to say, and will answer it at once.—I am convinced that I shall have to contend with difficulties of all sorts here also; but in what will they consist? Certainly in nothing but competition. The most eminent talents converge here, and offer their works for acceptance; managers are therefore compelled to exercise a searching scrutiny: a line must be drawn against bunglers, and none but works of exceptional merit can attain the honour of selection. Good! I have prepared myself for this examination, and ask for no distinction without deserving it. But what else have I to fear, beyond that competition? Am I to believe that here, too, one 'needs the wonted tactics of servility? (2) Here in Paris, the capital of free France, where a Press exists that unmasks and makes impossible all humbug and abuse; where merit alone can win the plaudits of a great incorruptible public?"

"The public?" I interrupted; "there you are right. I also am of opinion that, with your talent, you well might succeed, had you only the public to deal with. But as to the easiness of reaching that public you hugely err, poor friend! It is not the contest of talents, in which you will have to engage, but the contest of reputations and personal interests. If you are sure of firm and influential patronage, by all means venture on the fight; but without this, and without money,—give up, for you're sure to go under, without so much as being noticed. It will be no question of commending your work or talent (a favour unparalleled!), but what will be considered is the name you bear. Seeing that no renommée attaches to that name as yet, and it is to be found on no list of the moneyed, you and your talent remain in obscurity." (3)

My objection failed to produce the intended effect on my enthusiastic friend. He turned peevish, but refused to believe me. I went on to ask what he thought of doing as a preliminary, to earn some little renommée in another direction, which perchance might be of more assistance to the later execution of his soaring plan.

This seemed to dispel his ill-humour.

"Hear, then!" he answered: "You know that I have always had a great preference for instrumental music. Here, in Paris, where a regular cult of our great Beethoven appears to have been instituted, I have reason to hope that his fellow-countryman and most ardent worshipper will easily find entrance when he undertakes to give the public a hearing of his own attempts, however feeble, to follow in the footsteps of that unattainable example."

" Excuse me for cutting you short," I interposed. "Beethoven is getting deified,—in that you are right; but mind you, it is his name, his renown that is deified. That name, prefixed to a work not unworthy of the great master, will suffice to secure its beauties instant recognition. By any other name, however, the selfsame work will never gain the attention of the directorate of a concert-establishment for even its most brilliant passages." (4)

"You lie!"—my friend rather hastily exclaimed. "Your purpose is becoming clear, to systematically discourage me, and scare me from the path of fame. You shall not succeed, however!"

"I know you," I replied, "and forgive you. Nevertheless I must add that in your last proposal you will stumble on the very same difficulties, which rear themselves against every artist without renown, however great his talent, in a place where people have far too little time to bother themselves about hidden treasures. Both plans are modes of fortifying an already established position, and gaining profit from it, but by no manner of means of creating one. People will either pay no heed at all to your application for a performance of your instrumental compositions, or—if your works are composed in that daring individual spirit which you so much admire in Beethoven, they will find them turgid and indigestible, and send you home with a flea in your ears." (5)

"But," my friend put in, "what if I have already circumvented such a reproach? What if I have written works expressly to aid me with a more superficial public, and adorned them with those favourite modern effects which I abhor from the bottom of my heart, but are not despised by even considerable artists as preliminary bids for favour?"

"They will give you to understand," I replied, "that your work is too light, too shallow, to be brought to the public ear between the creations of a Beethoven and a Musard."

"Dear man!" my friend exclaimed, "That's good indeed! At last I see that you are making fun of me. You always were a wag!"

My friend stamped his foot in his laughter, and trod so forcibly upon the lordly paw of his splendid dog that the latter yelped aloud, then licked his master's hand, and seemed to humbly beg him to take no more of my objections as jokes.

"You see," I said, "it is not always well to take earnestness as jest. Passing that by, come tell me what other plans could have moved you to exchange your modest home for this monster of a Paris. In what other way, if you will please me by provisionally abandoning the two you have spoken of, do you propose to get the requisite renown?"

"So be it," was the reply I received. "In spite of your singular love of contradiction, I will proceed with the narration of my plans. Nothing, as I know, is more popular in Paris drawing-rooms than those charming sentimental ballads and romances, which are just to the taste of the French people, and some of which have even emigrated from our fatherland. Think of Franz Schubert's songs, and the vogue they enjoy here! This is a genre that admirably suits my inclination; I feel capable of turning out something worth noticing there. I will get my songs sung, and perchance I may share the good luck which has fallen to so many—namely of attracting by these unpretentious works the attention of some Director of the Opéra who may happen to be present, so that he honours me with the commission for an opera."

The dog again uttered a violent howl. This time it was I who, in an agony of laughter, had trodden on the paw of the excellent beast.

"What!" I cried, "is it possible that you seriously entertain such an idiotic idea? What on earth could entitle you—"

"My God!" the enthusiast broke in; "have not similar cases happened often enough? Must I bring you the newspapers in which I have repeatedly read how such-and-such a Director was so carried away by the hearing of a Romance, how such-and-such a famous poet was suddenly so impressed by the talent of a totally unknown composer, that both of them at once united in the resolve, the one to supply him with a libretto, the other to produce the opera to-be-written to order?"

"Ah! is that it?" I sighed, filled with sudden sadness; "Press notices have led astray your simple childlike head? Dear friend, of all you come across in that way take note of but a third, and even of that don't trust four quarters! Our Directors have something else to do, than to hear Romances sung and fall into raptures over them. (6) And, admitting that to be a feasible mode of gaining a reputation,— by whom would you get your Romances sung?"

"By whom else," was the rejoinder, "than the same world-famed singers who so often, and with the greatest amiability, have made it their duty to introduce the productions of unknown or downtrod talent to the public? Or am I here again deceived by lying paragraphs?"

"My friend," I replied, "God knows how far I am from wishing to deny that noble hearts of this kind beat below the throats of our foremost singers, male and female. But to attain the honour of such patronage, one needs at least some other essentials. You can easily imagine what competition goes on here also, and that it requires an infinitely influential recommendation, to make it dawn upon those noble hearts that one in truth is an unknown genius.—Poor friend, have you no other plans?"

Here my companion took leave of his senses. In a violent passion— though with some regard for his dog— he turned away from me. "And had I as many more plans as the sands of the sea," he shouted, "you should not hear a single one of them. Go! You are my enemy!— Yet know, inexorable man, you shall not triumph over me! Tell me— the last question I will put to you—tell me, wretch, how then have the myriads commenced, who first became known, and finally famous, in Paris ?"

"Ask one of them," I replied, in somewhat ruffled composure, "and perhaps you may discover. For my part, I don't know."

"Here, here!" called the infatuate to his wonderful dog. "You are my friend no longer,"—he volleyed at me,—"Your cold derision shall not see me blench. *In one year from* now—remember this—*in one year from now every gamin shall be able to tell you where I live, or you shall hear from me whither to come—to see me die.* Farewell!"

He whistled shrilly to his dog,—a discord. He and his superb companion had vanished like a lightning-flash. Nowhere could I overtake them.

It was only after a few days, when all my efforts to ascertain the dwelling of my friend had proved futile, that I began to realise the wrong I had done in not shewing more consideration for the peculiarities of so profoundly enthusiastic a nature, than unfortunately had been the case with my tart, perhaps exaggerated, objections to his very innocent plans. In the good intention of frightening him from his projects as much as possible, because I did not deem him fitted either by his outward or his inward condition to successfully pursue so intricate a path of fame—in this good intention, I repeat, I had not reckoned with the fact that I had by no means to do with one of those tractable and easily-persuaded minds, but with a man whose deep belief in the divine and irrefutable truth of his art had reached such a pitch of fanaticism, that it had turned one of the gentlest of tempers to a dogged obstinacy.

For sure—I could but think—he now is wandering through the streets of Paris with the firm conviction that he has only to decide which of his plans he shall realise first, in order to figure at once on one of those advertisements that, so to say, make out the vista of his scheme. For sure, he is giving an old beggar a sou to-day, with the determination to make it a napoleon a few months hence.

The more the time slipped by since our last parting, and the more fruitless became my endeavours to unearth my friend, so much the more—I admit my weakness—was I infected by the confidence he then displayed; so that I allowed myself at last to search the advertisements of musical performances, now and again, with eyes astrain to spy out in some corner of them the name of my assured enthusiast. Yes, the smaller my success in these attempts at discovery, the more—remarkable to say!—was my friendly interest allied with an ever-increasing belief that my friend might not impossibly succeed; that perchance even now, while I was seeking anxiously for him, his peculiar talent might already have been discovered and acknowledged by some important person or other; that perhaps he had received one of those commissions whose happy execution brings fortune, honour, and God knows what beside. And why not? Is there no star that rules the fate of each inspired soul? May not his be a star of luck? Cannot miracles take place, to expose a hidden treasure?—The very fact of my nowhere seeing the announcement of a single Romance, an Overture or the like, under the name of my friend, made me believe that he had gone straight for his grandest plan, and, despising those lesser adits to publicity, was already up to his eyes in work on an opera of at least five acts. True, I had never come across him in the haunts of artists, or met a creature who knew anything about him; still, as my own access to those sanctuaries was but rare, 'twas conceivable that it was *I* who was the unfortunate that could not penetrate where his fame maybe already shone with dazzling rays.—

You may easily guess that it needed a considerable time, for my first sad interest in my friend to change into a confident belief in his good star. It was only through all the phases of fear, of doubt, of hope, that I could arrive at this point. Such things are somewhat slow with me, and so it happened that almost a year had already elapsed since the day when I met a splendid dog and an enthusiastic friend in the Palais Royal. Meanwhile some wonderfully lucky speculations had brought me to so unprecedented a pitch of prosperity that, like Polycrates of old, I began to fear an imminent reverse. I fancied I could plainly see it coming; thus it was in a gloomy frame of mind, that I one day took my customary walk in the Champs Élysées.

'Twas autumn; the leaves fell withered from the trees, and the sky hung grey with age above the Elysian pomp below. But, nothing daunted, Punch renewed his old mad onslaught; in blind rage that scoundrel constantly defied the justice of this world, until at last the dæmonic principle, so forcibly depicted .by the chained-up cat, with super-human claws laid low the saucy bounce of the presumptuous mortal.

Close by my side, a few paces from the humble scene of Polichinel's misdeeds I heard the following remarkable soliloquy in German:—

"Excellent! excellent! Where, in the name of all the world, have I allowed myself to seek, when I could have found so near? What! Am I to despise this stage, on which the most thrilling political and poetic truths are set in realistic dress, so directly and intelligibly, before the most receptive and least assuming public? Is this braggart not Don Juan? Is that terribly fair white cat not the Commander on horseback, in very person?—How the artistic import of this drama will be heightened and transfigured when my music adds its quota!—What sonorous organs in these actors!—And the cat—ah, that cat! What hidden charms lie buried in her glorious throat!—Now she gives no sound—now she is still mere demon:—but how she will fascinate when she sings the roulades I'll write expressly for her! What a magnificent *portamento* she'll put into the execution of that supernatural chromatic scale!—How treacherous will be her smile, when she sings that famous passage of the future: "*O Polichinel, thou art lost!*"— —What a plan!—And then, what a splendid pretext for incessant use of the big drum, will Punch's constant truncheon-beats afford me!—Come, why delay? Quick, for the Director's favour! Here I can walk straight in,—no ante-chambers here! With one step I'm in the sanctuary—before him whose god-like piercing eye will recognise at once my genius. Or must I light on competition here as well ?—Should the cat—?—Quick, ere it is too late!"

With these last words the soliloquist was about to make straight for the Punch-and-Judy box. I had speedily recognised my friend, and determined to avert a scandal. I seized him by the arm, and span him round towards me.

"Who is it?"—he pettishly cried. He soon remembered me, quietly detached himself, and added coldly: "I might have known that it could only be *you*, that would thwart me in this step as well, the last for my salvation.—Leave me; it may become too late."

I grasped him afresh; but, though I was able to keep him from rushing forward to the little theatre, it was quite impossible to move him from the spot. Still, I gained the leisure to observe him closely. Great heavens, in what a condition he was ! I say nothing of his dress, but of his features; the former was poor and threadbare, but the latter were terrible. The free and open look was gone; lifeless and vacant, his eye travelled to and fro; his pallid, sunken cheeks told not alone of trouble,—the hectic flush upon them told of sufferings too,—of hunger!

As I studied him with deepest sorrow, he too seemed touched, for he struggled less to tear himself away from me.

"How goes it with you, dear R . . .?" I asked with choking voice. With a mournful smile I added: "Where is your beautiful dog?"

He looked black at once. "Stolen!" was the abrupt reply.

"Not sold?" I asked again.

"Wretch," he sullenly replied, "are you also like the Englishman?"

I did not understand his meaning. "Come," I said in faltering tones— "come! take me to your house; I have much to speak with you."

"You soon will know my house without my aid," he answered, "the year is not yet up. I'm now on the high road to recognition, fortune!—Go, you do not yet believe it! What boots it to preach to the deaf? You people must *see,* to believe; very good! You soon shall see. But loose me now, if I am not to take you for my sworn foe."

I held his hands the faster. "Where do you live?" I asked. "Come, take me there! We'll have a friendly, hearty chat,—about your plans, if it must be!"

"You shall learn them as soon as they are carried out," he answered. "Quadrilles, galops ! Oh, that is my forte!—You shall see and hear!— Do you see that cat?—She's to help me to fat fees!—See how sleek she is, how daintily she licks her chops! Imagine the effect when from that little mouth, between those pearly rows of teeth, the most inspired of chromatic scales well forth, accompanied by the most delicate moans and sobs in all the world ! Imagine it, dear friend! Oh, you have no fancy, you!—Leave me, leave me!—You have no phantasy!"

I held him tighter, and implored him to conduct me to his lodgings; without making the slightest impression, however. His eye was fixed with anxious strain upon the cat.

"Everything depends on her," he cried. "Fortune, honour, fame, reside within her velvet paws. May Heaven guide her heart, and turn on me her favour!—She looks friendly,—yes, that's the feline nature ! And she *is* friendly, polite, polite beyond measure! But she's a cat, a false and treacherous cat!—Wait,—thee at least I can rule! I have a noble dog; he'll make thee respect me.—Victory! I've won the day!—Where is my dog?"

He had shot forth the last few words in mad excitement, with a piercing cry. He looked hastily round, as if seeking for his dog. His eager glance fell on the roadway. There rode upon a splendid horse an elegant gentleman, by his physiognomy and the peculiar cut of his clothes an Englishman; by his side ran, proudly barking, a fine Newfoundland dog.

"Ha! my presentiment!" shrieked my friend, in a fury of wrath at the sight. "The cursed brute ! My dog; my dog !" My strength was unavailing against the violence with which the unhappy creature tore himself away. Like an arrow he fled after the horseman, who happened just then to be spurring his horse to a gallop, which the dog accompanied with the liveliest gambols. I rushed after—in vain! What effort of strength can compare with the feats of a madman?—I saw the rider, the dog, and my friend, all vanish down one of the side streets that lead to the Faubourg du Roule. When I reached the same street, they were gone.

Suffice it to mention that all my endeavours to track them were fruitless.—

Alarmed, and almost driven to madness myself I was forced at last to give up my inquiries for the moment. But you may readily imagine that I none the less bestirred myself each day to find some clue to the retreat of my unhappy friend. I sought for news in every place that had the remotest connection with music:—nowhere the smallest intimation ! It was only in the sacred ante-chambers of the Opéra that the subordinates remembered a pitiable apparition, which had often presented itself and waited for an audience, but of whose name or dwelling they naturally were ignorant. Every other path, even that of the police, led to no surer traces; the very guardians of the public safety seemed to have thought it needless to worry themselves about the poor soul.

I fell into despair. Then one day, about two months after that affair in the Champs Élysées, I received a letter sent me in a roundabout fashion through one of my acquaintances. I opened it with a heavy heart, and read the brief words:

"Dear friend, come and see me die!"

The address denoted a narrow little street on Montmartre.—It was no time for tears, and I ascended the hill of Montmartre. Following my directions, I arrived at one of those poverty-stricken houses which are common enough in the side-alleys of that little town. Despite its poor exterior, this building did not fail to rear itself to a *cinquième*; my unfortunate friend would appear to have welcomed the fact, and thus I also was compelled to mount to the same giddy height. It was worth the while, for, on asking for my friend, I was referred to the back attic; from this hinder side of the estimable building one certainly forwent all outlook on the four-foot-wide magnificence of the causeway, but was rewarded by the incomparably finer one on the whole of Paris.

I found my poor enthusiast propped-up on a wretched sick-bed, drinking in this wonderful prospect. His face, his whole body, were infinitely more haggard and emaciated than on that day in the Champs Élysées; nevertheless the expression of his features was far more reassuring. The scared, wild, almost maniacal look, the uncanny fire in his eyes, had vanished; his glance was dulled and half-extinguished; the dark and ghastly flecks upon his cheeks seemed quenched in a universal wasting.

Trembling, but still composed, he stretched his hand to me with the words: "Forgive me, old fellow, and take my thanks for coming."

The softness and sonority of the tone in which he uttered these few words produced on me an even more touching impression, if possible, than his appearance had already done. I pressed his hand, but could not speak for weeping.

"I think,"—went on my friend, after an affecting pause,—"it is already well over a year, since we met in that glittering Palais Royal;—I have not quite kept my word:—to become renowned within a year, was impossible to me, with the best will in the world; on the other hand it's no fault of mine that I could not write you punctually upon the year's elapse, where you must come to see me die:'spite all my struggles, I had not yet got quite so far.—Nay, do not weep, my friend ! There was a time when I must beg you not to laugh."

I tried to speak, but speech forsook me.—"Let me speak!" the dying man put in: "it is becoming easy to me, and I owe you a long account. I'm sure that I shall not be here to-morrow, so listen to my narrative to-day 'Tis a simple tale, my friend!—most simple. In it you'll find no wondrous complications, no hair-breadth strokes of luck, no ostentatious details. Fear not that your patience will be wearied by the easiness of speech which now is granted me, and certainly might tempt me to long-windedness; for there have been days, dear old man, when I couldn't utter a sound. Listen!—When I reflect on the state in which you find me, I hold it needless to assure you that my fate has been no bright one. Nor do I altogether need to count you up the trivialities among which my enthusiasm has come to ground. Suffice it to say, that they were no *breakers*, on which I foundered!—Happy the shipwrecked who goes down in *storm!*—No: they were *quagmires* and *swamps*, in which I sank. These swamps, dear friend, surround all proud and dazzling Art-fanes, to which we poor fools make such ardent pilgrimage, as though they held the saving of our souls. Happy the feather-brained ! With one successful entrechat he leaps the quagmire. Happy the rich ! His well-trained horse needs but one prick of the golden spur, to bear him swiftly over. But woe to the enthusiast who, taking that swamp for a flowery meadow, is swallowed in it past all rescue, a meal for frogs and toads!—See, dear friend, this vermin has devoured me; there's not a drop of blood left in me!— —Must I tell you how it happened? But why? You see me done for;—be content to hear that I was not vanquished on the field of battle, but—horrible to utter—in *the Ante-chambers of Hunger I fell*!—They are something terrible, those Ante-chambers; and know that there are many, very many of them in Paris,—with seats of wood or velvet, heated and not heated, paved and unpaved!—"

"In those Ante-chambers,"—continued my friend,—"I dreamed away a fair year of my life. I dreamt of many wondrous mad and fabled stories from the 'Thousand-and-one Nights,'' of men and beasts, of gold and offal. My dreams were of gods and contrabassists, of jewelled snuff-boxes and prima-donnas, of satin gowns and lovesick lords, of chorus-girls and five-franc pieces. Between I sometimes seemed to hear the wailing, ghost-like note of an oboe; that note thrilled through my every nerve, and cut my heart. One day when I had dreamed my maddest, and that oboe-note was tingling through me at its sharpest, I suddenly awoke and found I had become a madman. At least I recollect, that I had forgotten to make my usual obeisance to the theatre-lackey as I left the anteroom,—the reason, I may add, of my never daring to return to it; for *how* would the man have received me?—With tottering steps I left the haven of my dreams; on the threshold of the building I fell of a heap. I had stumbled over my poor dog, who, after his wont, was ante-chambering in the street, in waiting for his fortunate master who was allowed to ante-chamber among men. This dog, I must tell you, had been of the utmost service to me, for to him and his beauty alone I owed it that now and then the lackey of the ante-chamber would honour me with a passing glance. Alas ! with every day he lost a portion of his beauty, for hunger gnawed his entrails too. This gave me fresh alarm, as I clearly foresaw that the servant's favour would soon be lost to me; already a contemptuous smile would often purse his lips.—As said, I fell over this dog of mine. How long I lay, I know not; of the kicks which I may have received from passers-by I took no notice; but at last I was awoken by the tenderest kisses,—the warm licks of my dear beast. I leapt to my feet, and in a lucid interval I recognised at once my weightiest duty: to buy the dog some food. A shrewd *Marchand d'Habits* gave me a handful of sous for my villainous waistcoat. My dog ate, and what he left I devoured. With *him* this answered admirably, but I was past mending. The produce of an heirloom, an old ring of my grandmother's, sufficed to restore the dog to his ancient beauty; he bloomed afresh—oh, fatal blooming!

"With my brain it grew ever darker; I know not rightly what took place within it,—but I remember being seized one day by an irresistible longing to seek out the Devil. My dog, in all his former glory, accompanied me to the gates of the *Concerts Musard*. Did I hope to meet the Devil, there? That also I cannot tell. I scanned the people trooping in, and whom did I espy among them? The abominable *Englishman*: the same, as large as life, and not one atom changed from when, as I related to you, he harmed me so with Beethoven!—Fear took me; I was prepared to face a demon from the nether world, but never more this phantom of the upper. O how I felt, when the wretch also recognised *me*! I couldn't avoid him,—the crowd was pressing us towards each other. Involuntarily, and quite against the customs of his countrymen, he was compelled to fall into my arms, raised up to force myself an exit. There he lay, wedged tight against my breast, with its thousand torturing emotions. It was a fearful moment ! We were soon released a little, and he shook me off with a shade of indignation. I tried to escape; but it still was impossible.—'Welcome, mein Herr!'—the Briton shouted:—'I always meet you on the ways of Art This time we'll go to *Musard!*'—For very wrath I could say nothing but: 'To the Devil!'—'Quite so,' he answered, 'it seems that things go devilish there!—Last Sunday I threw off a composition, which I shall offer to Musard. Do you know this Musard? Will you introduce me to him?'

"My horror at this bugbear turned to speechless fear; impelled by it, I gained the strength to free myself and flee towards the Boulevard; my lovely dog rushed barking after me. But in a trice the Englishman was by my side once more, holding me, and asking in excited tones: 'Sir, does this splendid dog belong to you? Yes.'—'But it is superb!

Sir, I will pay you fifty guineas for this dog. A dog like this, you know, is the proper thing for a gentleman, and I have already owned a number of them. Unfortunately, the beasts were all unmusical; they could not stand my practising the horn or flute, and so they always ran away. But I take it for granted that, as you have the good fortune to be a musician, your dog is musical also; I accordingly may hope that he will stop with me. So I offer you fifty guineas for the beast.' — 'Villain!' I cried: — 'not for the whole of Britain would I sell my friend !' So saying, I hurried off, my dog in front. I dodged down the back streets that led to my usual night's-lodging — It was bright moonshine; now and then I looked furtively back: — to my alarm, I thought I saw the Englishman's long figure following me. I redoubled my pace, and peered round still more anxiously; now I caught sight of the shadow, now lost it. Panting for breath, I reached my refuge, gave my dog to eat, and threw myself all hungry on my rough, hard bed. — I slept long, and dreamt of horrors. When I awoke, — my beautiful dog had vanished. How he had got away from me, or been enticed through the badly fastened door, to this day is a mystery to me. I called, I hunted for him, till sobbing I fainted away. —

"You remember that I saw the faithless one again one day in the Champs Élysées; — you know what efforts I made to regain possession of him; — but you do not know that this animal recognised me, yet fled from my call like an untamed beast of the wilderness ! Nevertheless I followed him and his Satanic cavalier till the latter dashed into a gateway, whose doors were slammed behind him and the dog. In my anger I thundered at the gates; — a furious bark was the answer. — Dazed and crushed, I leant against the archway, — until at last a hideous scale on the horn aroused me from my stupefaction; it reached me from the ground-floor of the mansion, and was followed by the agonised moan of a dog. Then I laughed out loud, and went my way. — "

My friend here ceased; though speech had become easy, his inward agitation taxed him terribly. It was no longer possible for him to hold himself erect in bed, — with a smothered groan he sank back. — A long pause occurred; I watched the poor fellow with painful feelings:

that faint flush so peculiar to the consumptive had risen to his cheeks. He had closed his eyes, and lay as if in slumber; his breath came lightly, almost in ethereal waves.

I waited anxiously for the moment when I durst speak to him, and ask what earthly service I could render.—At last he opened his eyes once more; a dim but wondrous light was in the glance he straightway fixed on me.

"My poor friend,"—I began—"I came here with the sad desire to serve you somehow. Have you a wish, O speak it !"

With a smile he resumed: "So impatient, friend, for my last testament?—Nay, have no care; you too are mentioned in it.—But will you not first learn how it befell that your poor brother came to die? Look you, I wished my history to be known to *one* soul at the least; but I know of no one who would worry himself about me, unless it be *yourself*— —Fear not that I am overexerting myself! 'Tis well with me and easy—no laboured breath oppresses me—the words come freely to my lips.—And see, I have little left to narrate. You can imagine that, from the point where I broke off my story, I had no more outer incidents to do with. From there begins the history of my inner life, for then I knew I soon should die. That terrible scale on the horn in the Englishman's hôtel filled me with so overpowering a weariness of life, that I there and then resolved to die. Indeed, I should not boast of that decision, for I must confess that it no longer lay entirely within my own free will. Something had cracked within my breast, that left a long and whirring sound behind;—when this died out 'twas light and well with me, as never before, and I knew my end was near. O how happy that conviction made me ! How the presage of a speedy dissolution cheered me, as I suddenly perceived its work in every member of this wasted body!— Insensible to outward things, unconscious where my faltering steps were bearing me, I had gained the summit of Montmartre. Thrice welcoming the Mount of Martyrs, I resolved on it to die. I too was dying for the wholeness of my faith; I too could therefore call myself a martyr, albeit this my faith was challenged by none else—than Hunger.

"Houseless, I took this lodging, asking nothing further than this bed, and that they would send for my scores and papers, which I had stowed in a wretched hovel of the city; for, alas ! I had never succeeded in pawning them. So here I lie, determined to pass away in God and pure Music. A friend will close my eyes, my effects will cover all my debts, and for a decent grave I shall not want.—Say, what more could I wish?"

At last I gave vent to my pent-up feelings.—"What !" I cried, "was it only for this last mournful service, that you could use me? Could your friend, however powerless, have helped you in nothing else? I conjure you, for my peace of mind tell me this: Was it a doubt of my friendship, that kept you from discovering my whereabouts and acquainting me before with your distress?"

"O don't be angry," he answered coaxingly, "don't chide me if I own that I had fallen into the stubborn belief that you were my enemy! When I recognised that you were not, my brain was already in a condition that robbed me of all responsibility of will. I felt that I was no longer fit to associate with men of sense. Forgive me, and be kindlier toward me, than I have been to you!—Give me your hand, and let this debt of my poor life be cancelled!"

I could not resist, but seized his hand, and melted into tears. Yet I saw how markedly the powers of my friend were ebbing; he was now too weak to raise himself in bed; that flickering flush came ever paler to his sunken cheeks.

"A little business, dear chum," he began afresh. "Call it my last Will ! For I will, in the first place: that my debts be paid. The poor people who took me in, have nursed me willingly and dunned me little; they must be paid. The same with a few other creditors, whose names you will find on that paper. I bequeath all my property in payment, there my compositions and here my diary, in which I have jotted down my musical whims and reflections. I leave it to your judgment, my experienced friend, to sell so much of these remains as will liquidate my earthly debts.—I will, in the second place: that you do not beat my dog, if you ever should meet him; I assume that, in punishment of his faithlessness, he has already suffered torments from the Englishman's horn. I forgive him!—Thirdly, I will that the history of my Paris sufferings, with omission of my name, be published as a wholesome warning to all soft fools like me.—Fourthly, I wish for a decent grave, yet without any fuss or parade; few persons suffice for my following; their names and addresses you'll find in my diary. The costs of the burial must be mustered up by you and them.—Amen !"

"Now,"—the dying man continued, after a pause occasioned by his growing weakness,—"now one last word on my belief.—I believe in God, Mozart and Beethoven, and likewise their disciples and apostles;—I believe in the Holy Spirit and the truth of the one, indivisible Art;—I believe that this Art proceeds from God, and lives within the hearts of all illumined men;—I believe that he who once has bathed in the sublime delights of this high Art, is consecrate to Her for ever, and never can deny Her;—I believe that through this Art all men are saved, and therefore each may die for Her of hunger;—I believe that death will give me highest happiness;—I believe that on earth I was a jarring discord, which will at once be perfectly resolved by death. I believe in a last judgment, which will condemn to fearful pains all those who in this world have dared to play the huckster with chaste Art, have violated and dishonoured Her through evilness of heart and ribald lust of senses;—I believe that these will be condemned through all eternity to hear their own vile music. I believe, upon the other hand, that true disciples of high Art will be transfigured in a heavenly fabric of sun-drenched fragrance of sweet sounds, and united for eternity with the divine fount of all Harmony.—May mine be a sentence of grace!—Amen!"

I could almost believe that my friend's fervent prayer had been granted already, so heavenly a light shone in his eye, so enraptured he remained in breathless quiet. But his gentle, scarce palpable breathing assured me that he yet lived on.—Softly, but quite audibly, he whispered: "Rejoice, ye faithful ones; the joy is great, toward which ye journey!"

Then he grew dumb,—the radiance of his glance was quenched; a smile still wreathed his lips. I closed his eyes, and prayed God for such a death.— —

Who knows what died in this child of man, leaving no trace behind? Was it a Mozart,—a Beethoven? Who can tell, and who 'gainsay me when I claim that in him there fell an artist who would have enriched the world with his creations, had he not been forced to die too soon of hunger?—I ask, who will prove me the contrary?—

None of those who followed his body. Besides myself there were but two, a philologist and a painter; a third was hindered by a cold, and others had no time to spare.—As we were modestly approaching the churchyard of Montmartre, we noticed a beautiful dog, who anxiously sniffed at the bier and coffin. I recognised the animal, and Looked behind me;—bolt-upright on his horse, I perceived the Englishman. He seemed unable to understand the strange behaviour of his dog, who followed the coffin into the graveyard; he dismounted, gave the reins to his groom, and overtook us in the cemetery.

"Whom are you burying, mein Herr?" he asked me.—"The master of that dog," I gave for answer.

"Goddam!" he cried, "it is most annoying that this gentleman should have died without receiving the money for his beast. I set it aside for him, and have sought an opportunity of sending it, although this animal howls at my musical exercises like all the rest. But I will make good my omission, and devote the fifty guineas for the dog to a memorial stone, which shall be erected on the grave of the estimable gentleman!"—He left us, and mounted his horse; the dog remained beside the grave,—the Briton rode away. (7)

Notes

1

Under the title "Un musicien étranger à Paris," this story appeared in the *Gazette Musicale* of Jan. 31 and Feb. 7 and 11, 1841. Its German original was first printed in Nos. 187-91 of the *Abend-Zeitung* (Aug. 6 to 11, 1841) as a sequel to the "Pilgrimage ", and with the special title "Das Ende zu Paris. (Aus der Feder eines in Wahrheit noch lebenden Notenstechers.)" — i.e. "The end at Paris: from the pen of an in reality still living note-engraver." The title in the *Ges. Schr.* becomes "Ein Ende in Paris," but otherwise the two German texts are identical, saving for one or two quite trifling stylistic alterations and the appearance in the *A.Z.* of "—denn ich bin mehr Banquier als Notenstecher—", i.e. "—for I am more of a banker than a note-engraver—", following the words "as my own access to those sanctuaries was but rare" on page 55 *infra.*—Tr.

2

In the French this sentence ran, "Me faudrait-il craindre par hasard de me trouver, ici comme en Allemagne, dans l'obligation d'avoir recours à des voies tortueuses pour me procurer l'entrée des théâtres royaux?"—and was immediately followed by "Dois-je croire que, pendant des années entières, il me faudra mendier la protection de tel on tel laquais de cour pour finir par arriver, grâce à un mot de recommandation qu'aura daigné m'accorder quelque femme de chambre, à obtenir pour mes œuvres l'honneur de la réprésentation? Non sans doute, et à quoi bon dailleurs des démarches si serviles, ici, à Paris" etc.—Some specific case appears to be referred to here, for, although the passage drops out of this connection in the *Abendzeitung* and *Ges. Schr.*, we meet with an identical allusion in the essay on "Conducting," see Vol. IV., pp. 294 and 297.—Tr.

3

Between this paragraph and the next there appeared in the *Gazette Musicale* "(Je n'ai nul besoin, je pense, de faire remarquer au lecteur que, dans les objections dont je me sers et dont j'aurai encore à me servir vis-à-vis de mon ami, il ne s'agit nullement de voir l'expression complète de ma conviction personelle, mais seulement une série d'arguments que je regardais comme urgent d'employer pour amener mon enthousiaste à abandonner ses plans chimériques, sans diminuer pourtant en rien sa confiance en son talent.)"—Tr.

4

In the *Gazette* here appeared "(Le lecteur voudra bien ne pas oublier de faire ici une nouvelle application de la remarque que je lui ai recommandée ci-dessus.)" — Tr.

5

Here, as also at the end of the next paragraph but one, the *Gazette* had "(Le lecteur voudra bien ne pas oublier, etc.)" — Tr.

6

Here again, and after the first sentence of the next paragraph but one, the *G. M.* had "(Le lecteur voudra bien ne pas oublier, etc.)" — Tr.

7

Translator's note: — In the *Gazette Musicale* there was an additional paragraph: "Il me reste maintenant à exécuter le testament. Je publierai dans les prochains numéros de cette gazette, sous le titre de *Caprices esthétiques d'un musicien*, les differentes parties du journal du défunt, pour lesquels l'éditeur a promis de payer un prix élevé, par égard pour la destination respectable de cet argent. Les partitions qui composent le reste de sa succession sont à la disposition de MM. les directeurs d'Opéra, qui peuvent, pour cet objet, s'addresser, par lettres non affranchies, à l'exécuteur testamentaire,

RICHARD WAGNER."

THE ARTIST AND PUBLICITY

(1)

WHEN I am alone, and the musical strings begin to stir within me, strange whirling sounds take shape of chords, until at last a melody springs forth, revealing to me the idea of my whole being; when the heart beats time thereto in loud impatient strokes, and inspiration streams in tears immortal through the mortal eye, no longer seeing,—I often tell myself: Fool that thou art, not to bide forever by thyself, to live for these unequalled blisses, in lieu of rushing out to face that awful mass yclept the Public, to earn thee by its nothing-saying nod the fatuous authority to go on practising thy gift of composition! (2) What can the most brilliant welcome of this public give thee worth a hundredth fraction of that hallowed joy which wells from thine own heart? Why do mortals fired with a spark divine forsake their sanctuary, run breathless through the city's muddy streets, and seek in hottest haste for dull and sated men on whom to force a happiness indicible? And what exertions, turmoils and illusions, before they can even arrive at compassing the sacrifice! What plots and artifices must they ply, for a good part of their life, to bring to the ears of the crowd what it can never understand! Is it for fear the history of Music might one fine day stand still? Is it for that, they pluck the fairest pages from the secret history of their heart, and snap the magic chain that fastens sympathetic souls to one another throughout the centuries, whilst here the only talk can be of schools and manners? (3)

There must be some inexplicable force at work: who feels himself subjected to its power, must hold it ruinous. Certainly the first assumption to occur to one, would be that it was the bent of Genius to impart itself without regard to consequences: loud does it sound in thyself, aloud let it ring out to others! Eh, folk say 'tis the *duty* of Genius, to live for Man's pleasure; who imposed it, God alone knows! Merely it so happens that this duty never comes to consciousness, and least of all when Genius is engaged in its ownest function, of creation. But that perhaps is not the question; when it has created, it is then to feel the obligation to divest itself of the immense advantage it has above all other mortals, by surrendering its creation to them. In respect of Duty, however, Genius is the most conscienceless of beings: nothing does it bring to birth thereby, and I believe it neither regulates by that its traffic with the world. No, it abides by its nature for ever and ever: in its most foolish act it still stays Genius, and I rather fancy that at bottom of its bent to gain publicity there lies a motive of ill moral import, which again does not come to clear consciousness, but yet is serious enough to expose the very greatest artist to contemptuous treatment. In any case this passion for publicity is hard to comprehend: each experience teaches it that it is in an evil sphere, and can only hope to move a little smoothly by putting on an evil look itself. Genius,—would not all men run away from it, were it once to shew itself in its god-like nakedness as it is? Perhaps this really is its saving instinct; for nursed it not the knowledge of its purest chastity, how might it not be ravished by a ribald self-delight in its own fashionings? But the first contact with the outer world compels all genius to clothe itself. Here reads the rule: the Public wills to be amused, and thou must seek to smuggle in thine Own beneath the mantle of Amusement. Very well, we will say that Genius draws the needful act of self-denial from a feeling of duty: for Duty holds alike the command and compulsion to self-denial, self-sacrifice. Yet what duty bids a man to sacrifice his honour, a woman her shame? For sake of these they ought to offer up all personal welfare, if need so be. But more than to man his honour, to woman her shame, to Genius is itself; and if it bears the smallest wound in its own essence, compact of shame and honour in the very highest measure, then is it nothing, absolutely nothing more.

Impossible, that Duty urges Genius to the fearful act of self-denial whereby it makes itself away to public life. Some dæmonic secret must lie hidden here. He, the blest, the over-joyed, the over-rich,—goes begging. He begs for your favour, ye victims of boredom, ye seekers after amusement, ye vain presumptuous, ye ignorant all-wise, bad-hearted, venal, envious reporters,—and God knows of what else thou mayst consist, thou modern Art-public, thou institute of Public Opinion! And what humiliations he endures! The tortured

Saint can smile transfigured: for what no rack can ever reach, is just the hallowed soul; the wounded warrior dragging through the shades of night may smile, for what stays whole is his honour, his courage; the woman smiles, who suffers shame and scorn for sake of love: for the soul's salvation, honour, love, now first shine all transfigured in a higher glory. But Genius, that gives itself a mark for scorn when it gives itself the air of *pleasing?* — Happy may the world regard itself, that to it the pains of Genius can be so relatively little known!

No! These sufferings no one seeks from sense-of-duty, and whoever could imagine it, his duty necessarily rises from a very different source. One's daily bread, the maintenance of a family: most weighty motors. Only, they do not operate in the genius. They prompt the journeyman, the hand-worker; they may even move the man of genius to handiwork, but they cannot spur him to create, nor even to bring his creations to market. Yet that's the point we are discussing, namely how to explain the impulse that drives a man with demon force to carry just his noblest, ownest good to open market.

Certainly a mixture of the most mysterious sort here comes to pass, and could we ever clearly see it, 'twould shew the spirit of the highly-gifted artist quite strictly hovering 'twixt heaven and hell. Undoubtedly the god-like longing to impart an own interior bliss to human hearts, is the predominant motive, and in hours of awful stress the only strength-giver. This impulse feeds at all times on the genius's belief in self, to which no other can compare in vigour, and this faith again informs the artist with that very pride which works his fall in commerce with the miseries of earthly squalor. He feels himself free, and in life, too, will he be it: he will have nothing in common with his want; he will be wafted, light and quit of every care. This may happen in fact when his genius is generally recognised, and so the object is to bring it to acknowledgment. Though he thus appear to be ambitious (*ehrgeizig*), he yet is not; for he wants no honour (*Ehre*) paid him; but its fruit he wants, in Freedom. He only meets ambitious men, or such as dwell content with fruits apart from honour. How mark himself from these? He falls into a throng midst which he necessarily must pass for other than he truly is. What exceptional prudence, what cautiousness in every tiniest step, would it need for him to always walk securely here, and ward off all misapprehension! But he is awkwardness personified; confronted with the meannesses of Life, he can only use the privilege of Genius to get entangled in a constant contradiction with himself: and so, a prey for every springe, his own prodigious gift he casts before the swine, and squanders on the aimlessest of objects.—In truth he merely longs for freedom to give full play to his beneficence. To him it seems so natural a claim, that he can never fathom why its due should be denied him: is it not a mere question of manifesting Genius clearly to the world? That, he never ceases thinking, he is bound to bring about, if not to-morrow, assuredly the next day after. As if death were nothing! And Bach, Mozart, Beethoven, Weber?—Nay, but it yet might happen!—A sad, sad tale!—

And with it all to be so laughable!—

Could he only see himself, as we now see him, he must end by laughing at his very self. And that laughter is perhaps his direst danger, for it alone can move him to begin the frantic dance again. Yet his laughter is quite another thing from yours: the latter is mockery, the former Pride. For he just sees himself; and his self-recognition, in this infamous *quid-pro-quo* that he has tumbled into, attunes him to that monstrous merriment of which no other man is capable. So levity rescues him, to bear him to yet more fearful pains. Now he credits himself with the strength to play with even Evil: he knows that, lie as much as he will, his truthfulness will ne'er be sullied, for he feels with every gnaw of grief that Truth is his very soul; and he finds a curious consolation in the fact that not one of his lies is believed, that he can dupe no man. Who would take him for a jester?—But why does he give himself the look? The world leaves him no other road to freedom: and this latter (as dressed for the world's understanding) resembles little else than—*money*. That is to win him recognition of his genius, and for that is the whole mad game laid out. Then he dreams: "God, if only I were so-and-so, for instance *Meyerbeer*!" So *Berlioz* lately dreamt of what he would do, were he one of those unfortunates who pay five hundred francs for the singing of a Romance not worth five sous: then would he take the finest orchestra in the world to the ruins of Troy, to play him the "*Sinfonia eroica.*" (4) —You see, what heights the genius-beggar's phantasy can climb!—But such a thing seems possible. Now and then there really passes something quite unusual. Berlioz himself experienced it, when the marvellously stingy *Paganini* paid him the homage of a handsome present. That kind of thing is the beginning. To everyone there once comes such an omen: 'tis the wages of Hell; you now have conjured Envy up for good: now the world won't any longer give you even pity, for "You have already had more than you deserved." —

Happy the genius that Fortune ne'er has smiled on!—It is so wondrous precious to itself: what more could Fortune give it?

And that's what he tells himself, smiles and—laughs, renews his strength; it glimmers and leaps up in him: anew it rings from him, brighter and fairer than ever. A work, such as he himself had ne'er yet dreamt of, is growing up in silent solitude. This is it! That's the right thing! All the world must be entranced by this: to hear it once, and then—! Look how the madman is running! 'Tis the old, old road, that seems to him so new and glorious: mud splashes him; here he bumps against a lackey, whose finery he takes for a General's, and bows respectfully; there against a no less worshipful bank-porter, whose heavy gold-bag slung across the shoulders makes his nose bleed. They are all good omens. He runs and trips, until at last he stands once more within the temple of his shame! And everything comes back again: for, as Schiller sings, "each crime itself on earth avenges."

And yet a good spirit protects him, apparently his own: for he is spared fulfilment of his wishes. If he once succeeded in gaining welcome to that wondrous sanctuary, what else than a stupendous misunderstanding could have helped him thither? What Hell could compare with the slow torture of its dissolution day by day? We took you for a sensible fellow who would accommodate yourself, as you really were so anxious for "success": here it is, all guaranteed; only set this and that to rights; there is the prima donna, there the ballerina, here the great virtuoso: arrange affairs with them! There they stand, and group themselves into that strangely curtained porch through which you travel to the one Supreme, the great Public itself. Why! everyone who passed through here to the realms of bliss, had to make his little sacrifice. What the devil! do you think the "grand" Opera could have ever held on, had it raised such a fuss about trifles? —

Can you lie? —

No! — —

Then you are done for, dismissed, as in England the "Atheists." No respectable person will talk to you again. — Well, well: still hope that thy good genius will spare thee that. — Laugh, be light-minded, — but have patience and suffer: then all will be well. —

Dream! 'Tis the best thing! —

Notes

1

"Der Künstler und die Öffentlichkeit" appeared in the *Gazette Musicale* of April 1, 1841, under the title "Caprices esthétiques extraits du journal d'un musicien défunt. Le Musicien et la Publicité." After the first paragraph, however, the French again materially differs, besides bearing marks of the editorial scissors, for it is reduced to about a quarter of the usual length. In the first sentence "die als Idee mir mein ganzes Wesen offenbart" so strikingly resembles Schopenhauer's philosophy of Music that one might have taken it for an interpolation of 1871, did not the French of 1841 (i.e. thirteen years before the master read a line of Schopenhauer) give us its counterpart in "et que j'en sens jaillir enfin l'idée qui révéle tout mon être." — Tr.

2

From "to earn," to the end of the sentence, did not appear in the French.—Tr.

3

As said, from this point the French diverges: "Il y a là quelque puissance occulte et inexplicable, dont moi-même, hélas ! je subis l'influence funeste. Plus j'y songe, moins je puis me rendre compte des motifs qui poussent les artistes à rechercher le grand jour de a publicité. Est-ce l'ambition, le désir du bien-être? motifs bien puissants sans doute; mais quel est l'homme sur lequel ils aient prise à l'heure de l'enthousiasme on dont ils puissent émouvoir le génie? Dans la vie ordinaire, je conçois qu'on cède à ces motifs, quand il est question d'un bon dîner, d'un article louangeur dans les journaux; mais jamais quand il s'agit de sacrifier les plus hautes jouissances qu'il soit donné à l'homme de goûter. Pour les cœurs aimants, ce pourrait bien être le désir irrésistible de laisser s'épancher le surplus de l'enthousiasme qui les enivre et de faire participer le monde entier leur extase. Malheureusement l'artiste ne voit point le monde tel qu'il est ; il se le représente comme étant à sa hauteur, il oublie qu'il n'est composé que de gens en fracs à la dernière mode et en mantilles de soie.

"Ce désir immodéré et funeste de la publicité paraît être tellement vivace, que même aux heures où l'inspiration a cessé, il continue à nous travailler le cerveau, et c'est dans ces heures qu'il faut lui donner le nom d'ambition. O ambition pernicieuse, à qui nous devons tous les airs, airs variés, etc., c'est toi qui nous enseignes à ravager systématiquement le sanctuaire de la poésie que nous portons en nous! c'est toi qui dans ton ironie démoniaque nous pousses à souiller de roulades impudiques un chaste et pur accord ; à resserrer une pensée vigoureuse et large dans un lit étroit de cadences et de niaiseries!

"O vous, *heureux infortunés*, aux joues creuses et pâles, aux yeux usés, vous vous êtes flétris au souffle brûlant de l'étude et du travail, afin que le public vous criât bravo! pour l'enveloppe mensongère dont vous entouriez votre poésie dans les moments de calcul et de réflexion prosaïque, et que vous lui arracheriez avec joie si vous ne craigniez que votre création, si elle se montrait dans sa nudité, ne fût obligée de fuir honteuse et éperdue devant les railleries du vulgaire. Oh ! si vous étiez tous mes frères et mes amis, je vous ferais une proposition à l'aimable: je vous engagerais faire de la musique pour votre compte, et à exercer en même temps quelque bon métier ou à spéculer à la Bourse. Vous seriez alors tout-à-fait heureux et vous pourriez mener bonne et joyeuse vie. Je veux vous donner l'exemple; deux heures sonnent, je vais à la Bourse; si j'échoue dans mes opérations, j'écrirai des quadrilles; c'est un bon métier, qui fort heureusement n'a rien de commun avec la musique."

With that the article ends : it was signed "Werner," but a note to the Index of the *Gaz. Mus.* corrects the error.—Tr.

4

Proof positive that at least this portion of the article was contained in the original M. S. for the *Gazette Musicale*, as it was only two months previously (Jan. 28, 1841) that Berlioz had written in that journal: "Si j'étais riche, bien riche, riche comme ces malheureux du siècle qui donnent cinq cents francs à un chanteur pour une cavatine de cinq sous, . . . je partirais pour la Troade . . . j'en ferais à peu près une solitude . . . je bâtirais un temple sonore au pied de mont Ida, deux statues en décoreraient seules l'intérieur, et un soir, au soleil couchant, après avoir lu Homère et parcouru les lieux qu'immortalisa son génie, je me ferais réciter par le roi des orchestres l'autre poëme du roi des musiciens, la symphonie héroïque de Beethoven." Is it too much to fancy that this passage of Berlioz may have sown in Wagner's mind the first seed of the "Bayreuth idea," which came to its earliest recorded expression just ten years later, and twenty-one years after that, again, was celebrated by the crowning of a certain foundation-stone ceremony with the performance of Beethoven's Ninth Symphony?—Tr.

Summary

Solitude and the inner chords vibrating into melody. What drives the genius to bring to the ears of the crowd what it can never understand? It cannot be Duty; for all men would run away from Genius, did it shew itself naked. The saint, the wounded soldier, the taunted woman, bear less humiliation than the genius: happy the world, that knows so little of his pains! Duty of supporting one's family can never prompt a work of genius. Freedom he wants, not honour or money. Laughter his only salvation Happy the genius whom Fortune ne'er has smiled on! His awkwardness in dealing with the world; concessions asked of him. Wait and dream; 'tis the best!

A HAPPY EVENING

IT was a fine Spring evening; the heat of Summer had already sent its messengers before, delicious breaths that thronged the air like sighs of love and fired our senses. We had followed the stream of people pouring toward a public garden; here an excellent orchestra was to give the first of its annual series of summer-evening concerts. It was a red-letter day. My friend R . . ., not dead in Paris yet, (1) was in the seventh heaven; even before the concert began, he was drunk with music: he said it was the inner harmonies that always sang and rang within him when he felt the happiness of a beautiful Spring evening.

We arrived, and took our usual places at a table beneath a great oak-tree; for careful comparison had taught us, not only that this spot was farthest from the buzzing crowd, but that here one heard the music best and most distinctly. We had always pitied the poor creatures who were compelled, or actually preferred to stay in the immediate vicinity of the orchestra, whether in or out of doors; we could never understand how they found any pleasure in *seeing* music, instead of hearing it; and yet we could account no otherwise for their rapt attention to the various movements of the band, their enthusiastic interest in the kettle-drummer when, after an anxious counting of his bars of rest, he came in at last with a rousing thwack. We were agreed that nothing is more prosaic and upsetting, than the hideous aspect of the swollen cheeks and puckered features of the wind-players, the unæsthetic grabbings of the double-bass and violoncelli, ay, even the wearisome sawing of the violin-bows, when it is a question of listening to the performance of fine instrumental music. For this reason we had taken our seats where we could hear the lightest nuance of the orchestra, without being pained by its appearance.

The concert began: grand things were played; among others, Mozart's Symphony in E flat, and Beethoven's in A.

The concert was over. Dumb, but delighted and smiling, my friend sat facing me with folded arms. The crowd departed, group by group, with pleasant chatter; here and there a few tables still were occupied. The evening's genial warmth began to yield to the colder breath of night.

"Let's have some punch!" cried R . . ., suddenly changing his attitude to look for a waiter.

Moods like that in which we found ourselves, are too precious not to be maintained as long as possible. I knew how comforting the punch would be, and eagerly chimed in with my friend's proposition. A decent-sized bowl soon steamed on our table, and we emptied our first glasses.

"How did you like the performance of the symphonies?" I asked.

"Eh? Performance!" exclaimed R . . . . "There are moods in which, however critical at other times, the worst execution of one of my favourite works would transport me. These moods, 'tis true, are rare, and only exercise their sweet dominion over me when my whole inner being stands in blissful harmony with my bodily health. Then it needs but the faintest intimation, to sound in me at once the whole piece that answers to my full conception; and in so ideal a completeness, as the best orchestra in the world can never bring it to my outward sense. In such moods my else so scrupulous musical ear is complaisant enough to allow even the quack of an oboe to cause me but a momentary twinge; with an indulgent smile I let the false note of a trumpet graze my ear, without being torn from the blessed feeling that cheats me into the belief that I am hearing the most consummate execution of my favourite work. In such a mood nothing irritates me more, than to see a well-combed dandy airing high-bred indignation at one of those musical slips that wound his pampered ear, when I know that to-morrow he will be applauding the most excruciating scale with which a popular prima donna does violence to nerves alike and soul. Music merely ambles past the ear of these super-subtle fools; nay, often merely past their eye: for I remember noticing people who never stirred a muscle when a brass instrument really went wrong, but stopped their ears the instant they saw the wretched bandsman shake his head in shame and confusion."

"What?"—I interposed—"Must I hear you girding at people of delicate ear? How often have I seen you raging like a madman at the faulty intonation of a singer?"

"My friend," cried R . . ., "I simply was speaking of now, of to-night. God knows how often I have been nearly driven mad by the mistakes of a famous violinist; how often have I cursed the first of prima-donnas when she thought her tone so pure in vocalising somewhere between *mi fa sol*; eh! how often I have been unable to find the smallest consonance among the instruments of the very best-tuned orchestra. But look you! that is on the countless days when my good spirit has departed from me, when I put on my Sunday coat and squeeze between the perfumed dames and frizzled sirs to woo back happiness into my soul through these ears of mine. O you should feel the pains with which I then weigh every note and measure each vibration! When my heart is dumb I'm as subtle as any of the prigs who vexed me to-day, and there are hours when a Beethoven Sonata with violin or 'cello will put me to flight.—Blessed be the god who made the Spring and Music: to-night I'm happy, I can tell you." With that he filled our glasses again, and we drained them to the dregs.

"Need I declare,"—I began in turn,—"that I feel as happy as yourself? Who would not be, after listening in peace and comfort to the performance of two works which seem created by the very god of high æsthetic joy? I thought the conjunction of the Mozartian and the Beethovenian Symphony a most apt idea; I seemed to find a marked relationship between the two compositions; in both the clear human consciousness of an existence meant for rejoicing, is beautifully transfigured by the presage of a higher world beyond. The only distinction I would make, is that in Mozart's music the language of the heart is shaped to graceful longing, whereas in Beethoven's conception this longing reaches out a bolder hand to seize the Infinite. In Mozart's symphony the fulness of Feeling predominates, in Beethoven's the manly consciousness of Strength."

"It does me good to hear such views expressed about the character and meaning of such sublime instrumental works," replied my friend. "Not that I believe you have anything like exhausted their nature with your brief description; but to get to the bottom of that, to say nothing of defining it, lies just as little within the power of human speech as it resides in the nature of Music to express in clear and definite terms what belongs to no organ save the Poet's. 'Tis a great misfortune that so many people take the useless trouble to confound the musical with the poetic tongue, and endeavour to make good or replace by the one what in their narrow minds remains imperfect in the other. It is a truth for ever, that where the speech of man stops short there Music's reign begins. Nothing is more intolerable, than the mawkish scenes and anecdotes they foist upon those instrumental works. What poverty of mind and feeling it betrays, when the listener to a performance of one of Beethoven's symphonies has to keep his interest awake by imagining that the torrent of musical sounds is meant to reproduce the plot of some romance! These gentry then presume to grumble at the lofty master, when an unexpected stroke disturbs the even tenour of their little tale; they tax the composer with unclearness and inconsequence, and deplore his lack of continuity!—The idiots!"

"Never mind!" said I. "Let each man trump up scenes and fancies according to the strength of his imagination; by their aid he perhaps acquires a taste for these great musical revelations, which many would be quite unable to enjoy for themselves. At least you must admit that the number of Beethoven's admirers has gained a large accession this way, eh! that it is to be hoped the great musician's works will thereby reach a popularity they could never have attained if left to none but an ideal understanding."

"Preserve us Heaven!" R . . . exclaimed.—"Even for these sublimest sanctities of Art you ask that banal Popularity, the curse of every grand and noble thing? For *them* you would also claim the honour of their inspiring rhythms—their only temporal manifestation—being danced-to in a village-tavern?"

"You exaggerate," I calmly answered: "I do not claim for Beethovenas symphonies the vogue of street and tavern. But would you not count it a merit the more, were they in a position to give a gladder pulse to the blood in the cribbed and cabined heart of the ordinary man of the world ?,"

"They shall have no merit, these Symphonies!"—my friend replied, in a huff "They exist for themselves and their own sake, not to flip the circulation of a philistine's blood. Who *can*, for his eternal welfare let him earn the merit of understanding those revelations; on them there rests no obligation to force themselves upon the understanding of cold hearts."

I filled up, and exclaimed with a laugh: "You're the same old phantast, who declines to understand me on the very point where we both are certainly agreed at bottom! So let's drop the Popularity question. But give me the pleasure of learning your own sensations when you heard the two symphonies to-night."

Like a passing cloud, the shade of irritation cleared from my friend's lowered brow. He watched the steam ascending from our punch, and smiled. "My sensations?—I felt the soft warmth of a lovely Spring evening, and imagined I was sitting with you beneath a great oak and looking up between its branches to the star-strewn heavens. I felt a thousand things besides, but them I cannot tell you (2): there you have all."

"Not bad!" I remarked.—"Perhaps one of our neighbours imagined he was smoking a cigar, drinking coffee, and making eyes at a young lady in a blue dress."

"Without a doubt," R . . . pursued the sarcasm, "and the drummer apparently thought he was beating his ill-behaved children, for not having brought him his supper from town.—Capital! At the gate I saw a peasant listening in wonder and delight to the Symphony in

A:—I would wager my head he understood it best of all, for you will have read in one of our musical journals a short while ago that Beethoven had nothing else in mind, when he composed this symphony, than to describe a peasant's wedding. The honest rustic will thus at once have called his wedding-day to memory, and revived its every incident: the guests' arrival and the feast, the march to church and blessing, the dance and finally the crowning joy, what bride and bridegroom shared alone."

"A good idea!" I cried, when I had finished laughing.—"But for heaven's sake tell me why you would prevent this symphony from affording the good peasant a happy hour of his own kind? Did he not feel, proportionately, the same delight as yourself when you sat beneath the oak and watched the stars of heaven through its branches?"

"There I am with you,"—my friend complacently replied,—"I would gladly let the worthy yokel recall his wedding-day when listening to the Symphony in A. But the civilised townsfolk who write in musical journals, I should like to tear the hair from their stupid heads when they foist such fudge on honest people, and rob them of all the ingenuousness with which they would otherwise have settled down to hear Beethoven's symphony.—Instead of abandoning themselves to their natural sensations, the poor deluded people of full heart but feeble brain feel obliged to look out for a peasant's wedding, a thing they probably have never attended, and in lieu of which they would have been far more disposed to imagine something quite within the circle of their own experience."

"So you agree with me," I said, "that the nature of those creations does not forbid their being variously interpreted, according to the individual ? On the contrary," was the answer, "I consider a stereotype interpretation altogether inadmissible. Definitely as the musical fabric of a Beethovenian Symphony stands rounded and complete in all artistic proportions, perfect and indivisible as it appears to the higher sense,—just as impossible is it to reduce its effects on the human heart to one authoritative type. This is more or less the case with the creations of every other art: how differently will one and the same picture or drama affect two different human beings, nay, the heart of one and the same individual at different times! Yet how much more definitely and sharply the painter or poet is bound to draw his figures, than the instrumental composer, who, unlike them, is not compelled to model his shapes by the features of the daily world, but has a boundless realm at his disposal in the kingdom of the supramundane, and to whose hand is given the most spiritual of substances in that of Tone! It would be to drag the musician from this high estate, if one tried to make him fit his inspiration to the semblance of that daily world; and still more would that instrumental composer disown his mission, or expose his weakness, who should aim at carrying the cramped proportions of purely worldly things into the province of his art."

"So you reject all tone-painting," I asked?

"Everywhere," answered R . . ., "save where it either is employed in jest, or reproduces purely musical phenomena. In the province of Jest all things are allowed, for its nature is a certain purposed angularity, and to laugh and let laugh is a capital thing. But where tone-painting quits this region, it becomes absurd. The inspirations and incitements to an instrumental composition must be of such a kind, that they can arise in the soul of none save a musician."

"You have just said something you will have a difficulty in proving," I objected. "At bottom, I am of your opinion; only I doubt if it is quite compatible with our unqualified admiration for the works of our great masters. Don't you think that this maxim of yours flatly contradicts a part of Beethoven's revelations?"

"Not in the slightest: on the contrary, I hope to found my proof on Beethoven."

"Before we descend to details," I continued, "don't you feel that Mozart's conception of instrumental music far better corresponds with your assertion, than that of Beethoven?"

"Not that I am aware," replied my friend. "Beethoven immensely enlarged the form of Symphony when he discarded the proportions of the older musical 'period,' which had attained their utmost beauty in Mozart, and followed his impatient genius with bolder but ever more conclusive freedom to regions reachable by *him* alone; as he also knew to give these soaring flights a philosophical coherence, it is undeniable that upon the basis of the Mozartian Symphony he reared a wholly new artistic genre, which he at like time perfected in every point. But Beethoven would have been unable to achieve all this, had Mozart not previously addressed his conquering genius to the Symphony too; had his animating, idealising breath not breathed a spiritual warmth into the soulless forms and diagrams accepted until then. From here departed Beethoven, and the artist who had taken Mozart's divinely pure soul into himself could never descend from that high altitude which is true Music's sole domain."

"By all means,"—I resumed. "You will hardly deny, however, that Mozart's music flowed from none but a musical source, that his inspiration started from an indefinite inner feeling, which, even had he had a poet's faculty, could never have been conveyed in words, but always and exclusively in tones. I am speaking of those inspirations which arise in the musician simultaneously with his melodies, with his tone-figures. Mozart's music bears the characteristic stamp of this instantaneous birth, and it is impossible to suppose that he would ever have drafted the plan of a symphony, for instance, whereof he had not all the themes, and in fact the entire structure as we know it, already in his head. On the other hand, I cannot help thinking that Beethoven first planned the order of a symphony according to a certain philosophical idea, before he left it to his phantasy to invent the musical themes."

"And how do you propose proving that?"—my friend ejaculated. "By this evening's Symphony perhaps?"

"With *that* I might find it harder," I answered,—"but is it not enough to simply name the Heroic Symphony, in support of my contention? You know, of course, that this symphony was originally meant to bear the title: 'Bonaparte.' Can you deny, then, that Beethoven was inspired and prompted to the plan of this giant work by an idea outside the realm of Music?"

"Delighted at your naming that symphony!" R. . . . quickly put in. "You surely don't mean to say that the idea of a heroic force in mighty struggle for the highest, is outside the realm of Music? Or do you find that Beethoven has translated his enthusiasm for the young god of victory into such petty details as to make you think he meant this symphony for a musical bulletin of the first Italian campaign?"

"Where are you off to?"—I interposed: "Have I said anything like it?"

"It's at the back of your contention," my friend went passionately on.—"If we are to assume that Beethoven sat down to write a composition in honour of Bonaparte, we must also conclude that he would have been unable to turn out anything but one of those 'occasional' pieces which bear the stamp of still-born, one and all. (3) But the Sinfonia eroica is all the breadth of heaven from justifying such a view! No: had the master set himself a task like that, he would have fulfilled it most unsatisfactorily:—tell me, where, in what part of this composition do you find one colourable hint that the composer had his eye on a specific event in the heroic career of the young commander? What means the Funeral March, the Scherzo with the hunting-horns, the Finale with the soft emotional Andante woven in? Where is the bridge of Lodi, where the battle of Arcole, where the victory under the Pyramids, where the 18th Brumaire? Are these not incidents which no composer of our day would have let escape him, if he wanted to write a biographic Symphony on Bonaparte?—Here, however, the case was otherwise; and permit me to tell you my own idea of the gestation of this symphony.—When a musician feels prompted to sketch the smallest composition, he owes it simply to the stimulus of a feeling that usurps his whole being at the hour of conception. This mood may be brought about by an outward experience, or have risen from a secret inner spring; whether it shews itself as melancholy, joy, desire, contentment, love or hatred, in the musician it will always take a musical shape, and voice itself in tones or ever it is cast in notes. But grand, passionate and lasting emotions, dominating all our feelings and ideas for months and often half a year, these drive the musician to those vaster, more intense conceptions to which we owe, among others, the origin of a Sinfonia eroica. These greater moods, as deep suffering of soul or potent exaltation, may date from outer causes, for we all are men and our fate is ruled by outward circumstances; but when they force the musician to production, these greater moods have already turned to music in him, so that at the moment of creative inspiration, it is no longer the outer event that governs the composer, but the musical sensation which it has begotten in him. Now, what phenomenon were worthier to rouse and keep alive the sympathy, the inspiration of a genius so full of fire as Beethoven's, than that of the youthful demigod who razed a world to mould a new one from its ruins? Imagine the musician's hero-spirit following from deed to deed, from victory to victory, the man who ravished friend and foe to equal wonder! And the republican Beethoven, to boot, who looked to that hero for the realising of his ideal dreams of universal human good! How his blood must have surged, his heart glowed hot, when that glorious name rang back to him wherever he turned to commune with his Muse!—His strength must have felt incited to a like unwonted sweep, his will-of-victory spurred on to a kindred deed of untold grandeur. He was no General,—he was Musician; and in his domain he saw the sphere where he could bring to pass the selfsame thing as Bonaparte in the plains of Italy. His musical force at highest strain bade him conceive a work the like of which had ne'er before been dreamt of; he brought forth his Sinfonia eroica, and knowing well to whom he owed the impulse to this giant-work, he wrote upon its title-page the name of "Bonaparte." And in fact is not this symphony as grand an evidence of man's creative power, as Bonaparte's glorious victory? Yet I ask you if a single trait in its development has an immediate outer connection with the fate of the hero, who at that time had not even reached the zenith of his destined fame? I am happy enough to admire in it nothing but a gigantic monument of Art, to fortify myself by the strength and joyous exaltation which swell my breast on hearing it; and leave to learned other folk to spell out the fights of Rivoli and Marengo from its score's mysterious hieroglyphs!"

The night air had grown still colder; during this speech a passing waiter had taken my hint to remove the punch and warm it up again; he now came back, and once more the grateful beverage was steaming high before our eyes. I filled up, and reached my hand to R . . . .

"We are at one," I said, "as ever, when it touches the innermost questions of art. However feeble our forces, we shouldn't deserve the name of musicians, could we fall into such blatant errors about the nature of our art as you have just denounced. What Music expresses is eternal, infinite, and ideal; she expresses not the passion, love, desire, of this or that individual in this or that condition, but Passion, Love, Desire itself, and in such infinitely varied phases as lie in her unique possession and are foreign and unknown to any other tongue. Of her let each man taste according to his strength, his faculty and mood, what taste and feel he can" —

"And to-night," — my friend broke in, in full enthusiasm, — "'tis joy I taste, the happiness, the presage of a higher destiny, won from the wondrous revelations in which Mozart and Beethoven have spoken to us on this glorious Spring evening. So here's to Happiness, to Joy! Here's to Courage, that enheartens us in fight with our fate! Here's to Victory, gained by our higher sense over the worthlessness of the vulgar! To Love, which crowns our courage; to friendship, that keeps firm our Faith! To Hope, which weds itself to our foreboding! To the day, to the night! A cheer for the sun, a cheer for the stars! And three cheers for Music and her high priests! Forever be God adored and worshipped, the god of Joy and Happiness, — the god who created Music! Amen. —

Arm-in-arm we took our journey home; we pressed each other's hand, and not a word more did we say.

Notes

1

"Not dead in Paris yet" did not appear in the French. The tale was originally styled "Une soirée heureuse: Fantaisie sur la musique pittoresque," and published in the *Gazette Musicale* of Oct. 24 and Nov. 7, 1841.—Tr.

2

Cf. "Wo ich erwacht, weilt' ich nicht; doch wo ich weilte, das kann ich dir nicht sagen. . . . Ich war—wo ich von je gewesen, wohin auf je ich gehe: im weiten Reich der Welten Nacht." *Tristan,* act iii.—Tr.

3

In the *Gazette* there was a footnote here: "Il y a huit ans, à l'époque où cette conversation eut lieu, mon ami R... ne pouvait connaître la symphonie de Berlioz pour la translation des victimes de Juillet."—Tr.

ROSSINI'S STABAT MATER

Preface

The account of this remarkable occurrence in the highest Paris world of music our friend despatched to Robert Schumann, who at that time was editor of the "Neue Zeitschrift für Musik" and headed the skit—signed with an inexplicable pseudonym—with the following motto:

> "Das ist am allermeisten unerquickend,
> Dass sich so breit darf machen das Unächte,
> Das Ächte selbst mit falscher Scheu umstrickend."
> ("Of all our evils 'tis the sorriest token
> How wide the spurious has spread its rule,
> That e'en the genuine with false shame is spoken.")

RÜCKERT.

Rossini's Stabat Mater

WHILE waiting for other musical treats in preparation for the glorious Paris public; while waiting for Halévy's "Maltese Knight," the "Water-carrier" of Cherubini, and finally, in the dimmest background, the *"Nonne Sanglante"* of Berlioz,—nothing so excites and captivates the interest of this fevered world of dilettanti, as— *Rossini's* piety. (1) Rossini is pious,—all the world is pious, and the Parisian salons have been turned into praying-cells.—It is extraordinary! So long as this man lives, he'll always be the mode. Makes he the Mode, or makes it him? 'Tis a ticklish problem. True, that this piety took root a long time since, especially in high society;—what time this ardour has been catered-for in Berlin by philosophic Pietism; what time the whole of Germany lays bare its heart to' the musical gospel according to Felix Mendelssohn,—the Paris world of quality has no idea of being left behind. For some while past they have been getting their first quadrille-composers to write quite exquisite *Ave Marias* or *Salve Reginas*; and themselves, the duchesses and countesses, have made it their duty to study the two, or three parts of them, and edify therewith their thronging guests, groaning for very reverence and overcrowding. This glowing stress of piety had long burnt through the charming corsets of these lion-hearted duchesses and countesses, and threatened to singe the costly tulles and laces which theretofore had heaved so blamelessly and unimpassioned on their modest chests—when at last, at a most appropriate opportunity, it kindled into vivid flame. That opportunity was none other than the *in memoriam* service for the Emperor Napoleon, in the chapel of the Invalides. All the world knows that for these obsequies the most entrancing singers of the Italian and French Operas felt themselves impelled to render Mozart's Requiem, and all the world may see that that was no small matter. Above all, however, the *high* world of Paris was quite carried away by this flash of insight: it is wont to melt, without conditions, in presence of *Rubini's* and *Persiani's* singing; to close its fan with nerveless hand, to sink back upon its satin mantle, to close its eyes, and lisp: "*c'est ravissant!*" Further is it wont, when recovering from the exhaustion of its transports, to breathe out the yearning question: "By whom, this composition?" For this it really is quite requisite to know, if in one's stress to imitate those singers one means to send one's gold-laced chasseur next morning to the music-sellers, to fetch one home that heavenly aria or that divine duet. By strict observance of this custom the high Parisian world had come to learn that it was *Rossini, Bellini, Donizetti,* who had provided those intoxicating singers with the wherewithal to melt it; it recognised the merit of these masters, and it loved them.

So the destiny of France would have it that, to hear the adored *Rubini* and the bewitching *Persiani,* instead of in the *Théâtre des Italiens* one must assemble beneath the dome of the Invalides. In view of all the circumstances, the Ministry of Public Affairs had formed the wise resolve that this time, in lieu of Rossini's *Cenerentola,* Mozart's Requiem should be sung; and thus it came to pass, quite of itself, that our dilettantist duchesses and countesses were given something very different to hear, for once, from what they were accustomed-to at the Italian Opera. With the most touching lack of prejudice, however, they accommodated themselves to everything: they heard Rubini and Persiani,—they melted away; instead of their fans, they dropped their muffs; they leant back on their costly furs (for it was mortal cold in church on December 15, 1840)—and, just as at the Opera, they lisped: "*c'est ravissant!*" Next day one sends for Mozart's Requiem, and turns its first few pages over: it has plenty of *colorature*! One tries them,—but: "Good Heavens! It tastes like physic! They're fugues!" "Powers above! where have we got to?" "How is it possible? This can't be the right thing!", "And yet!"— What's to be done?—One tortures oneself,—one tries,—it won't go at all!—But there's no help for it; sacred music must be sung! Did not Rubini and Persiani sing sacred music?—Then kindly music-dealers, beholding the anguish of these pious ladies' hearts, rush in to the rescue: "Here you have brand-new Latin pieces by Clapisson, by Thomas, by Monpou, by Musard, &c., &c. All cut and dried for you! Made expressly for you! Here an *Ave*; there a *Salve*!"

Ah! how happy they were, the pious Paris duchesses, the fervent countesses! They all sing Latin: two soprani in thirds, with occasionally the purest fifths in all the world,—a tenor *col basso*! Their souls are calmed; no one now need be afraid of purgatory!—

Yet,—quadrilles of Musard's, or Clapisson's, one only dances *once*,— their *Ave*! and *Salve*!, with any good grace, one can sing but *twice* at most; that, however, is too little for the fervour of our high-class world; it asks for edifying songs which one may sing at least fifty times over, just like the lovely operatic arias and duets of Rossini, Bellini and Donizetti. Someone had read indeed, in a theatrical report from Leipzig, that Donizetti's *Favorite* was full of old-Italian church-style; however, the fact that this opera's church-pieces were composed to a French, and not to a Latin text, obstructed our high world from giving vent to its religious stress by singing them; and it still remained to find the man whose church-songs one might sing with orthodox belief.

About this time it happened that *Rossini* had let nothing be heard of him for ten long years: he sat in Bologna, ate pastry, and made wills. Among the pleadings in the recent action between Messieurs *Schlesinger* (2) and *Troupenas,* an inspired advocate declared that during those ten years the musical world had "moaned" beneath the silence of the giant master; and *we* may assume that, on this occasion, the Parisian *high* world even "groaned." Nevertheless there circulated dismal rumours about the extraordinary mood the maëstro was in; at one moment we heard that his hypogastrium was much incommoded, at another—his beloved father had died [April 29, 1839];—one said that he meant to turn fishmonger; another, that he refused to hear his operas any more. But the truth of it seems to have been, he felt penitent and meant to write church-music; for this one relied on an old, a well-known proverb, and the fact is that Rossini evinced an invincible longing to make this proverb's second half come true, since he positively had no more need to verify its first. The earliest stimulus to carry out his expiation seems to have come to him in Spain: in Spain, where Don Juan found the amplest, choicest opportunities of sin, Rossini is said to have found the spur to penance.

It was on a journey which he was making with his good friend the Paris banker, Herr *Aguado*;—they were sitting at ease in a well-appointed chariot, and admiring the beauties of Nature,—Herr Aguado was nibbling chocolate, Rossini was munching pastry. Then it suddenly occurred to Herr Aguado that he really had robbed his compatriots more than was proper, and, smitten with remorse, he drew the chocolate from his mouth;—not to be behind such a beautiful example, Rossini gave his teeth a rest, and confessed that all through life he had devoted too much time to pastry. Both agreed that it would well beseem their present mood to stop their chariot at the nearest cloister, and go through some fit act of penance: no sooner said than done. The Prior of the nearest monastery received the travellers like a friend: he kept a capital cellar, excellent *Lacrymæ Christi* and other good sorts, which quite uncommonly consoled the contrite sinners. Nevertheless it struck Messrs Aguado and Rossini, as they were in the right humour, that they really had meant to undergo a penance: Herr Aguado seized his pocket-book in haste, drew out a few telling banknotes, and dedicated them to the sagacious Prior. Behind this fine example of his friend's, again, Rossini felt he must not linger,—he produced a solid quire of music-paper, and what he wrote on it post-haste was nothing less than a whole *Stabat mater* with grand orchestra; that *Stabat* he presented to the estimable Prior. The latter gave them absolution, and they both got back into their chariot. But the worthy Prior soon was raised to lofty rank, and translated to Madrid; where he lost no time in having the *Stabat* of his confessional child performed, and dying at the earliest opportunity. Among a thousand memorable relics, his executors found the score of that contrite *Stabat mater*; they sold it, at not at all a bad figure, for good of the poor—and thus, from hand to 'hand, this much-prized composition became at last the property of a Paris music-publisher.

Now this music-publisher, deeply moved by its countless beauties, and no less touched on the other side by the growing pain of unallayed religious fervour among the high Parisian dilettanti, resolved to make his treasure public. With stealthy haste he was having the plates engraved when up there sprang another publisher, who with astounding cruelty clapped an injunction on his busy, hidden offering. That other publisher, a stiff-necked man by the name of *Troupenas*, maintained he had far better claims to the copyright of that *Stabat mater*, for his friend Rossini had pledged it to him against a huge consignment of pastry. He further averred that the work had been in his possession quite a number of years, and his only reason for not publishing it had been Rossini's wish to first provide it with a fugue or two, and a counterpoint in the seventh; these, however, were still a hard task for the master, as he had not quite completed his many years' study with that end in view; nevertheless, the master of late had gained so profound an insight into double counterpoint that his *Stabat* no longer pleased him in its present shape, and he had decided under no conditions to lay it thus—without fugues and such-like—before the world. (3) Unfortunately Herr Troupenas' letters of authorisation date merely from quite recent times; so that it would be difficult for this publisher to prove his prior rights, did he not believe he had one crushing argument, namely that so long ago as the obsequies of the Emperor Napoleon on December 15th, 1840, he had proposed this *Stabat* for performance in the chapel of the Invalides.

A shriek of horror and indignation rose from every salon of high Paris, when this latter statement was made known. "What!" cried everyone: "A composition of Rossini's was in existence,—it was offered you, and you Minister of Public Affairs, you rejected it? You dared, instead, to foist on us that hopeless Requiem by Mozart?"—In effect, the Ministry trembled; all the more, as its uncommon popularity had made it most obnoxious to the upper classes. It feared dismissal, an indictment for high treason, and therefore held it opportune to spread a secret rumour that Rossini's *Stabat mater* wouldn't at all have done for the Emperor's obsequies as its text was concerned with quite other things than were meet for Napoleon's shade to hear, and so forth.—That this was merely a herring drawn across the scent, one thought one saw at once; for one could justly reply that not a creature understood this Latin text, and finally— what mattered the text at all, if *Rossini's* heavenly melodies were to be sung by the most ravishing singers in the world?—

But the strife of parties round this fateful *Stabat mater* rages all the fiercer, since there is a further point involved in those awaited fugues. At last, then, is this mysterious class of composition about to be made presentable for salons of the higher dilettanti! At last, then, shall they learn the secret of that silly stuff which so racked their brains in Mozart's Requiem! At last will *they* be able, too, to boast of singing fugues; and these fugues will be oh! so charming and adorable, so delicate, so aërial! And these *counterpointlets*—they'll make everything else quite foolish,—they'll look like Brussels lace, and smell like patchouli!—What?—And without these fugues, without these counterpointlets, we were to have had the *Stabat*? How shameful! No, we'll wait till Herr Troupenas receives the fugues.— Heavens!—but there arrives a *Stabat*, straight from Germany! Finished, bound in a yellow cover There, too, are publishers who maintain they have sent baked goods to Rossini, at heavy prices! Is the bewilderment to have no end? Spain, France, Germany, all fall to blows around this *Stabat*:—Action! Fight! Tumult! Revolution! Horror!—

Then Herr *Schlesinger* decides to shed a friendly ray upon the night of trouble: he publishes a *Waltz by Rossini*. All smooth the wrinkles from their brow,—eyes beam with joy,—lips smile: ala! what lovely waltzes!—But Destiny descends:—Herr Troupenas impounds the friendly ray! That dreadful word: *Copyright*—growls through the scarce laid breezes. Action! Action! Once more, Action! And money is fetched out, to pay the best of lawyers, to get documents produced, to enter caveats.— — —O ye foolish people, have ye lost your hiking for your gold? I know somebody who for five francs will make you five waltzes, each of them better than that misery of the wealthy master's!

Paris, 15th December, 1841.

Notes

1

This article (to which a little editorial note was added, "From a new correspondent") formed the 'leader' in the *N.Z.f.M.* of December 28, 1841, and was signed "H. Valentino." The quotation from Friedrich Rückert (a celebrated German poet, 1788-1866) appears to have been Schumann's own selection, for it was assigned the usual place of honour beneath the journal's superscription. The text in the *Ges. Schr.* is absolutely identical with that in the *N.Z.*—Tr.

2

Publisher of the *Gazette Musicale.*—Tr.

3

According to Grove's Dictionary of Music, it was at the request of Aguado that Rossini composed six numbers of his *Stabat Mater* in 1832 for the Spanish Minister, Señor Valera, the work being then completed with four numbers by Tadolini. In 1839 the heirs of Valera sold the MS. for 2,000 fr. to a Paris publisher, at which Rossini was most indignant and instructed Troupenas to stop the publication and performance. He then wrote the remaining four numbers, and sold the whole to Troupenas for 6,000 fr. The first six numbers were produced at the Salle Herz in Paris on Oct. 31, 1841; the complete work was first performed at the Salle Ventadour, Jan. 7, 1842, by Grisi, Albertazzi, Mario and Tamburini.—Tr.

Summary

Religious fervour in Parisian salons; duchesses and countesses singing their little *Ave* etc.; re-interment of Bonaparte's remains to accompaniment of Mozart's *Requiem*—they melt away, then try its music, "it tastes like physic"; so they get their quadrille-composers to write Latin pieces Rossini's retirement at Bologna; his tour in Spain with Aguado; a *Stabat Mater* of contrition. Disputes about its copyright The maestro learning counterpoint; at last the duchesses will be able to sing fugues. A "friendly ray" impounded

AUTOBIOGRAPHIC SKETCH

Translator's Note

This sketch of his life, down to the year *1842*, was drawn up by Wagner, at the request of his friend Heinrich Laube, for publication (*1843*) in a Journal edited by the latter, and called the "*Zeitung für die Elegante Welt.*" The editor then prefaced it by the following remark:—

"The storm and stress of Paris have rapidly developed the Musician into a Writer. I should only spoil the life-sketch, did I attempt to alter a word of it."

Autobiographic Sketch

My name is *Wilhelm Richard Wagner*, and I was born at Leipzig on May the 22nd, 1813. My father was a police-actuary, and died six months after I was born. My step-father, Ludwig Geyer, was a comedian and painter; he was also the author of a few stage plays, of which one, "*Der Bethlehemitische Kindermord*" (The Slaughter of the Innocents), had a certain success. My whole family migrated with him to Dresden. He wished me to become a painter, but I showed a very poor talent for drawing.

My step-father also died ere long,—I was only seven years old. Shortly before his death I had learnt to play "*Üb' immer Treu und Redlichkeit*" and the then newly published "*Jungfernkranz*" upon the pianoforte; the day before his death, I was bid to play him both these pieces in the adjoining room; I heard him then, with feeble voice, say to my mother: "Has he perchance a talent for music?" On the early morrow, as he lay dead, my mother came into the children's sleeping-room, and said to each of us some loving word. To me she said: "He hoped to make *something* of thee." I remember, too, that for a long time I imagined that something indeed would come of me.

In my ninth year I went to the Dresden *Kreuzschule*: I wished to study, and music was not thought of. Two of my sisters learnt to play the piano passably; I listened to them, but had no piano lessons myself. Nothing pleased me so much as *Der Freischütz*; I often saw *Weber* pass before our house, as he came from rehearsals; I always watched him with a reverent awe. A tutor who explained to me *Cornelius Nepos*, was at last engaged to give me pianoforte instructions; hardly had I got past the earliest finger-exercises, when I furtively practised, at first by ear, the Overture to *Der Freischütz*; my teacher heard this once, and said nothing would come of me.—He was right; in my whole life I have never learnt to play the piano properly.—Thenceforward I only played for my own amusement, nothing but overtures, and with the most fearful 'fingering.' It was impossible for me to play a passage clearly, and I therefore conceived a just dread of all scales and runs. Of Mozart, I only cared for the *Magic Flute*; *Don Juan* was distasteful to me, on account of the Italian text beneath it: it seemed to me such rubbish.

But this music-strumming was quite a secondary matter: Greek, Latin, Mythology, and Ancient History were my principal studies. I wrote verses too. Once there died one of my schoolfellows, and our teacher set us the task of writing a poem upon his death; the best lines were then to be printed :—my own were printed, but only after I had cleared them of a heap of bombast. I was then eleven years old. I promptly determined to become a poet; and sketched out tragedies on the model of the Greeks, urged by my acquaintance with Apel's works: *Polyidos, Die Ätolier*, &c., &c. Moreover, I passed in my school for a good head *"in litteris;"* even in the 'Third form' I had translated the first twelve books of the Odyssey. For a while I learnt English also, merely so as to gain an accurate knowledge of Shakespeare; and I made a metrical translation of Romeo's monologue. Though I soon left English on one side, yet Shakespeare remained my exemplar, and I projected a great tragedy which was almost nothing but a medley of *Hamlet* and *King Lear*. The plan was gigantic in the extreme; two- and-forty human beings died in the course of this piece, and I saw myself compelled, in its working-out, to call the greater number back as ghosts, since otherwise I should have been short of characters for my last Acts. This play occupied my leisure for two whole years.

Meanwhile, I left Dresden and its *Kreuzschule,* and went to Leipzig. In the *Nikolaischule* of that city I was relegated to the 'Third form,' after having already attained to the 'Second' in Dresden. This circumstance embittered me so much, that thenceforward I lost all liking for philological study. I became lazy and slovenly, and my grand tragedy was the only thing left me to care about. Whilst I was finishing this I made my first acquaintance with Beethoven's music, in the Leipzig *Gewandhaus* concerts; its impression upon me was overpowering. I also became intimate with Mozart's works, chiefly through his *Requiem.* Beethoven's music to *Egmont* so much inspired me, that I determined—for all the world—not to allow my now completed tragedy to leave the stocks until provided with suchlike music. Without the slightest diffidence, I believed that I could myself write this needful music, but thought it better to first clear up a few of the general principles of thorough-bass. To get through this as swiftly as possible, I borrowed for a week Logier's "*Method of Thorough-bass,*" and studied it in hot haste. But this study did not bear such rapid fruit as I had expected: its difficulties both provoked and fascinated me; I resolved to become a musician.

During this time my great tragedy was unearthed by my family: they were much disturbed thereat, for it was clear as day that I had woefully neglected my school lessons in favour of it, and I was forthwith admonished to continue them more diligently. Under such circumstances, I breathed no word of my secret discovery of a calling for music; but, notwithstanding, I composed in silence a Sonata, a Quartet, and an Aria. When I felt myself sufficiently matured in my private musical studies, I ventured forth at last with their announcement. Naturally, I now had many a hard battle to wage, for my relations could only consider my penchant for music as a fleeting passion—all the more as it was unsupported by any proofs of preliminary study, and especially by any already won dexterity in handling a musical instrument.

I was then in my sixteenth year, and, chiefly from a perusal of E. A. Hoffmann's works, on fire with the maddest mysticism: I had visions by day in semi-slumber, in which the 'Keynote,' 'Third,' and 'Dominant' seemed to take on living form and reveal to me their mighty meaning: the notes that I wrote down were stark with folly.—At last a capable musician was engaged to instruct me: the poor man had a sorry office in explaining to me that what I took for wondrous shapes and powers were really chords and intervals. What could be more disturbing to my family than to find that I proved myself negligent and refractory in this study also? My teacher shook his head, and it appeared that here too no good thing could be brought from me. My liking for study dwindled more and more, and I chose instead to write Overtures for full orchestra—one of which was once performed in the Leipzig theatre. This Overture was the culminating point of my foolishness. For its better understanding by such as might care to study the score, I elected to employ for its notation three separate tints of ink: red for the' strings,' green for the 'wood-wind,' and black for the 'brass.' Beethoven's Ninth Symphony was a mere Pleyel Sonata by the side of this marvellously concocted Overture. Its performance was mainly prejudiced by a *fortissimo* thud on the big drum, that recurred throughout the whole overture at regular intervals of four bars; with the result, that the audience gradually passed from its initial amazement at the obstinacy of the drum-beater to undisguised displeasure, and finally to a mirthful mood that much disquieted me. This first performance of a composition of mine left on me a deep impression.

But now the July Revolution took place; with one bound I became a revolutionist, and acquired the conviction that every decently active being ought to occupy himself with politics exclusively. I was only happy in the company of political writers, and I commenced an Overture upon a political theme. Thus was I minded, when I left school and went to the university: not, indeed, to devote myself to studying for any profession—for my musical career was now resolved on—but to attend lectures on philosophy and aesthetics. By this opportunity of improving my mind I profited as good as nothing, but gave myself up to all the excesses of student life; and that with such reckless levity, that they very soon revolted me. My relations were now sorely troubled about me, for I had almost entirely abandoned my music. Yet I speedily came to my senses; I felt the need of a completely new beginning of strict and methodical study of music, and Providence led me to the very man best qualified to inspire me with fresh love for the thing, and to purge my notions by the thoroughest of instruction. This man was *Theodor Weinlig*, the Cantor of the Leipzig *Thomasschule*. Although I had previously made my own attempts at Fugue, it was with him that I first commenced a thorough study of Counterpoint, which he possessed the happy knack of teaching his pupils while playing.

At this epoch I first acquired an intimate love and knowledge of Mozart. I composed a Sonata, in which I freed myself from all buckram, and strove for a natural unforced style of composition. This extremely simple and modest work was published by Breitkopf und Härtel. My studies under Weinlig were ended in less than half a year, and he dismissed me himself from his tuition as soon as he had brought me so far forward that I was in a position to solve with ease the hardest problems of Counterpoint. "What you have made your own by this dry study," he said, "we call Self-dependence." In that same half year I also composed an Overture on the model of Beethoven; a model which I now understood somewhat better. This Overture was played in one of the Leipzig Gewandhaus concerts, to most encouraging applause. After several other works, I then engaged in a Symphony: to my head exemplar, Beethoven, I allied Mozart, especially as shewn in his great C major Symphony. Lucidity and force—albeit with many a strange aberration—were my end and aim.

My Symphony completed, I set out in the summer of 1832 on a journey to Vienna, with no other object than to get a hasty glimpse of this renowned music-city. What I saw and heard there edified me little; wherever I went, I heard *Zampa* and Straussian pot pourris on *Zampa*. Both—and especially at that time—were to me an abomination. On my homeward journey I tarried a while in Prague, where I made the acquaintance of Dionys Weber and Tomaschek; the former had several of my compositions performed in the conservatoire, and among them my Symphony. In that city I also composed an opera-book of tragic contents: *"Die Hochzeit."* I know not whence I had come by the mediaeval subject-matter : — a frantic lover climbs to the window of the sleeping chamber of his friend's bride, wherein she is awaiting the advent of the bridegroom; the bride struggles with the madman and hurls him into the courtyard below, where his mangled body gives up the ghost. During the funeral ceremony, the bride, uttering one cry, sinks lifeless on the corpse.

Returned to Leipzig, I set to work at once on the composition of this opera's first 'number,' which contained a grand Sextet that much pleased Weinlig. The textbook found no favour with my sister; I destroyed its every trace.

In January of 1833 my Symphony was performed at a Gewandhaus concert, and met with highly inspiriting applause. At about this time I came to know Heinrich Laube.

To visit one of my brothers, I travelled to Wurzburg in the spring of the same year, and remained there till its close; my brother's intimacy was of great importance to me, for he was an accomplished singer. During my stay in Wurzburg I composed a romantic opera in three Acts: *"Die Feen,"* for which I wrote my own text, after Gozzi's: *"Die Frau als Schlange."* Beethoven and Weber were my models; in the *ensembles* of this opera there was much that fell out very well, and the Finale of the Second Act, especially, promised a good effect. The 'numbers' from this work which I brought to a hearing at concerts in Wurzburg, were favourably received. Full of hopes for my now finished opera, I returned to Leipzig at the beginning of 1834, and offered it for performance to the Director of that theatre. However, in spite of his at first declared readiness to comply with my wish, I was soon forced to the same experience that every German opera-composer has nowadays to win: we are discredited upon our own native stage by the success of Frenchmen and Italians, and the production of our operas is a favour to be cringed for. The performance of my *Feen* was set upon the shelf.

Meanwhile I heard the *Devrient* sing in Bellini's *Romeo and Juliet*. I was astounded to witness so extraordinary a rendering of such utterly meaningless music. I grew doubtful as to the choice of the proper means to bring about a great success; far though I was from attaching to Bellini a signal merit, yet the subject to which his music was set seemed to me to be more propitious and better calculated to spread the warm glow of life, than the painstaking pedantry with which we Germans, as a rule, brought naught but laborious make-believe to market. The flabby lack of character of our modern Italians, equally with the frivolous levity of the latest Frenchmen, appeared to me to challenge the earnest, conscientious German to master the happily chosen and happily exploited means of his rivals, in order then to outstrip them in the production of genuine works of art.

I was then twenty-one years of age, inclined to take life and the world on their pleasant side. "*Ardinghello*" (by Heinse) and "*Das Junge Europa*" (by H. Laube) tingled through my every limb; while Germany appeared in my eyes a very tiny portion of the earth. I had emerged from abstract Mysticism, and I learnt a love for Matter. Beauty of material and brilliancy of wit were lordly things to me: as regards my beloved music, I found them both among the Frenchmen and Italians. I forswore my model, Beethoven; his last Symphony I deemed the keystone of a whole great epoch of art, beyond whose limits no man could hope to press, and within which no man could attain to independence. Mendelssohn also seemed to have felt with me, when he stepped forth with his smaller orchestral compositions, leaving untouched the great and fenced-off form of the Symphony of Beethoven; it seemed to me that, beginning with a lesser, completely unshackled form, he fain would create for himself therefrom a greater.

Everything around me appeared fermenting: to abandon myself to the general fermentation, I deemed the most natural course. Upon a lovely summer's journey among the Bohemian watering-places, I sketched the plan of a new opera, "*Das Liebesverbot*," taking my subject from Shakespeare's *Measure for Measure*—only with this difference, that I robbed it of its prevailing earnestness, and thus remoulded it after the pattern of *Das Junge Europa*; free and frank physicalism (*Sinnlichkeit*) gained, of its own sheer strength, the victory over Puritanical hypocrisy.

In the summer of this same year, 1834, I further took the post of Music-Director at the Magdeburg theatre. The practical application of my musical knowledge to the functions of a conductor bore early fruit; for the vicissitudes of intercourse with singers and singeresses, behind the scenes and in front of the footlights, completely matched my bent toward many-hued distraction. The composition of my *Liebesverbot* was now begun. I produced the Overture to *Die Feen* at a concert; it had a marked success. This notwithstanding, I lost all liking for this opera, and, since I was no longer able to personally attend to my affairs at Leipzig, I soon resolved to trouble myself no more about this work, which is as much as to say that I gave it up.

For a festival play for New Year's day, 1835, I hastily threw together some music, which aroused a general interest. Such lightly won success much fortified my views that in order to please, one must not too scrupulously choose one's means. In this sense I continued the composition of my *Liebesverbot*, and took no care whatever to avoid the echoes of the French and Italian stages. Interrupted in this work for a while, I resumed it in the winter of 1835-6, and completed it shortly before the dispersal of the Magdeburg opera troupe. I had now only twelve days before the departure of the principal singers; therefore my opera must be rehearsed in this short space of time, if I still wished them to perform it. With greater levity than deliberation, I permitted this opera—which contained some arduous rôles—to be set on the stage after a ten days' study. I placed my trust in the prompter and in my conductor's baton. But, spite of all my efforts, I could not remove the obstacle, that the singers scarcely half knew their parts. The representation was like a dream to us all: no human being could possibly get so much as an idea what it was all about; yet there was some consolation in the fact that applause was plentiful. From various reasons, a second performance could not be given.

In the midst of all this, the 'earnestness of life' had knocked at my door; my outward independence, so rashly grasped at, had led me into follies of every kind, and on all sides I was plagued by penury and debts. It occurred to me to venture upon something out of the ordinary, in order not to slide into the common rut of need. Without any sort of prospect, I went to Berlin and offered the Director to produce my *Liebesverbot* at the theatre of that capital. I was received at first with the fairest promises; but, after long suspense, I had to learn that not one of them was sincerely meant. In the sorriest plight I left Berlin, and applied for the post of Musical Director at the Königsberg theatre, in Prussia—a post which I subsequently obtained. In that city I got married in the autumn of 1836, amid the most dubious outward circumstances. The year which I spent in Königsberg was completely lost to my art, by reason of the pressure of petty cares. I wrote one solitary Overture: "*Rule Britannia.*"

In the summer of 1837 I visited Dresden for a short time. There I was led back by the reading of Bulwer's "*Rienzi*" to an already cherished idea, viz., of turning the last of Rome's tribunes into the hero of a grand tragic opera. Hindered by outward discomforts, however, I busied myself no further with dramatic sketches. In the autumn of this year I went to Riga, to take up the position of first Musical Director at the theatre recently opened there by Holtei. I found there an assemblage of excellent material for opera, and went to its employment with the greatest liking. Many interpolated passages for individual singers in various operas, were composed by me during this period. I also wrote the libretto for a comic opera in two Acts: "*Die Glückliche Bärenfamilie,*" the matter for which I took from one of the stories in the "Thousand and One Nights." I had only composed two 'numbers' for this, when I was disgusted to find that I was again on the high road to music-making *à la Adam*. My spirit, my deeper feelings, were wounded by this discovery, and I laid aside the work in horror. The daily studying and conducting of Auber's, Adam's, and Bellini's music contributed its share to a speedy undoing of my frivolous delight in such an enterprise.

The utter childishness of our provincial public's verdict upon any art-manifestation that may chance to make its first appearance in their own theatre—for they are only accustomed to witness performances of works already judged and accredited by the greater world outside—brought me to the decision, at no price to produce for the first time a largish work at a minor theatre. When, therefore, I felt again the instinctive need of undertaking a major work, I renounced all idea of obtaining a speedy representation of it in my immediate neighbourhood: I fixed my mind upon some theatre of first rank, that would some day produce it, and troubled myself but little as to where and when that theatre would be found. In this wise did I conceive the sketch of a grand tragic opera in five Acts: "Rienzi, the last of the Tribunes ;"and I laid my plans on so important a scale, that it would be impossible to produce this opera—at any rate for the first time—at any lesser theatre. Moreover, the wealth and force of the material left me no other course, and my procedure was governed more by necessity than set purpose. In the summer of 1838 I completed the poem; at the same time, I was engaged in rehearsing our opera troupe, with much enthusiasm and affection, in Méhul's *"Jacob and his Sons."*

When, in the autumn, I began the composition of my *Rienzi*, I allowed naught to influence me except the single purpose to answer to my subject. I set myself no model, but gave myself entirely to the feeling which now consumed me, the feeling that I had already so far progressed that I might claim something significant from the development of my artistic powers, and expect some not insignificant result. The very notion of being consciously weak or trivial—even in a single bar —was appalling to me.

During the winter I was in the full swing of composition, so that by the spring of 1839 I had finished the long first two Acts. About this time my contract with the Director of the theatre terminated, and various circumstances made it inconvenient to me to stay longer at Riga. For two years I had nursed the plan of going to Paris, and with this in view, I had, even while at Königsberg, sent to Scribe the sketch of an opera plot, with the proposal that he should elaborate it for his own benefit and procure me, in reward, the commission to compose the opera for Paris. Scribe naturally left this suggestion as good as unregarded. Nevertheless, I did not give up my scheme; on the contrary, I returned to it with renewed keenness in the summer of 1839; and the long and the short of it was, that I induced my wife to embark with me upon a sailing vessel bound for London.

This voyage I never shall forget as long as I live; it lasted three and a half weeks, and was rich in mishaps. Thrice did we endure the most violent of storms, and once the captain found himself compelled to put into a Norwegian haven. The passage among the crags of Norway made a wonderful impression on my fancy; the legends of the Flying Dutchman, as I heard them from the seamen's mouths, were clothed for me in a distinct and individual colour, borrowed from the adventures of the ocean through which I then was passing.

Resting from the severe exhaustion of the transit, we remained a week in London; nothing interested me so much as the city itself and the Houses of Parliament,—of the theatres, I visited not one. At Boulogne-sur-mer I stayed four weeks, and there made the acquaintance of Meyerbeer. I brought under his notice the two finished Acts of my *Rienzi*; he promised me, in the friendliest fashion, his support in Paris. With very little money, but the best of hopes, I now set foot in Paris. Entirely without any personal references, I could rely on no one but Meyerbeer. He seemed prepared, with the most signal attentiveness, to set in train whatever might further my aims; and it certainly seemed to me that I should soon attain a wished-for goal—had it not unfortunately so turned out that, during the very period of my stay in Paris, Meyerbeer was generally, nay almost the whole time, absent from that city. It is true that he wished to serve me even from a distance; but, according to his own announcement, epistolary efforts could avail nothing where only the most assiduous personal mediation is of any efficacy.

First of all, I entered upon negotiations with the *Théâtre de la Renaissance*, where both comedy and opera were then being given. The score of my *Liebesverbot* seemed best fitted for this theatre, and the somewhat frivolous subject appeared easily adaptable to the French stage. I was so warmly recommended by Meyerbeer to the Director of the theatre, that he could not help receiving me with the best of promises. Thereupon, one of the most prolific of Parisian dramatists, *Dumersan*, offered to undertake the poetical setting of the subject. He translated three 'numbers,' destined for a trial hearing, with so great felicity that my music looked much better in its new French dress than in its original German; in fact, it was music such as Frenchmen most readily comprehend, and everything promised me the best success — when the *Théâtre de la Renaissance* immediately became bankrupt. All my labours, all my hopes, were thus in vain.

In the same winter, 1839-40, I composed — besides an Overture to the first part of Goethe's Faust — several French Ballads; among others, a French translation made for me of H. Heine's *The Two Grenadiers*. I never dreamt of any possibility of getting my *Rienzi* produced in Paris, for I clearly foresaw that I should have had to wait five or six years, even under the most favourable conditions, before such a plan could be carried out; moreover, the translation of the text of the already half-finished composition would have thrown insuperable obstacles in the way.

Thus I began the summer of 1840, completely bereft of immediate prospects. My acquaintance with Habeneck, Halévy, Berlioz, &c., led to no closer relations with these men: in Paris no artist has time to form a friendship with another, for each is in a red hot hurry for his own advantage. Halévy, like all the composers of our day, was aflame with enthusiasm for his art only so long as it was a question of winning a great success: so soon as he had carried off this prize, and was enthroned among the privileged ranks of artistic 'lions,' he had no thought for anything but making operas and pocketing their pay. Renown is everything in Paris: the happiness and ruin of the artist. Despite his stand-off manners, Berlioz attracted me in a far higher degree. He differs by the whole breadth of heaven from his Parisian colleagues, for he makes no music for gold. But he cannot write for the sake of purest art; he lacks all sense of beauty. He stands, completely isolated, upon his own position; by his side he has nothing but a troup of devotees who, shallow and without the smallest spark of judgment, greet in him the creator of a brand new musical system and completely turn his head; — the rest of the world avoids him as a madman.

My earlier easy-going views of the means and ends of music received their final shock—from the Italians. These idolised heroes of song, with Rubini at their head, finished by utterly disgusting me with their music. The public to whom they sang, added their quota to this effect upon me. The Paris Grand Opera left me entirely unsatisfied, by the want of all genius in its representations: I found the whole thing commonplace and middling. I openly confess that the *mise en scène* and the decorations are the most to my liking of anything at the *Académie Royale de Musique*. The *Opéra Comique* would have had much more chance of pleasing me — it possesses the best talents, and its performances offer an *ensemble* and an individuality such as we know nothing of in Germany—but the stuff that is nowadays written for this theatre belongs to the very worst productions of a period of degraded art. Whither has flown the grace of Méhul, Isouard, Boieldieu, and the *young* Auber, scared by the contemptible quadrille rhythms which rattle through this theatre to-day? The only thing worthy the regard of a musician that Paris now contains, is the *Conservatoire* with its orchestral concerts. The renderings of German instrumental compositions at these concerts produced on me a deep impression, and inducted me afresh into the mysteries of noble art. He who would fully learn the Ninth Symphony of Beethoven, must hear it executed by the orchestra of the Paris Conservatoire. But these concerts stand alone in utter solitude; there is naught that answers to them.

I hardly mixed at all with musicians: scholars, painters, &c., formed my *entourage*, and I gained many a rare experience of friendship in Paris.—Since I was so completely bare of present Paris prospects, I took up once more the composition of my *Rienzi*. I now destined it for Dresden: in the first place, because I knew that this theatre possessed the very best material—Devrient, Tichatschek, &c; secondly, because I could more reasonably hope for an *entrée* there, relying upon the support of my earliest acquaintances. My *Liebesverbot* I now gave up almost completely; I felt that I could no longer regard myself as its composer. With all the greater freedom, I followed now my true artistic creed, in the prosecution of the music to my *Rienzi*. Manifold worries and bitter need besieged my life. On a sudden, Meyerbeer appeared again for a short space in Paris. With the most amiable sympathy he ascertained the position of my affairs, and desired to help. He therefore placed me in communication with Léon Pillet, the Director of the Grand Opera, with a view to my being entrusted with the composition of a two- or three-act opera for that stage. I had already provided myself for this emergency with an outline plot. The "Flying Dutchman," whose intimate acquaintance I had made upon the ocean, had never ceased to fascinate my phantasy; I had also made the acquaintance of H. Heine's remarkable version of this legend, in a number of his 'Salon'; and it was especially his treatment of the redemption of this Ahasuerus of the seas—borrowed from a Dutch play under the same title—that placed within my hands all the material for turning the legend into an opera-subject. I obtained the consent of Heine himself; I wrote my sketch, and handed it to M. Léon Fillet, with the proposal that he should get me a French text-book made after my model. Thus far was everything set on foot when Meyerbeer again left Paris, and the fulfilment of my wish had to be relinquished to destiny. I was very soon astounded by hearing from Pillet that the sketch I had tendered him pleased him so much that he should be glad if I would cede it to him. He explained: that he was pledged by a previous promise to supply another composer with a libretto as soon as possible; that my sketch appeared to be the very thing for such a purpose, and I should probably not regret consenting to the surrender he begged, when I reflected that I could not possibly hope to obtain a direct commission for an opera before the lapse of four years, seeing that he had in the interval to keep faith with several candidates for grand opera; that such a period would naturally be too long for myself to be brooding over this subject; and that I should certainly discover a fresh one, and console myself for the sacrifice. I struggled obstinately against this suggestion, without being able, however, to effect anything further than a provisional postponement of the question. I counted upon the speedy return of Meyerbeer, and held my peace.

During this time I was prompted by Schlesinger to write for his "Gazette Musicale." I contributed several longish articles on "German Music," &c., &c., among which the one which found the liveliest welcome was a little romance entitled, "A Pilgrimage to Beethoven." These works assisted not a little to make me known and noticed in

Paris. In November of this year I put the last touches to my score of *Rienzi*, and sent it post-haste to Dresden. This period was the culminating point of the utter misery of my existence. I wrote for the *Gazette Musicale* a short story: "The Life's End of a German Musician in Paris," wherein I made the wretched hero die with these words upon his lips: "I believe in God, Mozart, and Beethoven."

It was well that my opera was finished, for I saw myself now compelled to bid a long farewell to any practice of my art. I was forced to undertake, for Schlesinger, arrangements of airs for all the instruments under heaven, even the *cornet à piston*; thus only was a slight amelioration of my lot to be found. In this way did I pass the winter of 1840-1, in the most inglorious fashion. In the spring I went into the country, to Meudon; and with the warm approach of summer I began to long again for brain-work. The stimulus thereto was to touch me quicker than I had thought for; I learnt, forsooth, that my sketch of the text of the *Flying Dutchman* had already been handed to a poet, Paul Fouché, and that if I did not declare my willingness to part therewith, I should be clean robbed of it on some pretext or other. I therefore consented at last to make over my sketch for a moderate sum. (01) I had now to work post-haste to clothe my own subject with German verses. In order to set about its composition, I required to hire a pianoforte; for, after nine months' interruption of all musical production, I had to try to surround myself with the needful preliminary of a musical atmosphere. As soon as the piano had arrived, my heart beat fast for very fear; I dreaded to discover that I had ceased to be a musician. I began first with the "Sailors' Chorus" and the "Spinning-song"; everything sped along as though on wings, and I shouted for joy as I felt within me that I still was a musician. In seven weeks the whole opera was composed; but at the end of that period I was overwhelmed again by the commonest cares of life, and two full months elapsed before I could get to writing the overture to the already finished opera— although I bore it almost full-fledged in my brain. Naturally nothing now lay so much at my heart as the desire to bring it to a speedy production in Germany; from Munich and Leipzig I had the disheartening answer: the opera was not at all fitted for Germany.

Fool that I was! I had fancied it was fitted for Germany alone, since it struck on chords that can only vibrate in the German breast.

At last I sent my new work to Meyerbeer, in Berlin, with the petition that he would get it taken up for the theatre of that city. This was effected with tolerable rapidity. As my *Rienzi* had already been accepted for the Dresden Court theatre, I therefore now looked forward to the production of two of my works upon the foremost German stages; and involuntarily I reflected on the strangeness of the fact, that Paris had been to me of the greatest service for Germany. As regards Paris itself, I was completely without prospects for several years: I therefore left it in the spring of 1842. For the first time I saw the Rhine—with hot tears in my eyes, I, poor artist, swore eternal fidelity to my German fatherland.

Notes

01

Herr C. F. Glasenapp, in his *"Richard Wagner's Leben und Wirken,"* tells us that the name of the composer for whom Fouché adapted Wagner's sketch was Dietsch; that his opera was called *"Le Vaisseau Fantôme,"* was produced a few years later at the Paris Grand Opera, and was so overloaded with minor personages that it had no more dramatic than musical success.—A righteous nemesis!—Tr.

THE NIBELUNGEN-MYTH

As Sketch for a Drama

From the womb of Night and Death was spawned a race that dwells in Nibelheim (Nebelheim), i.e. in gloomy subterranean clefts and caverns: *Nibelungen* are they called; with restless nimbleness they burrow through the bowels of the earth, like worms in a dead body; they smelt and smith hard metals. The pure and noble Rhine-gold *Alberich* seized, divorced it from the waters' depth, and wrought there from with cunning art a ring that lent him rulership of all his race, the Nibelungen: so he became their master, forced them to work for him alone, and amassed the priceless *Nibelungen-Hoard*, whose greatest treasure is the Tarnhelm, conferring power to take on any shape at will, a work that Alberich compelled his own brother Reigin (Mime = Eugel) to weld for him. Thus armoured, Alberich made for mastery of the world and all that it contains.

The race of *Giants*, boastful, violent, ur-begotten, is troubled in its savage ease: their monstrous strength, their simple mother-wit, no longer are a match for Alberich's crafty plans of conquest: alarmed they see the Nibelungen forging wondrous weapons, that one day in the hands of human heroes shall cause the Giants' downfall.—This strife is taken advantage of by the race of *Gods*, now waxing to supremacy. *Wotan* bargains with the Giants to build the Gods a Burg from whence to rule the world in peace and order; their building finished, the Giants ask the Nibelungen-Hoard in payment. The utmost cunning of the Gods succeeds in trapping Alberich; he must ransom his life with the Hoard; the Ring alone he strives to keep:— the Gods, well knowing that in it resides the secret of all Alberich's power, extort from him the Ring as well: then he curses it; it shall be the ruin of all who possess it. Wotan delivers the Hoard to the Giants, but means to keep the Ring as warrant of his sovereignty: the Giants defy him, and Wotan yields to the counsel of the three Fates (Norns), who warn him of the downfall of the Gods themselves.

Now the Giants have the Hoard and Ring safe-kept by a monstrous Worm in the Gnita- (Neid-) Haide [the Grove of Grudge]. Through the Ring the Nibelungs remain in thraldom, Alberich and all. But the Giants do not understand to use their might; their dullard minds are satisfied with having bound the Nibelungen. So the Worm lies on the Hoard since untold ages, in inert dreadfulness: before the lustre of the new race of Gods the Giants' race fades down and stiffens into impotence; wretched and tricksy, the Nibelungen go their way of fruitless labour. Alberich broods without cease on the means of gaining back the Ring.

In high emprise the Gods have planned the world, bound down the elements by prudent laws, and devoted themselves to most careful nurture of the Human race. Their strength stands over all. Yet the peace by which they have arrived at mastery does not repose on reconcilement: by violence and cunning was it wrought. The object of their higher ordering of the world is moral consciousness: but the wrong they fight attaches to themselves. From the depths of Nibelheim the conscience of their guilt cries up to them: for the bondage of the Nibelungen is not broken; merely the lordship has been reft from Alberich, and not for any higher end, but the soul, the freedom of the Nibelungen lies buried uselessly beneath the belly of an idle Worm: Alberich thus has justice in his plaints against the Gods. Wotan himself, however, cannot undo the wrong without committing yet another: only a free Will, independent of the Gods themselves, and able to assume and expiate itself the burden of all guilt, can loose the spell; and in Man the Gods perceive the faculty of such free-will. In Man they therefore seek to plant their own divinity, to raise his strength so high that, in full knowledge of that strength, he may rid him of the Gods' protection, to do of his free will what his own mind inspires. So the Gods bring up Man for this high destiny, to be the canceller of their own guilt; and their aim would be attained even if in this human creation they should perforce annul themselves, that is, must part with their immediate influence through freedom of man's conscience. Stout human races, fruited by the seed divine, already flourish: in strife and fight they steel their strength; Wotan's Wish-maids shelter them as Shield-maids, as *Walküren* lead the slain-in-fight to Walhall, where the heroes live again a glorious life of jousts in Wotan's company. But not yet is the rightful hero born, in whom his self-reliant strength shall reach full consciousness, enabling him with the free-willed penalty of death before his eyes to call his boldest deed his own. In the race of the *Wälsungen* this hero at last shall come to birth: a barren union is fertilised by Wotan through one of Holda's apples, which he gives the wedded pair to eat: twins, *Siegmund* and *Sieglinde* (brother and sister), spring from the marriage. Siegmund takes a wife, Sieglinde weds a man (Hunding); but both their marriages prove sterile: to beget a genuine Wälsung, brother and sister wed each other. Hunding, Sieglinde's husband, learns of the crime, casts off his wife, and goes out to fight with Siegmund. *Brünnhild*, the Walküre, shields Siegmund counter to Wotan's commands, who had doomed him to fall in expiation of the crime; already Siegmund, under Brünnhild's shield, is drawing sword for the death-blow at Hunding—the sword that Wotan himself once had given him—when the god receives the blow upon his spear, which breaks the weapon in two pieces. Siegmund falls. Brünnhild is punished by Wotan for her disobedience: he strikes her from the roll of the Walküren, and banishes her to a rock, where the divine virgin is to wed the man who finds and wakes her from the sleep in which Wotan plunges her; she pleads for mercy, that Wotan will ring the rock with terrors of fire, and so ensure that none save the bravest of heroes may win her.—After long gestation the outcast Sieglinde gives birth in the forest to *Siegfried* (he who brings Peace through Victory): Reigin (*Mime*), Alberich's brother, upon hearing her cries, has issued from a cleft and aided her: after the travail Sieglinde dies, first telling Reigin of her fate and committing the babe to his care. Reigin brings up Siegfried, teaches him smithery, and brings him the two pieces of the broken sword, from which, under Mime's directions, Siegfried forges the sword Balmung. Then Mime prompts the lad to slay the Worm, in proof of his gratitude. Siegfried first wishes to avenge his father's murder: he fares out, falls upon Hunding, and kills him: only thereafter does he execute the wish of Mime, attacks and slays the Giant-worm. His fingers burning from the Worm's hot blood, he puts them to his mouth to cool them; involuntarily he tastes the blood, and understands at once the language of the woodbirds singing round him. They praise Siegfried for his glorious deed, direct him to the Nibelungenhoard in the cave of the Worm, and warn him against Mime, who has merely used him as an instrument to gain the Hoard, and therefore seeks his life. Siegfried thereon slays Mime, and takes the Ring and Tarnhelm from the Hoard: he hears the birds again, who counsel him to win the crown of women, Brünnhild. So Siegfried sets forth, reaches Brünnhild's mountain, pierces the billowing flames, and wakes her; in Siegfried she joyfully acclaims the highest hero of the Wälsung-stem, and gives herself to him: he marries her with Alberich's ring, which he places on her finger. When the longing spurs him to new deeds, she gives him lessons in her secret lore, warns him of the dangers of deceit and treachery: they swear each other vows, and Siegfried speeds forth.

A second hero-stem, sprung likewise from the Gods, is that of the *Gibichungen* on the Rhine: there now bloom *Gunther* and *Gudrun*, his sister. Their mother, Grimhild, was once overpowered by Alberich, and bore him an unlawful son, *Hagen*. As the hopes and wishes of the Gods repose on Siegfried, so Alberich sets his hope of gaining back the Ring on his hero-offspring Hagen. Hagen is sallow, glum and serious; his features are prematurely hardened; he looks older than he is. Already in his childhood Alberich had taught him mystic lore and knowledge of his father's fate, inciting him to struggle for the Ring: he is strong and masterful; yet to Alberich he seems not strong enough to slay the Giant-worm. Since Alberich has lost his power, he could not stop his brother Mime when the latter sought to gain the Hoard through Siegfried: but Hagen shall compass Siegfried's ruin, and win the Ring from his dead body. Toward Gunther and Gudrun Hagen is reticent,—they fear him, but prize his foresight and experience: the secret of some marvellous descent of Hagen's, and that he is not his lawful brother, is known to Gunther: he calls him once an Elf-son.

Gunther is being apprised by Hagen that Brünnhild is the woman most worth desire, and excited to long for her possession, when Siegfried speeds along the Rhine to the seat of the Gibichungs. Gudrun, inflamed to love by the praises he has showered on Siegfried, at Hagen's bidding welcomes Siegfried with a drink prepared by Hagen's art, of such potence that it makes Siegfried forget his adventure with Brünnhild and marriage to her. Siegfried desires Gudrun for wife: Gunther consents, on condition that he helps him win Brünnhild. Siegfried agrees: they strike blood-brothership and swear each other oaths, from which Hagen holds aloof.—Siegfried and Gunther set out, and arrive at Brünnhild's rocky fastness: Gunther remains behind in the boat; Siegfried for the first and only time exerts his power as Ruler of the Nibelungen, by putting on the Tarnhelm and thereby taking Gunther's form and look; thus masked, he passes through the flames to Brünnhild. Already robbed by Siegfried of her maidhood, she has lost alike her superhuman strength, and all her runecraft has she made away to Siegfried—who does not use it; she is powerless as any mortal woman, and can only offer lame resistance to the new, audacious wooer; he tears from her the Ring—by which she is now to be wedded to Gunther—, and forces her into the cavern, where he sleeps the night with her, though to her astonishment he lays his sword between them. On the morrow he brings her to the boat, where he lets the real Gunther take his place unnoticed by her side, and transports himself in a trice to the Gibichenburg through power of the Tarnhelm. Gunther reaches his home along the Rhine, with Brünnhild following him in downcast silence: Siegfried, at Gudrun's side, and Hagen receive the voyagers.—Brünnhild is aghast when she beholds Siegfried as Gudrun's husband: his cold civility to her amazes her; as he motions her back to Gunther, she recognises the Ring on his finger: she suspects the imposture played upon her, and demands the ring, for it belongs not to him, but to Gunther who received it from her: he refuses it. She bids Gunther claim the ring from Siegfried: Guimther is confused, and hesitates. Brünnhild: So it was Siegfried that had the ring from her? Siegfried, recognising the Ring: "From no woman I had it; my right arm won it from the Giant-worm; through it am I the Nibehungen's lord, and to none will I cede its might." Hagen steps between them, and asks Brünnhild if she is certain about the Ring? If it be hers, then Siegfried gained it by deceit, and it can belong to no one but her husband, Gunther. Brünnhild loudly denounces the trick played on her; the most dreadful thirst for vengeance upon Siegfried fills her. She cries to Gunther that he has been duped by Siegfried: "Not to thee—to this man am I wed; he won my favour."—Siegfried charges her with shamelessness: Faithful had he been to his blood-brothership,—his sword he laid between Brünnhilde and himself:—he calls on her to bear him witness.—Purposely, and thinking only of his ruin, she will not understand him.—The clansmen and Gudrun conjure Siegfried to clear himself of the accusation, if he can. Siegfried swears solemn oaths in confirmation of his word. Brünnhild taxes him with perjury: All the oaths he swore to her and Gunther, has he broken: now he forswears himself, to lend corroboration to a lie. Everyone is in the utmost commotion. Siegfried calls Gunther to stop his wife from shamefully slandering her own and husband's honour: he withdraws with Gudrun to the inner hall.—Gunther, in deepest shame and terrible dejection, has seated himself at the side, with hidden face: Brünnhild, racked by the horrors of an inner storm, is approached by Hagen. He offers himself as venger of her honour: she mocks him, as powerless to cope with Siegfried: One look from his glittering eye, which shone upon her even through that mask, would scatter Hagen's courage. Hagen: He well knows Siegfried's awful strength, but she will tell him how he may be vanquished? So she who once had hallowed Siegfried, and armed him by mysterious spells against all wounding, now counsels Hagen to attack him from behind; for, knowing that the hero ne'er would turn his back upon the foe, she had left it from the blessing.—Gunther must be made a party to the plot. They call upon him to avenge his honour: Brünnhild covers him with reproaches for his cowardice and trickery; Gunther admits his fault, and the necessity of ending his shame by Siegfried's death; but he shrinks from committing a breach of blood-brotherhood. Brünnhild bitterly taunts him: What crimes have not been wreaked on her? Hagen inflames him by the prospect of gaining the Nibelung's Ring, which Siegfried certainly will never part with until death. Gunther consents; Hagen proposes a hunt for the morrow, when Siegfried shall be set upon, and perhaps his murder even concealed from Gudrun; for Gunther was concerned for her sake: Brünnhilde's lust-of-vengeance is sharpened by her jealousy of Gudrun. So Siegfried's murder is decided by the three.— Siegfried and Gudrun, festally attired, appear in the hall, and bid them to the sacrificial rites and wedding ceremony. The conspirators feigningly obey: Siegfried and Gudrun rejoice at the show of peace restored.

Next morning Siegfried strays into a lonely gully by the Rhine, in pursuit of quarry. Three mermaids dart up from the stream: they are soothsaying Daughters of the waters' bed, whence Alberich once had snatched the gleaming Rhine-gold to smite from it the fateful Ring: the curse and power of that Ring would be destroyed, were it regiven to the waters, and thus resolved into its pure original element. The Daughters hanker for the Ring, and beg it of Siegfried, who refuses it. (Guiltless, he has taken the guilt of the Gods upon him, and atones their wrong through his defiance, his self-dependence.) They prophesy evil, and tell him of the curse attaching to the ring: Let him cast it in the river, or he must die to-day. Siegfried: "Ye glibtongued women shall not cheat me of my might: the curse and your threats I count not worth a hair. What my courage bids me, is my being's law; and what I do of mine own mind, so is it set for me to do: call ye this curse or blessing, it I obey and strive not counter to my strength." The three Daughters: "Wouldst thou outvie the Gods?" Siegfried: "Shew me the chance of mastering the Gods, and I must work my main to vanquish them. I know three wiser women than you three; they wot where once the Gods will strive in bitter fearing. Well for the Gods, if they take heed that then I battle *with* them. So laugh I at your threats: the ring stays mine, and thus I cast my life behind me." (He lifts a clod of earth, and hurls it backwards over his head.)—The Daughters scoff at Siegfried, who weens himself as strong and wise as he is blind and bond-slave. "Oaths has he broken, and knows it not: a boon far higher than the Ring he's lost, and knows it not: runes and spells were taught to him, and he's forgot them. Fare thee well, Siegfried! A lordly wife we know; e'en to-day will she possess the Ring, when thou art slaughtered. To her! She'll lend us better hearing."— Siegfried, laughing, gazes after them as they move away singing. He shouts: "To Gudrun were I not true, one of you three had ensnared me!" He hears his hunting-comrades drawing nearer, and winds his horn: the huntsmen—Gunther and Hagen at their head—assemble round Siegfried. The midday meal is eaten: Siegfried, in the highest spirits, mocks at his own unfruitful chase: But water-game had come his way, for whose capture he was not equipped, alack! or he'd have brought his comrades three wild water-birds that told him he must die to-day. Hagen takes up the jest, as they drink: Does he really know the song and speech of birds, then?—Gunther is sad and silent Siegfried seeks to enliven him, and sings him songs about his youth: his adventure with Mime, the slaying of the Worm, and how he came to understand bird-language. The train of recollection brings him back the counsel of the birds to seek Brünnhilde, who was fated for him; how he stormed the flaming rock and wakened Brünnhild. Remembrance rises more and more distinct. Two ravens suddenly fly past his head. Hagen interrupts him: "What do these ravens tell thee?" Siegfried springs to his feet. Hagen: "*I* rede them; they haste to herald thee to Wotan." He hurls his spear at Siegfried's back. Gunther, guessing from Siegfried's tale the true connection of the inexplicable scene with Brünnhilde, and suddenly divining Siegfried's innocence, had thrown himself on Hagen's arm to rescue Siegfried, but without being able to stay the blow. Siegfried raises his shield, to crush Hagen with it; his strength fails him, and he falls of a heap. Hagen has departed; Gunther and the clansmen stand round Siegfried, in sympathetic awe; he lifts his shining eyes once more: "Brünnhild, Brünnhild! Radiant child of Wotan! How dazzling bright I see thee nearing me! With holy smile thou saddlest thy horse, that paces through the air dew-dripping: to me thou steer'st its course; here is there Lot to choose (*Wal zu küren*)! Happy me thou chos'st for husband, now lead me to Walhall, that in honour of all heroes I may drink All-father's mead, pledged me by thee, thou shining Wish-maid! Brünnhild, Brünnhild! Greeting!" He dies. The men uplift the corpse upon his shield, and solemnly bear it over the rocky heights, Gunther in front.

In the Hall of the Gibichungs, whose forecourt extends at the back to the bank of the Rhine, the corpse is set down: Hagen has called out Gudrun; with strident tones he tells her that a savage boar had gored her husband.—Gudrun falls horrified on Siegfried's body: she rates her brother with the murder; Gunther points to Hagen: He was the savage boar, the murderer of Siegfried. Hagen: "So be it; an I have slain him, whom no other dared to, whatso was his is my fair booty. The ring is mine!" Gunther confronts him: "Shameless Elf-son, the ring is mine, assigned to me by Brünnhild: ye all, ye heard it."— Hagen and Gunther fight: Gunther falls. Hagen tries to wrench the Ring from the body,—it lifts its hand aloft in menace; Hagen staggers back, aghast; Gudrun cries aloud in her sorrow;—then Brünnhild enters solemnly: "Cease your laments, your idle rage! Here stands his wife, whom ye all betrayed. My right I claim, for what must be is done!"—Gudrun: "Ah, wicked one! 'Twas thou who brought us ruin." Brünnhild: "Poor soul, have peace! Wert but his wanton: his wife am I, to whom he swore or e'er he saw thee." Gudrun: "Woe's me! Accursed Hagen, what badest thou me, with the drink that filched her husband to me? For now I know that only through the drink did he forget Brünnhilde." Brünnhild: "O he was pure! Ne'er oaths were more loyally held, than by him. No, Hagen has not *slain* him; for Wotan has he marked him out, to whom I thus conduct him. And I, too, have atoned; pure and free am I: for he, the glorious one alone, o'erpowered me." She directs a pile of logs to be erected on the shore, to burn Siegfried's corpse to ashes: no horse, no vassal shall be sacrificed with him; she alone will give her body in his honour to the Gods. First she takes possession of her heritage; the Tarnhelm shall be burnt with her: the Ring she puts upon her finger. "Thou froward hero, how thou held'st me banned! All my rune-lore I bewrayed to thee, a mortal, and so went widowed of my wisdom; thou usedst it not, thou trustedst in thyself alone: but now that thou must yield it up through death, my knowledge comes to me again, and this Ring's runes I rede. The ur-law's runes, too, know I now, the Norns' old saying! Hear then, ye mighty Gods, your guilt is quit: thank him, the hero, who took your guilt upon him! To mine own hand he gave to end his work: loosed be the Nibelungs' thraldom, the Ring no more shall bind them. Not Alberich shall receive it; no more shall he enslave you, but he himself be free as ye. For to you I make this Ring away, wise sisters of the waters' deep; the fire that burns me, let it cleanse the evil toy; and ye shall melt and keep it harmless, the Rhinegold robbed from you to weld to ill and bondage. One only shall rule, All-father thou in thy glory! As pledge of thine eternal might, this man I bring thee: good welcome give him; he is worth it!"—Midst solemn chants Brünnhilde mounts the pyre to Siegfried's body. Gudrun, broken down with grief, remains bowed over the corpse of Gunther in the foreground. The flames meet across Brünnhild and Siegfried:—suddenly a dazzling light is seen: above the margin of a leaden cloud the light streams up, shewing Brünnhild, armed as Walküre on horse, leading Siegfried by the hand from hence. At like time the waters of the Rhine invade the entrance to the Hall: on their waves the three Water-maids bear away the Ring and Helmet. Hagen dashes after them, to snatch the treasure, as if demented,—the Daughters seize and drag him with them to the deep.

Summary

(Preliminary draft of *Siegfried's Tod*, which later on, with certain radical changes, became *Götterdämmerung*.—311).

ON THE PERFORMING OF "TANNHÄUSER."

Translator's Note

Considerable portions of this "Address" were printed in the *Neue Zeitschrift* for December 3 and 24, 1852, and January 1, 7 and 14, 1853—the extracts being chosen by the editor of that journal and arranged in a sequence other than, that of the *Ges. Schr.*, vol. v, which latter would appear to have been also the order of the original pamphlet To the first extract the editor appended a footnote: "This brochure is neither obtainable from the book-trade, nor destined for publication. It lies before us with the author's permission to make a *partial* use of it in this journal." The reasons for the "partial" permission are evident, for all the merely personal and local allusions were omitted in the *Zeitschrift*.

In *'Letters to Uhlig'* (Letter 74, August 14, '52) we read: "I am busy working at a concise address, . . . Unfortunately I can only work very slowly, as any work now tries my head extremely. Yet I hope to have done in four or five days at latest"; and in Letter 75 (August 23, '52) "Only to-day have I finished the manuscript of my 'Address on the performance of *Tannhäuser*.' It had to be more detailed than I at first thought, and I am now glad that I hit upon this way of removing a great weight from my mind. I am again much exhausted by the work, and I must now try to thoroughly recover from the effects. After ripe reflection, I found it necessary to give the manuscript at once to be printed here, so as to be able to send as quickly as possible a sufficient quantity of copies to the theatres (*privatim* and *gratis*). I have ordered two hundred, of which I will at once send you a good share, so thatyoti may be able to deliver them to the theatres, together with the scores." —

On the Performing of "Tannhäuser."

(An Address to the Directors and Performers of this Opera.)

A CONSIDERABLE number of theatres are entertaining the idea of producing my "Tannhäuser" before long. This unexpected situation, by no means due to my own initiative, has made me so keenly feel the hurtfulness of my inability to personally attend the preparations for the performances proposed, that for a long time I was in doubt as to whether I ought not to refuse my sanction to those undertakings for the present.—If the artist's work first approaches its actual fulfilment, when it is in course of preparation for direct presentment to the senses; if, therefore, the dramatic poet or composer *there* first begins to exert his definitive influence, where he has to bring his aim to intimate knowledge of the artistic organs for its realisement, and through their perfect understanding to make possible an utmost intelligible re-presentment of it: then this influence is nowhere more indispensable to him, than in the case of works with whose composition he has looked aside from customary methods of performance by the sole artistic organs forthcoming, and for their needful method has kept in eye a hitherto unwonted and un-evolved conception of the nature of the art-genre in question. To none can this have been brought more clearly home, than to myself; and it is among my greatest torments of later years, that I have not been able to be present at the individual attempts already made to perform my dramatic works, so that I might have arranged with those concerned the infinite variety of details by whose exact observance alone can the executant artists gain a thoroughly correct conception of the whole.

If paramount reasons have now inclined me to place no unconditional obstacles in the way of further performances of my earlier works, it has been in the belief that, so far as lay within my power, I might succeed in making-up for the impossibility of personal and oral intervention, by written communications to the respective managers and performers. But the number of the theatres which have announced themselves for "Tannhäuser" has so very much increased of late, that private correspondence with each several manager and performer would prove a task beyond my strength. Wherefore I seize on the expedient of the present summary, in pamphlet form, which I primarily address to all to whose understanding and goodwill I have to entrust my work.

———————————

The *Musical Directors* of our theatres have accustomed themselves, almost without exception, to allow the inscenation, and everything connected with it, to be entirely withdrawn from their concernment; in correspondence herewith, our *Regisseurs* (Stage-managers) confine their attention to the scenery, leaving the orchestra wholly out of count. From this ill state of things results the want of inner harmony, and the dramatic inefficiency, of our operatic representations. In necessary sequence, the performer has lost the habit of observing the slightest connection with a whole, and, in his isolated position toward the public, has gradually evolved to what we see him now— the opera-singer pure and simple. Now, if the musical-director regards the orchestra as a thing entirely for itself, he can only take the measure for its understanding from works of absolute Instrumental-music, such as the Symphony, and everything which departs from the forms of that genre must stay ununderstood by him. But the very thing which departs from the said forms, is just *that* whose own particular form is conditioned by an action or an emotional incident of the play; thus it cannot possibly find its explanation in Absolute Instrumental-music, but solely in that scenic incident. The conductor, therefore, who omits a strict observance of the latter, will detect nothing but caprice in the corresponding musical passages, and by his own capricious, purely-musical interpretation of them, will make them prove as much in execution; for, as he lacks any standard whereby to measure out the purely-musical essence of such passages, he is also sure to go astray in their tempo and expression. This result, again, suffices to so mislead the stage-manager and performers in their part of the business, that, losing the thread of dramatic connection between the stage and orchestra, and at last giving up all continuity of any kind, they feel urged to caprices of another sort in their performance; to caprices which, in their whole wonderful concordance, make out the stereotype conventions of our modern operatic style.

It is manifest that spirited dramatic compositions must in this wise be crippled past all recognition; it is equally certain that even the sickliest of modern Italian operas would gain immeasurably in representation, were due heed paid to that coherence which subsists in even such operas (albeit in merely the grotesquest phase). But I declare that a dramatic composition like my "Tannhäuser," whose sole potentiality of effect rests simply on the said connec- tion between scene and music, must be ruined out and out if Musical and Scenic Directors apply to its performance the methods I have just denounced. I therefore beg that musical-director whom fancy or injunction has assigned the task of producing my work, to read through my score with the very closest attention to the poem, and finally to the countless special indications for the stage performance. When convinced of the necessity for a careful handling of the Scene, it will be for him to acquaint the Regisseur with the full compass of his task. The latter will gain a most inadequate notion of that task by studying the "book" alone; were this otherwise, it would only prove the musical setting unneedful and superfluous. The majority of the stage-instructions are only to be found in the score, against the appropriate musical passages, and the Regisseur has therefore to gain a thorough knowledge of them by aid of the *Kapellmeister* (Conductor).

The Regisseur's next care will be, to come to the precisest agreement with the *Scene-painter*. In ordinary the latter, also, goes to work with no reference whatever to the musical and scenic directors; he has the "book" given him to look through, and he pays no heed to anything in it but what appears to touch himself alone, namely the bracketed passages bearing on his special work. In course of this Address, however, I shall shew how indispensable it is that this companion factor, too, should enter into the inmost intentions of the whole artwork, and how necessarily I must insist upon his reaching the clearest knowledge of those aims from the very outset.

For their dealings with the *Performers*, I have first to point out to the musical-director and stage-manager that the so-called "vocal rehearsals" should not begin until the players have become acquainted with the poem itself, in its whole extent and compass. To this end we must not content ourselves with the book's being sent to each member of the company, for his or her perusal; we desire on their part no critical knowledge of the subject, but a living, an artistic one. I must therefore press for a meeting of the whole body of performers, under conduct of the Regisseur and attended by the Kapellmeister, at which the poem shall be gone through in the fashion usual with a spoken play, each individual performer reading his rôle aloud; the chorus-singers should likewise attend this reading, and their passages are to be recited by either the Chorus-director himself or one of the chorus-leaders. Care should also be taken, that this trial-reading is given with full dramatic accent; and if, from lack of practice or understanding, the right expression proper to the subject as a poem is not attainable at once, then this rehearsal must be repeated until the needful expression is won from a thorough understanding both of the situations and the inner organism of the plot. Such a demand upon a modern opera-troupe, just as it is in fact a quite unusual one, will certainly be deemed exorbitant, pedantic, and altogether needless; but this very fear of mine throws light enough on the lamentable condition of our Opera affairs. Our singers are wont to busy themselves with the How of execution before they have learnt to know its What: they study the notes of their voice-parts at their own pianos, and, when got by heart, pick up the dramatic by-play in a few stage-rehearsals —too often, only at the dress-rehearsal—in whatever fashion may be dictated by operatic routine and certain fixed suggestions of the Regisseur's for their comings and goings. That they are to be Players in the first place, and only after adequate preparation for their office as such should they venture on concernment with the enhanced, the musical expression of their talk—this, at any rate in the present state of Opera, can by no means fall within their reckoning. Their habit may perhaps seem justified by the products of most opera-composers, yet I must state that my work demands a method of performance directly opposite to the customary. That singer who is not equal to reciting his "part" as a play-rôle, with an expression duly answering to the *poet's* aim, will certainly be neither able to sing it in accordance with the aim of the *composer*, to say nothing of representing the character in its general bearings. By this assertion of mine I stand so firmly, and I hold so definitely to the fulfilment of my stipulation for sufficient reading-rehearsals, that, as against this claim on my side, I once for all express the wish—nay, the will—that, should these reading-rehearsals fail to rouse among those concerned an all-round interest in the subject and its projected exposition, my work shall be laid on the shelf and its production given up.

Upon the results of the reading-rehearsals, and the spirit in which they have been carried out, I therefore make depend the happy outcome of all further study. It is in them that the performers and the ordainers of the performance have to come to an exact and exhaustive agreement upon *everything* which in usual course is left to the helter-skelter of the final stage-rehearsals. More especially will the musical- director have gained a fresh, an essentially heightened view-point for his later labours; led by the first material impression of the whole, as furnished him by the hearing of an expressive lection, in his subsequent rehearsing of the purely-musical detail he will go to work with needful knowledge of the artist's aim—as to which he must otherwise have cherished doubt and error of all kinds, however sincere his zeal for the enterprise.

As concerns the musical study with the Singers, I have the following general remarks to make. In my opera there exists no distinction between so-called "declaimed" phrases and phrases "sung," but my declamation is song withal, and my song declamation. A definite arrest of "song" and definite commencement of the usual "recitative"— whereby, in Opera, the singer's method of delivery is wont to be divided into two completely different kinds—does not take place with me. To the true Italian Recitative, in which the composer leaves the rhythm of the notes almost entirely undefined, and hands over its completion to the singer's good pleasure, I am an utter stranger; no, in passages where the poem drops from a more impassioned lyric flight, to the mere utterance of feeling discourse, I have never made away the right to prescribe the phrasing just as strictly as in the purely lyric measures. Whoever, therefore, confounds these passages with the customary Recitative, and in consequence transforms from pure caprice their stated rhythm, he defaces my music quite as much as though he fathered other notes and harmonies upon my lyric Melody. As in the said recitative-like passages I have throughout laboured to denote their phrasing in exact rhythmic accordance with the 'aim' of my Expression, so I crave of conductors and singers that they first should execute these passages in the strict value both of notes and bars, and in a tempo corresponding to the sense of the words. If I have been so fortunate, however, as to find rny indications for the delivery correctly felt, and thereafter definitely adopted, by the singers: then at last I urge an almost entire abandonment of the rigour of the musical beat, which was up to then a mere mechanical aid to agreement between composer and singer, but with the complete attainment of that agreement is to be thrown aside as a worn-out, useless, and thenceforth an irksome tool. From the moment when the singer has taken into his fullest knowledge my intentions for the rendering, let him give the freest play to his natural sensibility, nay, even to the physical necessities of his breath in the more agitated phrases; and the more creative he can become, through the fullest freedom of Feeling, the more will he pledge me to delighted thanks. The conductor will then have only to follow the singer, to keep untorn the bond which binds the vocal rendering with the orchestral accompaniment; on the other hand, this will be possible to him only when the orchestra itself is brought to exactest knowledge of the vocal phrasing—a result only to be brought about, on the one side, by the words and music for the voice being copied into each single orchestral part, and on the other, by sufficiently frequent rehearsals. The surest sign of the conductor's having completely solved his task in this respect would be the ultimate experience, at the production, that his active lead is scarcely noticeable. (I need hardly say that the mode of execution above-denoted—this highest point attainable in artistic phrasing—is not to be confounded with that too customary, where the conductor is held to have acquitted himself most ably when he places his whole intelligence and practised skill at the command of our prima-donnas' wayward whims, as their heedful, cringing lackey: here he is the bounden cloaker of revolting solecisms, but there the co-creative artist)

I now turn from these general observations on the chief lines of study, to impart my particular wishes as regards the special points in "Tannhäuser"; and here, again, I first shall keep in eye the functions of the Musical Director.

In view of certain circumstances unfavourable to the original production of "Tannhäuser," I saw myself forced at the time into various *omissions*. That most of them, however, were mere concessions wrung from me by utmost Want concessions, in truth, equivalent to a half surrender of my real artistic aim, this I would make clear to future conductors and performers of the opera, in order to convince them that, if they regard those concessions as conditions *sine quâ non*, I must necessarily assume withal their surrender of my intrinsic aim in crucial places. —

At Dresden, then, as early as the scene between *Tannhäuser* and *Venus* in the First Act I saw myself compelled (in the above sense) to plan an omission for the later representations: I cut the second verse of Tannhäuser's song and the immediately-preceding speech of Venus. This was by no means because these passages in themselves had proved flat, unpleasing, or ineffective, but the real reason was as follows: the whole scene failed in performance, above all because we had not succeeded in finding a thoroughly suitable representatrix for the difficult rôle of Venus; the rare and unwonted demands of this rôle were doomed to non-fulfilment by one of the greatest artists herself, because inexpugnable circumstances deprived her of the unconstraint required by her task. Thus the portrayal of the whole scene was involved in an embarrassment that became at last a positive torture, to the actress, to the public, and most of all to myself. I therefore resolved to make that torture as short as possible, and consequently shortened the scene by omitting a passage which (if anything was to be cut at all) not only was the best adapted for excision, but was also of such a nature, in itself, that Its omission spared the principal male singer no insignificant exertion. This was the sole cause of the abbreviation, and every inducement to continue it would vanish at once where there was no real ground for fear about the success of this scene as a whole. In fact, the very portion of this scene which failed at Dresden, despite the efforts of one of our greatest female artists, succeeded perfectly at Weimar later on, where Venus had a representatrix who certainly could not compare in general with my Dresdener, as artist, yet was so favourably disposed to this particular rôle, and discharged her task with such warmth and freedom from constraint, that this same distressing Dresden scene made the most profound impression here. Under like circumstances the said omission will become nothing less than a senseless mutilation, the verdict whereon I leave to whoever will take the trouble to closely examine the structure of the whole scene, with its gradual growth of mood and situation from their first beginnings to their final outburst; he will bear me witness, I trust, that that cut lops off an organically essential member from the natural body of this scene; and only where the effect of this extremely weighty scene must be given up in advance, could I consent again to its omission—though in such a case I would far rather advise the whole production being given up.

A second omission affects the orchestral postlude of the closing-scene of the First Act The passage struck-out was intended to accompany a scenic incident (the joyous tumult of the chase, as huntsmen fill the stage from every side) of such animation as I was unable to get enacted upon even the Dresden boards. Owing to the uncommon stiffness and conventionality of our usual stage-supers and such-like, the effect could not be brought to that exuberance of spirits which I had intended, and which should have offered the fitting climax to a mood (*Stimmung*) led over into keenest feeling of life's freshness. Where this effect cannot be brought about, then, the music also must keep to its shortened form. On the other hand, where a combination of favourable circumstances shall enable the regisseur to bring-out the full scenic effect intended by me, there nothing but an undocked rendering of the postlude can realise my whole original aim: namely, through an entirely adequate impression of the scene, to raise to its utmost height the *Stimmung* roused by the previous situation—to a height whereon alone can a bustling passage for the violins, omitted from the prelude to the Second Act, be rightly understood.

In the scores sent to the theatres a third omission will be found marked down in the long closing-scene of the Second Act, from page 326 to 331. This bracketed passage comprises one of the weightiest moments in the drama. In its predecessor we had been shewn the effect of Elisabeth's sacrificial courage, her profoundly moving and assuaging plea for her lover, upon those to whom she had immediately addressed herself—the prince, the knights and minstrels in very act of hounding Tannhäuser to the death: Elisabeth and this surrounding, with their mutual attitude toward one another, took all our interest, which concerned itself but indirectly with Tannhäuser himself. But when this first imperative interest is satiated, our sympathy turns back at last to the chief figure in the whole complex situation, the outlawed knight of Venus; Elisabeth and all the rest become a mere surrounding of the man about whom our urgent Feeling demands to be in so far set at rest, as it shall gain clear knowledge of the impression made by this appalling catastrophe upon its prime originator. After his fanatical defiance of the men's attack, *Tannhäuser*—most terribly affected by Elisabeth's intervention, the expression of her words, the tone of her voice, and the conscience of his hideous blasphemy against her— has fallen to the ground in final outbreak of the shattering sense of utter humiliation, thus plunging from the height of frenzied ecstasy to awful recognition of his present lot: as though unconscious, he has lain with face turned earthwards while we listened breathless to the effect proclaimed by his surrounding. Now Tannhäuser lifts up his head, his features blanched and seared by fearful suffering; still lying on the ground and staring vacantly before him, he begins with more and more impetuous accents to vent the feelings of his bursting heart:

(01)

> To lead the sinner to salvation,
> God's messeng'ress to me drew nigh;
> but, ah! that vilest desecration
> should lift to her its scathing eye!

O Mary Mother, high above earth's dwelling
who sent'st to me the angel of my weal—
have mercy on me, sunk in sin's compelling,
who shamed the heavenly grace thou didst reveal!

These words, with the expression lent them by this situation, contain the pith of Tannhäuser's subsequent existence, and form the axis of his whole career; without our having received with absolute certainty the impression meant to be conveyed by them at this particular crisis, we are in no position to maintain any further interest in the hero of the drama. If we have not been here at last attuned to deepest fellow-suffering with Tannhäuser, the drama will run its whole remaining course without consistence, without necessity, and all our hitherto-aroused awaitings will halt unsatisfied. Even Tannhäuser's recital of his sufferings, in the Third Act, can never compensate us for the missed impression; for that recital can only make the full effect intended, when it links itself to our memory of this earlier, this decisory impression.

What could have determined me, then, to omit this very passage from the second, and all later Dresden performances? My answer might well include the history of all the troubles I have had to suffer, both as poet and musician, from our Opera-affairs; but I here will put the matter "briefly. The first representative of Tannhäuser—unable, in his capacity of eminently-gifted singer, to grasp anything beyond the "Opera" proper—could not succeed in seizing the characteristic nature of a claim which addressed itself more to his acting powers, than to his vocal talent In keeping with the situation, the aforesaid passage is accompanied by whispered phrases for all the singers on the stage, their voices at times, however, threatening to hastily break short Tannhäuser's motif with warnings of their smothered anger: in the eyes of our singers, this gave the passage all the semblance of an ordinary concerted piece, in which no individual thinks himself entitled to take a prominent lead. Now the obstinacy of this error must bear the blame that this passage's true import, the high relief given to Tannhäuser's personality, was completely lost in the performance, and that the whole situation, with its needful breadth of musical treatment, acquired the character of one of those

Adagio-ensembles which we are wont to hear precede the closing *Stretto* of an opera-Finale. In the light of such an Adagio-section, dragging itself along without a change, the whole thing must necessarily appear too spun-out and fatiguing; and when the question of a cut arose, to stem the manifest displeasure, it was just this passage that —seeing it had been robbed, in performance, of its proper import—appeared to me a tedious 'length', i.e., a *void*. But I ask any intelligent person to judge my humour toward the external success of my work at Dresden, and whether a twenty-fold performance, with regularly repeated "calls" for the author, could repay me for the gnawing consciousness that a large portion of the received applause was due to nothing but a misunderstanding, or at least a thoroughly defective understanding, of my real artistic aim! If in future my intentions are to be better met, and my aim realised in fact, I must especially insist on a correct rendering of the passage just discussed at length, since it is no longer to be excised. In those days its omission, and the consequent abandonment of its whole import, resulted in all interest in Tannhäuser completely vanishing at the close of the Second Act, and centering simply in his environment and opposites—thus altogether nullifying my intrinsic aim. In the Third Act Tannhäuser was met by this lack of interest to such a point, that people troubled themselves about his subsequent fate merely insofar as the fate of Elisabeth and even Wolfram, now raised into the virtual protagonists, appeared to hang upon it: only the truly marvellous ability and staying-power of the singer of the chief rôle, when in sonorous and energetic accents he told the story of his pilgrimage, could laboriously re-awaken interest in himself. Wherefore my prayer goes out to every future exponent of Tannhäuser, to lay utmost weight -on the passage in question; his delivery of it will not succeed till, even in midst of that delivery, he gets full feeling that at this moment he is master of the dramatic, as well as the musical situation, that the audience is listening exclusively to *his* utterance, and that this latter is of such a kind as to instil the deepest sense of awe. The cries: *"Ach! erbarm' dich mein!"* demand so piercing an accent, that he here will not get through as a merely well-trained singer; no, the highest dramatic art must yield him all the energy of grief and desperation, for tones which must seem to break from the very bottom of a heart distraught by fearful suffering, like an outcry for redemption. It must be the conductor's duty, to see to it that the desired effect be made possible to the chief performer through the most discreet accompaniment, on part alike of the other singers and the orchestra.—

Yet another omission was I obliged to make in this closing scene of the Second Act, namely of the passage occupying pages 348 to 356 of the score. It came about for precisely the same reasons as in the case of the passage last referred-to, and was merely a consequence of the prior cut having grown inevitable: i.e., I felt that any interest in Tannhäuser, in this Act, was past praying for. The essence of the present passage is the renewed assumption of supremacy by Elisabeth, and more especially by Tannhäuser, as they approach their surrounding, which hitherto has filled the centre of the stage: here the theme of the men, with its command to Rome, is taken up by Elisabeth in fashion of an ardent prayer for her lover; Tannhäuser adds to the song the impassioned cries of broken-hearted penitence, athirst for action; while the remainder of the men break forth anew with threats and execrations. Whether this passage—which certainly belongs to the strictest sequence of the situation—shall be retained in future representations, I must make dependent on its outcome in the stage-rehearsals. If in the long run it should not entirely succeed, i.e., should it not bring about a heightening of the situation through the animation displayed by the surrounding; above all, if the singer of Tannhäuser should feel himself and his voice too sorely taxed by what has gone before, and especially by that aforesaid passage in *adagio*, to sing this too with fullest energy,—then I myself must strenuously advise that the cut shall here hold good: for only by the amplest force of acting and delivery, will the effect intended here be still attainable. In that event I must console myself that the chief matter, the focusing of the main interest on himself, has been compassed through Tannhäuser's enthralling effect in the Adagio, and must content myself with the further effect reserved for him to produce at the supreme moment of his exit. To that moment I should wish this performer's attention most emphatically directed. The men, affronted and incensed afresh at sight of the hated one's delay, are in act to carry out their threats with hand upon the sword-hilt; an adjuring gesture of Elisabeth's holds them back to the path which *she* has won: then suddenly there rings from out the valley the chant of the Younger Pilgrims, like a voice of promise and atonement; as it enchains the rest, so it falls on Tannhäuser with a summons from the tempest of his blind remorse. Like a flash from heaven, a sudden ray of hope invades his tortured soul; tears of ineffable woe well from his eyes; an irresistible impulse carries him to the feet of Elisabeth; he dares not lift to her his look, but presses the hem of her garment to his lips with passionate ardour. Hastily he leaps to his feet once more; hurls from his breast the cry: "To Rome!" with an expression as though the whole swift-kindled hope of a new life were urged into the sound; and rushes from the stage with burning steps. This action, which must be carried out with greatest sharpness and in briefest time, is of the most determinant weight for the final impression of the whole Act; and it is this impression that is absolutely indispensable, through the mood in which it leaves the public, for making possible the full effect of the difficult Third Act.—

The abridged version of the long instrumental introduction to the Third Act, as contained in the scores revised for the theatres, is the one I now wish kept-to. When first composing this piece, I allowed the subject of expression to betray me into almost recitative-like phrases for the orchestra; at the performance, however, I felt that their meaning might well be intelligible to myself, who carried in my head the fancy-picture of the incidents thus shadowed, but not to others. Nevertheless I must insist on a complete rendering of this tone-piece in its new shape, since I deem it indispensable for establishing the *Stimmung* needed by what follows.

For similar reasons to those given above, after the first representation I saw myself compelled to effect an omission in Elisabeth's Prayer, namely that marked on pages 396 to 398. That the weightiest motivation of Elisabeth's self-offering and death thus went by the board, must be obvious to anyone who will examine carefully the words and music here. Certainly, if the simple outlines of this tone-piece, completely bare of musical embroidery, are to avoid the effect of monotonous length for that of an outflow of sincere emotion, its delivery demands a conception and devotion to the task such as we can seldom hope to meet among our dainty opera-singeresses. Here the mere technical cultivation of even the most brilliant of voices will not suffice us; by no art of absolute-musical execution can this Prayer be made interesting; but *that* actress alone can satisfy my aim, who is able to feel-out Elisabeth's piteous situation, from the first quick budding of her affection for Tannhäuser, through all the phases of its growth, to the final efflorescence of the death-perfumed bloom—as it unfolds itself in this prayer,—and to feel this with the finest organs of a true woman's sensibility. Yet that only the highest dramatic, and particularly the highest *vocal* art, can make it possible to bring this sensibility to outward operation this is a thing that just *those* lady-singers will be the first to recognise, who have erewhile been clever enough at tricking a feelingless heap of loungers out of their ennui through their own most blinding arts, but cannot help perceiving the utter futility of their juggling-feats when confronted with the present task. —The initial inexperience of my Dresden actress must bear the blame, that I was forced to immolate the passage here referred-to; in course of the later performances I had reason to hope for a successful issue of the *whole* Prayer, were I to restore it to its integrity. But another experience made me hold my hand, and I consider this a most appropriate place for imparting it to the conductors and performers of my opera, in form of the following exhortation. — Whatever characteristic feature of a dramatic work we deem expedient to omit from the first few representations, can never be restored in subsequent performances. The first impression, even when a faulty one, fixes itself alike for public and performers as a definite, a given thing; and any subsequent change, albeit for the better, will always take the light of a derangement The performers in particular, after once getting over the worry and excitement of the first few nights, soon accustom themselves to holding their achievements, as set and moulded during this incubatory process, for something inviolable by any meddling hand; whilst carelessness and gradual indifference add their share, at last, toward making it impossible to deal afresh with a problem now considered solved. For this reason I entreat directors and performers to come to an agreement, upon everything I here am bringing under their notice, *before* the first production. What they are able to achieve, or not, must be definitely established in the stage-rehearsals, if not earlier; and, saving under utmost stress, one should therefore not decide upon omissions with the sorry hope that what has been neglected may be made good again in later performances: for this it never comes to. In like manner one must not at once feel prompted to lop away this or that passage because of insufficient success at the first public performance, but rather have care that its success shall not be lacking in the next; for where one attempts to make an organically-coherent work more palatable through excisions, one merely bears witness to one's own incapacity, and the enjoyment that seems hereby brought within reach at last is no enjoyment of the work as such, but only a self-deception, inasmuch as the work is taken for something other than it really is.

Now the genuine triumph of the representress of Elisabeth would consist in this: that she not only should give due effect to the Prayer in its entirety, but should further maintain that effect at such a pitch, by the magic of her acting, as to make possible an unabridged performance of its pantomimic postlude. I am well aware that this task is no less difficult than the vocal rendering of the Prayer itself; therefore only where the actress feels quite confident of her effect in this solemn dumb-show, do I wish sanction given to the undocked execution of this scene.

As regards the *revision of the opera's close,* upon whose observance I rigidly insist, I have first to beg all those who do not like this change—owing to impressions harboured from its earlier arrangement,—to consider what I have just said about first performances and repetitions. The revised Close stands towards its first version as the working-out to the sketch, and I soon experienced the pressing need of this working-out; whilst the very fact of my effecting it, may prove to every one that I do not obstinately abide by my first draughts, and therefore, when I press for the reinstatement of passages omitted earlier, that it is not from any blind affection for my works. When I first composed this closing scene I had just as complete an image of it in my brain, as I since have worked-out in its second version; not an atom here is changed in the intention, but merely that intention is more distinctly realised. The truth is, I had built too much on certain scenic effects, which proved inadequate when brought to actual execution: the mere glowing of the

Venusberg, in the farthest background, was not enough to produce the disquieting impression which I meant to lead up to the denouement; still less could the lighting of the windows of the Wartburg (also in the most distant background) and the far-off strains of the Dirge bring the catastrophic moment, which enters with Elisabeth's death, to instantaneous perception by an unbiased spectator not familiar with the literary and artistic details of the subject My experiences hereanent were so painfully convincing, that the very non-understanding of this situation afforded me a cogent reason for remodelling the closing-scene; and in no other way could this be accomplished, than by making Venus herself draw near, with witchcraft sensible to ear and eye, whilst Elisabeth's death is no longer merely hinted at, but the dying Tannhäuser sinks down upon her actual corse. Although the effect of this change was complete and decisive on the unbiased public, yet I can easily imagine how the art-connoisseur, already familiar with the earlier form—and that through his having acquired a clue to the situation by a study of the poem and music apart from representment,—must have found it disconcerting. This I the more readily comprehend, as the new Close could only be represented in a very halting style at Dresden: it had to be carried-out with the existing scenic material from the First Act, and with none of the fresh scenery which it required; moreover (as I have already mentioned) the rôle of Venus was one of the least satisfactorily rendered in that production, and thus her reappearance in itself could make no favourable impression. These grounds, however, are quite untenable against the validity of the new Close when it is a question, as now, of producing Tannhäuser for the first time on other stages and under quite other conditions, and therefore I cannot grant them the least regard.

Still reserving my discussion of this closing-scene with the regisseur, and especially the scene-painter, I have next to inform the musical-director that I deemed necessary to omit from the second edition the final chorus of the Younger Pilgrims, occurring in the first arrangement; after what has gone before, it is easy for this chorus to appear a length too much, if by the amplest vocal forces, on the one side, and a striking portrayal of the scene on the other, it be not brought to a powerful effect of its own. The chant is sung exclusively by soprano and alto voices: these must be available in considerable number and great beauty of tone; the approach of the singers must be so contrived that, despite the mere gradual arrival of the whole choir upon the stage, yet the chant is sounded from the ver) r first with utmost possible fulness; and finally, the scene must very effectively reproduce the valley's glowing flush at break of dawn, — if the Director is to feel justified in carrying out this Close of the opera in its entirety. Only the largest and amplest-equipped theatres, however, can command the needful means for the effect last-named; but these alone, by supplying the conditions necessary for retaining this Pilgrims'-chant, could also fully meet my aim; for, with its announcement of the miracle, and as forming the counterpart to Tannhäuser's story of his reception in Rome, this chant at any rate rounds off the whole in a thoroughly satisfying manner. (02)

Before I quite turn my back on the musical-director, (03) I have a few things to discuss with him as regards the *Orchestra*, and chiefly in reference to the phrasing of the *Overture*.—The theme with which this tone-piece begins, will at once be correctly grasped by the wind-instrumentists, if the conductor insists on their all taking breath together at the right caesura in the melody; this invariably precedes the upstroke leading to the 'good' bar of the rhythm, and thus occurs in the third, fifth, seventh, &c., of the melody, as follows:

In order to gain the effect intended, in imitation of a chorus sung to words, I further beg an alteration in the fourth and twelfth bars of the bassoon-parts, resolving the rhythm

into

When the trombones later take up the same theme *forte*, this breathing-mark will not of course hold good, but, for sake of the needful strength and duration of tone, the blowers must take breath as often as they require.—The *fortissimo* passage, from the third bar of page 5 to the second bar of page 10, should be executed by the accompanying instruments (i.e., the whole orchestra except the trombones, tuba, and drums) in such a manner that, whereas a full *fortissimo* marks the first beat of every bar, the second and third crotchets are played with decreasing force. Thus:

Only the instruments named above, as directly occupied with the theme itself, must maintain an even strength.—At the sixth bar of page 22 the conductor should somewhat restrain the pace, which had shortly before grown almost too rapid, yet without causing any conspicuous retardation; the expression of this passage should merely be sharply contrasted with that of the former, through its obtaining a yearning— I might almost say, a panting—character, both in phrasing and in tempo. On page 23, bar 2, the accent is to be removed from the first note of the first violins; similarly in the first bar of page 24 the *fp* is to be changed to a simple *p*, for all the instruments. On page 25 the time is to be again taken somewhat more briskly; only, the conductor must guard against the theme which enters with page 26 being played too fast: for all the fire with which it is to be rendered, a too rapid tempo would give it a certain taint of levity, which I should like kept very far away from it.—In the distribution of the violins into eight groups, from page 34 onwards, it must be seen-to that the six lower groups are of equal strength, while the two upper, from page 35 on, are manned in such a fashion that the second group is stronger than the first; the first part might even be entrusted to one solitary leader, whereas the second must be numerically stronger than all the others.—The clarinetist generally mistakes the 'slur' in the first bar of page 35, and connects the first note of the triplet with the preceding ¾ crotchet; it must, on the contrary, be emphasised apart. On page 36 particular heed should be paid to the clarinet's standing sharply out from all the other instruments; even the first violin must not overshadow it, and the clarinetist must fully realise that, from its first entry on this page down to the fifth bar of page 37, his instrument takes the absolutely leading part.—A moderately brisk accelerando must commence with page 39, and not slacken until the fifth bar of page 41, when it passes into the energetic tempo there required.—From the third bar of page 50 onwards, the conductor must maintain an unbroken body of fullest tone in all the instruments; any abatement in the first eight bars must be strenuously avoided.—It is of the greatest moment for an understanding of the whole closing section of the Overture, that from page 54 onwards the violins be played in utmost *piano*, so that above their wave-like figure—almost merely whispered—the theme of the wind-instruments may be heard with absolute distinctness; for this theme, albeit it is not to be played at all loud, must forthwith rivet the attention of the hearer.— Beginning with the third bar on page 66, the conductor must accelerate the pace in regular progression, though with marked effect—in such a way that with the entry of the *fortissimo* on page 68 that pitch of rapidity is reached in which alone the trombone-theme, so greatly 'augmented' in rhythm, can be given an intelligible enunciation through its notes losing all appearance of detached and disconnected sounds.—Finally, I scarcely need lay to the heart of the conductor and band that it is only by expenditure of the utmost energy and force, that the intended effect of this unbroken *fortissimo* can be attained. After yet another acceleration of the six preceding them, the last four bars are to be slackened to a solemn breadth of measure.—

As to the "tempi" of the whole work in general, I here can only say that if conductor and singers are to depend for their time-measure on the metronomical marks alone, the spirit of their work must stand indeed in sorry case; only *then* will both discern the proper measure, when an understanding of the dramatic and musical situations, an understanding won by lively sympathy, shall let them find it as a thing that comes quite of itself, without their further seeking.

For what concerns the *manning of the orchestra*—seeing that the body of wind-instruments in this opera exceeds in no essential the usual complement of all good German orchestras—I have only to draw attention to one point, though certainly of great importance to me: I mean, the requisite effective number of *string-instruments*. German orchestras are invariably too poorly manned with 'strings'; upon the grounds of this lack of fine feeling for the truest needs of good orchestral delivery much might be said, and that pretty decisive of any verdict on the state of Music in Germany; but, to be sure, it here would lead us too far afield. Thus much is certain, that the French—however we may cry out against their frivolity—keep their smallest orchestras better manned with 'strings' than we find in Germany, often in quite celebrated bands. Now in the instrumentation of "Tannhäuser" I so deliberately kept in view a particularly strong muster of strings, that I must positively insist on all the theatres increasing their string-instruments beyond the usual tally; and my requirements may be measured by this very simple standard—I declare that an orchestra which cannot muster at least four good viola-players, can bring to hearing but a mutilation of my music.

For the musical equipment of the stage itself I have made still more unwonted demands. If I stand by the exactest observance of my instructions for the stage-music, I am justified by the knowledge that in all the more important cities of Germany there exist large and well-manned music-corps, especially belonging to the military, and from these the stage-music-corps required for "Tannhäuser" can readily be combined. Further, I know that any opposition to the fulfilment of my demand will come chiefly from the parsimony—often alas! most warrantable, as I admit—of the theatrical Directors. I must tell these Directors, however, that they can expect no manner of success from the production of my "Tannhäuser," saving when the representation is prepared with the most exceptional care in every respect; with a care such as needs must give this representation, when contrasted with customary operatic performances, the character of something quite Unwonted. And as this character has to be evinced by the whole thing, under its every aspect, it must be also shewn on the side of its external mounting; for which I count on no mere tinsel pomp and blinding juggleries, but precisely on a supplanting of these trumpery effects by a really rich and thoughtfully-planned artistic treatment of the whole alike with every detail.

I must now devote a few lines to the *Regisseur*, begging him to lay to heart what I hitherto have chiefly addressed to the Musical Director, and thence to derive a measure for my claims on the character of his own collaboration. Nothing I have said about the representation from the musical side can succeed at all, unless the most punctilious carrying-out of every scenic detail makes possible a general prospering of the dramatic whole. The stage-directions in the score, to which I drew his marked attention in my opening statement, will mostly give him an exact idea of my aim; my circumstantial instructions, with reference to certain habitually-omitted passages, may shew him what unusual weight I lay on the precisest motivation of the situations through the dramatic action; and he thence may perceive the value I attach to his solicitous co-operation in the arrangement of even the most trifling scenic incidents. I therefore entreat the regisseur to cast to the winds that indulgence alas! too customarily shewn to operatic favourites, which leaves them almost solely in the hands of the musical-director. Though, in their general belittlement of Opera as a *genre*, people have thought fit to let a singer perpetrate any folly he pleases in his conception of a situation, because "an opera-singer isn't an actor, you know, and one goes to the opera simply to hear the singing, not to see a play," —yet I declare that if this indulgence is applied to the present case, my work may as well be given up at once for lost. What I ask of the performer, will certainly not be drummed into him by sheer weight of talk; and the whole course of study laid down by me, especially the holding of reading-rehearsals, aims at making the performer a fellow-feeling, a fellow-knowing, and finally, from his own convictions, a fellow-creative partner in the production: but it is just as certain that, under prevailing conditions, this result can only be brought about by the most active co-operation of the regisseur.

So I beg the stage-director to pay special heed to the scenic action's synchronising in the precisest fashion with the various features of the orchestral accompaniment. Often it has happened to me, that a piece of by-play—a gesture, a significant glance—has escaped the attention of the spectator because it came too early or too late, and at any rate did not exactly correspond in tempo or duration with the correlated passage for the orchestra which was Influencing that same spectator in his capacity of listener. Not only does this heedlessness damage the effect of the performer's acting, but this inconsequence in the features of the orchestra confuses the spectator to such a pitch, that he can only deem them arbitrary caprices of the composer. What a chain of misunderstandings is hereby given rise to, it is easy enough to see.

I further urge the regisseur to guard against the processions in "Tannhäuser" being carried out by the stage-personnel in the manner of the customary March, now stereotyped in all our operatic productions. Marches, in the ordinary sense, are not to be found in my later operas; therefore if the entry of the guests into the Singers' Hall (Act II. Scene 4) be so effected that the choir and supers march upon the stage in double file, draw the favourite serpentine curve around it, and take possession of the wings like two regiments of well-drilled troops, in wait for further operatic business,—then I merely beg the band to play some march from "Norma" or "Belisario," but not my music. If on the contrary one thinks it as well to retain my music, the entry of the guests must be so ordered as to thoroughly imitate real life, in its noblest, freest forms. Away with that painful regularity of the traditional marching-order! The more varied and unconstrained are the groups of oncomers, divided into separate knots of friends or relatives, the more attractive will be the effect of the whole Entry. Each knight and dame must be greeted with friendly dignity, on arrival, by the Landgrave and Elisabeth; but, naturally, there must be no visible pretence of conversation—a thing that under any circumstances should be strictly prohibited in a musical drama.—A most important task, in this sense, will then be the ordering of the whole Singers'-Tourney, the easy grouping of its audience, and especially the portrayal of their changing and waxing interest in the main action. Here the regisseur must tax the full resources of his art; for only through his most ingenious tactics can this complex scene attain its due effect.

He must treat in a similar fashion the bands of Pilgrims in the First and Third Acts; the freer the play, and the more natural the groupings, the better will my aim be answered. As to the close of the First Act, where (in fact during this whole scene, albeit unobtrusively at first) the stage is gradually occupied by the full hunting retinue; and as to the close of the Third Act, where I have been obliged to make the giving of the Younger Pilgrims' chorus depend in great measure on a skilful handling of the stage—I believe I have already said enough. But one most weighty matter still remains for me to clear up with the regisseur: the execution of the opera's first scene, the *dance*—if so I may call it—in the Venusberg. I need scarcely point out that we here have nothing to do with a dance such as is usual in our operas and ballets; the ballet-master, whom one should ask to arrange such a dance-set for this music, would soon send us to the right-about and declare the music quite unsuitable. No, what I have in mind is an epitome of everything the highest choreographic and pantomimic art can offer: a wild, and yet seductive chaos of movements and groupings, of soft delight, of yearning and burning, carried to the most delirious pitch of frenzied riot. For sure, the problem is not an easy one to solve, and to pro- duce the desired chaotic effect undoubtedly requires most careful and artistic treatment of the smallest details. The 'argument' of this wild scene is plainly set forth in the score, as concerns its essential features, and I must entreat whoever undertakes its carrying out, for all the freedom I concede to his invention, to strictly maintain the prescribed chief-moments; a frequent hearing of the music, rendered by the orchestra, will be the best means of inspiring any person in the least expert with the devices whereby to make the action correspond therewith.—

This scene now brings me into contact with the *Scene-painter*, whom I shall henceforth figure to myself as in close alliance with the Machinist Only through an accurate knowledge of the whole poetic subject, and after a careful agreement as to the scheme of its portrayal with the Regisseur—and the Kapellmeister—too will the scene-painter and machinist succeed in giving the stage its needful aspect In the absence of such an agreement, how often must it happen that, for mere sake of employing work already executed by the scene-painter and machinist after a one-sided acquaintance with the subject, one is forced at the last moment to embark on violent distortions of the intrinsic aim!

The main features of the Venusberg scenery, whose mechanical structure must accurately fit-in with that for the Wartburg valley set in readiness behind it (an arrangement favoured by the mountainous projections common to both), are sufficiently indicated in the score. However, the shrouding of this scene with a veil of rosy mist, to narrow down its space, Is a somewhat difficult matter: all the intended witchery would be destroyed, if this were clumsily effected by pushing forward, and dropping down, a massive cloud-piece. After many a careful trial, this veiling was most effectively carried-out at Dresden by gradually lowering a number of vaporous sheets of painted gauze, let slowly fall behind each other; so that not until the contours of the previous scene had become quite unrecognisable, was a massive rose-tinted canvas back-cloth let down behind these veils, thus completely shutting-in the scene. The tempo also was accurately reckoned, so as to coincide with the music.—The main change of scene is then effected at one stroke, as follows: the stage is suddenly plunged in darkness, and first the massive cloud-cloth, and immediately thereafter the veils of gauze, are drawn swiftly up; where-upon the light is instantly turned on again, revealing the new scene, the valley bathed in brilliant sunshine. The effect of this valley-picture—which must be mounted in strict accordance with the directions in the score—should be so overpoweringly fresh, so invitingly serene, that the poet and musician may be allowed to leave the spectator to its impression for a while.

The decorations for the Second Act, shewing the Singers'-Hall in the Wartburg, were so admirably designed for the Dresden production, by an eminent French artist, that I can only advise each theatre to procure a copy and mount this scene in accordance with it. The arrangement of the stage, as regards the tiers of seats for the guests at the Singers'-tourney, was also so happily effected there, that I have only to urge an employment of the plans, which may easily be obtained from Dresden.

Less happily did the scenery for the Third Act turn out at Dresden; not until after the production of the opera did it become evident that a special canvas should have been painted for this Act, whereas I had fancied we could manage with the second back-cloth from the First But it proved beyond the most ingenious artifice of lighting, to give to the same canvas, previously reckoned for the brightest eifect of a spring morning, the autumn-evening aspect so needful to the Third Act Above all, the magic apparition of the Venusberg could not be effectually rendered with this scenery, so that—as already said —for the second version I had to content myself with somewhat mconsequently letting drop once more the veilings of the First Act; whereby the whole apparition of Venus was driven much too much into the foreground, and thus quite missed its effect of a beckoning from afar. I therefore engage the scene-painter, to whom the mounting of this opera is confided, to insist on a special canvas being provided for the Third Act, and to treat it in such a way that it shall reproduce the last scene of the First Act in the tones of autumn and evening, but with strict observance of the fact that the valley is eventually to be shewn in the glowing flush of dawn.—Then for the spectral apparition of the Venusberg something like the following mode might be adopted. At the passage indicated in the score the lights should be very much lowered, while half-way up the stage two veils are dropped, one after the other, completely concealing the contours of the valley in the background; immediately afterwards the distant Venusberg, now painted as a transparency, must be lit with a roseate glow. The inventive talent of the scene-painter and machinist should next devise some means whereby the effect may be produced as though the glowing Venusberg were drawing nearer, and stretching wide enough—now that we can see through it—to hold within it groups of dancing figures, whose whirling movements must be plainly visible to the spectator. When the whole hinder stage is occupied by this apparition, Venus herself will then be seen, reclining on a litter. The perspective, however, must still appear as distant as is consistent with the size of actual human figures. The phantom's vanishing will then be brought about by a rapid diminution and final extinction of the rosy lighting of the background, which till then had grown more and more vivid— therefore by the stage being momentarily plunged in total darkness, during which the whole apparatus required by this vision of the Venusberg is to be speedily removed. Next, and while the dirge is being chanted, one perceives through the two still-hanging veils the lights and torches of the funeral train, as it descends from the heights at the back. Then the veils are drawn slowly up, one after the other, and at like time the gradual grey of early morn fills all the scene; to pass at last, as said, into the glowing flush of dawn.

The scene-painter may see, then, how infinitely important to me is his intelligent collaboration—nay, how alone enabling—and that I assign to him a certainly not un-decisive share in the success of the whole; a success only to be won through a clear and instant understanding of the most unwonted situations. But only a close and genuinely artistic acquaintance with my inmost aims, on his part, can secure me that collaboration.

––––––––––

After this somewhat circumstantial disquisition, I must turn at last to the *Actors* in particular. I cannot, however, attempt to discuss with them the minutiæ of their rôles; to gain a full and fitting opportunity for this, I should need to enter on a personal and friendly intercourse with each performer. Therefore I must confine myself to what I have already said about the needful mode of approaching the general study, in the hope that through familiarity with my intentions the performers will of themselves attain the power of executing them. But in all that I have addressed to the Musical Director, in the first place, my claims upon the players are so markedly involved, and in dealing with individual situations I have found occasion to so exactly motivate these claims, that I need only add that my requirements for the conception of those single passages must hold good for every other detail of the performance.—

Yet I deem it as well to go a little deeper into the character of the principal rôles.

Indisputably the hardest rôle is that of *Tannhäuser* himself, and I must admit that it may be one of the hardest problems ever set before an actor. The essentials of this character, in my eyes, are an ever prompt and active, nay, a brimming-over saturation with the emotion woken by the passing incident, and the lively contrasts which the swift changes of situation produce in the utter- ance of this fill of feeling. Tannhäuser is nowhere and never "a little" anything, but each thing fully and entirely. With fullest transport has he revelled in the arms of Venus; with keenest feeling of the necessity for his breaking from her, does he tear the bonds that bound him to Love's Goddess, without one moment's railing at her. With fullest unreserve he gives himself to the overpowering impression of re-entered homely Nature, to the familiar round of old sensations, and lastly to the tearful outburst of a childlike feeling of religious penitence; the cry: "Almighty, Thine the praise! Great are the wonders of Thy grace!" is the instinctive outpour of an emotion which usurps his heart with might resistless, down to its deepest root. So strong and upright is this emotion, and the felt need of reconciliation with the world—with the World in its widest, grandest sense—that he sullenly draws back from the encounter with his former comrades, and shuns their proffered reconcilement: no turning-back will he hear of, but only thrusting-on towards a thing as great and lofty as his new-won feeling of the World itself. This one, this nameless thing, that alone can satisfy his present longing, is suddenly named for him with the name "Elisabeth": Past and Future stream together, with lightning quickness, at mention of this name; while he listens to the story of Elisabeth's love they melt in one great flood of flame, and light the path that leads him to new life. Wholly and entirely mastered by this latest, this impression never felt before, he shouts for very joy of life, and rushes forth to meet the loved one. The whole Past now lies behind him like a dim and distant dream; scarce can he call it back to mind: one thing alone he knows of, a tender, gracious woman, a sweet maid who loves him; and one thing alone lies bare to him within this love, one thing alone in its rejoinder,—the burning, all-consuming fire of Life.— With this fire, this fervour, he tasted once the love of Venus, and instinctively must he fulfil what he had freely pledged her at his parting: "'gainst all the world, henceforth, her doughty knight to be." This World tarries not in challenging him to the combat In it— where the Strong brims full the sacrifice demanded of it by the Weak—man finds his only passport to survival in an endless accommodation of his instinctive feelings to the all-ruling mould of use and wont (*Sitte*). Tannhäuser, who is capable of nothing but the most direct expression of his frankest, most instinctive feelings, must find himself in crying contrast with this world; and so strongly must this be driven home upon his Feeling, that for sake of sheer existence, he has to battle with this his opposite in a struggle for life or death. It is this one necessity that absorbs his soul, when matters come to open combat in the "Singers'-tourney"; to content it he forgets his whole surrounding, and casts discretion to the winds: and yet his heart is simply fighting for his love to Elisabeth, when at last he flaunts his colours openly as Venus' knight. Here stands he on the summit of his life-glad ardour, and naught can dash him from the pinnacle of transport whereon he plants his solitary standard 'gainst the whole wide world,—nothing but the one experience whose utter newness, whose variance with all his past, now suddenly usurps the field of his emotions: the woman who *offers up herself* for love of him.—Forth from that excess of bliss on which he fed in Venus' arms, he had yearned for—Sorrow: this profoundly human yearning was to lead him to the woman who *suffers* with him, whilst Venus had but joyed. His claim is now fulfilled, and no longer can he live aloof from griefs as overwhelming as were once his joys. Yet these are no sought-for, no arbitrarily chosen griefs; with irresistible might have they forced an entrance to his heart through fellow-feeling, and it nurtures them with all the energy of his being, even to self-annihilation. It is here that his love for Elisabeth proclaims the vastness of its difference from that for Venus: her whose gaze he can no longer bear, whose words pierce his breast like a sword—to her must he atone, and expiate by fearsome tortures the torture of her love for him, though Death's most bitter pang should only let him distantly forebode that last atonement—Where is the suffering that he would not gladly bear? Before that world, confronting which he stood but now its jubilant foe, he casts himself with willing fervour in the dust, to let it tread him under foot No likeness shews he to his fellow-pilgrims, who lay upon themselves convenient penance for healing of their own souls: only "*her* tears to sweeten, the tears she weeps o'er his great sin," seeks he the path of healing, amid the horriblest of torments; for this healing can consist in nothing but the knowledge that those tears are dried. We must believe him, that never did a pilgrim pray for pardon with such ardour. But the more sincere and total his prostration, his remorse and craving for purification, the more terribly must he be overcome with loathing at the heartless lie that reared itself upon his journey's goal It is just his utter singlemindedness, recking naught of self, of welfare for his individual soul, but solely of his love towards another being, and thus of that beloved being's weal—it is just this feeling that at last must kindle into brightest flame his hate against this world, which must break from off its axis or ever it absolved his love and him; and these are the flames whose embers of despair scorch up his heart When he returns from Rome, he is nothing but embodied wrath against a world that refuses him the right of Being for simple reason of the wholeness of his feelings; and not from any thirst for joy or pleasure, seeks he once more the Venusberg; but despair and hatred of this world he needs must flout now drive him thither, to hide him from his "angel's" look, whose "tears to sweeten" the wide world could not afford to him the balm.—Thus does he love Elisabeth; and this love it is that she returns. What the whole moral world could not, that could she when, defying all the world, she clothed her lover in her prayer, and in hallowed knowledge of the puissance of her death she dying set the culprit free. And Tannhäuser's last breath goes up to her, in thanks for this supernal gift of Love. Beside his lifeless body stands no man but must envy him; the whole world, and God Himself—must call him blessed.—

Now I declare that not even the most eminent *actor*, of our own or bygone times, could solve the task of a perfect portrayal of Tannhäuser's character on the lines laid down in the above analysis; and I meet the question: "How could I hold it possible for an opera-singer to fulfil it?" by the simple answer that to *Music* alone could the draft of such a task be offered, and only a dramatic *singer*, just through the aid of Music, can be in the position to fulfil it Where a Player would seek in vain among the means of recitation, for the expression wherewithal to give this character success, to the Singer that expression is self-offered in the music; I therefore merely beg the latter to approach his task with unrestricted warmth, and he may be certain also of achieving it.—But above all, I must ask the singer of Tannhäuser to completely give over and forget his quondam standing as Opera-singer; *as such* he cannot even dream of a possibility of solving this task. To our *tenors*, in particular, there cleaves a downright curse as outcome of their rendering of the usual tenor-rôles— giving them for the most part an unmanly, vapid, and utterly invertebrate appearance. Under the influence, and in consequence, of the positively criminal school of singing now in vogue, during the whole of their theatrical career they are accustomed to so exclusively devote their attention to the paltriest details of vocal trickery, that they seldom attain to anything beyond the care whether that G or A-flat will come out roundly, or the delight that this G-sharp or A has "taken" well. Besides this care and this delight, they generally know nothing but the pleasure of fine clothes, and the toil to make their finery and voice together bring-in as much applause as possible—above all with an eye to higher wages. (04) I grant, then, that the mere attempt to handle such a task as that of my Tannhäuser will be sufficient in itself to ruffle the composure of the singer, and that this very disquietude will induce him to alter many of his old stage habits; in fact I go so far as to hope that, if the study of Tannhäuser is conducted on the lines laid down by me, so great a change will come over the habits and notions of the singer, in favour of his task, that of itself it will lead him to the right and needful thing. But a thoroughly successful issue of his labours I can only expect when this change shall compass a total revolution in himself and his former methods of conception and portrayal—a revolution such as to make him conscious that for this project he has to become something entirely different from what he has been, the diametric opposite of his earlier self. Let him not reply that already he has had tasks set before him which made unusual demands on his gift for acting: I can prove to him that what he haply has made his own in the so-called dramatic-tenor rôles of latter days will by no means help him out with Tannhäuser; for I could shew him that in the operas of Meyerbeer, for instance, the character for which I have blamed the modern tenor is regarded as unalterable, from top to toe, in means and end, and with the utmost shrewdness. Whoever, then, relying on his previous successes in the said operas, should attempt to play Tannhäuser with merely the same expenditure on the art of portrayal as has sufficed to make those operas both widely given and universally popular, would turn this rôle into the very opposite of what it is. Above all, he would not grasp the energy of Tannhäuser's nature, and thus would turn him into an undecided, vacillating, a weak and unmanly character; since for the *superficial* observer there certainly might exist temptation to such a false conception of the part (lending it somewhat of a resemblance to "Robert the Devil"). But nothing could make the whole drama less intelligible and more disfigure the chief character, than if Tannhäuser were displayed weak, or even by fits and starts "well-meaning," bourgeoisely devout, and at most afflicted with a few reprehensible cravings. This I believe I have substantiated by the foregoing characterisation of his nature; and as I can await no understanding of my work if its chief rôle be not conceived and rendered in consonance with that characterisation, so the singer of Tannhäuser may perceive not only what an unwonted demand I make upon him, but also to what joyful thanks he'll pledge me should he fully realise my aim. I do not hesitate to say that a completely successful impersonation of Tannhäuser will be the highest achievement in the record of his art.—

After this exhaustive talk with the singer of Tannhäuser, I have but little to tell the interpreters of the remaining rôles; the main gist of what I have said to him concerns them all. The hardest tasks, after that of Tannhäuser himself, are certainly those which fall to the two ladies, the exponents of *Venus* and *Elisabeth*. As to Venus, this rôle will only succeed when to a favourable exterior the actress joins a full belief in her part; and this will come to her so soon as she is able to hold Venus completely justified in her every utterance,—so justified that she can 3 r ield to no one but the woman who offers up herself for Love. The difficulty in the rôle of Elisabeth, on the other hand, is for the actress to give the impression of the most youthful and virginal unconstraint, without betraying how experienced, how refined a womanly feeling it is, that alone can fit her for the task.— The other male parts are less exacting, and even *Wolfram*—whose rôle I can by no means hold for unconditionally easy—needs little more than to address himself to the sympathy of the finer-feeling section of our public, to be sure of winning its interest. The lesser vehemence of his directly physical instincts has allowed him to make the impressions of Life a matter of meditation; he thus is pre-eminently Poet and Artist, whereas Tannhäuser is before all Man. His standing toward Elisabeth, which a noble manly pride enables him to bear so worthily, no less than his final deep fellow-feeling for Tannhäuser—whom he certainly can never comprehend —will make him one of the most prepossessing figures. Let the singer of this part, however, be on his guard against imagining the music as easy as might at first appear: more particularly his first song in the "Singers'-tourney"—comprising, as it does, the story of the whole evolution of Wolfram's life-views, both as artist and as man—will demand a phrasing (*Vortrag*) thought-out with the most sensitive care, after a minutest pondering of the poetic subject, while it will need the greatest practice to pitch the voice to that variety of expression which alone can give this piece the right effect.—In conclusion I would gladly turn from the "Performers" to the "Singers" in particular, did I not on the one hand fear to weary, and on the other, venture to assume that what I have already said will suffice to make clear my wishes to the representants in their function, too, of vocal artists.—

So I will now close this Address, albeit with a mournful feeling that I have most imperfectly attained my object: namely, to make good by it a thing denied me, and yet the thing I deem so needful—a personal and word-of-mouth address to all concerned. (05) Amid my deep feeling of the insufficience of this by-way that I have struck, my only solace is a firm reliance on the good will of my artistic comrades; a good will such as never an artist needed more for making possible his artwork, than I need in my present plight May all whom I have addressed take thought on my peculiar lot, and above all ascribe to the mood which consequently has grown upon me any stray sentence wherein I may have shewn myself too exacting, too anxious, or even too mistrustful, rigorous and harsh.—In view of the unwontedness of such an Address as the preceding, I certainly must prepare myself for its being wholly or for the most part disregarded— perhaps not even understood—by many of those to whom it is directed. With this knowledge I therefore can only regard it as an experiment, which I cast like a die on the world, uncertain whether it shall win or lose. Yet if merely among a handful of individuals I fully reach my aim, that attainment will richly compensate me for all mischanced besides; and cordially do I grasp in anticipation the hand of those valiant artists who shall not have been ashamed to concern themselves more closely with me, and more familiarly to befriend me, than is wonted In our modern Art-world's intercourse.

Notes

01

"Zum Heil den Sündiger zu führen," &c.

02

The theatres must apply to me for the music of this chorus.—R. WAGNER.

03

Touching the vocal parts, I must mate one more request to the Kapellmeister: viz., if the singer of *Walther*, whose solos in the "Minstrel's Tourney" are pitched somewhat low (yet in any case are to be maintained in the key prescribed), should find any difficulty with the persistently high register of the concerted pieces,—to effect a change by having the notes assigned to *Heinrich der Schreiber* copied into the music-part of the former, in addition to his own solo-passages, while the higher voice is made over to Heinrich.—R. WAGNER.

04

As I direct these remarks to a whole class, and in such general terms, it naturally is impossible for me to take notice of the manifold varieties which more or less depart from the generic character; wherefore in dealing with crying faults I here must necessarily employ superlatives, which, at any rate, can find no application to many an individual case.—R. WAGNER.

05

This "Address" was written when Wagner had already spent over three years in exile,—an exile destined to last for nearly ten years more.—TR.

Summary

Unexpectedly a number of theatres now applying for its performing-rights; one of my greatest torments that I cannot be present, but must convey instructions by pen; personal correspondence being beyond my strength, I print this pamphlet.

Anarchy among Conductors, Regisseurs and Scene-painters, each working independently at German theatres. Even the sickliest Italian opera would gain immensely by heed paid to "dramatic coherence; a work like "Tannhäuser" must be ruined out and out by present methods of performance —The poem to be first read aloud by the assembled performers, in presence of chorus, with full dramatic accent; singers generally pick up their rdles at their own pianos, but until they can *recite* their parts they can never sing them in accord with even the *composer's* aim. If this not complied with, I withdraw my work. Advantage of the Conductor's attending these rehearsals. In *Tann.* no real Recitative; strict tempo to be observed by singers in the recitative-like phrases till they have mastered my aim, *then* they should give free play to natural feeling; for full agreement, words should be written out in each *orchestral part.*—Caution against misunderstanding— The cuts (to be restored) necessitated at Dresden: I, second strophe of T.'s song to Venus, because Fr. Devrient unsuited for rôle of Venus, and thus to shorten scene this entire scene at Weimar, however, made a good effect; 2, orchestral postlude to act i, because of stiffness of supers; 3, bustling violin-passage in prelude to act ii, consequent thereon. Cut 4, *Adagio* in act ii: this situation forms the axis of T.'s career, nothing can compensate us for missing its due impression; omitted because singers treated it as an ordinary ensemble, instead of simply accompanying in whispers; could a twenty-times-repeated performance at Dresden, with regular calls for author, repay me for the gnawing consciousness that my aim was misunderstood? T. must here feel that he is master of the *dramatic* situation, that the audience is listening to him alone: "*Ach! erbarm dich mein!*". Cut 5, in closing ensemble of act ii, because all interest in T. past praying for—if this passage too sorely tries singer etc. cut must be maintained, and trust to supreme effect of exit, which is indispensable for the mood in which public approaches act iii; 6, abridged version of prelude to act iii—to remain; 7, in Elisabeth's Prayer, because of Johanna Wagner's inexperience, and could not be restored later at Dresden since first impressions fix themselves on public and performers as a definite unalterable thing—the dumb-show after Prayer difficult, but vital. Revision of opera's close: first version contains same idea, but merely sketched and thus not understood; public *v* art-connoisseurs. Younger Pilgrims' Chant only to be given where scenery quite satisfactory and voices good, full and ample in number; this chant at any rate rounds off the whole in a satisfactory manner. Tempi and dynamics of overture; in general an artistic understanding v metronomical marks. Manning of orchestra, usual deficiency of strings in German theatres compared with French; 'stage-music' to be recruited from military bands. Avoid parsimony, for performance must be unwonted, in character with work.

Duties of the Regisseur: "an opera-singer isn't an actor"; discard deference to operatic favourites, and make the performer a partner in the artist's creation from his own convictions; gesture and by-play to synchronise with orchestra. Freedom of grouping in the 'Processions': Entry of Guests and a march from *Norma*; usual serpentine curve, double file, and stage-conversation, prohibited; Minstrels' Tourney; entries and exits of Pilgrims; Dance in Venusberg, a wild and yet seductive chaos—freedom of invention to Regisseur, but must follow chief indications and strictly observe the music. *Scene-painter and Machinist*: necessity of intelligent acquaintance with subject, and agreement thereon with Conductor and Regisseur. The cloud-veilings in Venusberg scene; lighting of stage; Wartburg valley to be so fresh that spectator may be left a while to its impression. French designs for Dresden mounting of act ii. Necessity of separate canvas for Wartburg valley in act iii; arrangements for making glowing Venusberg seem to draw nearer; funeral train and flush of dawn.

The rôles. That of Tannhäuser himself may be one of the hardest problems ever set before an actor: his saturation with the passing incident, and the dramatic contrasts hence arising. Never "a little" anything; naming of the nameless, 'Elisabeth;' the whole Past now lies behind him like a dream; one thing alone in this love, the all-consuming fire of Life. The moral world and how it treats the strong; a struggle for life or death; his colours flaunted openly; only one thing can daunt him—the woman who *offers up herself* for love of him. Sorrow, once yearned for, now drunk deep, "her tears to sweeten"; unlike his self-saving fellow-pilgrims. The heartless lie at his journey's end; in despair and hatred of this self-righteous world, he seeks again the Venusbcrg, to hide him from his "angel's" look. Her love-death sets the culprit free; the world, and God Himself, must call him blessed. To Music alone could such a task be proposed, and only a dramatic *singer* could fulfil it, but not as *opera-singer*. Curse that cleaves to tenors, through present criminal school of singing; vocal trickery, fine clothes, applause and high wages. This rôle will ruffle singer's composure, and force him to change his habits; but a *total* revolution needed. Not a bit like Meyerbeer's so popular "dramatic-tenor" rôles, neither vapid and unmanly like *Robert*, nor "well-meaning" with a few reprehensible cravings. A completely successful impersonation will be the highest triumph of his art. Venus must have a full *belief* in her part; so justified, that she can yield to none but the *self-offering* woman. Elisabeth needs virginal unconstraint, without betraying how much experience that requires. Wolfram addresses sympathy of more refined section of audience; pre-eminently Poet and Artist—Tannhäuser being before all Man. Performers as singers also.— Valediction: a die cast on the world, unknowing whether it shall win or lose; cordially do I giasp the hands of valiant artists who shall not be ashamed to realise my aim.

ON STATE AND RELIGION

Translator's Note

The article on *"State and Religion"* was written at the request of King Ludwig II. of Bavaria, in the same year in which Richard Wagner was summoned to his intimate companionship. It does not appear to have been printed, at least for public circulation, until nine years later *(1873)*, when it was included in Vol. viii. of the *Gesammelte Schriften*. Undoubtedly to its intimate character we owe those deeper glimpses into Wagner's inmost thought, such as we meet so often in his private correspondence.

On State and Religion.

A HIGHLY-PRIZED young friend desires me to tell him whether, and if so in what way, my views on State and Religion have changed since the composition of my art-writings in the years 1849 to 1851.

As a few years ago, at the instigation of a friend in France, I was persuaded to re-survey my views on Music and Poetry, and assemble them in one concise synopsis (namely the preface to a French prose-translation of some of my opera-poems (01)), so it might not be unwelcome to me to clear and summarise my thoughts upon that other side as well, were it not that precisely here, where everyone considers he has a right to his opinion, a definite utterance becomes more and more difficult the older and more experienced one grows. For here is shewn again what Schiller says: *"ernst ist das Leben, heiter ist die Kunst"* ("Life is earnest, Art is gay"). Perhaps, however, it may. be said of me that, having taken Art in such special earnest, I ought to be able to find without much difficulty the proper mood for judging Life. In truth I believe the best way to inform my young friend about myself, will be to draw his foremost notice to the earnestness of my artistic aims; for it was just this earnestness, that once constrained me to enter realms apparently so distant as State and Religion. What there I sought, was really never aught beyond my art—that art which I took so earnestly, that I asked for it a basis and a sanction in Life, in State, and lastly in Religion. That these I could not find in modern life, impelled me to search out the cause in my own fashion; I had to try to make plain to myself the tendence of the State, in order to account for the disdain with which I found my earnest art-ideal regarded everywhere in public life.

But it certainly was characteristic of my inquiry, that it never led me down to the arena of *politics* proper; that is to say, the politics of the day remained as entirely untouched by me, as, despite the commotion of those times, they never truly touched myself. (02) That this or that form of Government, the jurisdiction of this or that party, this or that alteration in the mechanism of our State affairs, could furnish my art-ideal with any veritable furtherance, I never fancied; therefore whoever has really read my art-writings, must rightly have accounted me unpractical; but whoever has assigned me the rôle of a political revolutionary, with actual enrolment in the lists of such, manifestly knew nothing at all about me, and judged me by an outer semblance of events which haply might mislead a police-officer, but not a statesman. Yet this misconstruction of the character of my aims is entangled also with my own mistake: through taking Art in such uncommon earnest, I took Life itself too lightly; and just as this avenged itself upon my personal fortunes, so my views thereon were soon to be given another tinge. To put the matter plainly, I had arrived at a reversal of Schiller's saying, and desired to see my earnest art embedded in a gladsome life; for which Greek life, as we regard it, had thus to serve me as a model.

From all my imaginary provisions for the entry of the Artwork into Public Life, it is evident that I pictured them as a summons to self-collection (*Sammelung*) from amid the distractions of a life which was to be conceived, at bottom, merely as a gladsome occupation (*heitere Beschäftigung*), and not as a fatiguing toil. Hence the political movements of that time did not attract my serious attention until they touched the purely social sphere, and thus appeared to offer prospects of the realisation of my ideal premises—prospects which, I admit, for some time occupied my earnest thought. The line my fancy followed was an organisation of public life in common, as also of domestic life, such as must lead of itself to a beauteous fashioning of the human race. The calculations of the newer Socialists therefore lost my sympathy from the moment they seemed to end in systems that took at first the repellent aspect of an organisation of Society for no other purpose but an equally-allotted toil. (03) However, after sharing the horror which this aspect kindled in aesthetically-cultured minds, (04) a deeper glance into the proposed condition of society made me believe I detected something very different from what had hovered before the fancy of those calcu lating Socialists themselves. I found to wit that, when equally divided among all, actual *labour*, with its crip pling burthen and fatigue, would be downright done away with, leaving nothing in its stead but an *occupation*, which necessarily must assume an artistic character of itself. A clue to the character of this occupation, as substitute for actual labour, was offered me by Husbandry, among other things; this, when plied by every member of the commonalty [or "parish" — *Gemeinde*], I conceived as partly developed into more productive tillage of the Garden, partly into joint observances for times and seasons of the day and year, which, looked at closer, would take the character of strengthening exercises, (05) ay, of recreations and festivities. Whilst trying to work out all the bearings of this transformation of one-sided labour, with its castes in town and country, into a more universal occupation lying at the door of every man, (06) I became conscious on the other hand that I was meditating nothing so intensely new, but merely pursuing problems akin to those which so dearly had busied our greatest poets themselves, as we may see in "Wilhelm Meister's Wanderjahre." I, too, was therefore picturing to myself a world that I deemed possible, but the purer I imagined it, the more it parted company with the reality of the political tendencies-of-the-day around me; so that I could say to myself, my world will never make its entry until the very moment when the present world has ceased—in other words, where Socialists and Politicians came to end, should *we* commence. (07) I will not deny that this view became with me a positive mood (*Stimmung*): the political relations of the beginning of the bygone 'fifties kept everyone in a state of nervous tension, sufficient to awake in me a certain pleasurable feeling which might rightly seem suspicious to the practical politician.

Now, on thinking back, I believe I may acquit myself of having been sobered from the aforesaid mood—not unlike a spiritual intoxication—first and merely through the turn soon taken by European politics. It is an attribute of the poet, to be riper in his inner intuition (*Anschauung*) of the essence of the world than in his conscious abstract knowledge: precisely at that time I had already sketched, and finally completed, the poem of my "Ring des Nibelungen." With this conception I had unconsciously admitted to myself the truth about things human. Here everything is tragic through and through, and the Will, that fain would shape a world according to its wish, at last can reach no greater satisfaction than the breaking of itself in dignified annulment. (08) It was the time when I returned entirely and exclusively to my artistic plans, and thus, acknowledging Life's earnestness with all my heart, withdrew to where alone can "gladsomeness" abide.—

My youthful friend will surely not expect me to give a categorical account of my later views on Politics and State: under any circumstances they could have no practical importance, and in truth would simply amount to an expression of my horror of concerning myself professionally with matters of the sort. No; he can merely be wishful to learn how things so remote from its ordinary field of action may shape themselves in the brain of a man like myself, cut out for nothing but an artist, after all that he has gone through and felt. But lest I might appear to have meant the above as a disparagement, I must promptly add that whatever I might have to put forward would strictly and solely be a witness to my having arrived at a full valuation of the great, nay, terrible earnest of the matter. The artist, too, may say of himself: "My kingdom is not of this world;" and, perhaps more than any artist now living, I may say this of myself, for very reason of the earnestness wherewith I view my art. Amid that's the hardship of it; for with this beyond-the-worldly realm of ours we stand amid a world itself so serious and so careworn, that it deems a fleeting dissipation its only fitting refuge, whereas the need for earnest elevation (*Erhebung*) has quite become a stranger to it.—

Life is earnest, and—has always been.

Whoever would wholly clear his mind on this, let him but consider how in every age, and under ever freshly-shaped, but ever self-repeating forms, this life and world have spurred great hearts and spacious minds to seek for possibility of its bettering; and how 'twas always just the noblest, the men who cared alone for others' weal and offered willingly their own in pledge, that stayed without the slightest influence on the lasting shape of things. The small success of all such high endeavours would shew him plainly that these world-improvers were victims to a fundamental error, and demanded from the world itself a thing it cannot give. Should it even seem possible that much might be ordered more efficiently in man's affairs, yet the said experiences will teach us that the means and ways of reaching this are never rightly predetermined by the single thinker; never, at least, in a manner enabling him to bring them with success before the knowledge of the mass of men. Upon a closer scrutiny of this relation, we fall into astonishment at the quite incredible pettiness and weakness of the average human intellect, and finally into shamefaced wonder that it should ever have astonished us; for any proper knowledge of the world would have taught us from the outset that blindness is the world's true essence, and not Knowledge prompts its movements, but merely a head-long impulse, a blind impetus of unique weight and violence, which procures itself just so much light and knowledge as will suffice to still the pressing need experienced at the moment. So we recognise that nothing really happens but what has issued from this not far-seeing Will, from this Will that answers merely to the momentarily-experienced need; and thus we see that practical success, throughout all time, has attended only those politicians who took account of nothing but the momentary need, neglecting all remoter, general needs, all needs as yet unfelt to-day, and which therefore appeal so little to the mass of mankind that it is impossible to count on its assistance in their ministration.

Moreover we find personal success and great, if not enduring influence on the outer fashioning of the world allotted to the violent, the passionate individual, who, unchaining the elemental principles of human impulse under favouring circumstances, points out to greed and self-indulgence the speedy pathways to their satisfaction.

To the fear of violence from this quarter, as also to a modicum of knowledge thus acquired of basic human nature, we owe the *State*. In it the Need is expressed as the human Will's necessity of establishing some workable agreement among the myriad blindly-grasping individuals into which it is divided. It is a contract whereby the units seek to save themselves from mutual violence, through a little mutual practice of restraint. As in the Nature-religions a portion of the fruits of the field or spoils of the chase was brought as offering to the Gods, to make sure of a right to enjoy the remainder, so in the State the unit offered up just so much of his egoism as appeared necessary to ensure for himself the contentment of its major bulk. (09) Here the tendence of the unit naturally makes for obtaining the greatest possible security in barter for the smallest possible sacrifice: but to this tendence, also, he can only give effect through equal-righted fellowships; and these diverse fellowships of individuals equally-entitled in their groups make up the parties in the State, the larger owners striving for a state of permanence, the less favoured for its alteration. But even the party of alteration desires nothing beyond the bringing about a state of matters in which it, too, would wish no further change; and thus the State's main object is upheld from first to last by those whose profit lies in permanence.

Stability is therefore the intrinsic tendence of the State. And rightly; for it constitutes withal the unconscious aim in every higher human effort to get beyond the primal need: namely to reach a freer evolution of spiritual attributes, which is always cramped so long as hindrances forestall the satisfaction of that first root-need. Everyone thus strives by nature for stability, for maintenance of quiet: ensured can it only be, however, when the maintenance of existing conditions is not the preponderant interest of *one* party only. Hence it is in the truest interest of all parties, and thus of the State itself, that the interest in its abidingness should not be left to a single party. There must consequently be given a possibility of constantly relieving the suffering interests of less favoured parties: in this regard the more the nearest need is kept alone in eye, the more intelligible will be itself; and the easier and more tranquillising will be its satisfaction. General laws in provision of this possibility, whilst they allow of minor alterations, thus aim alike at maintenance of stability; and that law which, reckoned for the possibility of constant remedy of pressing needs, contains withal the strongest warrant of stability, must therefore be the most perfect law of State.

The embodied voucher for this fundamental law is the *Monarch*. In no State is there a weightier law than that which centres its stability in the supreme hereditary power of one particular family, unconnected and un-commingling with any other lineage in that State. Never yet has there been a Constitution in which, after the downfall of such families and abrogation of the Kingly power, some substitution or periphrasis has not necessarily, and for the most part necessitously, reconstructed a power of similar kind. It therefore is established as the most essential principle of the State; and as in it resides the warrant of stability, so in the person of the King the State attains its true *ideal*.

For, as the King on one hand gives assurance of the State's solidity, on the other his loftiest interest soars high beyond the State. Personally he has naught in common with the interests of parties, but his sole concern is that the conflict of these interests should be adjusted, precisely for the safety of the whole. His sphere is therefore equity, and where this is unattainable, the exercise of grace (*Gnade*). Thus, as against the party interests, he is the representative of purely-human interests, and in the eyes of the party-seeking citizen he therefore occupies in truth a position welinigh superhuman. To him is consequently accorded a reverence such as the highest citizen would never dream of distantly demanding for himself; and here, at this summit of the State where we see its ideal reached, we therefore meet that side of human apperception (*Anschauungsweise*) which, in distinction from the faculty of recognising the nearest need, we will call the power of *Wahn*. (10) All those, to wit, whose simple powers of cognisance do not extend beyond what bears upon their nearest need—and they form by far the largest portion of mankind—would be unable to recognise the importance of a Royal Prerogative whose exercise has no directly cognisable relation with their nearest need, to say nothing of the necessity of bestirring themselves for its upholding, nay, even of bringing the King their highest offerings, the sacrifice of goods and life, if there intervened no form of apperception entirely opposed to ordinary cognisance.

This form is *Wahn*.

Before we seek to gain intelligence of the nature of *Wahn* from its most wondrous phases, let us take for guide the uncommonly suggestive light thrown by an exceptionally deep-thinking and keen-sighted philosopher of the immediate past (11) upon the phenomena, so puzzling in themselves, of animal instinct.—The astounding aimfulness (*Zweckmässigkeit*) in the procedures (*Verrichtungen*) of insects, among whom the bees and ants lie handiest for general observation, is admittedly inexplicable on the grounds that account for the aimfulness of kindred joint procedures in human life; that is to say, we cannot possibly suppose that these arrangements are directed by an actual knowledge of their aimfulness indwelling in the individuals, nay, even of their aim. In explanation of the extraordinary, ay, the self-sacrificing zeal, as also the ingenious manner, in which such animals provide for their eggs, for instance, of whose aim and future mission they cannot possibly be conscious from experience and observation, our philosopher infers the existence of a *Wahn* that feigns to the individual insect's so scanty intellectual powers an end which it holds for the satisfaction of its private need, whereas that end in truth has nothing to do with the individual, but with the species. The individual's egoism is here assumed, and rightly, to be so invincible that arrangements beneficial merely to the species, to coming generations, and hence the preservation of the species at cost of the transient individual, would never be consummated by that individual with labour and self-sacrifice, were it not guided by the fancy (*Wahn*) that it is thereby serving an end of its own; nay, this fancied end of its own must seem weightier to the individual, the satisfaction reapable from its attainment more potent and complete, than the purely-individual aim of everyday, of satisfying hunger and so forth, since, as we see, the latter is sacrificed with greatest keenness to the former. The author and incitor of this Wahn our philosopher deems to be the spirit of the race itself; the almighty Will-of-life (*Lebenswille*) supplanting the individual's limited perceptive-faculty, seeing that without its intervention the individual, in narrow egoistic care for self; would gladly sacrifice the species on the altar of its personal continuance.

Should we succeed in bringing the nature of this Wahn to our inner consciousness by any means, we should therewith win the key to that else so enigmatic relation of the individual to the species. Perhaps this may be made easier to us on the path that leads us out above the State. Meanwhile, however, the application of the results of our inquiry into animal instinct to the products of certain constant factors of the highest efficacy in the human State—factors unbidden by any extraneous power, but arising ever of their own accord—will furnish us with an immediate possibility of defining Wahn in terms of general experience.

In political life this Wahn displays itself as *patriotism*. As such it prompts the citizen to offer up his private welfare, for whose amplest possible ensurement he erst was solely concerned in all his personal and party efforts, nay, to offer up his life itself; for ensuring the State's continuance. The Wahn that any violent transmutation of the State must affect him altogether personally, must crush him to a degree which he believes he never could survive, here governs him in such a manner that his exertions to turn aside the danger threatening the State, as 'twere a danger to be suffered in his individual person, are quite as strenuous, and indeed more eager than in the actual latter case; whereas the traitor, as also the churlish realist, finds it easy enough to prove that, even after entry of the evil which the patriot fears, his personal prosperity can remain as flourishing as ever.

The positive renunciation of egoism accomplished in the patriotic action, however, is certainly so violent a strain, that it cannot possibly hold out for long together; moreover the Wahn that prompts it is still so strongly tinctured with a really egoistic notion, that the relapse into the sober, purely egoistic mood of everyday occurs in general with marked rapidity, and this latter mood goes on to fill the actual breadth of life. Hence the Patriotic Wahn requires a lasting symbol, whereto it may attach itself amid the dominant mood of everyday—thence, should exigence again arise, to promptly gain once more its quickening force; something like the colours that led us formerly to battle, and now wave peacefully above the city from the tower; a sheltering token of the meeting-place for all, should danger newly enter. This symbol is the King; in him the burgher honours unawares the visible representative, nay, the live embodiment of that same Wahn which, already bearing him beyond and above his common notions of the nature of things, inspirits and ennobles him to the point of shewing himself a patriot.

Now, what lies above and beyond Patriotism—that form of Wahn sufficient for the preservation of the State—will not be cognisable to the state-burgher as such, but, strictly speaking, can bring itself to the knowledge of none save the King or those who are able to make his personal interest their own. Only from the Kinghood's height can be seen the rents in the garment wherewithal Wahn clothes itself to reach its nearest goal, the preservation of the species, under the form of a State-fellowship. Though Patriotism may sharpen the burgher's eyes to interests of State, yet it leaves him blind to the interest of mankind in general; nay, its most effectual force is spent in passionately intensifying this blindness, which often finds a ray of daylight in the common intercourse of man and man. The patriot subordinates himself to his State in order to raise it above all other States, and thus, as it were, to find his personal sacrifice repaid with ample interest through the might and greatness of his fatherland. Injustice and violence toward other States and peoples have therefore been the true dynamic law of Patriotism throughout all time. Self-preservation is still the real prime motor here, since the quiet, and thus the power, of one's own State appears securable in no other way than through the powerlessness of other States, according to Machiavelli's telling maxim: "What you don't wish put on yourself; go put upon your neighbour!" But this fact that one's own quiet can be ensured by nothing but violence and injustice to the world without, must naturally make one's quiet seem always problematic in itself: thereby leaving a door forever open to violence and' injustice within one's own State too. The measures and acts which shew us violently-disposed towards the outer world, can never stay without a violent reaction on ourselves. When modern state-political optimists speak of a state of International Law, (12) in which the [European] States stand nowadays toward one another, one need only point to the necessity of maintaining and constantly increasing our enormous standing armies, to convince them, on the contrary, of the actual lawlessness of that state (*Rechtslosigkeit dieses Zustandes*). Since it does not occur to me to attempt to shew how matters could be otherwise, I merely record the fact that we are living in a perpetual state of war, with intervals of armistice, and that the inner condition of the State itself is not so utterly unlike this state of things as to pass muster for its diametric opposite. If the prime concern of all State systems is the ensurance of stability, and if this ensurance hinges on the condition that no party shall feel an irresistible need of radical change; if; to obviate such an event, it is indispensable that the moment's pressing need shall always be relieved in due season ; and if the practical common-sense of the burgher may be held sufficient, nay alone competent, to recognise this need: on the other hand we have seen that the highest associate tendence of the State could only be kept in active vigour through a form of Wahn; and as we were obliged to recognise that this particular Wahn, namely that of Patriotism, neither was truly pure, nor wholly answered to the objects of the human race as such, — we now have to take this Wahn in eye, withal, under the guise of a constant menace to public peace and equity.

The very Wahn that prompts the egoistic burgher to the most self-sacrificing actions, can equally mislead him into the most deplorable embroglios, into acts the most injurious to Quiet.

The reason lies in the scarcely exaggerable weakness of the average human intellect, as also in the infinitely diverse shades and grades of perceptive-faculty in the units who, taken all together, create the so-called *public opinion*. Genuine respect for this "public opinion" is founded on the sure and certain observation that no one is more accurately aware of the community's true immediate life-needs, nor can better devise the means for their satisfaction, than the community itself: it would be strange indeed, were man more faultily organised in this respect than the dumb animal. Nevertheless we often are driven to the opposite view, if we remark how even for this, for the correct perception of its nearest, commonest needs, the ordinary human understanding does not suffice—not, at least, to the extent of jointly satisfying them in the spirit of true fellowship the presence of beggars in our midst, and even at times of starving fellow-creatures, shews how weak the commonest human sense must be at bottom. So here already we have evidence of the great difficulty it must cost to bring true reason (*wirkliche Vernunft*) into the joint determinings of Man: though the cause may well reside in the boundless egoism of each single unit, which, outstripping far his intellect, prescribes his portion of the joint resolve at the very junctures where right knowledge can be attained through nothing but repression of egoism and sharpening of the understanding,—yet precisely here we may plainly detect the influence of a baneful Wahn. This Wahn has always found its only nurture in insatiable egoism; it is dangled before the latter from without, however, to wit by ambitious individuals, just as egoistic, but gifted with a higher, though in itself by no means high degree of intellect This intentional employment and conscious or unconscious perversion of the Wahn can avail itself of none but the form alone accessible to the burgher, that of Patriotism, albeit in some disfigurement or other; it thus will always give itself out as an effort for the common good, and never yet has a demagogue or intriguer led a Folk astray without in some way making it believe itself inspired by patriotic ardour. Thus in Patriotism itself there lies the holdfast for misguidance; and the possibility of keeping always handy the means of this misguidance, resides in the artfully inflated value which certain people pretend to attach to "public opinion."

What manner of thing this "public opinion" is, should be best known to those who have its name forever in their mouths and erect the regard for it into a positive article of religion. Its self-styled organ in our times is the "Press": were she candid, she would call herself its generatrix, but she prefers to hide her moral and intellectual foibles—manifest enough to every thinking and earnest observer,— her utter want of independence and truthful judgment, behind the lofty mission of her subservience to this sole representative of human dignity, this Public Opinion, which marvellously bids her stoop to every indignity, to every contradiction, to to-day's betrayal of what she dubbed right sacred yesterday. Since, as we else may see, every sacred thing seems to come into the world merely to be employed for ends profane, the open profanation of Public Opinion might perhaps not warrant us in arguing to its badness in and for itself: only, its actual existence is difficult, or wellnigh impossible to prove, for *ex hypothesi* it cannot manifest as such in the single individual, as is done by every other noble Wahn; such as we must certainly account true Patriotism, which has its strongest and its plainest manifestation precisely in the individual unit. The pretended vicegerent of "public opinion," on the other hand, always gives herself out as its will-less slave; and thus one never can get at this wondrous power, save— by making it for oneself. This, in effect, is what is done by the "press," and that with all the keenness of the trade the world best understands, industrial business. Whereas each writer for the papers represents nothing, as a rule, but a literary failure or a bankrupt mercan tile career, *many* newspaper-writers, or all of them together, form the awe-commanding power of the *"press,"* the sublimation of public spirit, of practical human intellect, the indubitable guarantee of manhood's constant progress. Each man uses her according to his need, and she herself expounds the nature of Public Opinion through her practical behaviour—to the intent that it is at all times havable for gold or profit.

It certainly is not as paradoxical as it might appear, to aver that with the invention of the art of printing, and quite certainly with the rise of journalism, mankind has gradually lost much of its capacity for healthy judgment: demonstrably the plastic memory, (13) the widespread aptitude for poetical conception and reproduction, has considerably and progressively diminished since even written characters first gained the upper hand. No doubt a compensatory profit to the general evolution of human faculties, taken in the very widest survey, must be likewise capable of proof; but in any case it does not accrue to us immediately, for whole generations—including most emphatically our own, as any close observer must recognise— have been so degraded through the abuses practised on the healthy human power of judgment by the manipulators of the modern daily Press in particular, and consequently through the lethargy into which that power of judgment has fallen, in keeping with man's habitual bent to easygoingness, that, in flat contradiction of the lies they let themselves be told, men shew themselves more incapable each day of sympathy with truly great ideas.

The most injurious to the common welfare is the harm thus done to the simple sense of equity: there exists no form of injustice, of onesidedness and narrowness of heart, that does not find expression in the pronouncements of "public opinion," and—what adds to the hatefulness of the thing—forever with a passionateness that masquerades as the warmth of genuine patriotism, but has its true and constant origin in the most self-seeking of all human motives. Whoso would learn this accurately, has but to run counter to "public opinion," or indeed to defy it: he will find himself brought face to face with the most implacable tyrant; and no one is more driven to suffer from its despotism, than the Monarch, for very reason that he is the representant of that selfsame Patriotism whose noxious counterfeit steps up to him, as "public opinion," with the boast of being identical in kind.

Matters strictly pertaining to the interest of the King, which in truth can only be that of purest patriotism, are cut and dried by his unworthy substitute, this Public Opinion, in the interest of the vulgar egoism of the mass; and the necessitation to yield to its requirements, notwithstanding, becomes the earliest source of that higher form of suffering which the King alone can personally experience as his own. If we add hereto the personal sacrifice of private freedom which the monarch has to bring to "reasons of State," and if we reflect how he alone is in a position to make purely-human considerations lying far above mere patriotism—as, for instance, in his intercourse with the heads of other States—his personal concern, and yet is forced to immolate them upon the altar of his State: then we shall understand why the legends and the poetry of every age have brought the tragedy of human. life the plainest and the oftenest to show in just the destiny of Kings. In the fortunes and the fate of Kings the tragic import of the world can first be brought completely to our knowledge. Up to the King a clearance of every obstacle to the human Will is thinkable, so far as that Will takes on the mould of State, since the endeavour of the citizen does not outstep the satisfaction of certain needs allayable within the confines of the State. The General and Statesman, too, remains a practical realist; in his enterprises he may be unlucky and succumb, but chance might also favour him to reach the thing not in and for itself impossible: for he ever serves a definite, practical aim. But the King desires the Ideal, he wishes justice and humanity; nay, wished he them not, wished he naught but what the simple burgher or party-leader wants,—the very claims made on him by his office, claims that allow him nothing but an ideal interest, by making him a traitor to the idea he represents, would plunge him into those sufferings which have inspired tragic poets from all time to paint their pictures of the vanity of human life and strife. (14) True justice and humanity are ideals irrealisable: to be bound to strive for them, nay, to recognise an unsilenceable summons to their carrying out, is to be condemned to misery. What the throughly noble, truly kingly individual directly feels of this, in time is given also to the individual unqualified for knowledge of his tragic task, and solely placed by Nature's dispensation on the throne, to learn in some uncommon fashion reserved for kings alone: upon the height allotted to it by an unavoidable destiny, the vulgar head, the ignoble heart that in a humbler sphere might very well subsist in fullest civic honour, in thorough harmony with itself and its surroundings, here falls into a dire contempt, far-reaching and long-lasting, often in itself unreasoning, and therefore to be accounted wellnigh tragic. The very fact that the individual called to the throne has no personal choice, may allow no sanction to his purely human leanings, and needs must fill a great position for which nothing but great natural parts can qualify, foreordains him to a superhuman lot that needs must crush the weakling into personal nullity. The highly fit, however, is summoned to drink the full, deep cup of life's true tragedy in his exalted station. Should his construction of the Patriotic ideal be passionate and ambitious, he becomes a warrior-chief and conqueror, and thereby courts the portion of the violent, the faithlessness of Fortune; but should his nature be noble-minded, full of human pity, more deeply and more bitterly than every other is he called to see the futility of all endeavours for true, for perfect justice.

To him more deeply and more inwardly than is possible to the State-citizen, as such, is it therefore given to feel that in Man there dwells an infinitely deeper, more capacious need than the State and its ideal can ever satisfy. Wherefore as it was Patriotism that raised the burgher to the highest height by him attainable, it is *Religion* alone that can bear the King to the stricter dignity of manhood (*zur eigentlichen Menschenwürde*).

Religion, of its very essence, is radically divergent from the State. The religions that have come into the world have been high and pure in direct ratio as they seceded from the State, and in themselves entirely upheaved it. We find State and Religion in complete alliance only where each still stands upon its lowest step of evolution and significance. The primitive Nature-religion subserves no ends but those which Patriotism provides for in the adult State: hence with the full development of patriotic spirit the ancient Nature-religion has always lost its meaning for the State. So long as it flourishes, however, so long do men subsume by their gods their highest practical interest of State; the tribal god is the representant of the tribesmen's solidarity; the remaining Nature-gods become Penates, protectors of the home, the town, the fields and flocks. Only in the wholly adult State, where these religions have paled before the full-fledged patriotic duty, and are sinking into inessential forms and ceremonies; only where "Fate" has shewn itself to be Political Necessity (15) —could true Religion step into the world. Its basis is a feeling of the unblessedness of human being, of the State's profound inadequacy to still the purely human need. Its inmost kernel is denial of the world— i.e. recognition of the world as a fleeting and dreamlike state [of mind] reposing merely on illusion (*auf einer Täuschung*)—and struggle for Redemption from it, prepared-for by renunciation, attained by Faith.

In true Religion a complete reversal thus occurs of all the aspirations to which the State had owed its founding and its organising: what is seen to be unattainable here, the human mind desists from striving-for upon this path, to ensure its reaching by a path completely opposite. To the religious eye (*der religiösen Vorstellung*) the truth grows plain that there must be another world than this, because the inextinguishable bent-to-happiness cannot be stilled within this world, and hence requires another world for its redemption. What, now, is that other world? So far as the conceptual faculties of human Understanding reach, and in their practical application as intellectual Reason, it is quite impossible to gain a notion that shall not clearly shew itself as founded on this selfsame world of need and change: wherefore, since this world is the source of our unhappiness, that other world, of redemption from it, must be precisely as different from this present world as the mode of cognisance whereby we are to perceive that other world must be different from the mode which shews us nothing but this present world of suffering and illusion. (16)

In Patriotism we have already seen that a Wahn usurps the single individual prompted merely by personal interests, a Wahn that makes the peril of the State appear to him an infinitely intensified personal peril, to ward off which he then will sacrifice himself with equally intensified ardour. But where, as now, it is a question of letting the personal egoism, at bottom the only decisor, perceive the nullity of all the world) of the whole assemblage of relations in which alone contentment had hitherto seemed possible to the individual; of directing his zeal toward free-willed suffering and renunciation, to detach him from dependence on this world: this wonder-working intuition—which, in contradistinction from the ordinary practical mode of ideation, we can only apprehend as Wahn (17) —must have a source so sublime, so utterly incomparable with every other, that the only notion possible to be granted us of that source itself; in truth, must consist in our necessary inference of its existence from this its supernatural effect.—

Whosoever thinks he has said the last word on the essence of the Christian faith when he styles it an attempted satisfaction of the most unbounded egoism, a kind of contract wherein the beneficiary is to obtain eternal, never-ending bliss on condition of abstinence [or "renunciation"—*Entsagung*] and free-willed suffering in this relatively brief and fleeting life, he certainly has defined therewith the sort of notion alone accessible to unshaken human egoism, but nothing even distantly resembling the Wahn-transfigured concept proper to the actual practiser of free-willed suffering and renunciation. Through voluntary suffering and renunciation, on the contrary, man's egoism is already practically upheaved, and he who chooses them, let his object be whate'er you please, is thereby raised already above all notions bound by Time and Space; for no longer can he seek a happiness that lies in Time and Space, e'en were they figured as eternal and immeasurable. That which gives to him the superhuman strength to suffer voluntarily, must itself be felt by him already as a profoundly inward happiness, incognisable by any other, a happiness quite incommunicable to the world except through outer suffering: it must be the measurelessly lofty joy of world-overcoming, compared wherewith the empty pleasure of the world-conqueror seems downright null and childish. (18)

From this result, sublime above all others, we have to infer the nature of the Divine Wahn itself; and, to gain any sort of notion thereof; we have therefore to pay close heed to how it displays itself to the religious world-Overcomer, simply endeavouring to reproduce and set before ourselves this conception of his in all its purity, but in nowise attempting to reduce the Wahn itself; forsooth, to terms of *our* conceptual method, so radically distinct from that of the Religious.—

As Religion's highest force proclaims itself in *Faith*, its most essential import lies within its *Dogma*. (19)   Not through its practical importance for the State, i.e. its moral law, is Religion of such weight; for the root principles of all morality are to be found in every, even in the most imperfect, religion: but through its measureless value to the Individual, does the Christian religion prove its lofty mission, and that through its Dogma. The wondrous, quite incomparable attribute of religious Dogma is this: it presents in positive form that which on the path of reflection (*des Nachdenkens*), and through the strictest philosophic methods, can be seized in none but negative form. That is to say, whereas the philosopher arrives at demonstrating the erroneousness and incompetence of that natural mode of ideation in power whereof we take the world, as it commonly presents itself; for an undoubtable reality: religious Dogma shews the other world itself; as yet unrecognised; and with such unfailing sureness and distinctness, that the Religious, on whom that world has dawned, is straightway possessed with the most unshatterable, most deeply-blessing peace. We must assume that this conception, so indicibly beatifying in its effect, this idea which we can only rank under the category of Wahn, or better, this immediate vision seen by the Religious, to the ordinary human apprehension remains entirely foreign and unconveyable, in respect of both its substance and its form. What, on the other hand, is imparted thereof and thereon to the layman (*den Profanen*), to the people, can be nothing more than a kind of allegory; to wit, a rendering of the unspeakable, impalpable, and never understandable through [their] immediate intuition, into the speech of common life and of its only feasible form of knowledge, erroneous *per se*. In this sacred allegory an attempt is made to transmit to wordly minds (*der weltlichen Vorstellung*) the mystery of the divine revelation: but the only relation it can bear to what the Religious had immediately beheld, is the relation of the day-told dream to the actual dream of night. As to the part the most essential of the thing to be transmitted, this narration will be itself so strongly tinctured with the impressions of ordinary daily life, and through them so distorted, that it neither can truly satisfy the teller—since he feels that just the weightiest part had really been quite otherwise—nor fill the hearer with the certainty afforded by the hearing of something wholly comprehensible and intelligible in itself. If; then, the record left upon our own mind by a deeply moving dream is strictly nothing but an allegorical paraphrase, whose intrinsic disagreement with the original remains a trouble to our waking consciousness; and therefore if the knowledge reaped by the hearer can at bottom be nothing but an essentially distorted image of that original: yet this [allegorical] message, in the case both of the dream and of the actually received divine revelation, remains the only possible way of proclaiming the thing received to the layman. Upon these lines is formed the Dogma; and this is the revelation's only portion cognisable by the world, which it therefore has to take on authority, so as to become a partner, at least through Faith, in what its eye has never seen. Hence is Faith so strenuously commended to the Folk: the Religious, become a sharer in salvation through his own eye's beholding (*durch eigene Anschauung*), feels and knows that the layman, to whom the vision (*die Anschauung*) itself remains a stranger, has no path to knowledge of the Divine except the path of Faith; and this Faith, to be effectual, must be sincere, undoubting and unconditional, in measure as the Dogma embraces all the incomprehensible, and to common knowledge contradictory-seeming, conditioned by the incomparable difficulty of its wording. (20)

The intrinsic distortion of Religion's fundamental essence, beheld through divine revelation, that is to say of the true root-essence incommunicable *per se* to ordinary knowledge, is hence undoubtedly engendered in the first instance by the aforesaid difficulty in the wording of its Dogma; but this distortion first becomes actual and perceptible, from the moment when the Dogma's nature is dragged before the tribune of common causal apprehension. The resulting vitiation of Religion itself; whose holy of holies is just the indubitable Dogma that blesses through an inward Faith, is brought about by the ineluctable requirement to defend that Dogma against the assaults of common human apprehension, to explain and make it seizable to the latter. This requirement grows more pressing in degree as Religion, which had its primal fount within the deepest chasms of the world-fleeing heart, comes once again into a relation with the State. The disputations traversing the centuries of the Christian religion's development into a Church and its complete metamorphosis into a State-establishment, the perpetually recurring strifes in countless forms anent the rightness and the rationality of religious Dogma and its points, present us with the sad and painfully instructive history of an attack of madness. Two absolutely incongruous modes of view and knowledge, at variance in their entire nature, cross one another in this strife, without so much as letting men detect their radical divergence: not but that one must allow to the truly religious champions of Dogma that they started with a thorough consciousness of the total difference between their mode of knowledge and that belonging to the world; whereas the terrible wrong, to which they were driven at last, consisted in their letting themselves be hurried into zealotism and the most inhuman use of violence when they found that nothing was to be done with human reason (*Vernunft*), thus practically degenerating into the utmost opposite of religiousness. On the other hand the hopelessly materialistic, industrially commonplace, entirely un-Goded aspect of the modern world is debitable to the counter eagerness of the common practical understanding to construe religious Dogma by laws of cause-and-effect deduced from the phenomena of natural and social life, and to fling aside whatever rebelled against that mode of explanation as a reasonless chimera. After the Church, in her zeal, had clutched at the weapons of State-jurisdiction (*staatsrechtlichen Exekution*), thus transforming herself into a political power, the contradiction into which she thereby fell with herself— since religious Dogma assuredly conveyed no lawful title to such a power—was bound to become a truly lawful weapon in the hands of her opponents; and, whatever other semblance may still be toilsomely upheld, to-day we see her lowered to an institution of the State, employed for objects of the State-machinery; wherewith she may prove her use, indeed, but no more her divinity.

But does this mean that Religion itself has ceased ?—

No, no! It lives, but only at its primal source and sole true dwelling-place, within the deepest, holiest inner chamber of the individual; there whither never yet has surged a conflict of the rationalist and supranaturalist, the Clergy and the State. For *this* is the essence of true Religion: that, away from the cheating show of the day-tide world, it shines in the night of man's inmost heart, with a light quite other than the world-sun's light, and visible nowhence save from out that depth. (21) —

'Tis thus indeed! Profoundest knowledge teaches us that only in the inner chamber of our heart, in nowise from the world presented to us without, can true assuagement come to us. Our organs of perception of the outer world are merely destined for discovering the means wherewith to satisfy the individual unit's need, that unit which feels so single and so needy in face of just this world; with the selfsame organs we cannot possibly perceive the basic Oneness of all being; it is allowed us solely by the new cognitive faculty that is suddenly awoken in us, as if through Grace, so soon as ever the vanity of the world comes home to our inner consciousness on any kind of path. Wherefore the truly religious knows also that he cannot really impart to the world on a theoretic path, forsooth through argument and controversy, his inner beatific vision, and thus persuade it of that vision's truth: he can do this only on a practical path, through *example*, (22) through the deed of renunciation, of sacrifice, through gentleness unshakable, through the sublime serenity of earnestness (*Heiterkeit des Ernstes*) that spreads itself o'er all his actions. The saint, the martyr, is therefore the true mediator of salvation; through his example the Folk is shewn, in the only manner to it comprehensible, of what purport must that vision be, wherein itself can share through Faith alone, but not yet through immediate knowledge. Hence there lies a deep and pregnant meaning behind the Folk's addressing itself to God through the medium of its heart-loved saints; and it says little for the vaunted enlightenment of our era, that every English shopkeeper for instance, so soon as he has donned his sunday-coat and taken the right book with him, opines that he is entering into immediate personal intercourse with God. No: a proper understanding of that Wahn wherein a higher world imparts itself to common human ideation, and which proves its virtue through man's heartfelt resignation (*Unterworfenheit*) to this present world, alone is able to lead to knowledge of man's most deep concerns; and it must be borne in mind, withal, that we can be prompted to that resignation only through the said example of true saintliness, but never urged into it by an overbearing clergy's vain appeal to Dogma pure and simple.—

This attribute of true religiousness, which, for the deep reason given above, does not proclaim itself through disputation, but solely through the active example—this attribute, should it be indwelling in the King, becomes the only revelation, of profit to both State and Religion, that can bring the two into relationship. As I have already shewn, no one is more compelled than he, through his exalted, well-nigh superhuman station, to grasp the profoundest earnestness of Life; and—if he gain this only insight worthy of his calling—no one stands in more need, than he, of that sublime and strengthening solace which Religion alone can give. What no cunning of the politician can ever compass, to him, thus armoured and equipped, will then alone be possible: gazing out of that world into this, the mournful seriousness wherewith the sight of mundane passions fills him, will arm him for the exercise of strictest equity; the inner knowledge that all these passions spring only from the one great suffering of unredeemed mankind, will move him pitying to the exercise of grace. *Unflinching justice, ever ready mercy—here is the mystery of the King's ideal!* But though it faces toward the State with surety of its healing, this ideal's possibility of attainment arises not from any tendence of the State, but purely from Religion. Here, then, would be the happy trysting-place where State and Religion, as erst in their prophetic days of old, met once again.

We here have ascribed to the King a mission so uncommon, and repeatedly denoted as almost superhuman, that the question draws near: how is its constant fulfilment to be compassed by the human individual, even though he own the natural capacity for which alone its possibility is reckoned, without his sinking under it? In truth there rules so great a doubt as to the possibility of attaining the Kingly ideal, that the contrary case is provided for in advance in the framing of State-constitutions. Neither could we ourselves imagine a monarch qualified to fulfil his highest task, saving under conditions similar to those we are moved to advance when seeking to account for the working and endurance of everything uncommon and unordinary in this ordinary world. For, when we regard it with closer sympathy, each truly great mind—which the human generative-force, for all its teeming productivity, brings forth so vastly seldom—sets us a-wondering how twas possible for it to hold out for any length of time within this world, to wit for long enough to acquit itself of its tale of work.

Now, the great, the truly noble spirit is distinguished from the common organisation of everyday by this: to *it* every, often the seemingly most trivial, incident of life and world-intercourse is capable of swiftly displaying its widest correlation with the essential root-phenomena of all existence, thus of shewing Life and the World themselves in their true, their terribly earnest meaning. The naïve, ordinary man—accustomed merely to seize the outmost side of such events, the side of practical service for the moment's need—when once this awful earnestness suddenly reveals itself to him through an unaccustomed juncture, falls into such consternation that self-murder is very frequently the consequence. The great, the exceptional man finds himself each day, in a certain measure, in the situation where the ordinary man forthwith despairs of life. Certainly the great, the truly religious man I mean, is saved from this consequence by the lofty earnest of that inner ure-knowledge (*Ur-erkenntniss*) of the essence of the world which has become the standard of all his beholdings; at each instant he is prepared for the terrible phenomenon: also, he is armoured with a gentleness and patience which never let him fall a-storming against any manifestation of evil that may haply take him unawares.

Yet an irrecusable yearning to turn his back completely on this world must necessarily surge up within his breast, were there not for him— as for the common man who lives away a life of constant care—a certain distraction, a periodical turning-aside from that world's-earnestness which else is ever present to his thoughts. What for the common man is entertainment and amusement, must be forthcoming for him as well, but in the noble form befitting him; and that which renders possible this turning aside, this noble illusion, must again be a work of that man-redeeming Wahn which spreads its wonders wherever the individual's normal mode of view can help itself no farther. But in this instance the Wahn must be entirely candid; it must confess itself in advance for an illusion, if it is to be willingly embraced by the man who really longs for distraction and illusion in the high and earnest sense I mean. The fancy-picture brought before him must never afford a loophole for re-summoning the earnestness of Life through any possible dispute about its actuality and provable foundation upon fact, as religious Dogma does: no, it must exercise its specific virtue through its very setting of the conscious Wahn in place of the reality. This office is fulfilled by *Art*; and in conclusion I therefore point my highly-loved young friend to Art, as the kindly Life-saviour who does not really and wholly lead us out beyond this life, but, within it, lifts us up above it and shews it as itself a game of play; a game that, take it ne'er so terrible and earnest an appearance, yet here again is shewn us as a mere Wahn-picture, as which it comforts us and wafts us from the common truth of our distress (*Noth*). The work of noblest Art will be given a glad admittance by my friend, the work that, treading on the footprints of Life's earnestness, shall soothingly dissolve reality into that Wahn wherein itself in turn, this serious reality, at last seems nothing else to us but Wahn: and in his most rapt beholding of this wondrous Wahn-play (*Wahnspiel*) there will return to him the indicible dream-picture of the holiest revelation, of meaning ure-akin (*urverwandt sinnvoll*), with clearness unmistakable,—that same divine dream-picture which the disputes of sects and churches had made ever more incognisable to him, and which, as wellnigh unintelligible Dogma, could only end in his dismay. The nothingness of the world, here is it harmless, frank, avowed as though in smiling: for our willing purpose to deceive ourselves has led us on to recognise the world's real state without a shadow of illusion.—

Thus has it been possible for me, even from this earnest sally into the weightiest regions of Life's earnestness, and without losing myself or feigning, to come back to my beloved Art. Will my friend in sympathy understand me, when I confess that first upon this path have I regained full consciousness of Art's serenity?

Notes

01

See Volume vii., "Zukunftsmusik."—Richard Wagner.—Volume III. of the present series. —Tr.

02

"Gewiss war es aber für meine Untersuchung charakteristisch, dass ich hierbei nie auf das Gebiet der eigentlichen *Politik* herabstieg, namentlich die Zeitpolitik, wie sie mich trotz der Heftigkeit der Zustände nicht wahrhaft berührte, auch von mir gänzlich unberührt blieb." In confirmation of this statement, which has been disputed by Wagner's enemies and by one so-called "friend," the late Ferdinand

Praeger, I may refer to the facts collected in my little brochure "1849: A Vindication," published in 1892 by Messrs Kegan Paul & Co.—Tr.

03

"Nicht eher nahmen daher die politischen Bewegungen jener Zeit meine Aufmerksamkeit ernster in Anspruch, als his durch den Übertritt derselben auf das rein soziale Gebiet in mir Ideen angeregt wurden, die, weil sie meiner idealen Forderung Nabrung zu geben schienen, mich, wie ich gestehe, eine Zeit lang ernstlich erfüllten. Meine Richtung ging darauf, mir eine Organisation des gemeinsamen öffentlichen, wie des hauslichen Lebens vorzustellen, welche von selbst zu einer schonen Gestaltung des menschlichen Geschlechtes führen müsste. Die Berechnungen der neueren Sozialisten fesselten demnach meine Theilnahme von da ab, wo sie in Systeme auszugehen schienen, welche zunächst nichts Anderes als den widerlichen Anblick einer Organisation der Gesellschaft zu gleichmässig vertheilter Arbeit hervorbrachten." As I have been compelled to slightly paraphrase the first of these sentences, and as there are minor difficulties in the other two, I give all three in the original.—Tr.

04

C:. Vol. I., 30-31.—Tr.

05

C:. Vol. I., 58.—Tr.

06

Cf. *Letters to Uhlig*, pp. 81-82, written October 22nd, 1850.—Tr.

07

Cf. Vol I., 24, and Vol II., 178.—Tr.

08

"Zu schauen kam ich, nicht zu schaffen"—Wotan in *Siegfried*, act ii.—Tr.

09

Cf. Vol. II., 186-187.—Tr.

10

"Wahn-Vermögen." As the word "Wahn" is frequently used in these pages, and is absolutely untranslatable, I shall mostly retain it as it stands. It does not so much mean an "illusion" or "delusion," in general, as a "semi-conscious *feigning*" (such as the 'legal fiction'),a "dream," or a "symbolical aspiration"—its etymological kinship being quite as near to "fain" as to "feign"; but the context will leave the reader in no doubt as to its particular application in any sentence. It will be remembered that "Wahn" plays an important part in Hans Sachs' monologue in *Die Meistersinger*, act iii; the poem of that drama, containing the Wahn-monologue in a somewhat more extended form than its ultimate version, had already been published in 1862.—Tr.

11

Arthur Schopenhauer, in *"Die Welt als Wille und Vorstellung,"* vol. ii, cap. 27. The philosopher there compares the operations of this "animal instinct" with a case of what we now should call hypnotism, and says that "insects are, in a certain sense, natural somnambulists . . . They have the feeling that they *must* perform a certain action, without exactly knowing why." He also compares this "instinct" to the "daimonion" of Socrates, but does not absolutely employ the expression "Wahn" in this connection. Neither does the "spirit of the race" (or "species"), mentioned by Wagner a few sentences farther on, occur in so many words with Schopenhauer. Nowadays for "the spirit of the race" some of us might be inclined to read "the principle of the survival of the fittest"; but the explanation of its *mode* of action,

through a "Wahn," would hold as good to-day as thirty years ago.— Tr.

12

"Von einem allgemeinen Rechtszustande,"—literally, "of a general (or universal) state of right (or law);" the expression seems to refer to the so-called "Balance of power," and may also be paraphrased by the more modern European concert."—Tr.

13

"Das plastische Gedächtniss"—evidently the mental record of things in their visual, concrete form, as opposed to their abstract labels.— Tr.

14

Cf. Amfortas; at this epoch our author was drafting his *Parsifal.*—Tr.

15

Cf. Vol II., 178, 179. Upon coupling the present parallelism with that noted on page 11 *antea,* it would appear highly probable that King Ludwig had been studying Part II. of *Oper und Drama,* and had directed Wagner's attention to this section—surrounding the Œdipus-Antigone myth—in particular.—Tr.

16

"So weit die intellektualen Vorstellungfähigkeiten des menschlichen Verstandes reichen, und in ihrer praktischen Anwendung als Vernunft sich geltend machen, ist durchaus keine Vorstellung zu gewinnen, welche nicht genau immer nur wieder diese selbe Welt des Bedürfnisses und des Wechsels erkennen liesse: da diese der Quell unserer Unseligkeit ist, muss daher jene andere Welt der Erlösung von dieser Welt genau so verschieden sein, als diejenige Erkenntnissart, durch welche wir sie erkennen sollen, verschieden von derjenigen sein muss, welcher einzig diese täuschende leidenvolle Welt sich darstellt."

17

"Diese wunderwirkende Vorstellung, die wir, der gemeinen praktischen Vorstellungsweise gegenuber, nur als Wahn auffassen können" etc. I here have translated the first "Vorstellung" as "intuition," though "idea" is the word generally employed for rendering the Schopenauerian term; literally it signifies an image *"set before* the mind," and hence any "mental concept," but with a less *abstract* shade of meaning than "Begriff"—the bare "idea"; a difficulty arises at times, in the translation of this term, from its connoting not only the "mental picture" itself, but also the act of forming it.—Tr.

18

Cf. "Doch wenn der mich im Himmel hält, dann liegt zu Füssen mir die Welt." *Die Meistersinger*, act ii.—Tr.

19

"Wie die höchste Kraft der Religion sich im *Glauben* kundgiebt, liegt ihre wesentlichste Bedeutung in ihrem *Dogma*."

20

"Und dieser [Glaube] muss, soll er erfolgreich sein, in dem Maasse innig, unbedingt und zweifellos sein, als das Dogma in sich all' das Unbegreifliche, und der gemeinen Erkenntniss widerspruchvoll Dünkende enthält, welches durch die unvergleichliche Schwierigkeit seiner Abfassung bedingt war." The obscurity of this sentence— credo *ouia impossibile*—will be cleared up in the next paragraph.—Tr.

21

"Da erdämmerte mild erhab'ner Macht im Busen mir die Nacht; mein Tag war da vollbracht." *Tristan und Isolde*, act ii.—Tr.

22

"Nicht darf sie Zweifels Last beschweren; sie sahen meine gute That." *Lohengrin*, act ii.—Tr.

A REPORT ON THE PRODUCTION OF "TANNHÄUSER" IN
PARIS.

Translator's Notes

The letter on *"Tannhäuser" in Paris* was originally published in the supplement to the *Deutsche Allgemeine Zeitung* for April 7, 1861, and reprinted in the *Neue Zeitschrift* five days later.

A Report on the Production of "Tannhäuser" in Paris.

Paris, 27th March, 1861.

I PROMISED to give you a full report, some day, of my Tannhäuser affairs in Paris; now that they have reached a climax, and can be surveyed in their whole extent, it is some satisfaction to myself to come to a final settlement by a calm review of their leading features—as it were for my own behoof. But none of you can rightly grasp the nature of this business, unless I also touch upon the true motive of my coming to Paris at all. Let me therefore begin with that.

After wellnigh ten years' preclusion from all possibility of reinvigorating myself by assisting at good performances of my dramatic compositions—if only periodically—I felt driven at last to contemplate removal to a spot which might bring this needful living contact with my art within my reach, in time. I hoped to be able to find that spot in some modest nook of Germany itself. The Grand Duke of Baden had already promised me, with most touching kindness, the production of my latest work at Carlsruhe under my personal direction; in the summer of 1859 I pressed him most importunately, in lieu of the projected temporary sojourn, to use his influence to forthwith procure me a permanent domicile in his country, (01) as there would otherwise be nothing for me to do but settle down in Paris for good. My plea's fulfilment was—impossible.

However, when I removed to Paris in the autumn of that same year, I still kept in sight the production of my "Tristan," for which I hoped to be summoned to Carlsruhe for the 3rd December. Once brought to performance under my own supervision, I believed I then could entrust the work to the other theatres of Germany. The prospect of dealing in the same way with the rest of my works, in future, sufficed me; and on this assumption Paris offered me the solitary interest of hearing an excellent quartet, an admirable orchestra, from time to time, and thus keeping myself in refreshing touch with at least the living organs of my art. All this was changed at a blow when I received notice from Carlsruhe that it had turned out impossible to produce my "Tristan" there. My sorry plight at once inspired me with the notion of inviting certain firstrate singers of my acquaintance to Paris for the following spring, so as to bring about the desired model-performance of my new work, with their assistance, on the boards of the "Italian Opera"; to this I also meant to invite the Directors and Regisseurs of friendly German theatres, in order to compass the same result as I had had in eye with the Carlsruhe production. Since the execution of my plan was impossible without the assistance of the larger Paris public, I was bound to bespeak its interest for my music, and to that end I undertook the well-known three concerts in the Théâtre des Italiens. The highly encouraging result of these concerts, in the matter of applause and interest, unfortunately could not help forward the main enterprise I had in view; for it was just these concerts that plainly shewed me the difficulties of any such undertaking, whilst the impossibility of gathering at one time in Paris the singers I had chosen was sufficient in itself to make me abandon the plan.

Hemmed in on every hand, and once more casting a longing look on Germany, I learnt to my intense surprise that my lot had become the subject of animated discussion and advocacy at the court of the Tuileries. It was to the extraordinarily friendly interest—almost unknown to myself before—of several members of the German embassies here, that I had to thank this propitious turn of affairs. It went so far that the Emperor, having also heard the most flattering account of my "Tannhäuser" (the work most spoken of) from a German princess for whom he entertained a particular esteem, (02) at once gave orders for the performance of that opera in the *Académie impériale de musique*.

Now I don't deny that, though highly delighted at first by this quite unexpected evidence of my works' success in social circles from which I personally had stood so distant, I soon could think with naught but grave misgivings of a performance of "Tannhäuser" at that particular theatre. To whom was it clearer, that this great opera-house had long estranged itself from every earnest artistic tendence; that in it quite other claims, than those of Dramatic Music, had brought themselves to currency; that Opera itself had there become a mere excuse for Ballet? In fact, when of late years I had received repeated invitations to think about the performance of one of my works in Paris, I had never dreamt of the *Grand Opéra*, but rather—for a trial—of the unassuming *Théâtre Lyrique*. And for two definite reasons: firstly, that here no special class of the audience prescribes the tone; secondly, that—thanks to the poverty of its exchequer—the Ballet pure and simple has not as yet become the focus of its whole art-doings. But, after many times returning to the idea, of his own accord, the Director of this theatre had been obliged to renounce a performance of "Tannhäuser," mainly because he could find no tenor competent to fill the difficult chief rôle.

As a matter of fact, my first conference with the Director of the Grand Opéra shewed me that the introduction of a ballet into "Tannhäuser," and indeed in the second act, was considered a sine quâ non of its successful performance. I couldn't fathom the meaning of this requirement, until I had declared that I could not possibly disturb the course of just this second act by a ballet, which must here be senseless from every point of view; while on the other hand I thought the first act, at the voluptuous court of Venus, would afford the most apposite occasion for a choreographic scene of amplest meaning, since I myself had not deemed possible to dispense with dance in my first arrangement of that scene. Indeed I was quite charmed with the idea of strengthening an undoubtedly weak point in my earlier score, and I drafted an exhaustive plan for raising this scene in the Venusberg to one of great importance. This plan the Director most emphatically rejected, telling me frankly that in the production of an opera it was not merely a question of a ballet, but of a ballet to be danced in the middle of the evening's entertainment; for it was only at about this time that the subscribers to whom the ballet almost exclusively belonged, appeared in their boxes, as they were in the habit of dining very late; a ballet in the opening scene would therefore be of no use to them, since they were never by any chance present for the first act These and similar admissions were subsequently repeated to me by the Cabinet-minister himself, and all possibility of a good result was made so definitely dependent on the said conditions being fulfilled, that I began to believe I should have to renounce the whole undertaking.

But while I thus was thinking again, more actively than ever, of my return to Germany, and spying out for a foothold to be granted me for the performance of my new works, I was now to discover the full value of the Emperor's command; for he placed the whole institute of the Grand Opéra at my disposal, without conditions or reserve, and allowed me carte blanche for whatever engagements I deemed needful. Every acquisition desired by me was forthwith carried out, without the slightest counting of the cost; to the mise-en-scène a care was devoted such as I had never conceived before. Under circumstances so entirely novel to me, I soon was more and more persuaded of the possibility of seeing a thoroughly complete, nay, an ideal performance. The vision of such a performance, wellnigh no matter of which of my works, had long occupied my mind since my withdrawal from our Opera-house; what nowhere and never had stood within my power, was unexpectedly to greet me here in Paris, and at a time when no efforts had availed to procure me an even remotely similar privilege on German soil. I openly admit that this thought inspired me with a warmth unknown for many a day, a warmth only intensified, perhaps, by a bitter feeling mixed therewith. I soon had eyes for nothing but the possibility of a splendid performance, and in the absorbing care to realise that possibility I allowed no other sort of consideration to influence me: if I attain what I may dare hold possible—said I to myself—what care I for the Jockey Club and its ballet?

Henceforth my eveiy thought was for the performance. There was no French tenor to be had, so the Director told me, for the rôle of Tannhäuser. Informed of the brilliant talents of the youthful singer *Niemann*, though I had never heard him myself, I cast him for the title-rôle; after the most careful preliminaries, his engagement was concluded at great expense, especially as he was master of a very fluent French pronunciation. Several other artists, and in particular the barytone *Morelli*, owed their engagement to nothing but my wish to acquire them for my work. Moreover, instead of certain first singers already popular here, whose too settled method alarmed me, I gave the preference to youthful talents whom I might hope to mould more easily to my style. I was surprised by the carefulness, quite unknown among ourselves, with which the voice-and-pianoforte rehearsals are here conducted; under the intelligent and sensitive guidance of the *chef du chant*, Vauthrot, I soon found our studies progressing at a rapid pace. In particular was I rejoiced to see how the younger French artists arrived at a better and better understanding of the thing, and caught a genuine liking for their task.

Thus I myself was taken with a new liking- for this earlier work of mine: I most carefully revised the score afresh, entirely re-wrote the scene of Venus and the ballet-scene preceding it, and everywhere sought to bring the vocal parts into closest agreement with the translated text.

Now, as I had made the performance my unique aim, and left every other consideration out of count, so my real trouble at last began with the perception that this performance itself would not attain the height expected by me. It would be hard for me, to tell you exactly on what points I had finally to see myself undeceived. The most serious, however, was that the singer of the difficult chief rôle fell into greater and greater disheartenment the nearer we approached the actual production, in consequence of interviews it had been thought necessary for him to hold with the reporters, who assured him of the inevitable failure of my opera. (03) The most promising hopes, which I had harboured in the course of the pianoforte-rehearsals, sank deeper and deeper the more we came in contact with the stage and orchestra. I saw that we were getting back to the dead level of ordinary Operatic performances, that all the requirements meant to bear us far above it were doomed to stay unmet Yet in this sense, which I naturally had disallowed from the first, we lacked the only thing that could confer distinction on such an Operatic show: some noted 'talent' or other, some tried and trusted favourite of the public; whereas I was making my début with almost absolute novices. Finally what most distressed me, was that I had not been able to wrest the orchestral conductorship, through which I might still have exercised a great influence on the spirit of performance, from the hands of the official *chef d'orchestre*; and my being thus compelled to mournfully resign myself to a dull and spiritless rendering of my work (for my wish to withdraw the score was not acceded to) is what makes out my genuine trouble even to this day.

Under such circumstances it became almost a matter of indifference to me, what kind of reception my opera would meet at the hands of the public: the most brilliant could not have moved me to personally attend a longer series of performances, for I found far too little satisfaction in the thing. But hitherto you have been diligently kept in ignorance of the true character of that reception, as it seems to me, and you would do very wrong if you based thereon a judgment of the Paris public in general, however flattering to the German, yet in reality incorrect. On the contrary, I abide by my opinion that the Paris public has very agreeable qualities, in particular those of a quick appreciation and a truly magnanimous sense of justice. A public, I say: a whole audience to which I am a total stranger, which day by day has heard from the journals and idle chatterers the most preposterous things about me, and has been deliberately set against me with wellnigh unexampled care—to see such a public repeatedly taking up the cudgels in my behalf against a clique, with demonstrations of applause a quarter of an hour long, must fill me with a warmth of heart towards it, were I even the most indifferent of men. But, through the admirable foresight of those who have the sole distribution of seats on first nights, and had made it almost impossible for me to gain admission for my handful of personal friends, there was assembled on that evening in the Grand Opera-house an audience which every dispassionate person could see at once was prejudiced in the extreme against my work; add to this the whole Parisian Press, which is always invited officially on such occasions, and whose hostile attitude towards me you have simply to read its reports to discover: and you may well believe that I have a right to speak of a great victory, when I tell you in all sober earnest that this by no means exquisite performance of my work met with louder and more unanimous applause than ever I experienced personally in Germany. The actual leaders of an opposition perhaps almost universal at first—several, nay, very likely all of the musical reporters here—who up to then had done their utmost to distract the attention of the public, were seized towards the end of the second act by manifest terror of having to witness a complete and brilliant success of "Tannhäuser"; and now they fell on the expedient of breaking into roars of laughter after certain cues, pre-arranged among themselves at the general-rehearsals, whereby they created a diversion sufficiently disturbing to damp a considerable manifestation of applause at the curtain's second fall. These selfsame gentlemen, however, had observed at the stage-rehearsals, which I had also not been able to hinder them from attending, that the opera's real success lay guaranteed in the execution of its third act. At the rehearsals an admirable 'set' by Mons. Despléchin, representing the Wartburg valley in the light of an autumn evening, had already exerted on everyone present a charm which irresistibly gave birth to the *Stimmung* requisite for taking-in the following scenes; on the part of the performers these scenes were the bright spot in the whole day's work; quite insurpassably was the Pilgrims' Chorus sung and managed; the Prayer of Elisabeth, delivered in its entirety by Fraulein *Sax* with affecting expression, the 'fantasie' to the Evening-star, rendered by *Morelli* with perfect elegiac tenderness, so happily prepared the way for the best part of *Niemann's* performance, his narration of the Pilgrimage—which has always won this artist the liveliest commendation—that a quite exceptional success seemed assured for just this third act, even in the eyes of my most determined adversaries. So this was the act the aforesaid leaders fastened on, trying to hinder any onset of the needful mood of absorption (*Sammlung*) by outbursts of violent laughter, for which the most trivial occasion had to afford the childish pretext. Undeterred by these adverse demonstrations, neither did my singers allow themselves to be put out, nor the public refrain from devoting its sympathetic attention, and often its profuse applause, to their valiant exertions; and at the end, when the performers were vociferously called before the curtain, the opposition was at last entirely beaten down.

That I had made no mistake in viewing this evening's outcome as a complete victory, was proved to me by the public's demeanour on the night of the second performance; for here it became manifest with *what* opposition alone I should have to do in the future, to wit, with that of the Paris Jockey Club—whose name I need not scruple to give you, as the public itself, with its cry "*à la porte les Jockeys,*" both openly and loudly denounced my chief opponents. The members of this club—whose right to consider themselves the rulers of the Grand Opéra I need not here explain to you—feeling their interests deeply compromised by the absence of the usual ballet at the hour of their arrival, i.e. towards the middle of the representation, were horrified to discover that "Tannhäuser" had *not* made a fiasco, but an actual triumph at its first performance. Henceforth it was their business to prevent this ballet-less opera from being given night after night; to this end, on their way from dinner they had bought a number of dog-calls and such-like instruments, with which they manœuvred against "Tannhäuser" in the most unblushing manner directly they had entered the opera-house. Until then, that is to say from the beginning of the first to about the middle of the second act, not a single trace of the first night's opposition had been shewn, and the most prolonged applause had undisturbedly accompanied those passages of my opera which had become the speediest favourites. But from now on, no acclamation was of the least avail: in vain did the Emperor himself, with his Consort, demonstrate for a second time in favour of my work; by those who considered themselves masters of the house, and all of whom belong to France's highest aristocracy, the condemnation of "Tannhäuser" was irrevocably pronounced. Whistles and flageolets accompanied every plaudit of the audience, down to the very close.

In view of the management's utter impotence against this powerful club, in view of even the State-minister's obvious dread of making serious enemies of its members, I recognised that I had no right to expect my proved and faithful artists of the stage to expose themselves any longer to the abominable agitation put upon them by unscrupulous persons (naturally with the intention of forcing them to throw up their engagements). I told the management that I must withdraw my opera, and consented to a third performance only upon condition that it should take place on a Sunday: that is to say, on a night outside the subscription, and thus under circumstances which would not incur the subscribers' wrath, while on the other hand the house would be left completely clear for the public proper. My wish to have this performance announced on the posters as "the last" was not allowed, and all I could do was to personally inform my acquaintances of the fact These precautionary measures, however, were powerless to dissipate the Jockey Club's alarm; on the contrary, it fancied that it detected in this Sunday performance a bold stratagem against its dearest interests, after which — the opera once brought to an unqualified success — the hated work might be forced quite easily down its throat. In the sincerity of my assurance, that in case of such a success I should still more certainly withdraw my work, people hadn't the courage to believe. So the gentlemen forsook their other pleasures for this evening, returned to the Opéra in full battle-array, and renewed the scenes of the second night. This time the public's exasperation, at the attempt to downright hinder it from following the opera at all, reached a pitch unknown before, as people have assured me; and it was only the, as it would seem, unassailable social standing of Messieurs Disturbers-of-the-peace, that saved them from positive rough handling. To put the matter briefly: astonished as I am at the outrageous behaviour of those gentlemen, I am equally touched and moved by the real public's heroic exertions to procure me justice; and nothing can be more distant from my mind, than to entertain the smallest doubt of the Paris Public whenever it shall find itself on a neutral terrain of its own.

My withdrawal of the score, at last announced officially, has placed the Directors of the Opéra in great and genuine perplexity. They frankly and openly confess to regarding my opera as one of their greatest successes, for they cannot remember having ever seen the public side so actively in favour of a contested work. The most abundant receipts appear to them assured with "Tannhäuser," the house being already sold-out for several performances in advance. They are informed of a growing irritation on the part of the public, which sees its rights of hearing and judging a new, much-talked-of work in peace and quietness, denied it by an infinitely small minority. I learn that the Emperor remains thoroughly well-disposed, that the Empress would gladly take upon herself the protection of my opera, and demand guarantees against further disturbances of the peace. At this moment there is circulating among the musicians, painters, artists and authors of Paris a protest against the unseemly occurrences in the Opera-house: a protest addressed to the Minister of State and, as I am told, already numerously signed. Under such circumstances folk think I might well feel encouraged to let my opera proceed. But a weighty artistic consideration holds me back. Hitherto my work has had no quiet, no collected hearing; its intrinsic character—lying in its intentional appeal to a *Stimmung* foreign to the customary opera-public, a *Stimmung* compassing the whole—has not dawned as yet upon the audience; up to the present they have only been able to catch at certain glittering points which served me, strictly speaking, merely as a garnish (*Staffage*), and to single these out for ready sympathy. But should they once arrive at a calm, attentive hearing of my opera, then, after what I have hinted to you about the character of the performance here, I fear they would soon unearth the latter's inner feebleness and want of verve— for these evils are no secret to those who really know my work, though I have been debarred from intervening personally for their removal; so that I could not dream for this time of a radical, not merely an external, success for my opera. Wherefore let all the inadequacies of this production lie buried decently beneath the dust of those three evenings' warfare, and may many a one, who bitterly deceived my hopes reposed in him, save his honour for the nonce with the belief that he fell fighting for a good cause!

So let us hold the Parisian "Tannhäuser" as played-out for the present. Should the wish of earnest friends of my art be fulfilled; should a project, seriously entertained of late by people who know their business, and aiming at nothing less than the speedy foundation of a new opera-house for the realisement of reforms which I have mooted here, as well as elsewhere—should this be carried out, then perhaps you may hear from Paris itself yet once again of "Tannhäuser."

As to what has been done with my work in Paris till to-day, rest assured that you now have heard the strictest truth. One simple thing may be your warranty: that it is impossible for me to content myself with a semblance, when my inmost wish stays unfulfilled; and that wish is only to be stilled by the consciousness of having evoked a really intelligent impression.

Hearty greetings from yours,

RICHARD WAGNER.

Notes

01

Referring to his exile; for the first, the partial, amnesty was not granted until the summer of 1860.—TR.

02

Princess Metternich, née Countess Pauline Sandór, wife of the Austrian ambassador.—TR.

03

The clause about the reviewers was omitted in the *Deutsche Allgemeine Zeitung*, and therefore in the *Neue Zeitschrift*.—TR.

Summary

Projects for *Tristan* at Carlsruhe in 1859; amnesty impossible then; removal to Paris in autumn, for sake of hearing good orchestra etc. at last; Carlsruhe plan falls through. Idea of *Tristan* at Théâtre des Italiens, inviting German Directors to a model-performance; the three Paris concerts were to prepare the public, but they proved the plan's impossibility. Princess Metternich and the Emperor; order for *Tannhäuser* at Grand Opéra a complete surprise. Difficulties about a ballet in act ii for the late diners; plan for new Venusberg scene; carte blanche for engagements and mise en scene; Niemann, Morelli and young talents; Vauthrot and his pains with pianoforte rehearsals; taken with a new liking for this early work, I carefully revised the .score. Gradual disheartenment; reporters prophesy failure to Niemann; spiritless orchestral conducting; offer to withdraw score. Performance and false accounts; magnanimity of Paris public proper. First night: clique of reviewers, cues and roars of laughter, especially in third act, which promised so well; uproar, but opposition beaten down at end by public—in reality a victory for the work. Second night: Jockey Club and dog-calls for the ballet-less opera. Second offer to withdraw the work, but management persisted, and refused to announce third night as "final." Jockey Club's alarm at stratagem of Sunday performance; scenes of second night renewed, indignation of public; only social standing of Messieurs Disturbors-of-peace saved them irom rough handling. Definite withdrawal prompted by artistic considerations—the house was sold-out for several nights in advance; circular protest signed by musicians, authors etc.; Empress's offer to intervene. Let the inadequacies of this production lie buried beneath the dust of its three nights' war! Project for a new theatre in Paris, to realise my reforms.

THE DESTINY OF OPERA

Translator's Note

This essay was published in the Spring of 1871 (E. W. Fritzsch, Leipzig), with the subsidiary title "An Academic Lecture by Richard Wagner." The author had in 1869 been elected a member of the Royal Academy of the Arts in Berlin, and "The Destiny of Opera" was intended as the thesis for his installation, which followed on April 28, 1871.

Preface

IN preparing the following essay for an Academic lecture, the author experienced the difficulty of having to enlarge once more on a subject he many years ago had treated exhaustively, as he believes, in a special book entitled *Oper und Drama*. As the requisite brevity of its present treatment would only allow of the main idea being sketched in outline, whoever might haply feel roused to more serious interest in the subject must needs be referred to that earlier book of mine. It then would scarcely escape his notice that, albeit a complete agreement holds between the older, lengthier, and the present conciser treatment of the subject itself—namely the character and importance ascribed by the author to the Musically-conceived drama—yet in many respects this recent setting offers new points of view, from whence regarded certain details necessarily assume another aspect; and that, perhaps, may make this newer treatment interesting even to those already familiar with the older one.

Certainly I have been given ample time to digest the topic started by myself, and I could have wished to have been diverted from the process by practical proof of the justice of my views being made more easy to me. The obtaining of single stage-performances, correct in my sense of the term, could not suffice me so long as they were not withdrawn completely from the sphere of modern operatic doings; for the ruling theatrical element of our day, with all its outward and inward attributes, entirely inartistic, un-German, both morally and mentally pernicious, invariably gathers again like a choking mist over any spot where the most arduous exertions may have given one for once an outlook on the sunlight. May the present writing therefore be not taken as an ambitious contribution to the field of Theory proper, but merely as a last attempt from that side to awaken interest and furtherance for the author's efforts on the realm of artistic Practice. It will then be understood why, prompted by this wish alone, he has constantly endeavoured to place his subject in new lights; for he was bound to keep on trying to propound the problem, that occupied his mind, in such a way that it finally might strike the minds of those alone qualified to give it serious attention. That this result has hitherto been so hard of attainment that he could but regard himself as a lonely wanderer soliloquising to a croaking accompaniment of the frogs in our stage-reporters' swamp, has simply shewn him how low had sunk the sphere to which he found himself and problem banned: but this sphere alone contains the elements capable of producing a higher Artwork, and thus the object of the following treatise, too, can only be to direct to those elements the gaze of those who at present stand entirely outside this sphere.

The Destiny of Opera

A WELL-MEANT cry of earnest friends of the Theatre lays the blame of its downfall on the Opera. The charge is founded on the unmistakable decline of interest in the spoken Play, as also on the degeneration of dramatic performances in general.

The correctness of this accusation must needs seem obvious. Merely, one might ask how it came to pass that the foundations of Opera were laid with the first beginnings of the modern Theatre, and why the most distinguished minds have repeatedly dwelt on the potentialities in a genre of dramatic art whose one-sided development has taken the shape of current Opera? In such an inquiry we might easily be led into regarding our greatest poets as, in a certain sense, the pioneers of Opera. Though such an allegation must be accepted with great reserve, on the other hand the issue of our great German poets labours for the theatre, and their effect on the whole spirit of our dramatic representations, can but cause us earnestly to ponder how it was that Opera could have acquired so overpowering a control over theatric taste in general, in face of just the influence of those great poetic works themselves. And here we perhaps may gain an answer if we limit ourselves at first to the actual result, upon the character of stage-doings in the stricter province of the *Play,* of the effect of the Goethe-and-Schiller Drama upon the spirit in which our actors approach their work.

That result we recognise at once as due to a disproportion between the capacity of our actors and the nature of the tasks proposed them. A full account of this misrelation belongs to the history of German Acting, and has already been undertaken in praiseworthy fashion. (1) Referring to that account, on the one hand, and on the other reserving the deeper aesthetic problem at bottom of the evil for the later course of our inquiry, our present concern is that our poets had to couch their idealising tendence in a dramatic form to which the natural parts and training of our actors could not adapt themselves. It needed the rarest talents, such as of a Sophie Schröder, to completely solve a task pitched far too high for our players; accustomed solely to their native element of German burgher life, the sudden demand could not but set them in the most ruinous bewilderment To that disproportion we owe the rise and eventual rampancy of "false pathos." This had been preceded, at an earlier epoch of the German stage, by the grotesque affectation peculiar to the "English comedians" so-called: a grotesquery applied by them to the rough-and-ready representation of old-English and even Shakespearian pieces, and to be met to this day at the degenerate English national theatre. In healthy opposition there had since arisen the so-called "true-to-nature," which found its suitable field of expression in the "Burgher" drama. Though Lessing himself, as also Goethe in his youth, wrote poems for this Burgher drama, we must note that it always derived its chief supply from pieces written by the foremost actors of this period. Now, the narrow sphere and scant poetic value of these products impelled our great poets to extend and elevate dramatic style; and though their original purpose was to continue the cultivation of the "true-to-nature," it was not long before the Ideal tendence shewed itself,—to be realised, as for expression, by *poetic pathos.* Those at all acquainted with this branch of our art-history, know how our great poets were disturbed in their endeavours to instil the new style into the players; however, it is much to be doubted whether in any event they would finally have proved successful, as they had previously been obliged to content themselves with a mere artificial semblance of success, which persistently developed into just that so-called "false pathos." In harmony with the German's modest talent for play-acting, this remained the sole but doubtful profit, as regards the character of performance of dramas of an Ideal trend, of that else so gigantic influence of our poets on the Theatre.

Now, what took the outward form of this "false pathos" became in turn the tendence of all the dramatic conceptions of our lesser stage-poets, whose matter from first to last was every whit as hollow as that pathos itself: we need but recall the products of a Houwald, Müllner, and the string of similar playwrights who have made for the Pathetic to the present day. The only adducible reaction against this tendence would be the constantly reviving Burgher play or prose-comedy of our time, had the French "Sensational piece" ("*Effektstück*") not overwhelmed us with its influence in this direction also. Hereby has the last trace of purity of type been wiped from our stage; and all that our Play has retained from the dramas of Goethe and Schiller themselves, is the now open secret of the employment of "false pathos," to wit "*Effect.*"

As everything written for, and acted at the theatre is nowadays inspired by nothing but this tendence to "Effect," so that whatever ignores it is promptly condemned to neglect, we need feel no surprise at seeing it systematically applied to the performance of pieces by Goethe and Schiller; for, in a certain sense, we here have the original model that has been misconstrued to this tendence. The need of "poetic pathos" made our poets deliberately adopt a *rhetorical mode of diction*, with the aim of working on the Feeling; and, as it was impossible for our unpoetic actors to either understand or carry out the ideal aim, this diction led to that intrinsically senseless, but melodramatically telling style of declamation whose practical object was just the said "Effect," i.e. a stunning of the spectator's senses, to be documented by the outburst of "applause." This "applause" and its unfailing provoker, the "exit"-tirade, became the soul of every tendence of our modern theatre: the "brilliant exits" in the rôles of our classical plays have been counted up, and the latters' value rated by their number—exactly as with an Italian operatic part. Surely we cannot scold our applause-dry priests of Thalia and Melpomene for casting envious glances at the Opera, where these "exits" are far more plentiful, and the storms of applause are raised with much greater certainty, than in even the most effective play; and since our playwrights live on the Effect of the rôles of our actors, 'tis easy to understand why the opera-composer appears to them a very hateful rival, for he can bring all this about by simply arranging for a good loud scream at the close of any vocal phrase you please.

In truth the outer reason, as also the most obvious character of the complaint we noted at starting, turns out to be thus and not otherwise. That I am far from thinking I have herewith shewn its deeper ground, I sufficiently hinted above: but, before we touch the inner core, I deem it more advisable to first weigh well its outer tokens, open to the experience of everyone. Let us therefore remember that in the character of all theatrical performances there inheres a tendency whose worst consequence comes out as the striving for "effect," and, though just as rampant in the spoken Play, in Opera it has the fullest opportunity of satiation. At bottom of the common actor's cry against the Opera there probably lies nothing but jealousy of its greater wealth of means of effect: but we must admit that the earnest actor has far more show of reason for annoyance, when he compares the seeming easiness and frivolity of these means of effect with the certainly much severer pains he has to take, to do some justice to the characters he represents. For, even from the standpoint of its outward effect on the public, the Play may boast of at least this merit:—that the plot itself, with the incidents that hold the plot together and the motives that explain it, must be intelligible, to rivet the spectator's interest; and that a piece composed of nothing but declamatory phrases, without an underlying plot intelligibly set forth and thereby centering the interest, is here as yet unthinkable. Opera, on the contrary, may be taxed with simply stringing together a number of means of exciting a purely physical sense, whilst a mere agreeable contrast in their order of sequence suffices to mask the absence of any understandable or reasonable plot.

Plainly, a very serious point in the indictment. Yet even of this we may have our doubts, on closer scrutiny. That the so-called text of an opera must be interesting, composers have felt so clearly in every age, and particularly of late, that to obtain a good "book" has been one of their most earnest endeavours. An attractive, or if possible a rousing plot, has always been essential for an opera to make its mark, especially in our time; so that it would be difficult to argue wholly away the dramatic tendence in the flimsy structure of an operatic text In fact this side of the procedure has been so little unpretentious, that there is hardly a play of Shakespeare's, and there soon will be none of Schiller's and Goethe's, which Opera has not deemed just good enough for adaptation. Precisely this abuse, however, could only irritate our actors and playwrights still more, and this time with great justice; they might well protest: "Why should we take any pains in future to acquit ourselves of true dramatic tasks, when the public runs from us to where the selfsame themes, most frivolously distorted, are employed for mere multiplication of the vulgarest effects?" To this we at any rate might reply by asking how it would have been possible to set Herr Gounod's opera "Faust" before the German public, if our acting-stage had been able to make it really understand the "Faust" of Goethe? No: 'tis not to be disputed that the public has turned away from our actors' singular efforts to make something of the monologue of our own "Faust," to Herr Gounod's aria with the theme on the pleasures of youth, and here applauds whilst it there refused to move a hand.

Perhaps no instance could shew us more plainly and distressingly, to what a pass our Theatre has come. Yet even now we cannot admit the perfect equity of laying the whole blame of this undeniable downfall on the vogue enjoyed by Opera; rather, that very vogue should open our eyes alike to the failings of our Play and the impossibility of fulfilling within its bounds, and with the only expressional means at its command, the *ideal* scope of Drama. Precisely here, where the highest ideal is faced with its utmost trivialising, as in the above example, the horror of the thing must force us to look deeper into the nature of our problem. We still might shirk the obligation, if we merely meant to take a great depravation of public taste for granted, and to seek its causes in the wider field of our public life. But for ourselves, having reached that horrifying experience from just this standpoint, it is hopeless to contemplate an improvement of public art-taste, in particular, by the lengthy route of a regeneration of our public spirit itself; we deem wiser to take the direct path of an inquiry into the purely æsthetic problem lying at bottom, and thus to arrive at an answer which perchance may give us hopes of the possibility of an influence being exerted on the public spirit from this opposite side.

We therefore will formulate a thesis, whose working-out may haply guide us to that end. As follows:—

We grant that Opera has made palpable the downfall of the Theatre: though it may be doubted whether it really brought about that downfall, yet its present supremacy shews clearly that by it alone can our Theatre be raised again; but this restoration can never truly prosper till it conducts our Theatre to that Ideal to which it is so innately predisposed, that neglect and misapprehension thereof have done far greater harm to the German stage than to the French, since the latter had no idealistic aspirations and therefore could devote itself to the development of realistic correctness in a narrower sphere.—

An intelligent history of stage "pathos" would make plain what the idealistic trend in modern drama has ever aimed at. Here it would be instructive to note how the Italians, who sat at the feet of the Antique for wellnigh all their art-tendences, left the spoken drama almost quite in embryo; they promptly attempted a reconstruction of the antique drama on a basis of musical Lyrics, and, straying ever farther to one side, produced the Opera. While this was taking place in Italy under the omnipotent influence of the cultured upper circles of the nation, among the Spaniards and English the Folk-spirit itself was evolving the modern Play, after the antiquarian bent of lettered poets had proved incapable of any vital influence on the nation. Only by starting from this realistic sphere, wherein Lope de Vega had shewn such exuberant fertility, did Calderon lead the Spanish drama to that idealising tendence, which brought him so close to the Italians that many of his pieces we can but characterise as wellnigh operatic. Perhaps the English drama also would not have held aloof from a similar tendence, had not the inscrutable genius of a Shakespeare enabled the loftiest figures of history and legend to tread the boards of the realistic Folk-play with such a truth to nature that they passed beyond the reach of any rule erewhile misborrowed from the antique Form. Perhaps their awe at Shakespeare's unfathomable inimitability had no less share than their recognition of the true meaning of the Antique and its forms, in determining our great poets' dramatic labours. They pondered too the eminent advantages of Opera, though it finally passed their understanding how this Opera was to be dealt with from their standpoint. Schiller, transported by Gluck's "Iphigenia in Tauris," nevertheless could not discover a modus vivendi with the Opera; and Goethe appears to have plainly seen that the task was reserved for the musical genius, when he regarded the news of Mozart's death as effacing all the splendid prospects of a Musically-conceived Drama opened up to him by "Don Giovanni."

Through this attitude of Goethe and Schiller we are afforded a deep insight into the nature of the *poet* pure and simple. If on the one hand Shakespeare and his method to them seemed incomprehensible, and on the other they felt compelled to leave to the *musician*—whose method was equally incomprehensible—the unique task of breathing ideal life into the figures of the Drama, the question arises: how did they stand as poets toward the genuine Drama, and whether, solely as such, they could feel themselves equipped for Drama at all? A doubt of this seems to have invaded more and more these so profoundly truthful men, and the constant change of Form in their projects shews, of itself, that they felt as if engaged in one continual series of experiments. Were we to try to probe that doubt, we might find in it the confession of a certain insufficiency in the poetic nature (*das Bekenntniss einer Unzulänglichkeit des dichterischen Wesens*); for Poetry, taken by itself, is only to be conceived as an *abstractum*, and first becomes a *concretum* through the matter of its fashionings. If neither the Plastic artist nor the Musician is thinkable without a trace of the poetic spirit, the question simply is how that latent force, which in them brings forth the work of art, can lead to the same result in the Poet's shapings as a conscious agent?

Without embarking on an inquiry into the mystery just mooted, we yet must call to mind the distinction between the modern culture-poet and the naive poet of the ancient world. The latter was in the first place an inventor of Myths, then their word-of-mouth narrator in the Epos, and finally their personal performer in the living Drama. Plato was the first to adopt all three poetic forms for his "dialogues," so filled with dramatic life and so rich in myth-invention; and these scenes of his may be regarded as the foundation—nay, in the poet-philosopher's glorious "Symposium," the model unapproached—of strictly literary poetry, which always leans to the didactic. Here the forms of naive poetry are merely employed to set philosophic theses in a quasi-popular light, and conscious *tendence* takes the place of the directly-witnessed scene from life. To extend this "Tendence" to the acted drama, must have appeared to our great culture-poets the surest mode of elevating the existing popular play; and in this they may have been misled by certain features of the Antique Drama. The Tragedy of the Greeks having evolved from a compromise between the Apollinian and the Dionysian elements, upon the basis of a system of Lyrics wellnigh past our understanding, the didactic hymn of the old-Hellenian priests could combine with the newer Dionysian dithyramb to produce that enthralling effect in which this artwork stands unrivalled. Now the fact of the Apollinian element in Greek Tragedy, regarded as a literary monument, having attracted to itself the principal notice in every age, and particularly of philosophers and didacts, may reasonably have betrayed our later poets—who also chiefly viewed these tragedies as literary products—into the opinion that in this didactic tendence lay the secret of the antique drama's dignity, and. consequently into the belief that the existing popular drama was only to be raised and idealised by stamping it therewith. Their true artistic instinct saved them from sacrificing living Drama to Tendence bald and bare: but what was to put soul into this Drama, to lift it on the cothurnus of ideality, they deemed could only be the purposed elevation of its tendence; and that the more, as their sole disposable material, namely Word-speech, the vehicle of notions (*Begriffe*), seemed to exclude the feasibility, or even the advisability, of an ennoblement and heightening of expression on any side but this. The lofty *sentence* alone could match the higher *tendence*; and to impress the hearer's physical sense, unquestionably excited by the drama, recourse must be had to so-called *poetic diction*. But this diction lured the exponents of their pieces into that "false pathos," whose recognition must needs have given our great poets many a pang when they compared it with their deep delight in Gluck's "Iphigenia" and Mozart's "Don Juan."

What so profoundly moved them in these last, must surely have been that here they found the drama transported by its music to the sphere of the Ideal, a sphere where the simplest feature of the plot was at once transfigured, and motive and emotion, fused in one direct expression, appealed to them with noblest stress. Here hushed all desire to seize a Tendence, for the Idea had realised itself before them as the sovereign call of Fellow-feeling. "Error attends manes ev'ry quest," or "Life is not the highest good," was here no longer to be clothed in words, for the inmost secret of the wisest apothegm itself stood bared to them in limpid Melody. Whilst that had said "it means," this said "it is!" Here had the highest pathos come to be the very soul of Drama; as from a shining world of dreams, Life's picture stepped before us here with sympathetic verity.

But what a riddle must this artwork have seemed to our poets! — where was the Poet's place therein? Certainly not where their own strength lay, in the poetic thought and diction, of which these "texts" were absolutely destitute. There being, then, no possible question of the Poet, it was the Musician alone to whom this artwork appeared to belong. Yet, judged by their artistic standard, it fell hard to accord this latter a rank at all commensurate with the stupendous force he set in motion. In Music they saw a plainly irrational art, a thing half wild half foolish, not for a moment to be approached from the side of true artistic culture. And in Opera, forsooth, a paltry, incoherent pile of forms, without the smallest evidence of a sense for architectonics; whilst the last thing its capriciously assorted items could be said to aim at, was the consistence of a true dramatic plan. So that, admitting it was the dramatic groundwork that in Gluck's "Iphigenia" had held that jumble of forms together for once, and made of it a thrilling whole, there arose the question: Who would ever care to step into the shoes of its librettist, and write the threadbare text for the arias of even a Gluck, unless he were prepared to give up all pretence to rank as "poet"? The incomprehensible in the thing, was the supreme ideality of an effect whose artistic factors were not discoverable by analogy with any other art soever. And the incomprehensibility increased when one passed from this particular work of Gluck's, instinct with the nobility of a tragic subject taken bodily from the antique, and found that under certain circumstances, no matter how absurd or trivial its shape, one could not deny to Opera a power unrivalled even in the most ideal sense. These circumstances arose forthwith, whenever a great dramatic artist filled a rôle in such an opera. We need but instance the impersonation, surely unforgettable by many yet alive, once given us by Frau Schröder-Devrient of "Romeo" in Bellini's opera. Every fibre of the musician rebels against allowing the least artistic merit to the sickly, utterly threadbare music here hung upon an opera-poem of indigent grotesqueness; but ask anyone who witnessed it, what impression he received from the "Romeo" of Frau Schröder-Devrient as compared with the Romeo of our very best play-actor in even the great Briton's piece? And this effect by no means lay in any vocal virtuosity, as with the common run of our prime donne's successes, for in this case that was scant and totally unsupported by any richness of the voice itself: the effect was simply due to the dramatic power of the rendering. But that, again, could never possibly have succeeded with the selfsame Schröder-Devrient in quite the finest spoken play; and thus the whole achievement must have issued from the element of music, transfiguring and idealising even in this most meagre form.

Such an experience as this last, however, might set us on the high road to discover and estimate the veritable factor in the creation of the Dramatic Artwork.—As the Poet's share in it was so infinitesimal, Goethe believed he must ascribe the whole authorship of Opera to the Musician; and how much of serious truth resides in that opinion, we perhaps shall see if next we turn our notice to our great poets' second object of non-comprehension in the realm of Drama, to wit the singularity of *Shakespeare* and his artistic method.—

To the French, as representatives of modern civilisation, Shakespeare, considered seriously, to this day is a monstrosity; and even to the Germans he has remained a subject of constantly renewed investigation, with so little positive result that the most conflicting views and statements are forever cropping up again. Thus has this most bewildering of dramatists—already set down by some as an utterly irresponsible and untamed genius, without one trace of artistic culture—quite recently been credited again with the most systematic tendence of the didactic poet. Goethe, after introducing him in "Wilhelm Meister" as an "admirable writer," kept returning to the problem with increasing caution, and finally decided that here the higher tendence was to be sought, not in the poet, but in the embodied characters he brought before us in immediate action. Yet the closer these figures were inspected, the greater riddle became the artist's method: though the main plan of a piece was easy to perceive, and it was impossible to mistake the consequent development of its plot, for the most part pre-existing in the source selected, yet the marvellous "accidentiæ" in its working out, as also in the bearing of its dramatis personae, were inexplicable on any hypothesis of deliberate artistic scheming. Here we found such drastic individuality, that it often seemed like unaccountable caprice, whose sense we never really fathomed till we closed the book and saw the living drama move before our eyes; then stood before us life's own image, mirrored with resistless truth to nature, and filled us with the lofty terror of a ghostly vision. But how decipher in this magic spell the tokens of an "artwork"? Was the author of these plays a *poet*?

What little we know of his life makes answer with outspoken naïvety: he was a *play-actor* and *manager*, who wrote for himself and his troop these pieces that in after days amazed and poignantly perplexed our greatest poets; pieces that for the most part would not so much as have come down to us, had the unpretending prompt-books of the Globe Theatre not been rescued from oblivion in the nick of time by the printing-press. *Lope de Vega*, scarcely less a wonder, wrote his pieces from one day to the next in immediate contact with his actors and the stage; beside Corneille and Racine, the poets of *façon*, there stands the actor *Molière*, in whom alone production was alive; and midst his tragedy sublime stood *Æschylus*, the leader of its chorus.—Not to the Poet, but to the Dramatist must we look, for light upon the Drama's nature; and he stands no nearer to the poet proper than to the *mime* himself, from whose heart of hearts he must issue if as poet he means to "hold the mirror up to Nature."

Thus undoubtedly the essence of Dramatic art, as against the Poet's method, at first seems totally irrational; it is not to be seized, without a complete reversal of the beholder's nature. In what this reversal must consist, however, should not be hard to indicate if we recall the natural process in the beginnings of all Art, as plainly shewn to us in *improvisation*. The poet, mapping out a plan of action for the improvising mime, would stand in much the same relation to him as the author of an operatic text to the musician; his work can claim as yet no atom of artistic value; but this it will gain in the very fullest measure if the poet makes the improvising spirit of the mime his own, and develops his plan entirely in character with that improvisation, so that the mime now enters with all his individuality into the poet's higher reason. This involves, to be sure, a complete transformation of the poetic artwork itself, of which we might form an idea if we imagined the impromptu of some great musician noted down. We have it on the authority of competent witnesses, that nothing could compare with the effect produced by Beethoven when he improvised at length upon the pianoforte to his friends; nor, even in view of the master's greatest works, need we deem excessive the lament that precisely these inventions were not fixed in writing, if we reflect that far inferior musicians, whose penwork was always stiff and stilted, have quite amazed us in their 'free fantasias' by a wholly unsuspected and often very fertile talent for invention.—At anyrate we believe we shall really expedite the solution of an extremely difficult problem, if we define the Shakespearian Drama as *a fixed mimetic improvisation of the highest poetic worth*. For this explains at once each wondrous accidental in the bearing and discourse of characters alive to but one purpose, to be at this moment all that they are meant to seem to us to be, and to whom accordingly no word can come that lies outside this conjured nature; so that it would be positively laughable to us, upon closer consideration, if one of these figures were suddenly to pose as poet. This last is silent, and remains for us a riddle, such as Shakespeare. But his work is the only veritable Drama; and what that implies, as work of Art, is shewn by our rating its author the profoundest poet of all time.—

From the countless topics for reflection afforded by this Drama of Shakespeare's let us choose those attributes which seem of most assistance to our present inquiry. Firstly then, apart from all its other merits, it strictly belongs to the class of effective *stage-pieces*, such as have been devised in the most dissimilar ages by skilful authors either sprung from the Theatre itself or in immediate contact therewith, and such as have enriched, for instance, the popular stages of the French from year to year. The difference between these true dramatic products, similarly arisen, simply lies in their *poetic value*. At first sight this poetic value seems determined by the dignity and grandeur of the subject-matter. Whereas not only have the French succeeded in setting every incident of modern life with speaking truth upon the stage, but even the Germans—with their infinitely smaller talent for the Theatre—have done the like for the narrower burgher province of that life, this genuinely reproductive force has failed in measure as the scene was to picture forth events of higher life, and finally the fate of heroes of world-history and their myths, sublimely distant from the eye of everyday. For here the mime's improvisation fell too short, and needed to be wielded by the poet proper, i.e. the inventor and fashioner of Myths; and his genius had to prove its pre-election by raising the style of mimetic improvisation to the level of his own poetic aim. How Shakespeare may have succeeded in raising his players themselves to that level, must remain to us another riddle; the only certainty is, that our modern actors wreck their faculties at once upon the task he set. Possibly, what we above have called the grotesque affectation peculiar to English actors of nowadays is the remains of an earlier aptitude, and, springing from an inborn national idiosyncrasy, it may once have led, in the fairest age of English folk-life and through the contagious example of the poet himself, to so unheard a climax of the player's art that Shakespeare's conceptions could be realised thereby. If we are indisposed to assume so great a miracle however, we perhaps may explain this riddle by instancing the fate of great Sebastian Bach, whose difficult and prolific choral compositions tempt us at first to assume that the master had the most unrivalled vocal forces at command for their performance; whereas, on the contrary, we have unimpeachable documents to prove his complaints of the mostly altogether pitiable condition of his schoolboy choir. (2) Certain it is, that Shakespeare withdrew very early from his business with the stage; for which we may easily account by the immense fatigue the rehearsing of his pieces must have cost him, as also by the despair of a genius that towered high above the "possibility" of its surroundings. Yet the whole nature of this genius is explicable by nothing but that "possibility" itself, which assuredly existed in the nature of the mime, and was therefore very rightly presupposed by the genius; and, taking all the cultural efforts of the human spirit in one comprehensive survey, we may regard it as in a certain sense the task bequeathed to Shakespeare's aftercomers by the greatest Dramatist, to actually attain that highest possibility in the development of histrionic art.

To fulfil this task, appears to have been the inner aspiration of our great German poets. Starting, as here was indispensable, with the recognition of Shakespeare's inimitability, every form in which they cast their poetic conceptions was dictated by an aim we can readily understand on this assumption. The search for the ideal Form of the highest work of art, the Drama, must necessarily lead them away from Shakespeare to a fresh and ever deeper consideration of Antique Tragedy; in what sense they thought to draw profit thence, we have explained before, and we had to see them turning from this more than dubious path to the strangely powerful impression made on them by the noblest products of a genre that yet appeared so highly enigmatic, the genre of Opera.

Here were two chief points of notice: firstly, that a great master's music lent the doings of even poor dramatic exponents an ideal charm, denied to the most admirable of actors in the spoken play; secondly, that a true dramatic talent could so ennoble even entirely worthless music, as to move us with a performance inachievable by the self-same talent in the recited drama. That this phenomenon must be accounted to nothing but the might of *Music*, was irrefutable. Yet this could apply to Music solely in the general, and it still remained incomprehensible how the dramatic poet was to approach the singularly paltry fabric of her forms without falling into a subjection of the very vilest sort—Now, we have appealed to Shakespeare to give us, if possible, a glimpse into the nature, and more especially the method, of the genuine dramatist Mysterious as we found the most part of this matter too, yet we saw that the poet was here entirely at one with the art of the mime; so that we now may call this mimetic art the life-dew wherein the poetic aim was to be steeped, to enable it, as in a magic transformation, to appear as the mirror of life. And if every action, each humblest incident of life displays itself, when reproduced by mimicry, in the transfiguring light and with the objective effect of a mirror-image (as is shewn not only by Shakespeare, but by every other sterling playwright), in further course we shall have to avow that this mirror-image, again, displays itself in the transfiguration of purest Ideality so soon as it is dipped in the magic spring of Music and held up to us as nothing but pure Form, so to say, set free from all the realism of Matter.

'Tis not the *Form* of Music, therefore, but *the forms which music has evolved in history*, that we should have to consider before arguing to that highest possibility in the development of the latent powers of the mimo-dramatic artwork, that possibility which has hovered before the earnest seeker as a voiceless riddle, and yet a riddle crying out aloud for answer.

Music's Form, without a doubt, is synonymous with *Melody*; the latter's special evolution makes out the history of our music, just as its need determined the development of Lyric Drama, once attempted by the Italians, into the "Opera." If one meant to imitate the form of the Greek Tragedy, the first glance shewed it falling into two main sections, the choral chant and a dramatic recitation that mounted periodically to *melopöe*: so the "drama" proper was handed over to Recitative, whose oppressive monotony was at last to be broken by the academically-approved invention of the "Aria." In this last alone did Music here attain her independent Form, as Melody; and it therefore most rightly gained such a preponderance over the other factors of the musical drama, that the latter itself eventually sank to a mere pretext, a barren prop on which to hang the Aria. It thus is with the history of Melody chained to the Aria-form, that we should have to occupy ourselves, were it not sufficient for our present purpose to consider that one particular shape in which it offered itself to our great poets when they felt so deeply moved by its effect in general, but all the more bewildered at the thought of any poetic concern therewith. Beyond dispute it was always the particular genius, and he alone, who knew to put such life into this cramped and sterile cast of melody as to make it capable of that profound effect: consequently its expansion, its ideal unfolding, could be awaited from no one but the Musician; and the line of this development was already to be traced, if one compared the masterpiece of Mozart with that of Gluck. And here the greater store of musical invention turned out to be the unique measure of Music's dramatic capacity, since Mozart's "Don Juan" already displayed a wealth of dramatic characterisation whereof the far lesser musician Gluck could never have dreamt But it still was reserved for the German genius to raise musical Form, by the utmost vitalising of its tiniest fraction, to the infinite diversity the music of our great *Beethoven* now offers to a wondering world.

Now, Beethoven's musical fashionings bear marks that leave them equally inexplicable as those of Shakespeare have remained to the inquiring poet. Whilst the power of effect in both must needs be felt as different at once and equal, upon a deeper scrutiny of its essence the very difference appears to us to vanish, for suddenly the one unsolved peculiarity affords the only explanation of the other. Let us select the peculiarity of the Humour, as that most swiftly seizable, and we discover that what often seems to us an unaccountable caprice in the sallies given off by Shakespeare's characters, in the corresponding turns of Beethoven's motive-moulding becomes a natural occurrence of the utmost ideality, to wit a melody that takes the mind by storm. We cannot but here assume a blood-relationship, which to correctly define we must seek it, not between the musician and the poet, but between the former and the poet-mime.

Whereas no poet of any artistic epoch can be compared with Beethoven, we find his fellowship with Shakespeare in the very fact that the latter, as poet, would forever remain to us a problem, could we not detect in him before all else the poet-mime. The secret lies in the directness of the presentation, here by mien and gesture, there by living tone. That which both directly mould and fashion is the actual Artwork, for which the Poet merely drafts the plan,—and that itself successfully, only when he has borrowed it from their own nature.

We have found that the Shakespearian Drama was definable the most intelligibly as a "fixed mimetic improvisation"; and as we had to suppose that this Art-work's high poetic value, resting in the first place on the elevation of its subject, must be ensured by the heightening of the *style* of that improvisation, we can scarcely go astray if we look for the possibility of such an utmost heightening in a mode of music which shall bear thereto the same relation as Beethoven's Music to just this Drama of Shakespeare's.

The very difficulty of thus applying Beethovenian Music to the Shakespearian Drama might lead, when conquered, to the utmost perfecting of musical Form, through its final liberation from each remaining fetter. What still distressed our great German poets in regard of Opera, and what still left its manifest traces on Beethoven's instrumental music,—that scaffolding which in nowise rested on the essence of Music, but rather on that selfsame tendence which planned the operatic aria and the ballet-tune,—this conventional four-square structure, so wondrously wreathed already with the luxuriant life of Beethovenian melody, would vanish quite away before an ideal ordering of highest freedom; so that Music now would take the ineffably vital shape of a Shakespearian drama, and its sublime irregularity, compared with the antique drama, would wellnigh give it the appearance of a nature-scene as against a work of architecture, a scene whose skilful measurement would be evinced by nothing but the unfailing sureness of the artwork's effect And in this would lie withal the untold newness of this artwork's form: a form ideal alike and natural, and thus conceivable in no modern, racial language save the German, the most developed of them all; a form, on the other hand, which could be misconstrued only for so long as the artwork was measured by a standard it had thoroughly outgrown, whereas the new and fitting standard might haply be sought in the impression received by the fortunate hearers of one of those unwritten impromptus of the most peerless of musicians. Then would the greatest dramatist have taught us to fix that impromptu too; for in the highest conceivable Artwork the sublimest inspirations of them both should live with an undying life, as the essence of the world displayed with clearness past all measure in the mirror of the world itself.

Now if we abide by this definition, "a mimo-musical improvisation, of consummate poetical value, fixed by the highest artistic care," we may find experience throw a startling light on the practical side of our Artwork's execution.—Taken in a very weighty sense, our great poets' prime concern was to furnish Drama with a heightened Pathos, and finally to discover the technical means of securely fixing its delivery. Markedly as Shakespeare had derived his style from the instinct of mimetic art, for the performance of his dramas he nevertheless stayed bound to the accidental greater or less degree of talent in his players, who all, in a sense, would have had to be Shakespeares, just as he was certainly at all times the whole character he personated; nor have we any reason to suppose that in the representations of his pieces his genius would have recognised aught beyond his own bare shadow cast across the boards. What so chained our own great poets' hopes to Music, was its being not only 'purest Form, but the most complete physical presentation of that Form; the abstract cypher of Arithmetic, the figure of Geometry, here steps before us in a shape that holds the Feeling past denial, to wit as Melody; and whereas the poetic diction of the written speech falls prey to every personal caprice of its reciter, the physical reproduction of this Melody can be fixed beyond all risk of error. What to Shakespeare was practically impossible, namely to be the mime of all his rôles, the tone-composer achieves with fullest certainty, for from out his each executant musician he speaks to us directly. Here the transmigration of the poet's soul into the body of the player takes place by laws of surest technique, and the composer giving the beat (3) to a technically correct performance of his work becomes so entirely one with the executant that the nearest comparison would be that of a plastic artist and his work achieved in stone or colour, were it possible to speak of a metempsychosis into this lifeless matter.

If to this astounding might of the Musician we add that attribute of his art which we recognised at starting,—namely that even indifferent music, so long as it does not positively descend to the grotesque vulgarity of certain operatic genres in vogue to-day, enables a good dramatic artist to achieve results beyond his reach without it, as also that noble music virtually extorts from even inferior actors achievements of a type unreachable elsewhere at all,— we can scarcely doubt the reason of the utter dismay aroused in the Poet of our era who desires nobly to succeed in Drama with the only means at his disposal, that self-same speech in which to-day the very leading-articles address us. Precisely on this side, however, our hypothesis of the perfection destined for the Musically-conceived Drama should rather prove encouraging than the reverse, for its first effect would be to purge a great and many-sided genre of art, the Drama in general, from those errors which the modern Opera alike has heightened and exposed. To clear up this point, and at the same time to gain a survey of their future field of prosperous work, our dramatists perhaps might deem advisable to trace back the pedigree of the modern Theatre; not seeking its roots in Antique Drama, however, whose form is so distinctly a native product of the Hellenic spirit, its religion, ay, its State itself, that to assume the possibility of a modern imitation must necessarily lead to the gravest errors. No: the path of evolution of the Modern Theatre has such a wealth of products of the greatest worth to shew, that it fitly may be trodden farther without shame. The thorough "stage-piece," in the modernest of senses, assuredly would have to form the basis, and the only sound one, of all future dramatic efforts: for success in this, however, the very first essential is to rightly grasp the spirit of theatric art, which rests upon mimetic art itself, and to use it, not for the bolstering-up of tendences, but for the mirroring of scenes from actual life. The French, who not so long ago did admirably in this line, were certainly content to not expect a brand-new Molière every year; nor for ourselves would the birthdays of new Shakespeares be recorded in each calendar.

Coming at last to the contentment of ideal aspirations, from the working of that all-powerful dramatic Artwork itself we might see, with greater certainty than has hitherto been possible, the length to which such aspirations were justified in going. Their boundary would be found at the exact point in that Artwork where Song is thrusting toward the spoken Word. By this we in no sense imply an absolutely lowly sphere, but a sphere entirely different, distinct in kind; and we may gain an instant notion of this difference, if we call to mind certain instinctive transgressions on the part of our best dramatic singers, when in the full flow of song they have felt driven to literally *speak* a crucial word. To this, for example, the Schröder-Devrient found herself impelled by the cumulative horror of a situation in the opera "Fidelio"; in the sentence "one further step and thou art—*dead*," where she aims the pistol at the tyrant, with an awful accent of desperation she suddenly *spoke* the closing word. The indescribable effect upon the hearer was that of a headlong plunge from one sphere to the other, and its sublimity consisted in our being given, as by a lightning-flash, a glimpse into the nature of both spheres at once, the one the ideal, the other the real. Plainly, for one moment the ideal was unable to bear a certain load, and discharged it on the other: seeing how fond people are of ascribing to Music, particularly of the passionate and stirring type, a simply pathologic character, it may surprise them to discover through this very instance how delicate and purely ideal is her actual sphere, since the material terror of reality can find no place therein, albeit the soul of all things real in it alone finds pure expression.—Manifestly then, there is a side of the world, and a side that concerns us most seriously, whose terrible lessons can be brought home to our minds on none but a field of observation where Music has to hold her tongue: this field perhaps may best be measured if we allow Shakespeare, the stupendous mime, to lead us on it as far as that point we saw him reach with the desperate fatigue we assumed as reason for his early withdrawal from the stage. And that field might be best defined, if not exactly as the soil, at least as the phenomena of

History. To portray its material features for the benefit of human knowledge, must always remain the Poet's task.

So weighty and clearing an influence as this that we here could only undertake to sketch in broadest outline—an influence not merely upon its nearest relatives in Drama, but upon every branch of Art whose deepest roots connect with Drama—most certainly could never be made possible to our "Musically-conceived-and-carried-out Dramatic Artwork" until that Artwork could present itself to the public in an outward garb entirely corresponding with its inner nature, and thus facilitate the needful lack of bias in the judgment of its qualities. 'Tis so closely allied to "Opera," that for our present purpose we might justly term it the fulfilment of the Opera's destiny: not one of the said possibilities would ever have dawned on us, had it not already come to light in Opera, in general, and in the finest works of great Opera-composers in particular. Quite surely, too, it was solely the spirit of Music, whose ever ampler evolution so influenced the Opera as to enable those possibilities to arise therein. Once more then, if we wish to account for the degradation to which the Opera has been brought, we certainly must seek its reason in the attributes of Music herself. Just as in Painting, and even in Architecture, the "piquant" has taken the place of the "beautiful," so was it doomed that Music should turn from a sublime into a merely pleasing art. Though her sphere was that of purest ideality, and her effect on our mind so deeply calming and emancipating from all the anguish of reality, through her displaying herself as nothing but pure Form,—so that whatever threatened to disturb the latter, either fell away of itself, or had to be held aloof from her—this very unmixed Form, when set in a relation not completely suitable, might easily pass current for a mere agreeable toy; thus, once set in so indefinite a sphere as that on which the Opera rested, it could be employed in this sense alone, and finally be made to serve as a mere surface fillip to the ear or feeling.

On this point, however, we have the less need to dwell just now, as we started from the outcry raised against the Opera and its influence, whose ill effect we can express no better than by pointing to the notorious fact that the Theatre has long been given over to an intense neglect by all the truly cultured in the nation, though once they set great hopes thereon. Wherefore, as we cannot but desire to bring our suggested Artwork to the only notice of profit to it, namely of those who have turned with grave displeasure from the Theatre of to-day, it follows that we must shun all contact with that Theatre itself. But although the neutral ground for this must locally be quite cut off from our theatres' field of action, it could prove fruitful only if it drew its nurture from the actual elements of mimetic and musical art that have already developed in their own fashion at the theatres. In these alone consists, and will consist, the truly fertile material for genuine dramatic art; each attempt in other directions would lead, instead of Art, to a posing Artificiality. 'Tis our actors, singers and bandmen, on whose innate instinct must rest all hope of the attainment of even artistic ends as yet beyond their understanding; for it is they to whom those ends will become clear the swiftest, so soon as their instinct is rightly guided to a knowledge of them. That this instinct has been led by the tendence of our theatres to the exclusive development of the worst propensities in the profession,— it is this that needs must make us wish to snatch these irreplaceable artistic forces at least periodically from the influence of that tendence, and give them such a means of exercising their own good qualities as would rapidly and surely fit them for the realising of our Artwork. For only from the natural will of this mimetic fellowship, cutting so sorry a figure in its present misdirection, can issue now— as from of old have issued the best of things dramatic—the perfect Drama meant by us. Less by them, than by those who without the slightest calling have hitherto conducted them, has the downfall of the theatric art of our era been brought to pass. To name in one word what on German soil has shewn, and goes on proving itself least worthy of the fame of our great victories of to-day, we have only to point to this *Theatre*, whose tendence avows itself aloud and brazen the betrayer of German honour. Whoso should link himself to this tendence in any shape or form, must needs fall victim to a misconstruction that would assign him to a sphere of our publicity of the most questionable nature, whence to rise to the pure sphere of Art would be about as difficult and fatiguing as to arrive from Opera at what we have termed the Ideal Drama. Certain it is, however, that if Art has fallen solely through the artists,—according to Schiller's saying, here not exactly accurate,—it can be *raised again by the artists alone*, and not by those who have dishonoured it with their favour. *But to help forward from without, as well, that restoration of Art by the artists, would be the fitting national expiation for the national sin of our present German Theatre.*

Notes

1

Ed. Devrient's "*Geschichte der deutschen Schauspielkunst.*" — Tr.

2

A story, now become a commonplace among musicians, tells us how the master contrived to get his excessively difficult works performed at all: it concerns one of Bach's former choristers, who made the strange confession, "first he thrashed us, and then—it sounded horrible." — R. WAGNER.

3

It is all-important that this beat should be the right one, however, for a false tempo will undo the spell at once; as to which I have therefore expressed myself at length elsewhere. — R. WAGNER.

DAS LIEBESVERBOT

Translator's Note

The following "Account of a first Operatic Performance" is evidently an extract from Richard Wagner's as yet unpublished "Memoirs," as may be gathered from its second paragraph. Its publication in the first volume of the *Gesammelte Schriften* was also its first, and hitherto its only, appearance. Though I propose retaining the German title of the opera, it may be rendered in English by "Love's Penalty" or "Love Forbidden."

Das Liebesverbot

OF my second completed opera, *das Liebesverbot*, I will merely give an outline of the so-called text, with an account of the attempt at its performance and the circumstances connected therewith. Though I omit a similar report on my earliest opera, "die Feen," since it in no way came before the public, (1) I have felt it impermissible to quite pass by this second work of youth, as it really made a public appearance, already remarked on. (2)

I planned the poem of this opera in the summer of 1834, during a holiday at Teplitz, about which I have made the following notes in my life-recollections.

———

On a few fine mornings I stole away from my surroundings, to take my breakfast in solitude upon the "Schlackenburg," and seize the opportunity of jotting down the sketch of a new opera-poem in my notebook. I had annexed the subject of Shakespeare's *Measure for Measure*, and, in accordance with my then-prevailing mood, I adapted it very freely for a libretto to which I gave the title: "*das Liebesverbot.*" The ideas of "*Young Europe*" at that time in the air, as also a reading of "Ardinghello," united with the peculiar frame into which I had fallen in respect of German opera-music to supply the keynote of my conception, which struck at puritanical hypocrisy in particular, and therefore tended to a frank extolling of the "liberated senses." To this sense alone I wrested Shakespeare's earnest story; nothing would I see in it but the gloomy, rigorous moralist of a Stateholder aflame with passion for the beautiful novice who pleads his mercy for her brother, condemned to death for a love-offence, and kindles the most pernicious fire in the breast of the stony Puritan by the warmth of her human feeling. That Shakespeare simply develops these powerful motives the more conclusively to load the scale of justice in the end, was not my business to regard; my only object was to expose the sin of hypocrisy and the unnaturalness of a ruthless code of morals. So I left the "measure for measure" completely out of sight, and let avenging love alone arraign the hypocrite. From fabulous Vienna I transposed the scene to the capital of glowing Sicily, where a German Stateholder, aghast at the incomprehensible laxness of its populace, attempts to carry out a puritanical reform, and lamentably falls. Presumably the *Muette de Portici* [Masaniello] had something to do with it; reminiscences of the "Sicilian Vespers" may have had their share (3): when I reflect that even the gentle Sicilian *Bellini* must be numbered among the factors of this composition, I can but smile at the singular quid-pro-quo into which the oddest misunderstandings here had shaped themselves.

It was not till the winter of 1835-36, that I was able to finish the score of my opera. This occurred amid the most bewildering duties at the little town - theatre of Magdeburg, whose opera-performances I conducted for two winter - seasons as Musikdirektor. A strange confusion had been wrought in my taste by immediate contact with the German operatic stage, and so strongly did it stamp the cut and execution of my work, that the youthful enthusiast for Beethoven and Weber would surely have been traced by no one in this score.

Its fortune was as follows.

Despite a royal subsidy and the intervention of the theatre-committee in the management, our worthy Director was in a perennial state of bankruptcy, and a continuance of his undertaking in any shape or form was not to be thought of. So the performance of my opera, by the really excellent troop of singers at my disposal, was to constitute a turning-point in my career. I had the right to claim a 'benefit' in repayment of certain travelling-expenses from the previous summer: naturally I decided on a representation of my work, and did my best to make this managerial favour as little costly as possible. As the management had nevertheless to bear some outlay for the new opera, I agreed to surrender the receipts of the first performance and content myself with those of the second. Nor did the postponement of the rehearsals to the very end of the season appear to me an unmixed evil, since I might assume that the last performances of a company that had often been received with uncommon warmth would have a special interest for the public. Unfortunately, however, we never reached the season's stipulated close, fixed for the end of April, as in March the most popular members of our Opera announced their departure on account of unpunctuality in the payment of their salaries, and the offer of better engagements elsewhere; against which the impecunious management had no means of redress. That was bad news for me: the attainment of a performance of my *Liebesverbot* seemed more than doubtful. It was only through my being a favourite with the whole opera-company, that I induced the singers not merely to stay until the end of March, but also to undertake the study of my opera, most exhausting in view of the briefness of time. So scanty was it, that if two performances were to be given, we had no more than ten days for all the various rehearsals. As it was by no means a simple Singspiel, but, for all the slipshod character of its music, a grand opera with many lengthy ensemble numbers, the undertaking might rank as the height of folly. Nevertheless I built my hopes on the great exertions which the singers had willingly borne for my sake with their constant practice night and morning; and, notwithstanding that it had been clean impossible to drive them to a little conscious settledness of memory, I finally reckoned on a miracle to be wrought by my own acquired dexterity as conductor. The peculiar knack I had of giving the singers an illusive air of fluency, however uncertain they might really be, was shewn in our two or three full rehearsals, when I kept the whole afloat by incessant prompting, singing the notes aloud and shouting out the needful action, so that one might positively believe the thing would cut a decent figure after all. Unfortunately we had forgotten that on the night of performance [March 29, 1836], in presence of the public, all these drastic means of oiling the dramatic-musical machinery would have to shrink to the beat of my bâton and the dumb motion of my face. Indeed the singers, especially the male ones, were so extraordinarily shaky that their rôles were lamed of all effect from beginning to end. The first tenor, blest with the very weakest memory, tried to bolster up the mercurial character of the madcap *Luzio* by the routine of *Fra Diavolo* and *Zampa*, and in particular by an immoderately large and tossing plume of gaudy feathers. Moreover as the management could not afford to print any textbooks, it was scarcely the public's fault that it remained entirely in the dark as to the story's drift, for the piece was sung throughout. Whereas I had intended a brisk and energetic play of speech and action,—with exception of a few of the female parts, which were greeted with applause, the whole thing remained a musical shadow-play on the stage which the orchestra did its best to drown in inexplicable torrents. As characterising the treatment of my tone-colours, I may mention that the conductor of a Prussian military band, who was quite delighted with the work, felt it his duty to give me a well-meant hint on handling the Turkish drum in future operas. But, before proceeding with the history of this wonderful juvenile work, I must dwell awhile upon its character, especially as regards the poem.

The piece, which Shakespeare had kept to a very earnest basis, in my version had turned out as under:—

"An un-named King of Sicily leaves his country on a journey to Naples, as I suppose, and deputes to his appointed Stateholder— called simply *Friedrich*, to mark him for a German—the full authority to use all royal powers in an attempt to radically reform the manners of his capital, which had become an abomination to the strait-laced minister. At the commencement of the piece we see public officers hard at work on the houses of amusement in a suburb of Palermo, closing some, demolishing others, and taking their hosts and servants into custody. The populace interferes; great riot: after a roll of the drums the chief constable *Brighella* (basso buffo), standing at bay, reads out the edict of the Stateholder according to which these measures have been adopted to secure a better state of morals. General derision, with a mocking chorus; *Luzio*, a young nobleman and jovial rake (tenor), appears to wish to make himself the people's leader; he promptly finds occasion for espousing the cause of the oppressed when he sees his friend *Claudio* (likewise tenor) conducted on the road to prison, and learns from him that, in pursuance of an ancient law unearthed by *Friedrich*, he is about to be condemned to death for an amorous indiscretion. His affianced, whom the hostility of her parents has prevented his marrying, has become a mother by him; the hatred of the relatives allies itself with *Friedrich's* puritanic zeal: he fears the worst, and has one only hope of rescue, that the pleading of his sister *Isabella* may succeed in softening the tyrant's heart. *Luzio* promises to go at once to *Isabella* in the cloister of the Elisabethans, where she has lately entered her novitiate.

"Within the quiet cloister walls we make the acquaintance of this sister, in confidential converse with her friend *Marianne*, who also has entered as novice. *Marianne* discloses to her friend, from whom she has long been parted, the sad fate that has brought her hither. By a man of high position she had been persuaded to a secret union, under the pledge of eternal fidelity; in her hour of utmost need she had found herself abandoned, and even persecuted, for the betrayer proved to be the most powerful personage in all the state, no less a man than the King's present Stateholder. *Isabella's* horror finds vent in a tempest of wrath, only to be allayed by the resolve to leave a world where such monstrosities can go unpunished.—When *Luzio* brings her tidings of the fate of her own brother, her abhorrence of his misdemeanour passes swiftly to revolt against the baseness of the hypocritical Stateholder who dares so cruelly to tax her brother's infinitely lesser fault, at least attainted with no treachery. Her violence unwittingly exhibits her to *Luzio* in the most seductive light; fired by sudden love, he implores her to leave the nunnery for ever and take his hand. She quickly brings him to his senses, yet decides, without a moment's wavering, to accept his escort to the Stateholder in the House of Justice.

"Here the trial is about to take place, and I introduce it with a burlesque examination of various moral delinquents by the chief constable *Brighella*. This gives more prominence to the seriousness of the situation when the gloomy figure of *Friedrich* appears, commanding silence to the uproarious rabble that has forced the doors; he then begins the hearing of *Claudio* in strictest form. The relentless judge is upon the point of passing sentence, when *Isabella* arrives and demands a private audience of the Stateholder. She comports herself with noble moderation in this private colloquy with a man she fears and yet despises, commencing with nothing but an appeal to his clemency and mercy. His objections make her more impassioned: she sets her brother's misdemeanour in a touching light, and pleads forgiveness for a fault so human and in nowise past all pardon. As she observes the impression of her warmth, with ever greater fire she goes on to address the hidden feeling of the judge's heart, which cannot possibly have been quite barred against the sentiments that made her brother stray, and to whose own experience she now appeals for help in her despairing plea for mercy. The ice of that heart is broken: *Friedrich*, stirred to his depths by *Isabella's* beauty, no longer feels himself his master; he promises to *Isabella* whatever she may ask, at price of her own body. Hardly has she become conscious of this unexpected effect, than, in utmost fury at such incredible villainy, she rushes to door and window and calls the people in, to unmask the hypocrite to all the world. Already the whole crowd is pouring in to the judgment-hall, when *Friedrich's* desperate self-command succeeds in convincing *Isabella*, by a few well-chosen phrases, of the impossibility of her attempt: he would simply deny her accusation, represent his offer as a means of detection, and certainly find credence if it came to any question of repudiating a charge of wanton insult. *Isabella*, ashamed and bewildered, recognises the madness of her thought, and succumbs to mute despair. But while *Friedrich* is displaying his utmost rigour afresh to the people, and delivering sentence on the prisoner, *Isabella* suddenly remembers the mournful fate of *Marianne*; like a lightning-flash, she conceives the idea of gaining by stratagem what seems impossible through open force. At once she bounds from deepest sorrow to the height of mirth: to her lamenting brother, his downcast friend, the helpless throng, she turns with promise of the gayest escapade she will prepare for all of them, for the very Carnival which the Stateholder had so strenuously forbidden shall be celebrated this time with unwonted spirit, as that dread rigorist had merely donned the garb of harshness the more agreeably to surprise the town by his hearty share in all the sport he had proscribed. Everyone deems her crazy, and *Friedrich* chides her most severely for such inexplicable folly: a few words from her suffice to set his own brain reeling; for beneath her breath she promises fulfilment of his fondest wishes, engaging to despatch a messenger with welcome tidings for the following night.

"Thus ends the first act, in wildest commotion. What the heroine's hasty plan may be, we learn at the beginning of the second, where she gains admittance to her brother's gaol to prove if he is worth the saving. She reveals to him *Friedrich's* shameful proposals, and asks him if he craves his forfeit life at this price of his sister's dishonour? *Claudio's* wrath and readiness to sacrifice himself are followed by a softer mood, when he begins to bid his sister farewell for this life, and commit to her the tenderest greetings for his grieving lover; at last his sorrow causes him to quite break down. *Isabella*, about to tell him of his rescue, now pauses in dismay; for she sees her brother falling from the height of nobleness to weak avowal of unshaken love of life, to the shamefaced question whether the price of his deliverance be quite beyond her. Aghast, she rises to her feet, thrusts the craven from her, and informs him that he now must add to the shame of death the full weight of her contempt. As soon as she has returned him to the gaoler, her bearing once more passes to ebullient glee: she resolves indeed to chastise the weak-kneed by prolonging his uncertainty about his fate, but still abides by her decision to rid the world of the most disgraceful hypocrite that ever sought to frame its laws. She has arranged for *Marianne* to take her place in the rendezvous desired by *Friedrich* for the night, and now sends him the invitation, which, to involve him in the greater ruin, appoints a masked encounter at one of the places of amusement which he himself has closed. The madcap *Luzio*, whom she also means to punish for his impudent proposal to a novice, she tells of *Friedrich's* passion, and remarks on her feigned decision to yield to the inevitable in such a flippant fashion that she plunges him, at other times so feather-brained, into an agony of despair: he swears that even should the noble maid intend to bear this untold shame, he will ward it off with all his might, though all Palermo leap ablaze.

"In effect he induces every friend and acquaintance to assemble at the entrance to the Corso that evening, as if for leading off the prohibited grand Carnival procession. At nightfall, when the fun is already waxing wild there, *Luzio* arrives, and stirs the crowd to open bloodshed by a daring carnival-song with the refrain: 'Who'll not carouse at our behest, your steel shall smite him in the breast.' *Brighella* approaching with a company of the watch, to disperse the motley gathering, the revellers are about to put their murderous projects into execution; but *Luzio* bids them scatter for the present, and ambush in the neighbourhood, as he here must first await the actual leader of their movement: for this is the place that *Isabella* had tauntingly divulged to him as her rendezvous with the Stateholder. For the latter *Luzio* lies in wait: he soon detects him in a stealthy masker, whose path he bars, and as *Friedrich* tears himself away he is about to follow him with shouts and drawn rapier, when by direction of *Isabella*, concealed among the bushes, he himself is stopped and led astray. *Isabella* comes forth, rejoicing in the thought of having restored *Marianne* to her faithless mate at this very moment, and in the possession of what she believes to be the stipulated patent of her brother's pardon; she is on the point of renouncing all further revenge when, breaking open the seal by the light of a torch, she is horrified at discovering an aggravation of the order of execution, which chance and bribery of the gaoler had delivered into her hands through her wish to defer her brother's knowledge of his ransom. After a hard battle with the devouring flames of love, and recognising his powerlessness against this enemy of his peace, *Friedrich* has resolved that, however criminal his fall, it yet shall be as a man of honour. One hour on *Isabella's* bosom, and then his death—by the self-same law to whose severity the life of *Claudio* still shall stand irrevocably forfeit. *Isabella*, who perceives in this action but an additional villainy of the hypocrite, once more bursts out in frenzy of despairing grief. At her call to instant revolt against the odious tyrant the whole populace assembles, in wildest turmoil: *Luzio,* arriving on the scene at this juncture, sardonically adjures the throng to pay no heed to the ravings of a woman who, as she has deceived himself assuredly will dupe them all; for he still believes in her shameless dishonour. Fresh confusion, climax of *Isabella's* despair: suddenly from the back is heard *Brighella's* burlesque cry for help; himself entangled in the coils of jealousy, he has seized the disguised Stateholder by mistake, and thus leads to the latter's discovery. *Friedrich* is unmasked; *Marianne*, clinging to his side, is recognised. Amazement, indignation, joy: the necessary explanations are soon got through; *Friedrich* moodily asks to be led before the judgment-seat of the King on his return, to receive the capital sentence; *Claudio*, set free from prison by the jubilant mob, instructs him that death is not always the penalty for a love-offence. Fresh messengers announce the unexpected arrival of the King in the harbour; everyone decides to go in full carnival-attire to greet the beloved prince, who surely will be pleased to see how ill the sour puritanism of the Germans becomes the heat of Sicily. The word goes round: 'Gay festivals delight him more than all your gloomy edicts.' *Friedrich*, with his newly-married wife *Marianne*, has to head the procession; the Novice, lost to the cloister for ever, makes the second pair with *Luzio.*—"

I had worked out these bustling and, in many respects, ambitious scenes, with some regard to verse and diction. The police took offence at the title, which, if I had not altered it, would have dashed my whole plans of performance. We were in the week before Easter, a time when merry, to say nothing of frivolous, pieces were forbidden at the theatre. Fortunately the magistrate whom I had to consult in the matter had not gone any farther into the poem, and when I assured him that it was founded on a very serious play of Shakespeare's he contented himself with a change in the highly alarming title, for which we substituted the "Novice of Palermo"; that appearing to have nothing against it, no further scruples were raised on the score of propriety.—I found things otherwise at Leipzig shortly after, where I tried to insinuate my new work in place of the abandoned "Feen." There I meant to win over the Director of the theatre by offering his daughter, a débutante in Opera, the part of "Marianne"; but he had grasped the tendence of the story, and made it a not uncolourable pretext for rejection. He informed me that even were the Leipzig Magistrates to permit the representation, which his respect for those authorities caused him very much to doubt, as a conscientious father he could not possibly allow his daughter to appear in it.—

In the Magdeburg performance, remarkably enough, I had nothing at all to suffer from this dubious character of my opera-text; the story remained entirely unknown to the audience, as said above, on account of its utterly vague reproduction. This circumstance, with the consequent absence of any opposition to the *tendence,* enabled me to announce a second performance; against which no one raised his voice, since no one vexed his head. Perfectly aware that my opera had made no impression and left the audience in a complete haze as to what the whole thing was about, I counted nevertheless on the attraction of the very last appearance of our opera-troop to bring me in quite good, nay, large returns; so that I was not to be hindered from demanding the so-called "full" prices for admission. Whether a few seats would have been filled by the commencement of the overture, I can scarcely judge: about a quarter of an hour previously the only people I could see in the stalls were my landlady with her husband, and, strange to relate, a Polish Jew in full costume. I was hoping for an increase notwithstanding, when suddenly the most unheard-of scenes took place behind the wings. The husband of my prima donna (the actress of "Isabella") had fallen upon the second tenor, a very pretty young man who sang my "Claudio," and against whom the offended husband long had nursed a secret grudge. It seems that, having convinced himself of the nature of the audience when he accompanied me to the curtain, the lady's husband deemed the longed-for hour arrived for taking vengeance on his wife's pretender without damage to the theatrical enterprise. *Claudio* was so badly cuffed and beaten by him, that the unlucky wretch had to escape to the cloak-room with a bleeding face. *Isabella* was told of it, rushed in despair at her raging husband, and received such blows from him that she fell into convulsions. The uproar in the company soon knew no bounds: sides were taken, for and against, and little lacked of a general free-fight, as it appeared that this unhappy evening was held by all a fit occasion for paying off old scores. So much was certain,—the pair who had suffered from *Isabella's* husband's love-forbiddal were rendered quite incapable of coming on that night. The regisseur was sent before the curtain, to inform the singularly select company in the auditorium that "on account of unforeseen obstacles" the performance of the opera could not take place. —

To a further attempt to rehabilitate my work of youth it never came.

Notes

1

Not until June 29, 1888, when it was given at the Munich Court-theatre by way of indemnity for the right of performance of *Parsifal*, as claimed by King Ludwig's successors. — The work was written in 1833, when Wagner was just twenty years of age. — Tr.

2

In the "Autobiographic Sketch"; see Vol. I. of this series. — Tr.

3

This allusion to the historical "Sicilian Vespers" (13th century) has misled one or two writers into the assertion that Wagner's earliest works were influenced by Verdi. Nothing could be more ridiculous. Not till the year 1839 was Verdi's first opera, *Oberto*, produced in Milan; nor did he make any particular name until March 1842, with his *Nabucco*, some months after the score of *Rienzi* had been despatched to Dresden, and that of the *Flying Dutchman* to Berlin. Verdi's *Vêpres siciliennes*, composed for Paris, appeared in 1855. — Tr.

Summary

Sketched in 1834 from *Measure for Measure*, freely adapted to the idea of "the liberated senses"; an indictment of puritanical hypocrisy; various influences at work in text and music; completed and performed once in 1836 at Magdeburg, after insufficient rehearsals at a bankrupt theatre. Summary of the plot. Police objections to title circumvented—they were shrewder at Leipzig; a second performance that never came off, through a fight behind the scenes.

WHAT IS GERMAN?

Translator's Note

For a similar reason as in the case of the Vaterlandsverein Speech, I have chosen *"Was ist deutsch?"* to follow after "German Art and German Policy." The author's introductory note explains the intimate connexion of the two articles.

"Was ist deutsch?" was evidently written, either entirely or in part, towards the *end* of *1865*; for the review of C. H. Bitter's "Johann Sebastian Bach," quoted on page *163*, appeared in the Augsburg *Allgemeine Zeitung* of September 22nd *1865*.

The article itself was first printed in the second Number of the *Bayreuther Blätter*, namely for February *1878*. It was reprinted in the last, i.e. the tenth, volume of Richard Wagner's *Gesammelte Schriften*, *1883*, the contents whereof were collected by Baron Hans von Wolzogen soon after the author's death.

What is German?

WHEN lately searching through my papers, I found in disconnected paragraphs a manuscript of the year 1865; to-day, at wish of my younger friend and colleague in the publication of the "Bayreuther Blätter," I have decided to hand over the greater portion for issue to our more distant friends of the Patronatverein.

If the question "What is German?" was in itself so hard for me to answer, that I did not presume to include the all-unfinished article in the Collected Edition of my writings, my recent difficulty has been the matter of selection; for several of the points discussed in these paragraphs had already been treated by me at greater length in other essays, particularly in that on "German Art and German Policy." May this be my apology for the present article's shortcomings. In any case I have still to close the train of thought I then sketched out; and that close—to which, after thirteen years of fresh experience, I have certainly to give a colour of its own—will this time be my final word upon the sadly earnest theme.—

It has often weighed upon my mind, to gain a clear idea of what is really to be understood by the expression *"deutsch"* ["German"].

It is a commonplace of the Patriot's, to introduce his nation s name with unconditional homage; the mightier a nation is, however, the less store it seems to set on repeating its own name with all this show of reverence. It happens seldomer in the public life of England and France, that people speak of "English" and "French virtues"; whereas the Germans are always appealing to "German depth," "German earnestness," "German fidelity" (*Treue*) and the like. Unfortunately it has become patent, in very many cases, that this appeal was not entirely founded; yet we haply should do wrong to suppose that the qualities themselves are mere figments of the imagination, even though their name be taken in vain. It will be best to seek upon the path of History the meaning of this idiosyncrasy of the Germans.

The word "deutsch," according to the latest and most profound researches, is not a definite Folk's name in history there has been no people that could claim the original title "Deutsche." Jacob Grimm, on the contrary, has proved that "diutisk" or "deutsch" means nothing more than what is homelike to ourselves, "ourselves" being those who parley in a language mutually intelligible. It was early set in contrast with the "walsch," whereby the Germanic races signify. the "proper to the Gaels and Kelts." The word "deutsch" reappears in the verb "deuten" [to "point, indicate, or explain"]: thus "deutsch" is what is plain (*deutlich*) to us, the familiar, the wonted, inherited from our fathers, racy of our soil. Now it is a striking fact, that the peoples remaining on this side of the Rhine and Alps began to call themselves by the name of *"Deutsche"* only after the Goths, Vandals, Franks and Lombards had established their dominion in the rest of Europe. Whilst the "Franks" spread their name over the whole great conquered land of Gaul, but the races left on the hither side of the

Rhine consolidated themselves into Saxons, Bavarians, Swabians and East-Franks, it is at the division of the empire of Karl the Great [Charlemagne] that the name "Deutschland" makes its first appearance; and that as collective-name for all the races who had stayed this side the Rhine. Consequently it denotes those peoples who, remaining in their ancestral seat, continued to speak their ure-mother-tongue, whereas the races ruling in Romanic lands gave up that mother-tongue. It is to the speech and the ure-homeland, then, that the idea of *"deutsch"* is knit; and there came a time when these "Deutschen" could reap the advantage of fidelity to their homeland and their speech, for from the bosom of that home there sprang for centuries the ceaseless renovation and freshening of the soon decaying outland races. Moribund and weakened dynasties were recruited from the primal stock of home. To the enfeebled Merovingians succeeded the East-Frankish Carlovingians; from the degenerate Carlovingians, in their turn, Saxons and Swabians took the sceptre of the German lands; and when the whole might of Romanised Frankdom passed into the power of the purely-German stock, arose the strange, but pregnant appellation "the Roman Empire of the German Nation." (01) Finally, upon this glorious memory we could feed the pride that bade us look into the Past for consolation, amid the ruins of the Present. No great culture-Folk has fallen into the plight of building for itself a fanciful renown, as the Germans. What profit the obligation to build such a fantastic edifice from relics of the Past might haply bring us, will perchance grow clear if first we try to realise its drawbacks, free from prejudice.

These drawbacks, past dispute, are found above all in the realm of Politics. Curiously enough, the memory of the German name's historic glory (*Herrlichkeit*) attaches precisely to that period which was so fatal to the German essence, the period of the German's authority over non-German peoples. The King of the Germans had to fetch the confirmation of this authority from Rome; the Romish Kaiser belonged not strictly to the Germans: The cavalcades to Rome were hateful to the Germans, who could be made at most take kindly to them as predatory marches, during which, however, their chief desire was a speedy return to home. Peevishly they followed the Romish Kaiser into Italy, most cheerfully their German Princes back to home. This relation is responsible for the constant powerlessness of so-called German Glory. The idea of this Glory was an un-German one. What distinguishes the "Deutschen" proper from the Franks, Goths, Lombards &c., is that the latter found pleasure in the foreign land, settled there, and commingled with its people to the point of forgetting their own speech and customs. The German proper, on the contrary, weighed always as a stranger on the foreign people, because he did not feel himself at home abroad; and strikingly enough, we see the Germans hated to our day (1865) in Italy and in Slavonic lands, as foreigners and oppressors, whereas we cannot veil the shaming truth that German nationalities quite willingly abide beneath a foreign sceptre, if only they be not dealt with violently in regard of speech and customs, as we have before us in the case of Elsass [Alsace].—

With the fall of outer political might, i.e. with the lost significance of the Romish Kaiserdom, which we bemoan to-day as the foundering of German glory, there begins on the contrary the real development of genuine German essence (*Wesen*). Albeit in undeniable conjunction with the development of all other European nations, the German homeland assimilates their influences, especially those of Italy, in so individual a manner that in the last century of the Middle Ages the German costume actually becomes a pattern for the rest of Europe, whereas at the time of so-called German glory even the magnates of the German Reich were clad in Romo-Byzantine garb. In the German Netherlands German art and industry were powerful rivals of Italy's most splendid bloom. After the complete downfall of the German nature, after the wellnigh total extinction of the German nation in consequence of the indescribable devastations of the Thirty Years' War, it was this inmost world of Home from whence the German spirit was reborn. German poetry, German music, German philosophy, are nowadays esteemed and honoured by every nation in the world: but in his yearning after "German glory" the German, as a rule, can dream of nothing but a sort of resurrection of the Romish Kaiser-Reich, and the thought inspires the most good-tempered German with an unmistakable lust of mastery, a longing for the upper hand over other nations. He forgets how detrimental to the welfare of the German peoples that notion of the Romish State had been already.

To gain a clear idea of the only policy to help this welfare, to be worthy the name of German, we must before all ascertain the true meaning and peculiarity of that German essence which we have found to be the only prominent power in history itself. Therefore, still to keep an historical footing, let us somewhat more closely consider one of the weightiest epochs in the German people's evolution, that extraordinarily agitated crisis which it had to pass through at time of the so-called Reformation.

The Christian religion belongs to no specific national stock: the Christian dogma addresses purely - human nature. Only in so far as it has seized in all its purity this content common to all men, can a people call itself Christian in truth. However, a people can make nothing fully its own but what becomes possible for it to grasp with its inborn feeling, and to grasp in such a fashion that in the New it finds its own familiar self again. Upon the realm of aesthetics and philosophic Criticism it may be demonstrated, almost palpably, that it was predestined for the German spirit to seize and assimilate the Foreign, the primarily remote from it, in utmost purity and objectivity of intuition (*in höchster objektiver Reinheit der Anschauung*). One may aver, without exaggeration, that the Antique would have stayed unknown, in its now universal world-significance, had the German spirit not recognised and expounded it. The Italian made as much of the Antique his own, as he could copy and remodel; the Frenchman borrowed from this remodelling, in his turn, whatever caressed his national sense for elegance of Form: the German was the first to apprehend its purely-human originality, to seize therein a meaning quite aloof from usefulness, but therefore of the only use for rendering the Purely-human. Through its inmost understanding of the Antique, the German spirit arrived at the capability of restoring the Purely-human itself to its pristine freedom; not employing the antique form to display a certain given 'stuff,' but moulding the necessary new form itself through an employment of the antique conception of the world. (02) To recognise this plainly, let anyone compare Goethe's *Iphigenia* with that of Euripides. One may say that the true idea of the Antique has existed only since the middle of the eighteenth century, since Winckelmann and Lessing.

Now, that the German would have apprehended the Christian dogma in equally preeminent clearness and purity, and would have raised it to the only valid Confession-of-faith, just as he had raised the Antique to a dogma in AEsthetics,—this can not be demonstrated. Perhaps on evolutionary paths unknown to us, and by us unimaginable, he might have arrived hereat; and certain attributes would make it appear that, of all others, the German spirit was called thereto. In any case 'tis easier for us to see what hindered its solution of the problem, since we recognise what enabled it to solve a like one in the region of Æsthetics. For here there was nothing to hinder it: Æsthetics were neither interfered with by the State, nor converted to its ends. With Religion things were otherwise: it had become an interest of the State, and this State-interest obtained its meaning and its guidance, not from the German, but quite definitely from the un-German, the Romanic spirit. It was. the incalculable misfortune of Germany that, about the time when the German spirit was ripening for its task upon that high domain, the legitimate State-interests of all German peoples were entrusted to the counsels of a prince to whom the German spirit was a total stranger, to the most thorough-paced representative of the un-German, Romanic State-idea: Charles the Fifth, King of Spain and Naples, hereditary Archduke of Austria, elected Romish Kaiser and Sovereign of the German Reich, devoured by ambition for world-supremacy, which would actually have fallen to him if he had been able to master France,—this sovereign felt no other interest in Germany, than to weld it with his empire, an iron-bound monarchy like Spain.

With him arrived the grave fatality that later doomed weilnigh each German prince to misunderstanding of the German spirit; yet he was opposed by the majority of the Reichs-princes of that time, whose interests then coincided, as good fortune would have it, with those of the German Folk-spirit. One can never conjecture the mode in which the actual religious question, too, would have been answered to the honour of the German spirit if Germany then had had a sterling patriotic overchief for Kaiser, such as the Luxemburgian Heinrich VII. At any rate the original Reformatory movement in Germany made not for separation from the Catholic Church; on the contrary, it was an attempt to strengthen and reknit the Church's general union, by putting an end to the hideous abuses of the Roman Curia, so wounding to German religious feeling. What good and world-significant thing might here have come to life, we can scarce approximately measure; but we have before us the results of the disastrous conflict of the German spirit with the un-German spirit of the German Reich's supreme controller. Since that time—cleavage of religion: a dire misfortune! None but a universal religion is Religion in truth: divers confessions, politically established and ranged beside or over one another by contract with the State, simply confess that Religion is in act of dissolution. In that conflict the German Folk was brought near its total foundering, nay, wellnigh it altogether reached it through the outcome of the Thirty Years' War. If therefore the German Princes had mostly worked in common with the German spirit, I have already shewn how since that time, alas l our Princes themselves almost quite unlearnt an understanding of this spirit. The sequel we may see in our public State-life of to-day: the sterling German nature (*das eigentlich deutsche Wesen*) is withdrawing ever farther from it; in part the German is following his native bent to phlegma, in part that to fantasticism: and since the lordling and even the lawyer is becoming quite old-fashioned, the royal rights of Prussia and Austria have gradually to accustom themselves to being upheld before their peoples by—Israelites. (03)

In this singular phenomenon, this invasion of the German nature by an utterly alien element, there is more than meets the eye. Here, however, we will only notice that other nature in so far as its conjunction with us obliges us to become quite clear as to what we have to understand by the "German" nature which it exploits.—It everywhere appears to be the duty of the Jew, to shew the nations of modern Europe where haply there may be a profit they have overlooked, or not made use of. The Poles and Hungarians did not understand the value, to themselves, of a national development of trade and commerce: the Jew displayed it, by appropriating that neglected profit None of the European nations had recognised the boundless advantages, for the nation's general oeconomy, of an ordering of the relations of Labour and Capital in accordance with the modern spirit of burgher-enterprise: the Jews laid hand on those advantages, and upon the hindered and dwindling prosperity of the nation the Jewish banker feeds his enormous wealth. Adorable and beautiful is that foible of the German's which forbade his coining into personal profit the inwardness and purity of his feelings and beholdings, particularly in his public and political life: that a profit here, as well, was left unused, could be cognisable to none but a mind which misunderstood the very essence of the German nature. The German Princes supplied the misunderstanding, the Jews exploited it. Since the new-birth of German poetry and music, it only needed the Princes to follow the example of Frederick the Great, to make a fad of ignoring those arts, or wrongly and unjustly measuring them with French square and cornpasses, and consequently allowing no influence to the spirit which they manifested,—it only needed this, to throw open to the spirit of alien speculation a field whereon it saw much profit to be reaped. 'Tis as though the Jew had been astounded to find such a store of mind and genius yielding no returns but poverty and unsuccess. He could not conceive, when the Frenchman worked for "*gloire*," the Italian for the *denaro*, why the German did it simply "*pour le roi de Prusse*." The Jew set right this bungling of the German's, by taking German intellectual labour into his own hands; and thus we see an odious travesty of the German spirit upheld to-day before the German Folk, as its imputed likeness. It is to be feared, ere long the nation may really take this simulacrum for its mirrored image: then one of the finest natural dispositions in all the human race were done to death, perchance for ever.

We have to inquire how to save it from such a shameful doom, and therefore first of all will try to signalise the characteristics of genuine "German" nature.—

Once more let us briefly, but plainly recite the outer, historical documents of German nature. "Deutsche" is the title given to those Germanic races which, upon their natal soil, retained their speech and customs. Even from lovely Italy the German yearns back to his homeland. Hence he quits the Romish Kaiser, and cleaves the closer and the trustier to his native Prince. In rugged woods, throughout the lengthy winter, by the warm hearth-fire of his turret-chamber soaring high into the clouds, for generations he keeps green the deeds of his forefathers; the myths of native gods he weaves into an endless web of sagas. (04) He wards not off the influences incoming from abroad; he loves to journey and to look; but, full of the strange impressions, he longs to reproduce them; he therefore turns his steps toward home, for he knows that here alone will he be *understood*: here, by his homely hearth, he tells what he has seen and gone through there outside. Romanic, Gaelic (*wälische*), French books and legends he transposes for himself, and whilst the Latins, Gaels and French know nothing of him, he keenly studies all their ways. But his is no mere idle gaping at the Foreign, as such, as purely foreign; he wills to understand it "Germanly." He renders the foreign poem into German, to gain an inner knowledge of its content. Herewith he strips the Foreign of its accidentals, its externals, of all that to him is unintelligible, and makes good the loss by adding just so much of his own externals and accidentals as it needs to set the foreign object plain and undefaced before him. In these his natural endeavours he makes the foreign exploit yield to him a picture of its purely-human motives. Thus "Parzival" and "Tristan" were shaped anew by Germans: and whilst the originals have become mere curiosities, of no importance save to the history of literature, in their German counterparts we recognise poetic works of worth imperishable.—

In the same spirit the German borrows for his home the civic measures of abroad. Beneath the castle's shelter, expands the burghers' town; but the flourishing town does not pull down the Burg: the" Free Town" renders homage to the Prince; the industrial burgher decks the castle of his ancient lord. The German is conservative: his treasure bears the stamp of all the ages; he hoards the Old, and well knows how to use it. Fonder is he of keeping, than of winning: the gathered New has value for him only when it serves to deck the Old. He craves for nothing from without; but he wills no hindrances within. He attacks not, neither will he brook attack.— Religion he takes in earnest: the ethical corruption of the Roman Curia, with its demoralising influence on the clergy, irks him to the quick. By Religious Liberty he means nothing other than the right to deal honestly and in earnest with the Holiest. Here he waxes warm, and disputes with all the hazy passionateness of the goaded friend of peace and quiet. Politics get mixed therein: shall Germany become a Spanish monarchy, the free Reich be trodden under foot, his Princes made mere eminent courtiers? No people has taken arms against invasions of its inner freedom, its own true essence, as the Germans: there is no comparison for the doggedness with which the German chose his total ruin, rather than accommodate himself to claims quite foreign to his nature. This is weighty. The outcome of the Thirty Years' War destroyed the German nation; yet, that a German Folk could rise again, is due to nothing but that outcome. The nation was annihilated, but the German spirit had passed through. It is the essence of that spirit which we call "genius in the case of highly-gifted individuals, not to trim its sails to worldly profit. (05) What with other nations led at last to compromise, to a practical ensurance of that profit through accommodation, could not control the Germans: at a time when Richelieu forced the French to accept the laws of political advantage, the German nation was completing its shipwreck; but that which never could bend before the laws of this advantage, lived on and bore its Folk afresh: the German Spirit.

A Folk reduced to a tenth of its former numbers, its significance could nowhere survive but in the memory of units. Even that memory had first to be revived and toilsomely fed, to begin with, by the most prescient of minds. It is a wonderful trait of the German spirit's, that whereas in its earlier period of evolution it had most intimately assimilated the influences coming from without, now, when it quite had lost the vantage-ground of outward political power, it bore itself anew from out its own most inward store.— Recollection (*Erinnerung*) now became for it in truth a self-collection (*Er-Innerung*); for upon its deepest inner self it drew, to ward itself from the now immoderate Outer influences. 'Twas no question of its external existence, for that had been ensured by the continuance of the German Princes; ay! survived there not the title of "Romo-German Kaiser"? But its truest essence, now ignored by most of these its Princes,—that was the German spirit's object to preserve and quicken to new force. In the French livery and uniform, with periwig and pigtail (*Zopf*), and laughably set out with imitations of French gallantry, the scanty remnant of its people fronted it; while its language even the burgher, with his garnish of French flourishes, was about to abandon merely to the peasant—Yet when its native countenance, its very speech was lost, there remained to the German spirit one last, one undreamt sanctuary wherein to plainly tell itself the story of its heart of hearts. From the Italians the German had adopted Music, also, for his own. Whoso would seize the wondrous individuality, the strength and meaning of the German spirit in one incomparably speaking image, let him cast a searching glance upon the else so puzzling, welinigh unaccountable figure of Music's wonder-man SEBASTIAN BACH. He is the history of the German spirit's inmost life throughout the gruesome century of the German Folk's complete extinction. See there that head, insanely muffled in the French full-bottomed wig; behold that master, a wretched organist and cantor, slinking from one Thuringian parish to another, puny places scarcely known to us by name; see him so unheeded, that it required a whole century to drag his works from oblivion; finding even Music pinioned in an art-form the very effigy of his age, dry, stiff, pedantic, like wig and pigtail set to notes: then see what a world the unfathomably great Sebastian built from out these elements! I merely point to that Creation; for it is impossible to denote its wealth, its sublimity, its all-embracing import, through any manner of comparison. If, however, we wish to account for the amazing rebirth of the German spirit on the field of poetic and philosophic Literature too, we can do so only by learning from Bach what the German spirit is in truth, where it dwelt, and how it restless shaped itself anew, when it seemed to have altogether vanished from the world. A biography of this man has recently appeared, and the Ailgemeine Zeitung has reviewed it. I cannot resist quoting the following passages from that review: "With labour and rare force of will he struggles up from poverty and want to the topmost height of art, strews with full hands an almost incommensurable plenty of most glorious masterworks, strews it on an age which can neither comprehend nor prize him, and dies beneath a burden of downweighing cares, lonely and forgotten, leaving his family in poverty and privation. . . . The grave of the Song-dispenser closes over the weary home-gone man without a song or sound, because the household penury cannot afford the grave-chant fee. . . . Might the reason, why our composers so seldom find biographers, lie partly in the circumstance that their end is usually so mournful, so harrowing?"——And while this was happening with great Bach, sole harbourer and new-bearer of the German spirit, the large and little Courts of German princes were swarming with Italian opera-composers and virtuosi, bought with untold outlay, too, to shower on slighted Germany the leavings of an art that nowadays cannot be accorded the least consideration.

Yet Bach's spirit, the German spirit, stepped forth from the sanctuary of divinest Music, the place of its new-birth. When Goethe's "Götz" appeared, its joyous cry went up: "That's German!" And, beholding his likeness, the German also knew to shew himself, to shew the world, what Shakespeare is, whom his own people did not understand. These deeds the German spirit brought forth of itself, from its inmost longing to grow conscious of itself. And this consciousness told it—what it was the first to publish to the world— that *the Beautiful and Noble came not into the world for sake of profit, nay, not for sake of even fame and recognition*. And everything done in the sense of this teaching is *"deutsch"*; and *therefore* is the German great; and *only what is done in that sense, can lead Germany to greatness*.

To the nurture of the German Spirit, the greatness of the German Folk, nothing can lead, then, save its veritable understanding by the rulers. The German Folk arrived at its rebirth, at unfolding of its highest faculties, through its conservative temper, its inward cleaving to itself, to its own idiosyncrasy: once it shed its life's blood for the preservation of its Princes. 'Tis now for them to shew the German Folk that they belong to it; and where the German spirit achieved its (deed of rebearing the Folk, *there* is the realm whereon the Princes, too, have first to found their new alliance with the Folk. It is highest time the Princes turned to this re-baptism: the danger that menaces the whole of German public life, I have already pointed out. Woe to us and the world, if the nation itself were this time saved, but the German spirit vanished from the world! (06) —

How are we to conceive a state of things in which the German *Folk* remained, but the German *Spirit* had taken flight? The hardly-thinkable is closer to us than we fancy. When I defined the essence and functions of the German spirit, I kept in view a happy development of the German people's most significant attributes. But the birthplace of the German spirit is alike the basis of the German people's failings. The capacity of diving deep within, and thence observing lucidly and thoughtfully the world without, always presupposes a bent to meditation; which, in the less gifted individual, quite easily becomes a love of doing nothing, a positive phlegma. What in its happiest manifestation places us nearest the supremely gifted folk of ancient Indus,. may give the mass the character of common Oriental sloth (*Trägheit*); nay, even that neighbouring development to utmost power can become a curse for us, by betraying us into fantastic self-complacency. That Goethe and Schiller, Mozart and Beethoven have issued from the German people's womb, far too easily tempts the bulk of middling talents to consider these great minds their own by right of birth, to persuade the mass with demagogic flatulence that they themselves are Goethes and Schillers, Mozarts and Beethovens. Nothing flatters more the bent to sloth and easygoingness, than a high opinion of oneself, an opinion that quite of oneself one is something great and needs take no sort of pains to first become it. This leaning is root-German, and hence no people more requires to be flicked up and compelled to help itself, to act for itself, than the German. But German Princes and Governments have done the very opposite. It was reserved for Börne the Jew, to sound the first challenge to the German's sloth; and, albeit in this sense unintentionally, he thereby raised the Germans' great misunderstanding of themselves to the pitch of direfulest confusion. The misunderstanding that prompted the Austrian Chancellor, Prince Metternich, in the day of his leadership of German Cabinet-policy, to deem the aspirations of the German "Burschenschaft" identical with those of the bygone Paris club of Jacobins, and to take hostile measures accordingly,—that misunderstanding was most advantageous to the [Jewish] speculator who stood outside, seeking nothing but his personal profit. This time, if he played his game well, that speculator had only to swing himself into the midst of the German Folk and State, to exploit and, in the end, not merely govern it, but downright make it his own property.

After all that had gone before, it now had really become a difficult matter, to rule in Germany. Had the Governments made it a maxim to judge their German peoples by the measure of French events, there also soon arose adventurers to teach the downtrod German Folk-spirit to apply French maxims to its estimate of the Governments. The *Demagogue* had now arrived indeed: but what a doleful after-birth! Every new Parisian revolution was promptly 'mounted' in Germany: of course, for every new spectacular Paris opera had been mounted forthwith at the Court-theatres of Berlin and Vienna, a pattern for all Germany. I have no hesitation about styling the subse quent revolutions in Germany entirely un-German. (07) "Democracy" in Germany is purely a translated thing. It exists merely in the "Press"; and what this German Press is, one must find out for oneself. But untowardly enough, this translated Franco-Judaico-German Democracy could really borrow a handle, a pretext and deceptive cloak, from the misprised and maltreated spirit of the German Folk. To secure a following among the people, "Democracy" aped a German mien; and *Deutschthum*," "German spirit," "German honesty," "German freedom," "German morals," became catchwords disgusting no one more than him who had true German culture, who had to stand in sorrow and watch the singular comedy of agitators from a non-German people pleading for him without letting their client so much as get a word in edgewise. The astounding unsuccessfulness of the so loud-mouthed movement of 1848 is easily explained by the curious circumstance that the genuine German found himself; and found his name, so suddenly represented by a race of men quite alien to him. Whilst Goethe and Schiller had shed the German spirit on the world, without so much as talking of the "German" spirit, these Democratic speculators fill every book- and print-shop, every so-called "Volks-," i.e. joint-stock theatre, with vulgar, utterly vapid dummies, forever plastered with the puff of "deutsch," and "deutsch" again, to decoy the easygoing crowd. And really we have got so far, that we presently shall see the German Folk quite turned to gabies by it: the national propensity to sloth and phlegma is being lured into fantastic satisfaction with itself; already the German people is taking a large part, itself, in the playing of the shameful comedy; and not without a shudder can the thoughtful German spirit look upon those foolish festive gatherings, with their theatrical processions, their silly speeches, and the cheerless empty songs wherewith one tries to make the German Folk imagine it is something special and does not need to first endeavour to become it.—

So far the earlier article, from the year 1865. My project was to get a political journal founded for the purpose of advocating the tendences expressed therein: Herr Julius Fröbel declared his readiness to undertake that advocacy: the "Suddeutsche Presse" came to daylight. Unfortunately I soon discovered that Herr Fröbel's view of the problem in question was different from my own, and one fine day we parted; for the thought that Art should serve no end of usefulness, but only its own honour (*Werth*), so sorely went against his grain that he fell into a fit of tears and sobbing.

However, I certainly had other grounds for leaving my task unfinished.—"What is German?"—The question puzzled me more and more. What simply aggravated my bewilderment, were the impressions of the eventful years which followed the time when that article was begun. What German could have lived through the year 1870 without amazement at the forces manifested here, as also at the courage and determination with which the man who palpably knew something that we others did not know, brought those forces into action?—Many an objectionable feature one might overlook at the time. We who, with the spirit of our great masters at heart, witnessed the physiognomic bearing of our death-defiant landsmen in the soldier's coat, we cordially rejoiced when listening to the "Kutschkelied," (08) and deeply were we affected by the "feste Burg" before the war and "nun danket Alle Gott" when it was over. To be sure, it was precisely we who found it hard to comprehend how the deadly courage of our patriots could whet itself on nothing better than the "Wacht am Rhein"; a somewhat mawkish Liedertafel product, which the Frenchmen held for one of those Rhine-wine songs at which they earlier had made so merry. But no matter, they might scoff as they pleased, even their *"allons enfants de la patrie"* could not this time put down "lieb Vaterland, kannst ruhig sein," or stop their being soundly beaten.—When our victorious troops were journeying home I made private inquiries in Berlin as to whether, supposing one contemplated a grand solemnity for the slain in battle, I should be permitted to compose a piece of music for performance thereat, and to be dedicated to the sublime event. The answer was: upon so joyful a return, one wished to make no special arrangements for painful impressions. Still beneath the rose, I suggested another music-piece to accompany the entry of the troops, at the close of which, mayhap at the march past the victorious Monarch, the singing-corps so well supported in the Prussian army should join-in with a national song. No: that would have necessitated serious alterations in arrangements settled long before, and I was counselled not to make the proposal. My Kaisermarsch I arranged for the concert-room: there may it fit as best it can!—In any case, I ought not to have expected the "German spirit," new-risen on the field of battle, to trouble itself with the musical fancies of a presumably conceited opera-composer. However, divers other experiences made me gradually feel odd in this new "Reich;" so that when I came to editing the last volume of my Collected Writings, as already mentioned, I could find no right incitement to complete my article on "What is German?"

When once I spoke my mind about the character of the Berlin performances of my "Lohengrin," (09) I was reprimanded by the editor of the "Norddeutsche Allgemeine Zeitung," to the effect that I must not consider myself sole lessee of the "German spirit." I took the hint, and surrendered the lease. On the other hand, I was glad to find a coinage minted for the whole new German Reich, particularly when I heard that it had turned out so original-German that it would fit the currency of no other of the Great Powers, but remained subject to a "rate of exchange" with "franc" and "shilling": people told me this was tricky for the common trader, no doubt, but most advantageous to the banker. My German heart leaped high, too, when Liberally we voted for "Free-trade": there was, and still prevails, much want throughout the land; the workman hungers, and industry has fallen sick: but "business" flourishes. For "business" in the very grandest sense, indeed, the Reichs-" broker" has recently been patented; and, to grace and dignify the wedding-feasts of Highnesses, with oriental etiquette the newest Minister leads off the torch-dance.

This all may be good, and well beseem the novel Deutsches Reich; but no longer can I plumb its meaning, and therefore I must hold myself unqualified for further answering the question: "was ist Deutsch?" Could not Herr Constantin Frantz, for instance, afford us splendid aid? Herr Paul de Lagarde, too? May they consider themselves most friendlily invited to take up the answer to that fateful question, for instruction of our poor Bayreuther Patronatverein. If they haply then should reach the realm whereon we had to take Sebastian Bach in view, in course of the preceding article, I might perchance be able to relieve my hoped-for colleagues of their task again. How capital, if I should gain these writers' ear for my appeal!

Notes

01

"Und als die ganze Macht des romanisirten Frankenreiches in die Gewalt der reindeutschen Stämme überging, kam die seltsame, aber bedeutungsvolle Bezeichnung 'römisches Reich deutscher Nation auf."

02

"Durch das innigste Verständniss der Antike ist der deutsche Geist zu der Fähigkeit gelangt, das Reinmenschliche selbst wiederum in ursprünglicher Freiheit nachzubilden, nämlich, nicht durch die Anwendung der antiken Form einen bestimmten Stoff darzustellen, sondern durch eine Anwendung der antiken Auffassung der Welt die nothwendige neue Form selbst zu bilden."

03

In the original there occurs a Stabreim, unfortunately irreproducible, of "Junker, Jurist and Juden." —TR.

04

Cf. *Die Meistersinger*: "Am stillen Heerd in Winterszeit, wenn Burg und Hof mir eingeschnei't . . . ein altes Buch, vom Ahn' vermacht, gab das mir oft zu lesen." —TR.

05

"Es ist das Wesen des Geistes, den man in einzelnen hochbegabten Menschen 'Genie' nennt, sich auf den weltlichen Vortheil nicht zu verstehen." The colloquialism "not to be up to" is really the best translation for what I have rendered "not to trim its sails to." —TR.

06

Cf. *Die Meistersinger*, act iii: "Habt Acht! Uns drohen üble Streich':— zerfällt erst deutsches Volk und Reich, in falscher wälscher Majestät kein Fürst bald mehr sein Volk versteht; und wälschen Dunst mit wälschem Tand sie pflanzen uns in's deutsche Land." —TR,

07

"Ich stehe nicht an, die seitdem vorgekommenen Revolutionen in Deutschland als ganz undeutsch zu bezeichnen."

08

A song very popular with the German troops in the Franco-German War, originally attributed to a fusilier by name of Kutschke, but later ascertained to have been written by Field-chaplain Herm. Alex. Pistorius (1811-1877). —The "determined man" of two sentences back is, of course, Prince Bismarck. —TR.

09

Cf. Vol. III. p. 270—written in the year 1871.—TR.

Summary

History of M. S. for the article,—Meaning of "deutsch"; applies to those peoples who remained faithful to the fatherland and mother-tongue. Curiously enough, the memory of German glory is always attached to a period fatal to the German nature, when the Germans ruled over non-Germanic peoples; with the fall of outer political might began the real development of genuine German qualities. The Reformation contrasted with German evaluation of the Antique: had Germany's ruler, Charles V., been guided by the German Spirit, the Christian Church might then have been strengthened and re-knit; none but a universal religion is Religion in truth. Owing to the German's phlegma and fantasticism, gradual invasion of the Jew, usurping whole range of German public life and travestying the German spirit. Characteristics of genuine German Spirit: its openmindedness and introspection, conservatism and assimilation, love of intellectual liberty and refusal to trim its sails to worldly profit. Thirty Years' War decimated the nation, and dressed the remnant in French costume, but the German spirit survived: its sanctuary was Music; Bach as forerunner of Goethe. The *Beautiful and Noble not for profit, nor even Fame*—that is German, and alone can lead to German greatness. Let its Princes shew the German Folk they belong to it in this sense: it is high time, for fear the German spirit vanish again from the world, out of sheer inertia, and yield place to the Judaic. Franco-Judaico-German demagogues and Revolution of 1848: the genuine German represented by a race of men quite alien to him. German nation now being taught by blatant mediocrities to imagine it *is* already something great and does not need to first *become* it.

Experiences since 1865: the Franco-German War, courage of Bismarck and the army; Liedertafel songs. Return of the victorious troops. I offer to compose music in celebration of our fallen heroes; "upon so joyful an occasion we desire no painful impressions."

Kaisermarsch proposed for the march past: declined; let it fit the *concert-room* as best it may. New Coinage, Free Trade, and "Reichs-broker"; I surrender my "lease of the German Spirit," for I no longer (1878) can read the meaning of the new German Reich. Will some political writer enlighten us.

ON THE NAME "MUSIKDRAMA."

WE often read just now of a "Musikdrama," also hear of a society in Berlin, for instance, that proposes to help this Music-drama forward—yet without our being able to form an accurate idea of what is meant. I certainly have reason to suppose that this term was invented for sake of honouring my later dramatic works with a distinctive classification; but the less I have felt disposed to accept it, the more have I perceived an inclination in other quarters to adopt the name for a presumably new art-genre, which would appear to have been bound to evolve in answer to the temper and tendences of the day, even without my intervention, and now to lie ready as a cosy nest for everyone to hatch his musical eggs in.

I cannot indulge in the flattering view, that things are so pleasantly situate; and the less, as I don't know how to read the title "Musikdrama." When we unite two substantives to form one word, with any understanding of the spirit of our language, by the first we always signify in some sort of way the object of the second; so that "Zukunftsmusik," though invented in derision of me, had its sense as "music for the future." (01) But "Musikdrama" similarly interpreted as "drama for the object of music" would have no sense at all, were it not point-blank the old familiar libretto, which at anyrate was a drama expressly constructed for music. Yet this certainly is not what we mean: merely our sense of literary propriety has become so blunted through a constant reading of the farrago of our newspaper-writers and other beaux esprits, that we believe we may put any meaning we choose to the nonsensical words they coin, and in the present case we use "Musikdrama" to denote the very opposite of the sense the word implies.

Upon closer inspection, however, we find that the solecism here consists in the now favourite conversion of an adjectival predicate into a substantival prefix: one had begun by saying "musical drama." Yet it perhaps was not solely that evil habit, that brought about the abbreviation into "Musikdrama," but also a hazy feeling that no drama could possibly be "musical," like an instrument or (in rare enough events) a prima donna. A "musical drama," taken strictly, would be a drama that made music itself, or was good for making music with, or even that understood music, somewhat as our musical reporters. As this would not do, the mental confusion thought better to hide behind a wholly senseless word: for "Musikdrama" was a name which nobody had heard before, and one felt assured that nobody would ever dream of wilfully misconstruing so seriously-combined a word by its analogy with "Musikdosen" [musical snuffbox] and the like.

Now the serious meaning, intended by the term, was probably an actual "drama set to music." The mental emphasis would therefore fall on the "drama," which one regarded as differing from the former opera-libretto, and differing in that a dramatic plot was not to be simply trimmed to the needs of traditional operatic music, but the musical structure itself was to be shaped by the requirements characteristic of an actual drama. But if the "drama" was thus the main affair, it surely ought to have been placed before the "music" which it governed, and, somewhat like "Tanzmusik" or "Tafelmusik" [dance, and banquet-music], we then should have had to say "Dramamusik." Into this absurdity, however, one did not care to fall; twist and turn it as one might, "music" remained the real encumbrance to the naming, though everybody dimly felt that it was the chief concern in spite of all appearances, and the more so when that music was invited to develop and put forth its amplest powers through its association with an actual drama.

The obstacle to devising a name for this artwork was accordingly, in any event, the assumed necessity of indicating that the new whole had been formed by welding two disparate elements, music and drama, together. And certainly the greatest difficulty is to place "music" in a proper position toward "drama," since it can be brought into no equality therewith, as we have just seen, and must rank as either much more or much less than "drama." (02) The reason surely lies in the fact that the word "music" denotes an *art*, originally the whole assemblage of the arts, whilst "drama" strictly denotes a *deed* of art. In coupling words together it is easy to tell by the intelligibleness of the resulting compound whether we really still understand its constituent parts, taken separately, or merely employ them after a conventional usage. The primary meaning of "drama" is a *deed* or *action*: as such, displayed upon the stage, it at first formed but a portion of the Tragedy, i.e. the sacrificial choral chant, but at last invaded it from end to end and thus became the main affair. By its name one now denoted for all ages an action shewn upon the stage, and, to lay stress on this being a performance to look at, the place of assembly was called the "theatron," the looking-room. Our "Schauspiel" [strictly "look-game" or "show-play"] is therefore a very sensible name for what the Greeks more naïvely still called "drama," for it still more definitely expresses the characteristic development of an initial part into the ultimate main object. But Music is placed in an utterly false relation to this "show-play," if she now is to form but a part of that whole; as such she is wholly superfluous and disturbing, and for this reason has at last been quite excluded from the stricter Play. Of a truth she is "the part that once was all," and even now she feels called to re-assume her ancient dignity, as very mother-womb of Drama. Yet in this high calling she must neither stand before nor behind the Drama: she is no rival, but its mother. She sounds, and what she sounds ye see upon the stage; for that she gathered you together: what she is, ye never can but faintly dream; so she opens your eyes to behold her through the scenic likeness, as a mother tells her children legends shadowing the mysteries of religion.

The stupendous works of their Æschylus the Athenians called not dramas, but left them with the holy name of their descent: "tragedies," sacrificial chants in celebration of the god inspiring them. Happy they, to have to puzzle out no name for them! They had the most unheard-of artwork, and—left it nameless. But there came the great critics, the redoubtable reporters; abstract ideas were found, and where these ran short came words for word's sake. The good Polonius edifies us with a handsome list of them in "Hamlet." The Italians capped it with a *"Dramma per musica,"* which expresses much the same idea, though more grammatically phrased, as our "Musikdrama"; but one manifestly was not satisfied with this expression, and the curious outcome of the changes introduced by vocal virtuosi had to accept a name as nothing-saying as the genre itself. "Opera," plural of "opus," this new variety of "works" was dubbed; the Italians made a female of it, the French a male, so that the variety seemed to have turned out *generis utriusque.* I believe one could find no apter criticism of "Opera," than to allow this name as legitimate an origin as that of "Tragedy"; in neither case was it a matter of reason (*Vernunft*), but a deep-set instinct here expressed a thing of nameless nonsense, there a thing of sense indicibly profound.

Now I advise my professional competitors to retain the designation "opera," on second thought, for their musical works intended for the present theatre: it leaves them where they are, gives them no false colour, lifts them above all rivalry with their librettist, and if they are blest with good ideas for an aria, a duet, or even a drinking-chorus, they will please and give us something worth acknowledging, without having to overtax their strength to spoil their prettiest fancies. In every age there have been not only pantomimists, but cithern-players, flautists, and finally cantores: if some of their tribe were called for once to do a thing beyond their kind and custom, it was only very solitary units, whose unexampled rarity the finger of History underlines across the centuries and tens thereof; but never has a *genre* arisen thence, a genre in which, once given its proper name, the extra-ordinary lay ready for the common use of every fumbler. As for myself, with the best of will I should scarcely know what name to give the child that smiles from out my works a trifle shyly on a good part of the world we live in. Herr W. H. Riehl, as he somewhere has said, loses sight and hearing at my operas, for with some he hears, with others sees: how shall one name so inaudible, invisible a thing? I should almost have felt disposed to take my stand on its visibility, and abide by the "show-play," as I would gladly have called my dramas *deeds of Music brought to sight* (ersichtlich gewordene Thaten der Musik). But that would have been quite an art-philosophical title, fit to grace the catalogue of the future Polonii of our art-struck courts; since one may assume that, after their soldiers' successes, our Princes next will wish the Theatre led onward in a corresponding German sense. Only, in spite of all the "play" I offer, which many declare to touch the monstrous, there really would be far too little to see; as for instance I have been rebuked for not introducing into the second act of "Tristan" a brilliant court-ball, during which the hapless pair of lovers might hide themselves at the proper time in some shrubbery or other, where their discovery would create quite a startling scandal, with all the usual consequences. Instead there passes little more than music in this act, which unfortunately seems to be so very much music that people with the organisation of Herr W. H. Riehl quite lose their hearing through it; the more's the pity, as I give them next to nothing to see.

As folk would not let my poor works even pass for "operas," mainly because of their great dissimilarity to "Don Juan," I have had to console myself with handing them to the theatres without any designation of their genre at all; by this device I also think of abiding for just as long as I have to do with our theatres, which rightly recognise no other genre than "Opera," and, let one give them never so strict a "music-drama," would make of it an "opera" notwithstanding. To boldly emerge from the whole confusion, I lit, as known, on the thought of a *Bühnenfestspiel* [stage-festival-play], which I am hoping to bring about at Bayreuth with help from my friends. The name suggested itself through the character of my undertaking; for I knew of *Singing-festivals, Gymnastic-fêtes* and so forth, and could well imagine a theatre-feast—in which the *stage* and what takes place upon it, appropriately termed a *play*, would of course be the chief affair. But if any of the visitors to this Bühnenfestspiel shall chance to preserve a remembrance thereof, to him there may likewise occur a name for that thing I now propose to offer my friends as an unnamed deed of art.

Notes

01

Namely, for a time when one could get it performed without bungling.— R. WAGNER.

02

"Das Schwierigste hierbei ist jedenfalls, die 'Musik' in eine richtige Stellung zum 'Drama' zu bringen, da sie, wie wir dieses soeben ersehen mussten, mit diesem in keine ebenbürtige Verbindung zu bringen ist, und uns entweder viel mehr, oder viel weniger als das Drama gelten muss."

Summary

A senseless name, apparently invented in honour of my later works, and now usurped by imitators. Meaning of German compound words; this one a solecism, condensed from equally incorrect "musical drama." Music an *art*, Drama a *deed*. Music the part that once was all; Greek "Tragedy," Italian "Opera," and German "Schauspiel." Let my rivals stick to "opera," which will confuse no one, nor spoil their prettiest fancies. I should like to call my dramas "deeds of Music brought to sight," but people say I give them too little to see. Let "Bühnenfestspiel" serve for the nonce, for at Bayreuth the *stage* will be the main object of the *festival*.

JUDAISM IN MUSIC

Judaism in Music.

(01)

IN THE 'NEUE ZEITSCHRIFT FüR MUSIK' not long ago, mention was made of an "Hebraic art-taste": an attack and a defence of that expression neither did, nor could, stay lacking. Now it seems to myself not unimportant, to clear up the matter lying at bottom of all this—a matter either glossed over by our critics hitherto, or touched with a certain outburst of excitement. (02) It will not be a question, however, of saying something new, but of explaining that unconscious feeling which proclaims itself among the people as a rooted dislike of the Jewish nature; thus, of speaking out a something really existent, and by no means of attempting to artfully breathe life into an unreality through the force of any sort of fancy. Criticism goes against its very essence, if, in attack or defence, it tries for anything else.

Since it here is merely in respect of Art, and specially of Music, that we want to explain to ourselves the popular dislike of the Jewish nature, even at the present day, we may completely pass over any dealing with this same phenomenon in the field of Religion and Politics. In Religion the Jews have long ceased to be our hated foes,—thanks to all those who within the Christian religion itself have drawn upon themselves the people's hatred. (03) In pure Politics we have never come to actual conflict with the Jews; we have even granted them the erection of a Jerusalemitic realm, and in this respect we have rather had to regret that Herr v. Rothschild was too keen-witted to make himself King of the Jews, preferring, as is well known, to remain "the Jew of the Kings." It is another matter, where politics become a question of Society: here the isolation of the Jews has been held by us a challenge to the exercise of human justice, for just so long as in ourselves the thrust toward social liberation has woken into plainer consciousness. When we strove for emancipation of the Jews, however, we virtually were more the champions of an abstract principle, than of a concrete case: just as all our Liberalism was a not very lucid mental sport (04)—since we went for freedom of the Folk without knowledge of that Folk itself, nay, with a dislike of any genuine contact with it—so our eagerness to level up the rights of Jews was far rather stimulated by a general idea, than by any real sympathy; for, with all our speaking and writing in favour of the Jews' emancipation, we always felt instinctively repelled by any actual, operative contact with them.

Here, then, we touch the point that brings us closer to our main inquiry: we have to explain to ourselves the *involuntary repellence* possessed for us by the nature and personality of the Jews, so as to vindicate that instinctive dislike which we plainly recognise as stronger and more overpowering than our conscious zeal to rid ourselves thereof. Even to-day we only purposely belie ourselves, in this regard, when we think necessary to hold immoral and taboo all open proclamation of our natural repugnance against the Jewish nature. Only in quite the latest times do we seem to have reached an insight, that it is more rational (*vernünftiger*) to rid ourselves of that strenuous self-deception, (05) so as quite soberly instead to view the object of our violent sympathy and bring ourselves to understand a repugnance still abiding with us in spite of all our Liberal bedazzlements. (06) To our astonishment, we perceive that in our Liberal battles (07) we have been floating in the air and fighting clouds, whereas the whole fair soil of material reality has found an appropriator whom our aerial flights have very much amused, no doubt, yet who holds us far too foolish to reward us by relaxing one iota of his usurpation of that material soil. Quite imperceptibly the "Creditor of Kings" has become the King of Creeds, and we really cannot take this monarch's pleading for emancipation as otherwise than uncommonly naïve, seeing that it is much rather *we* who are shifted into the necessity of fighting for emancipation from the Jews. According to the present constitution of this world, the Jew in truth is already more than emancipate: he rules, and will rule, so long as Money remains the power before which all our doings and our dealings lose their force. That the historical adversity (08) of the Jews and the rapacious rawness of Christian-German potentates have brought this power within the hands of Israel's sons—this needs no argument of ours to prove. That the impossibility of carrying farther any natural, any 'necessary' and truly beauteous thing, upon the basis of that stage whereat the evolution of our arts has now arrived, and without a total alteration of that basis—that this has also brought the public Art-taste of our time between the busy fingers of the Jew, however, is the matter whose grounds we here have to consider somewhat closer. What their thralls had toiled and moiled to pay the liege-lords of the Roman and the Medieval world, to-day is turned to money by the Jew: who thinks of noticing that the guileless-looking scrap of paper is slimy with the blood of countless generations? What the heroes of the arts, with untold strain consuming lief and life, have wrested from the art-fiend of two millennia of misery, to-day the Jew converts into an art-bazaar (*Kunstwaarenwechsel*): who sees it in the mannered bricabrac, that it is glued together by the hallowed brow-sweat of the Genius of two thousand years?—

We have no need to first substantiate the be-Jewing of modern art; it springs to the eye, and thrusts upon the senses, of itself. Much too far afield, again, should we have to fare, did we undertake to explain this phenomenon by a demonstration of the character of our art-history itself. But if emancipation from the yoke of Judaism appears to us the greatest of necessities, we must hold it weighty above all to prove our forces for this war of liberation. Now we shall never win these forces from an abstract definition of that phenomenon *per se*, but only from an accurate acquaintance with the nature of that involuntary feeling of ours which utters itself as an instinctive repugnance against the Jew's prime essence. Through it, through this unconquerable feeling—if we avow it quite without ado—must there become plain to us *what* we hate in that essence; what we then know definitely, we can make head against; nay, through his very laying bare, may we even hope to rout the demon from the field, whereon he has only been able to maintain his stand beneath the shelter of a twilight darkness—a darkness we good-natured Humanists ourselves have cast upon him, to make his look less loathly.

The Jew—who, as everyone knows, has a God all to himself—in ordinary life strikes us primarily by his outward appearance, which, no matter to what European nationality we belong, has something disagreeably (09) foreign to that nationality: instinctively we wish to have nothing in common with a man who looks like that. This must heretofore have passed as a misfortune for the Jew: in more recent times, however, we perceive that in the midst of this misfortune he feels entirely well; after all his successes, he needs must deem his difference from us a pure distinction. Passing over the moral side, in the effect of this in itself unpleasant freak of Nature, and coming to its bearings upon Art, we here will merely observe that to us this exterior can never be thinkable as a subject for the art of re-presentment.: if plastic art wants to present us with a Jew, it mostly takes its model from sheer phantasy, with a prudent ennobling, or entire omission, of just everything that characterises for us in common life the Jew's appearance. But the Jew never wanders on to the theatric boards: the exceptions are so rare and special, that they only confirm the general rule. We can conceive no representation of an antique or modern stage-character by a Jew, be it as hero or lover, without feeling instinctively the incongruity of such a notion. (10) This is of great weight: a man whose appearance we must hold unfitted for artistic treatment—not merely in this or that personality, but according to his kind in general—neither can we hold him capable of any sort of artistic utterance of his (11) [inner] essence.

By far more weighty, nay, of quite decisive weight for our inquiry, is the effect the Jew produces on us through his *speech*; and this is the essential point at which to sound the Jewish influence upon Music. (12) —The Jew speaks the language of the nation in whose midst he dwells from generation to generation, but he speaks it always as an alien. As it lies beyond our present scope to occupy ourselves with the cause of this phenomenon, too, we may equally abstain from an arraignment of Christian Civilisation for having kept the Jew in violent severance from it, as on the other hand, in touching the sequelae of that severance we can scarcely propose to make the Jews the answerable party. (13) Our only object, here, is to throw light on the aesthetic character of the said results.—In the first place, then, the general circumstance that the Jew talks the modern European languages merely as learnt, and not as mother tongues, must necessarily debar him from all capability of therein expressing himself idiomatically, independently, and conformably to his nature. (14) A language, with its expression and its evolution, is not the work of scattered units, but of an historical community: only he who has unconsciously grown up within the bond of this community, takes also any share in its creations. But the Jew has stood outside the pale of any such community, stood solitarily with his Jehova in a splintered, soilless stock, to which all self-sprung evolution must stay denied, just as even the peculiar (Hebraïc) language of that stock has been preserved for him merely as a thing defunct. Now, to make poetry in a foreign tongue has hitherto been impossible, even to geniuses of highest rank. Our whole European art and civilisation, however, have remained to the Jew a foreign tongue; for, just as he has taken no part in the evolution of the one, so has he taken none in that of the other; but at most the homeless wight has been a cold, nay more, a hostile looker-on. In this Speech, this Art, the Jew can only after-speak and after-patch—not truly make a poem of his words, an artwork of his doings.

In particular does the purely physical aspect of the Jewish mode of speech repel us. Throughout an intercourse of two millennia with European nations, Culture has not succeeded in breaking the remarkable stubbornness of the Jewish *naturel* as regards the peculiarities of Semitic pronunciation. The first thing that strikes our ear as quite outlandish and unpleasant, in the Jew's production of the voice-sounds, is a creaking, squeaking, buzzing snuffle (15) : add thereto an employment of words in a sense quite foreign to our nation's tongue, and an arbitrary twisting of the structure of our phrases—and this mode of speaking acquires at once the character of an intolerably jumbled blabber (*eines unertraglich verwirrten Geplappers*); so that when we hear this Jewish talk, our attention dwells involuntarily on its repulsive *how*, rather than on any meaning of its intrinsic *what*. How exceptionally weighty is this circumstance, particularly for explaining the impression made on us by the music-works of modern Jews, must be recognised and borne in mind before all else. If we hear a Jew speak, we are unconsciously offended by the entire want of purely-human expression in his discourse: the cold indifference of its peculiar "blubber" ("*Gelabber*") never by any chance rises to the ardour of a higher, heartfelt passion. If, on the other hand, we find *ourselves* driven to this more heated expression, in converse with a Jew, he will always shuffle off, since he is incapable of replying in kind. Never does the Jew excite himself in mutual interchange of feelings with us, but—so far as we are concerned—only in the altogether special egoistic interest of his vanity or profit; a thing which, coupled with the wry expression of his daily mode of speech, always gives to such excitement a tinge of the ridiculous, and may rouse anything you please in us, only not sympathy with the interests of the speaker. Though we well may deem it thinkable that in intercourse with one another, and particularly where domestic life brings purely-human feelings to an outburst, even the Jews may be able to give expression to their emotions in a manner effective enough among themselves: yet this cannot come within our present purview, since we here are listening to the Jew who, in the intercourse of life and art, expressly speaks *to us*.

Now, if the aforesaid qualities of his dialect make the Jew almost (16) incapable of giving artistic enunciation to his feelings and beholdings through *talk*, for such an enunciation through *song* his aptitude must needs be infinitely smaller. Song is just Talk aroused to highest passion: Music is the speech of Passion. All that worked repellently upon us in his outward appearance and his speech, makes us take to our heels at last in his Song, providing we are not held prisoners by the very ridicule of this phenomenon. Very naturally, in Song—the vividest and most indisputable expression of the personal emotional-being—the peculiarity of the Jewish nature attains for us its climax of distastefulness; and on any natural hypothesis, we might hold the Jew adapted for every sphere of art, excepting that whose basis lies in Song.

The Jews' sense of Beholding has never been of such a kind as to let *plastic* artists arise among them: from ever have their eyes been busied with far more practical affairs, than beauty and the spiritual substance of the world of forms. We know nothing of a Jewish architect or sculptor in our times, (17) so far as I am aware: whether recent painters of Jewish descent have really created (*wirklich geschaffen haben*) in their art, I must leave to connoisseurs to judge; presumably, however, these artists occupy no other standing toward their art, than that of modern Jewish composers toward Music—to whose plainer investigation we now will turn.

The Jew, who is innately incapable of enouncing himself to us artistically through either his outward appearance or his speech, and least of all through his singing. has nevertheless been able in the widest-spread of modern art-varieties, to wit in Music, to reach the rulership of public taste.—To explain to ourselves this phenomenon, let us first consider *how* it grew possible to the Jew to become a musician.—

From that turning-point in our social evolution where Money, with less and less disguise, was raised to the virtual patent of nobility, the Jews—to whom money-making without actual labour, i.e. Usury, had been left as their only trade—the Jews not merely could no longer be denied the diploma of a new society that needed naught but gold, but they brought it with them in their pockets. Wherefore our modern Culture, accessible to no one but the well-to-do, remained the less a closed book to them, as it had sunk into a venal article of Luxury. Henceforward, then, the *cultured Jew* appears in our Society; his distinction from the uncultured, the common Jew, we now have closely to observe. The cultured Jew has taken the most indicible pains to strip off all the obvious tokens of his lower co-religionists: in many a case he has even held it wise to make a Christian baptism wash away the traces of his origin. This zeal, however, has never got so far as to let him reap the hoped-for fruits: it has conducted only to his utter isolation, and to making him the most heartless of all human beings; to such a pitch, that we have been bound to lose even our earlier sympathy for the tragic history of his stock. His connexion with the former comrades in his suffering, which he arrogantly tore asunder, it has stayed impossible for him to replace by a new connexion with that society whereto he has soared up. He stands in correlation with none but those who need his money: and never yet has money thriven to the point of knitting a goodly bond 'twixt man and man. Alien and apathetic stands the educated Jew in midst of a society he does not understand, with whose tastes and aspirations he does not sympathise, whose history and evolution have always been indifferent to him. In such a situation have we seen the Jews give birth to Thinkers: the Thinker is the backward-looking poet; but the true Poet is the foretelling Prophet. For such a prophet-charge can naught equip, save the deepest, the most heartfelt sympathy with a great, a like-endeavouring Community—to whose unconscious thoughts the Poet gives exponent voice. Completely shut from this community, by the very nature of his situation; entirely torn from all connexion with his native stock—to the genteeler Jew his learnt and payed-for culture could only seem a luxury, since at bottom he knew not what to be about with it.

Now, our modern arts had likewise become a portion of this culture, and among them more particularly that art which is just the very easiest to learn—the art of *music*, and indeed *that* Music which, severed from her sister arts, had been lifted by the force and stress of grandest geniuses to a stage in her universal faculty of Expression where either, in new conjunction with the other arts, she might speak aloud the most sublime, or, in persistent separation from them, she could also speak at will the deepest bathos of the trivial. Naturally, *what* the cultured Jew had to speak, in his aforesaid situation, could be nothing but the trivial and indifferent, because his whole artistic bent was in sooth a mere luxurious, needless thing. Exactly as his whim inspired, or some interest lying outside Art, could he utter himself now thus, and now otherwise; for never was he driven to speak out a definite, a real and necessary thing, but he just merely wanted to speak, no matter what (18) ; so that, naturally, the *how* was the only 'moment' left for him to care for. At present no art affords such plenteous possibility of talking in it without saying any real thing, as that of Music, since the greatest geniuses have already said whatever there was to say in it as an absolute separate-art. (19) When this had once been spoken out, there was nothing left but to babble after; and indeed with quite distressing accuracy and deceptive likeness, just as parrots reel off human words and phrases, but also with just as little real feeling and expression as these foolish birds. Only, in the case of our Jewish music-makers this mimicked speech presents one marked peculiarity—that of the Jewish style of talk in general, which we have more minutely characterised above.

Although the peculiarities of the Jewish mode of speaking and singing come out the most glaringly in the commoner class of Jew, who has remained faithful to his fathers' stock, and though the cultured son of Jewry takes untold pains to strip them off, nevertheless they shew an impertinent obstinacy in cleaving to him. Explain this mishap by physiology as we may, yet it also has its reason in the aforesaid social situation of the educated Jew. However much our Luxury-art may float in wellnigh nothing but the aether of our self-willed Phantasy, still it keeps below one fibre of connexion with its natural soil, with the genuine spirit of the Folk. The true poet, no matter in what branch of art, still gains his stimulus from nothing but a faithful, loving contemplation of instinctive Life, of that life which only greets his sight amid the Folk. Now, where is the cultured Jew to find this Folk? Not, surely, on the soil of that Society in which he plays his artist-rôle? If he has any connexion at all with this Society, it is merely with that offshoot of it, entirely loosened from the real, the healthy stem; but this connexion is an entirely loveless, and this lovelessness must ever become more obvious to him, if for sake of food-stuff for his art he clambers down to that Society's foundations: not only does he here find everything more strange and unintelligible, but the instinctive ill-will of the Folk confronts him here in all its wounding nakedness, since—unlike its fellow in the richer classes—it here is neither weakened down nor broken by reckonings of advantage and regard for certain mutual interests. Thrust back with contumely from any contact with this Folk, and in any case completely powerless to seize its spirit, the cultured Jew sees himself driven to the taproot of his native stem, where at least an understanding would come by all means easier to him. Willy-nilly he must draw his water from this well; yet only a *How*, and not a *What*, rewards his pains. The Jew has never had an Art of his own, hence never a Life of art-enabling import (*ein Leben von kunstfähigem Gehalte*): an import, a universally applicable, a human import, not even to-day does it offer to the searcher, but merely a peculiar method of expression—and that, the method we have characterised above. Now the only musical expression offered to the Jew tone-setter by his native Folk, is the ceremonial music of their Jehova-rites: the Synagogue is the solitary fountain whence the Jew can draw art-motives at once popular and *intelligible to himself*. However sublime and noble we may be minded to picture to ourselves this musical Service of God in its pristine purity, all the more plainly must we perceive that that purity has been most terribly sullied before it came down to us: here for thousands of years has nothing unfolded itself through an inner life-fill, but, just as with Judaism at large, everything has kept its fixity of form and substance. But a form which is never quickened through renewal of its substance, must fall to pieces in the end; an expression whose content has long-since ceased to be the breath of Feeling, grows senseless and distorted. Who has not had occasion to convince himself of the travesty of a divine service of song, presented in a real Folk-synagogue? Who has not been seized with a feeling of the greatest revulsion, of horror mingled with the absurd, at hearing that sense-and-sound-confounding gurgle, jodel and cackle, which no intentional caricature can make more repugnant than as offered here in full, in naïve seriousness? In latter days, indeed, the spirit of reform has shewn its stir within this singing, too, by an attempted restoration of the older purity: but, of its very nature, what here has happened on the part of the higher, the reflective Jewish intellect, is just a fruitless effort from Above, which can never strike Below to such a point that the cultured Jew—who precisely for his art-needs seeks the genuine fount of Life amid the Folk— may be greeted by the mirror of his intellectual efforts in that fount itself. He seeks for the Instinctive, and not the Reflected, since the latter is *his* product; and all the Instinctive he can light on, is just that out-of-joint expression.

If this going back to the Folk-source is as unpurposed with the cultured Jew, as unconsciously enjoined upon him by Necessity and the nature of the thing, as with every artist: with just as little conscious aim, and therefore with an insuperable domination of his whole field of view, does the hence-derived impression carry itself across into his art - productions. Those (20) rhythms and melismi of the Synagogue-song usurp his musical fancy in exactly the same way as the instinctive possession of the strains and rhythms of our

Folksong and Folkdance made out the virtual (21) shaping-force of the creators of our art-music, both vocal and instrumental. To the musical perceptive-faculty (22) of the cultured Jew there is therefore nothing seizable in all the ample circle of our music, either popular or artistic, but that which flatters his general sense of the intelligible: intelligible, however, and so intelligible that he may use it for his art, is merely That which in any degree approaches a resemblance to the said peculiarity of Jewish music. In listening to either our naïve or our consciously artistic musical doings, however, were the Jew to try to probe their heart and living sinews, he would find here really not one whit of likeness to *his* musical nature; and the utter strangeness of this phenomenon must scare him back so far, that he could never pluck up nerve again to mingle in our art-creating. Yet his whole position in our midst never tempts the Jew to so intimate a glimpse into our essence: wherefore, either intentionally (provided he recognises this position of his towards us) or instinctively (if he is incapable of understanding us at all), he merely listens to the barest surface of our art, but not to its life-bestowing inner organism; and through this apathetic listening alone, can he trace external similarities with the only thing intelligible to his power of view, peculiar to his special nature. To him, therefore, the most external accidents on our domain of musical life and art must pass for its very essence; and therefore, when as artist he reflects them back upon us, his adaptations needs must seem to us outlandish, odd, indifferent, cold, unnatural and awry; so that J udaic works of music often produce on us the impression as though a poem of Goethe's, for instance, were being rendered in the Jewish jargon.

Just as words and constructions are hurled together in this jargon with wondrous inexpressiveness, so does the Jew musician hurl together the diverse forms and styles of every age and every master. Packed side by side, we find the formal idiosyncrasies of all the schools, in motleyest chaos. As in these productions the sole concern is Talking at all hazards, and not the Object which might make that talk worth doing, so this clatter can only be made at all inciting to the ear by its offering at each instant a new summons to attention, through a change of outer expressional means. Inner agitation, genuine passion, each finds its own peculiar language at the instant when, struggling for an understanding, it girds itself for utterance: the Jew, already characterised by us in this regard, has no true passion (*Leidenschaft*), and least of all a passion that might thrust him on to art-creation. But where this passion is not forthcoming, *there* neither is any calm (*Ruhe*): true, noble Calm is nothing else than Passion mollified through Resignation. (23) Where the calm has not been ushered in by passion, we perceive naught but sluggishness (*Trägheit*): the opposite of sluggishness, however, is nothing but that prickling unrest which we observe in Jewish music-works from one end to the other, saving where it makes place for that soulless, feelingless inertia. What issues from the Jews' attempts at making Art, must necessarily therefore bear the attributes of coldness and indifference, even to triviality and absurdity; and in the history of Modern Music we can but class the Judaic period as that of final unproductivity, of stability gone to ruin.

By what example will this all grow clearer to us—ay, wellnigh what other single case could make us so alive to it, as the works of a musician of Jewish birth whom Nature had endowed with specific musical gifts as very few before him? All that offered itself to our gaze, in the inquiry into our antipathy against the Jewish nature; all the contradictoriness of this nature, both in itself and as touching us; all its inability, while outside our footing, to have intercourse with us upon that footing, nay, even to form a wish to further develop the things which had sprung from out our soil: all these are intensified to a positively tragic conflict in the nature, life, and art-career of the early-taken FELIX MENDELSSOHN BARTHOLDY. He has shewn us that a Jew may have the amplest store of specific talents, may own the finest and most varied culture, the highest and the tenderest sense of honour—yet without all these pre-eminences helping him, were it but one single time, to call forth in us that deep, that heart-searching effect which we await from Art (24) because we know her capable thereof, because we have felt it many a time and oft, so soon as once a hero of our art has, so to say, but opened his mouth to speak to us. To professional critics, who haply have reached a like consciousness with ourselves hereon, it may be left to prove by specimens of Mendelssohn's art-products our statement of this indubitably certain thing; by way of illustrating our general impression, let us here be content with the fact that, in hearing a tone-piece of this composer's, we have only been able to feel engrossed where nothing beyond our more or less amusement-craving Phantasy was roused through the presentment, stringing-together and entanglement of the most elegant, the smoothest and most polished figures—as in the kaleidoscope's changeful play of form and colour (25) —but never where those figures were meant to take the shape of deep and stalwart feelings of the human heart. (26) In this latter event Mendelssohn lost even all *formal* productive-faculty; wherefore in particular where he made for Drama, as in the Oratorio, he was obliged quite openly to snatch at every formal detail that had served as characteristic token of the individuality of this or that forerunner whom he chose out for his model. It is further significant of this procedure, that he gave the preference to our old master BACH, as special pattern for his inexpressive modern tongue to copy. Bach's musical speech was formed at a period of our history when Music s universal tongue was still striving for the faculty of more individual, more unequivocal Expression: pure formalism and pedantry still clung so strongly to her, that it was first through the gigantic force of Bach's own genius that her purely human accents (*Ausdruck*) broke themselves a vent. The speech of Bach stands toward that of Mozart, and finally of Beethoven, in the relation of the Egyptian Sphinx to the Greek statue of a Man: as the human visage of the Sphinx is in the act of striving outward from the animal body, so strives Bach's noble human head from out the periwig. It is only another evidence of the inconceivably witless confusion of our luxurious music-taste of nowadays, that we can let Bach's language be spoken to us at the selfsame time as that of Beethoven, and flatter ourselves that there is merely an individual difference of form between them, but nowise a real historic distinction, marking off a period in our culture. The reason, however, is not so far to seek: the speech of Beethoven can be spoken only by a whole, entire, warm-breathed human being; since it was just the speech of a music-man so perfect, that with the force of Necessity he thrust beyond Absolute Music—whose dominion he had measured and fulfilled unto its utmost frontiers—and shewed to us the pathway to the fecundation of every art through Music, as her only salutary broadening. (27) On the other hand, Bach's language can be mimicked, at a pinch, by any musician who thoroughly understands his business, though scarcely in the sense of Bach; because the Formal has still therein the upper hand, and the purely human Expression is not as yet a factor so definitely preponderant that its *What* either can, or must be uttered without conditions, for it still is fully occupied with shaping out the *How*. The washiness and whimsicality of our present musical style has been, if not exactly brought about, yet pushed to its utmost pitch by Mendelssohn's endeavour to speak out a vague, an almost nugatory Content as interestingly and spiritedly as possible. Whereas Beethoven, the last in the chain of our true music-heroes, strove with highest longing, and wonder-working faculty, (28) for the clearest, certainest Expression of an unsayable Content through a sharp-cut, plastic shaping of his tone-pictures: Mendelssohn, on the contrary, reduces these achievements to vague, fantastic shadow-forms, midst whose indefinite shimmer our freakish fancy is indeed aroused, but our inner, purely-human yearning for distinct artistic sight is hardly touched with even the merest hope of a fulfilment. Only where an oppressive feeling of this incapacity seems to master the composer's mood, and drive him to express a soft and mournful resignation, has Mendelssohn the power to shew himself characteristic—characteristic in the subjective sense of a gentle (29) individuality that confesses an impossibility in view of its own powerlessness. This, as we have said, is the tragic trait in Mendelssohn's life-history; and if in the domain of Art we are to give our sympathy to the sheer personality, we can scarcely deny a large measure thereof to Mendelssohn, even though the force of that sympathy be weakened by the reflection that the Tragic, in Mendelssohn's situation, hung rather over him than came to actual, sore and cleansing consciousness.

A like sympathy, however, can no other Jew composer rouse in us. A far-famed Jewish tone-setter of our day has addressed himself and products to a section of our public whose total confusion of musical taste was less to be first caused by him, than worked out to his profit. The public of our Opera-theatre of nowadays has for long been gradually led aside from those claims which rightly should be addressed, not only to the Dramatic Artwork, but in general to every work of healthy taste. (30) The places in our halls of entertainment are mostly filled by nothing but that section of our citizen society whose only ground for change of occupation is utter 'boredom' (*Langeweile*): the disease of boredom, however, is not remediable by sips of Art; for it can never be distracted of set purpose, but merely duped into another form of boredom. Now, the catering for this deception that famous opera-composer has made the task of his artistic life. (31) There is no object in more closely designating the artistic means he has expended on the reaching of this life's-aim: enough that, as we may see by the result, he knew completely how to dupe; and more particularly by taking that jargon which we have already characterised, and palming it upon his ennuyed audience as the modern-piquant utterance of all the trivialities which so often had been set before them in all their natural foolishness. That this composer took also thought for thrilling situations (*Erschütterungen*) and the effective weaving of emotional catastrophes (*Gefühlskatastrophen*), need astonish none who know how necessarily this sort of thing is wished by those whose time hangs heavily upon their hands; nor need any wonder that in *this* his aim succeeded too, if they but will ponder well the reasons why, in such conditions, (32) the whole was bound to prosper with him. In fact, this composer pushes his deception so far, that he ends by deceiving himself, and perchance as purposely as he deceives his bored admirers. We believe, indeed, that he honestly would like to turn out artworks, and yet is well aware he cannot: to extricate himself from this painful conflict between Will and Can, he writes operas for Paris, and sends them touring round the world—the surest means, to-day, of earning oneself an art-renown albeit not an artist. Under the burden of this self-deception, which may not be so toilless as one might think, (33) he, too, appears to us wellnigh in a tragic light: yet the purely personal element of wounded vanity turns the thing into a tragi-comedy, just as in general the un-inspiring, the truly laughable, is the characteristic mark whereby this famed composer shews his Jewhood in his music.—

From a closer survey of the instances adduced above—which we have learnt to grasp by getting to the bottom of our indomitable objection to the Jewish nature—there more especially results for us a proof of the *ineptitude of the present musical epoch*. Had the two aforesaid Jew composers (34) in truth helped Music into riper bloom, then we should merely have had to admit tha.t our tarrying behind them rested on some organic debility that had taken sudden hold of us: but not so is the case; on the contrary, as compared with bygone epochs, the specific musical powers of nowadays have rather increased than diminished. The incapacity lies in the spirit of our Art itself, which is longing for another life than the artificial one now toilsomely upheld for it. The incapacity of the musical art-*variety*, itself, is exposed for us in the art-doings of Mendelssohn, the uncommonly-gifted specific musician; but the nullity of our whole public system, its utterly un-artistic claims and nature, in the successes of that famous Jewish opera-composer grow clear for any one to see. These are the weighty points that have now to draw towards themselves the whole attention of everyone who means honestly by Art: here is what we have to ask ourselves, to scrutinise, to bring to plainest understanding. Whoever shirks this toil, whoever turns his back upon this scrutiny—either since no Need impels him to it, or because he waives a lesson that possibly might drive him from the lazy groove of mindless, feelingless routine—even him we now include in that same category, of "Judaism in Music." (35) The Jews could never take possession of this art, until *that* was to be exposed in it which they now demonstrably have brought to light— its inner incapacity for life. So long as the separate art of Music had a real organic life-need in it, down to the epochs of Mozart and Beethoven, there was nowhere to be found a Jew composer: it was impossible for an element entirely foreign to that living organism to take part in the formative stages of that life. Only when a body's inner death is manifest, do outside elements win the power of lodgment in it—yet merely to destroy it. Then indeed that body's flesh dissolves into a swarming colony of insect-life: but who, in looking on that body's self would hold it still for living? The spirit, that is: the *life*, has fled from out that body, has sped to kindred other bodies; and this is all that makes out Life. In genuine Life alone can we, too, find again the ghost of Art, and not within its worm-befretted carcase.—

I said above, the Jews had brought forth no true poet. We here must give a moment's mention, then, to HEINRICH HEINE. At the time when Goethe and Schiller sang among us, we certainly know nothing of a poetising Jew: at the time, however, when our poetry became a lie, when every possible thing might flourish from the wholly unpoetic element of our life, but no true poet—then was it the office of a highly-gifted poet-Jew to bare with fascinating taunts that lie, that bottomless aridity and jesuitical hypocrisy of our Versifying which still would give itself the airs of true poesis. His famous musical congeners, too, he mercilessly lashed for their pretence to pass as artists; no make-believe could hold its ground before him: by the remorseless demon of denial of all that seemed worth denying was he driven on without a rest, (36) through all the mirage of our modern self-deception, till he reached the point where in turn he duped himself into a poet, and was rewarded by his versified lies being set to music by our own composers.—He was the conscience of Judaism, just as Judaism is the evil conscience of our modern Civilisation.

Yet another Jew have we to name, who appeared among us as a writer. From out his isolation as a Jew, he came among us seeking for redemption: he found it not, and had to learn that only *with our redemption, too, into genuine Manhood*, would he ever find it. To become Man at once with us, however, means firstly for the Jew as much as ceasing to be Jew. And this had BÖRNE done. Yet Börne, of all others, teaches us that this redemption can not be reached in ease and cold, indifferent complacence, but costs—as cost it must for us—sweat, anguish, want, and all the dregs of suffering and sorrow. Without once looking back, take ye your part in this regenerative work of deliverance through self-annulment (37); then are we one and un-dissevered! But bethink ye, that one only thing can redeem you from the burden of your curse: the redemption of Ahasuerus—*Going under!*

K. Freigedank

Notes

01

To the opening of this article the editor of the *Neue Zeitschrift* appended the following footnote: "However faulty her outward conformation, we have always considered it a pre-eminence of Germany's, a result of her great learning, that at least in the scientific sphere she possesses intellectual freedom. This freedom we now lay claim to and rely on, in printing the above essay, desirous that our readers may accept it in this sense. Whether one shares the views expressed therein, or not, the author's breadth of grasp (*Genialität der Anschauung*) will be disputed by no one." — TR.

02

"Erregtheit" — in the *N.Z.* this stood as "Leidenschaftlichkeit," i.e. "passion." — Tr.

03

In the *N.Z.* this clause ran: "thanks to our pietists and Jesuits, who have led the Folk's entire religious hatred toward themselves, so that with *their* eventual downfall Religion, in its present meaning (which has been rather that of Hate, than Love), will presumably have also come to naught!" — TR.

04

"Nicht sehr hellsehendes (in the *N.Z.* "luxuriöses") Geistesspiel." — TR.

05

"Selbsttäuschung"; in the *N.Z.* "Lüge," i.e. "lie." — TR.

06

"Vorspiegelungen"; in the *N.Z.* "Utopien." —TR.

07

In the *N.Z.* "auf gut christlich," i.e. "like good Christians." —TR.

08

"Elend" may also mean "exile." In this sentence the *N.Z.* had "Romo-Christian Germans," in place of "Christian-Germanic potentates." —TR.

09

This adverb (*unangenehm*) was preceded in the *N.Z.* by another, "unüberwindlich," i.e. "unconquerably"; whereas "instinctively" (*unwillkürlich*) was absent from the next clause. —TR.

10

Note to the 1869, and later editions:—"To be sure, our later experiences of the work done by Jewish actors would afford food for many a dissertation, as to which I here can only give a passing hint. Since the above was written not only have the Jews succeeded in capturing the Stage itself, but even in kidnapping the poet's dramatic progeny; a famous Jewish "character-player" not merely has done away with any representment of the poetic figures bred by Shakespeare, Schiller, and so forth, but substitutes the offspring of his own effect-full and not quite un-tendentiose fancy—a thing which gives one the impression as though the Saviour had been cut out from a painting of the crucifixion, and a demagogic Jew stuck-in instead. On the stage the falsification of our Art has thriven to complete deception; for which reason, also, Shakespeare & Co. are now spoken of merely in the light of their qualified adaptability for the stage. —The Editor" (i.e. Richard Wagner).

11

In the *N.Z.* "purely human" stood in the place of "his." — TR.

12

The clause after the semicolon did not exist in the *N. Z.*

13

This sentence occurred as a footnote in the *N. Z.*, and the next sentence was absent. — TR.

14

In the *N.Z.*, "in any higher sense." — TR.

15

"Ein zischender, schrillender, summsender und murksender Lautausdruck."

16

In the *N.Z.* "durchaus," i.e. "altogether." — TR.

17

"In our times" did not appear in the *N.Z.* article. — TR.

18

In the *N.Z.* "but he just merely wanted to speak" appears to have been skipped by the printer, leaving a hiatus in the sense; moreover, after "no matter what," there occurred: "sheerly to make his existence noticeable." — TR.

19

In the *N.Z.* this sentence was continued by:—"and this was just the proclamation of its perfect *faculty* for the most manifold Expression, but not an *object* of expression in itself (*nicht aber ein* Ausdruckswerthes *selbst*). When this had happened, and *if one did not propose to express thereby a definite thing*, there was nothing left but to senselessly repeat the talk; and indeed" &c.—Perhaps I may be forgiven for again recalling Wagner's own parrot, from the *Letters to Uhlig* (see Preface to Vol. ii. of the present series).—TR.

20

In the *N.Z.* "wondrous";

21

"unconsciously";

22

"capacity," as also in the preceding sentence where now stands "fancy."—TR.

23

"Die durch Resignation beschwichtigte Leidenschaft." In the *N. Z.* this ran: "der Genuss der Sättigung wahrer und edler Leidenschaft," i.e. "the after-taste of true and noble passion satisfied." The change, or rather advance, of view-point is highly significant.—TR.

24

In the *N.Z.* "from Music."—TR.

25

A slight change has been made by our author in the construction of this sentence, since the time of the *Neue Zeitschrift* article; but, while improving the general 'run,' it has given rise to almost the sole instance of a "false relation" in all his prose.—TR.

26

Note to the 1869, and subsequent editions: "Of the Neo-Judaic system, which has been erected on this attribute of Mendelssohnian music as though in vindication of such artistic falling-off, we shall speak later!"

27

In the *N.Z.* this stood: "he yearned to pass beyond Absolute Music and mount up to a union with her human sister arts, just as the full and finished Man desires to mount to wide Humanity."—TR.

28

"Wunderwirkenden Vermögen" and "eines unsäglichen Inhaltes" did not occur in the *N.Z.*—TR.

29

"Zartsinnigen"—in the *N.Z.* "edlen," i.e. "noble."—TR.

30

The last clause, "but in general" &c., was absent from the *N.Z.* article.—TR.

31

Whoever has observed the shameful indifference and absent-mindedness of a Jewish congregation, throughout the musical performance of Divine Service in the Synagogue, may understand why a Jewish opera-composer feels not at all offended by encountering the same thing in a theatre-audience, and how he cheerfully can go on labouring for it; for this behaviour, here, must really seem to him less unbecoming than in the house of God.—R. WAGNER.

32

To the *N.Z.* article there here was added a foot-note: "'Man so thun!' sagt der Berliner," i.e. "' It's to be done!' as they say in Berlin,"—TR.

33

This subsidiary clause did not exist in the *N.Z.*—TR.

34

Characteristic enough is the attitude adopted by the remaining Jew musicians, nay, by the whole of cultured Jewry, toward their two most renowned composers. To the adherents of Mendelssohn, that famous opera-composer is an atrocity: with a keen sense of honour, they feel how much he compromises Jewdom in the eyes of better-trained musicians, and therefore shew no mercy in their judgment. By far more cautiously do that composer's retainers express themselves concerning Mendelssohn, regarding more with envy, than with manifest ill-will, the success he has made in the "more solid" music-world. To a third faction, that of the composition-at-any-price Jews, it is their visible object to avoid all internecine scandal, all self-exposure in general, so that their music-producing may take its even course without occasioning any painful fuss: the by all means undeniable successes of the great opera-composer they let pass as worth some slight attention, allowing there is something in them albeit one can't approve of much or dub it "solid." In sooth, the Jews are far too clever, not to know how their own goods are lined!—R WAGNER.—In the *Neue Zeitschrift* this note formed part of the body of the text.—TR.

35

In the *N Z*. this ran: "of Judaism in *Art*, whereto the actual Jews have merely given its most obvious physiognomy, but in nowise its

intrinsic meaning. The Jews could never take possession of our art"
&c. —TR.

36

In the *N.Z.* there appeared: "in cold, contemptuous complacency,"
and the sentence ended at the "self-deception"—a footnote being
added, as follows: "What he lied himself, our Jews laid bare again by
setting it to music." Moreover in place of "seemed" there stood "is,"
and in the next sentence the predicate "evil" did not occur.—TR.

37

In the *N.Z.* "an diesem selbstvernichtenden, blutigen Kampfe."—TR.

Lightning Source UK Ltd.
Milton Keynes UK
UKHW011245181021
392412UK00001B/77